WITTGENSTEIN

This collection of new essays deals with the relationship between Wittgenstein's life and his philosophy. The first two essays in the volume reflect on general problems inherent in philosophical biography itself. The essays that follow draw on recently published letters as well as recently published diaries from the 1930s to explore Wittgenstein's background as an engineer and its relation to the *Tractatus Logico-Philosophicus,* the impact of his schizoid personality on his approach to philosophy, his role as a diarist, letter writer, and polemicist, and finally the complex issue of Wittgenstein as a Jew.

Written by a first-rate team of Wittgenstein scholars, including two published biographers of the philosopher, Brian McGuinness and Ray Monk, this collection will appeal especially to anyone with a serious interest in the most influential philosopher of the 20th century.

Contributors: James Conant, Hans-Johann Glock, Kelly Hamilton, James C. Klagge, Brian McGuinness, Ray Monk, Alfred Nordmann, Louis Sass, Joachim Schulte, and David Stern

Wittgenstein

Biography and Philosophy

Edited by

JAMES C. KLAGGE

Virginia Polytechnic Institute and State University

CAMBRIDGE
UNIVERSITY PRESS

PUBLISHED BY THE PRESS SYNDICATE OF THE UNIVERSITY OF CAMBRIDGE
The Pitt Building, Trumpington Street, Cambridge, United Kingdom

CAMBRIDGE UNIVERSITY PRESS
The Edinburgh Building, Cambridge CB2 2RU, UK
40 West 20th Street, New York, NY 10011-4211, USA
10 Stamford Road, Oakleigh, VIC 3166, Australia
Ruiz de Alarcón 13, 28014 Madrid, Spain
Dock House, The Waterfront, Cape Town 8001, South Africa

http://www.cambridge.org

First published 2001

Printed in the United States of America

Typeface Times Roman 10/12 pt.   *System* DeskTopPro$_{/UX}$ [BV]

A catalog record for this book is available from the British Library.

Library of Congress Cataloging in Publication Data
Wittgenstein : biography and philosophy / edited by James C. Klagge.
p. cm.
ISBN 0-521-80397-7 – ISBN 0-521-00868-9 (pbk.)
1. Wittgenstein, Ludwig, 1889–1951.   2. Philosophers–Austria–Biography.   3.
Philosophers–Great Britain–Biography.   I. Klagge, James Carl, 1954–
B3376.W564 W56 2001
192—dc21
[B]   00-067497

ISBN 0 521 80397 7 hardback
ISBN 0 521 00868 9 paperback

Contents

List of Contributors

JAMES CONANT, Philosophy, University of Chicago

HANS-JOHANN GLOCK, Philosophy, University of Reading, England

KELLY HAMILTON, History, Saint Mary's College, Indiana

JAMES C. KLAGGE, Philosophy, Virginia Polytechnic Institute
    and State University

BRIAN MCGUINNESS, Philosophy, University of Siena, Italy

RAY MONK, Philosophy, University of Southampton, England

ALFRED NORDMANN, Philosophy, University of South Carolina

LOUIS SASS, Clinical Psychology and Comparative Literature,
    Rutgers University, New Jersey

JOACHIM SCHULTE, Philosophy, University of Bielefeld, Germany

DAVID STERN, Philosophy, University of Iowa

Editor's Preface

JAMES C. KLAGGE

Introduction

No one who reads, or tries to read, the *Tractatus* can help wondering what kind of person its author was. Upon reading the *Tractatus* but before meeting its author, Theodore Redpath, a student of Ludwig Wittgenstein's from the mid- to late 1930s, imagined Wittgenstein "with the facial appearance of a 'prophet,' with a thin long sensitive, El Grecoish kind of face, framed by long strands of silvery hair and set with large, dark, expressive eyes."[1] The contrast created by reading the *Philosophical Investigations* can only increase one's curiosity.

Until Wittgenstein's death in 1951, knowledge of him as a person was limited to friends and students and rumor. For the next three dozen years it was refracted by a growing stream of memoirs and recollections by friends, students, and acquaintances. Finally, near the centenary anniversary of his birth, we began to know Wittgenstein through two well-researched biographies.[2] The more we know of him as a person, the more interesting become the connections, and disconnections, to his philosophical work. With these biographies, the real work has now begun of understanding Wittgenstein as a person and a thinker. This collection of papers continues that work. What stands out in many of these papers is the attention to recently published material – Wittgenstein's diaries from the 1930s, his correspondence with his family, his engineering training.

The bulk of the papers that follow were delivered at the Virginia Tech Philosophy Department's annual spring conference, held 25–28 March 1999, on the topic "Wittgenstein: Biography and Philosophy." Some of the papers were solicited by the editor for the conference, while others were chosen from among submissions. Some of the papers in this collection were written for other occasions but have been included because of their relevance. The conference was made possible by financial support from a number of institutions, but particular thanks must go to the Franklin J. Matchette Foundation. This volume benefited from the editorial assistance of David Stern and Alfred Nordmann.

Coincidentally, the very week that the conference was held, *Time* magazine released its special issue (March 29, 1999) on "The Century's Greatest Minds," the fourth in its five-part series on the 100 most influential people of the century. Wittgenstein was the only philosopher chosen among the two dozen greatest scientists and thinkers, unless one counts Gödel and Turing. *Time* commissioned Daniel Dennett to write the three-page account, which includes the teaser, "Wittgenstein . . . continues to attract fanatics who devote their life to disagreeing with one another (and, presumably, with my brief summary)." While the contributors to this collection have found things to disagree about, a startling unity emerges in their belief that there is an intimate connection between Wittgenstein's life and his work; this connection is crucial to understanding both.

Alfred Nordmann, in his contribution to this volume, explores Wittgenstein's newly discovered diaries from the 1930s – in particular, Wittgenstein's comment that "the movement of thought in my philosophy should be discernible in the history of my mind, of its moral concepts and in the understanding of my situation."[3] Several essays in this volume search for these parallel movements.

It is impossible to summarize the wealth of issues that revolve around the relationship between Wittgenstein's life and his work probed in this collection, but I will illustrate such an issue, though it is not addressed by any of the contributors.

Wittgenstein and Wonder

In reflecting on Wittgenstein's life and work I begin at its end: I think it is a touchstone of any interpretation of Wittgenstein's life and work that it help us to make sense of his dying words for his close friends, said (in English) to the woman who helped nurse him through his last months: "Tell them I had a wonderful life."[4]

Is this an accurate statement about Wittgenstein's life? Did he mean to be saying something true, or something consoling? What did he mean by "wonderful"? Not only is this a poignant remark because of its timing and apparent content, but it also raises just the kind of issues that concern us here – issues about the relationship between Wittgenstein's life and his thoughts.

In 1925, while visiting England and staying with John Maynard Keynes, Wittgenstein had concluded a letter to his friend Engelmann: ". . . I wish now I could die in a moment of brilliance."[5] There is a sense in which Wittgenstein got his wish, since he was able to continue his philosophical writing until the day before he lapsed into a coma.[6] In other respects, however, the suffering of his last days could hardly have been conducive to brilliance. Joachim Schulte, in his contribution to this volume, stresses the importance to Wittgenstein of finding the right context and phrasing for his remarks. What is the right context for understanding this remark?

James Conant, in his contribution to this volume, compares writing about Wittgenstein to writing about Socrates. In the ancient tradition there was a presumption that a philosopher's life was relevant as an expression of his philosophy. Conant sees Wittgenstein as fitting into that tradition. And Wittgenstein's dying remark cries out for interpretation just as do Socrates' remarks at the end of his trial, such as "the unexamined life is not worth living for man" and "a good man cannot be harmed either in life or in death".[7] Of course these remarks are already put into a context by Plato, in his writing of the *Apology*. Just as Socrates had his Xenophon, who gave a different tone to the defense, and Aristophanes, who might have found yet a different tone if he had addressed this scene, so Wittgenstein had his Derek Jarman.

Jarman, surprisingly, does not include this scene in his film, "Wittgenstein," but an anonymous reviewer of the film on a gay film website commented that "Wittgenstein struggled with self-alienation throughout his life. He died of cancer in 1951. His final, mocking words were: 'Tell them I've had a wonderful life.' Jarman's film captures this life with energy and imagination."[8] I think it is likely that if Jarman had included this scene, it could well have been said caustically.

The paragraph in which Ray Monk quotes Wittgenstein's words certainly supports the caustic interpretation, surrounding them, as Monk does, with a foul mood and other caustic remarks. Yet Monk does not present them as an expression of a life-long alienation. As explained in Monk's contribution to this volume, he leaves us to draw our own conclusion about the tone of voice from the collage of surroundings he has accumulated.

Obviously Wittgenstein's close friends would not want to be bidden farewell in that way. Norman Malcolm, one of those friends, who first published these words in his memoir in 1958, found them to be a mystery. Then in a revised edition in 1984 he decided that, though Wittgenstein's life seemed unhappy, he must have derived considerable satisfaction from his work and friendships.[9]

In 1958 Malcolm interpreted "wonderful" as synonymous with "enjoyable." By 1984 he saw it as synonymous with "worthwhile." Perhaps the best model for this latter sense of "wonderful" is the 1946 Frank Capra film, "It's a Wonderful Life." (I wonder if Wittgenstein, a fan of popular American films, could have made his statement without being aware of its similarity to the title of this film.) We see already that Wittgenstein's parting words have all the potential for ambiguity that Schulte finds in the various letters he discusses. (Indeed, Wittgenstein's words were like a very brief letter to his friends.)

David Stern, in his contribution, raises the question of what stake we have in how Wittgenstein's remarks are interpreted. Perhaps some wish to see Wittgenstein as a companion in misery, as the gay review might suggest. Personal friends might wish to see something redemptive in Wittgenstein's struggles. Biographers may wish to find unity in a life. Philosophers of various stripes may wish to see Wittgenstein as an ally, or alternately as a purveyor of mistaken views.

Peter John has instead proposed to interpret "wonderful" literally as meaning "full of wonder."[10] Though this stretches its colloquial usage in English, Webster's second edition (1934) does offer: "adapted to excite wonder." It is clear that the capacity to wonder and remain in wonder was important for Wittgenstein. In 1929, in a lecture on ethics, he offered "wonder at the existence of the world" as an illustration of what had intrinsic value for him.[11] A year later Wittgenstein worried that this capacity for wonder was greatly endangered by modern conceptions of science and progress: "Man has to awaken to wonder [*Zum Staunen*] – and so perhaps do people. Science is a way of sending him to sleep again."[12]

While some may see this as an ignorantly prejudicial remark against science, Kelly Hamilton's paper reminds us of Wittgenstein's strong grounding in science. While Hamilton emphasizes the importance of models in turn-of-the-century German engineering training and of their relevance to Wittgenstein's model/picture theory of meaning in the *Tractatus,* the later Wittgenstein could well have come to see scientific models as limiting people's imagination by seeming to do the work of understanding by themselves – just as the later Wittgenstein did come to see the model/picture theory of meaning as defective because it appeared to do the work of meaning by itself, apart from human engagement.[13]

The focus on wonder is an example of the sort of second-order reflective state of mind that Louis Sass, in his contribution, finds so characteristic of Wittgenstein's personality. One cannot wonder at a state of affairs without placing it in a larger context, among other possibilities. Yet it is this very reflectiveness that makes acceptance of the given so difficult. Thus we get Wittgenstein's ambivalence, about philosophy and in his personal relations.

But fundamentally Wittgenstein strove to have a life full of wonder, and Peter John's construal of his remark would, in a sense, crown that life. On this interpretation, his dying remark crystallized the brilliance of his life as he sought to live it.[14] This is just one of many examples of the work that remains to be done in filling out our understanding of Wittgenstein, both as a person and as a philosopher.

Communication and Community

Students of Wittgenstein's life know that alienation was a recurring experience. Brian McGuinness, in his contribution, and David Stern, in his, examine the vexed question of Wittgenstein's alleged Jewishness and his own attitude to this attribution. It was a visceral source of alienation. Jarman's cinematic representation of Wittgenstein's philosophizing presents that as an expression of his alienation, as well, but philosophy was in fact Wittgenstein's way of reaching outside of himself. Hans-Johann Glock, in his essay, emphasizes the many ways in which Wittgenstein's philosophy engaged in a rational way not only with the philosophical traditions that preceded him, but also with various contemporary figures. Though Wittgenstein never managed to live in a setting of which he felt genuinely a part – perhaps he was, indeed, incapable of being anything but apart – and never managed to have more than a friend or two at a time, he offered up himself in his philosophizing.[15]

Jarman's film implies that this offering was not comprehended – a fact that Wittgenstein himself suspected. Wittgenstein closed the lectures of Easter term, 1939, with the lament: "The seed I'm most likely to sow is a certain jargon."[16] His work, however, was not hopeless, nor did he feel it to be hopeless. He did not seek disciples, and he invariably tried to steer his students away from careers in philosophy, but he did offer some four dozen courses of lectures at Cambridge over a period of 18 years.[17] And from his tens of thousands of manuscript pages, he sought constantly to refine and cast a satisfactory expression of his thoughts.[18]

Though he sometimes felt he was only "writing for friends who are scattered throughout the corners of the globe" still he never ceased in his effort to communicate his thoughts, and thereby establish a community:

> If I say that my book is meant for only a small circle of people (if it can be called a circle), I do not mean that I believe this circle to be the elite of mankind; but it does comprise those to whom I turn (not because they are better or worse than others but) because they form my cultural milieu, my fellow citizens as it were, in contrast to the rest who are *foreign* to me.[19]

The community for which he hoped was not just limited to his own time. As he said to Drury in 1949, "Perhaps in a hundred years people will really want what I am writing."[20]

So it is that we, his students in later decades, in a later century, still hold the key to the successful community that Wittgenstein sought. Through our ongoing attempts to understand him and his movements of thought, we seek to accept the offering of himself that he so painfully made through those many pages of notebooks and hours of lecturing. The papers in this volume, and the work they provoke, are part of that incipient community.

NOTES

1. Theodore Redpath, *Ludwig Wittgenstein: A Student's Memoir* (London: Duckworth, 1990), pp. 16–17.

2. Brian McGuinness, *Wittgenstein: A Life, The Young Ludwig (1889–1921)* (Berkeley: University of California Press, 1988); and Ray Monk, *Ludwig Wittgenstein: The Duty of Genius* (New York: Free Press, 1990).

3. *Denkbewegungen: Tagebücher 1930–32, 1936–37* (Innsbruck, Austria: Haymon Verlag, 1997), 7.11.31; to be reprinted with English translation in *Public and Private Occasions,* ed. J. Klagge and A. Nordmann (Totowa, NJ: Rowman and Littlefield, forthcoming).

4. First reported by Malcolm in the 1958 edition of *Ludwig Wittgenstein: A Memoir* (Oxford: Oxford University Press) [new edition 1984], and set in a context by Monk, op.cit., p. 579.

5. Postmarked 19.8.25, and published in *Letters from Ludwig Wittgenstein: with a Memoir,* ed. Paul Engelmann (Oxford: Basil Blackwell, 1967), pp. 54–57. Engelmann notes that, in the letter, Wittgenstein had originally written "conversation" and replaced it with "moment."

6. §§ 670–6 of *On Certainty* (Oxford: Basil Blackwell, 1969) dated 27.4[.51].

7. Plato, *Trial and Death of Socrates,* tr. G. Grube (Indianapolis: Hackett, 1983).

8. Derek Jarman and Ken Butler, "Wittgenstein: The Derek Jarman Film," in *Wittgenstein: The Terry Eagleton Script, The Derek Jarman Film* (British Film Institute, 1993); PopcornQ: The Ultimate Home for the Queer Moving Image, at *http://www.planetout.com/pno/popcornq/db/getfilm.html297.*

9. In the 1984 edition, the original remark and interpretation are given on p. 81, the later reinterpretation is on p. 84.

10. Peter John, "Wittgenstein's Wonderful Life," *Journal of the History of Ideas* 49, no. 3 July–September 1988: 495–510.

11. "Lecture on Ethics," in *Philosophical Occasions: 1912–1951,* ed., J. Klagge and A. Nordmann (Indianapolis: Hackett, 1993), p. 41. The lecture was given on 17.11.29.

12. *Culture and Value* (Chicago: University of Chicago Press, 1980; rev. ed. [Oxford: Basil Blackwell, 1998]), p. 5 (in 1980 edition)/p. 7 (in 1998 edition). The revised translation in the 1998 edition renders *Zum Staunen* as "in order to marvel."

13. Wittgenstein was not an opponent of science, but of certain attitudes towards science. Cf. Klagge, "Wittgenstein and Neuroscience," *Synthese* 78 (1989): 319–343.

14. The circumstances of his death made appropriate his 1925 "correction" that his time of dying would not involve a conversation after all (though in 1925 he must have been having brilliant conversations with Keynes).

15. See Klagge, "When Are Ideologies Irreconcilable? Case Studies in Diachronic Anthropology," *Philosophical Investigations* 21 (July 1998), Section VII: pp. 268–279; "Wittgenstein's Community," in *Metaphysics in the Post-Metaphysical Age: Papers of the 22nd International Wittgenstein Symposium,* vol. VII (1), ed. U. Meixner and P. Simons (Kirchberg am Wechsel: Austrian Ludwig Wittgenstein Society, 1999); and "Wittgenstein in Exile," in *Religion and Wittgenstein's Legacy,* ed., D. Z. Phillips (New York: Macmillan), in press.

16. *Wittgenstein's Lectures on the Foundations of Mathematics: Cambridge, 1939,* ed. Cora Diamond (Ithaca: Cornell University Press, 1976), p. 293.

17. See Klagge, "Wittgenstein's Lectures," to appear as an appendix in *Public and Private Occasions,* ed. J. Klagge and A. Nordmann (Totowa, NJ: Rowman and Littlefield, forthcoming).

18. See G. H. von Wright's "The Wittgenstein Papers," updated as an appendix in *Philosophical Occasions* 480–506; and David Stern, "The Availability of Wittgen-

stein's Philosophy," in *The Cambridge Companion to Wittgenstein,* ed. H. Sluga and D. Stern (Cambridge, 1996), pp. 442–476.

19. Wittgenstein, *Culture and Value,* pp. 6/9, 10/12–13.
20. M. Drury, "Conversations with Wittgenstein," in *Recollections of Wittgenstein,* ed. R. Rhees (Oxford: Oxford University Press, 1984), p. 160.

Biography and Philosophy

Philosophical Biography: The Very Idea

RAY MONK

The purpose of philosophical biography is very simply stated: it is to understand a philosopher. By "philosopher" here I do not necessarily mean someone who earns his or her living from writing and teaching philosophy. Jean-Paul Sartre, for example, wrote philosophical biographies of Charles Baudelaire, Jean Genet, and Gustave Flaubert, none of whom wrote or taught philosophy. To regard someone as a philosopher in this sense, that is, as an appropriate subject for a philosophical biography, it is enough to see them as someone whose thought – whether expressed in poetry, music, painting, fiction or works of philosophy – it is important and interesting to understand.

Now, of course, the central question is raised: to understand somebody's thought, why is it necessary to understand *them?* Can't we, for example, understand *The Critique of Pure Reason,* or indeed *Madame Bovary,* without knowing or understanding anything at all about Kant or Flaubert themselves? In one sense, the simple answer to this is "yes, of course we can." Indeed, not only can we separate life and work, but, for certain purposes we *must* do so. Whether the arguments in *Critique of Pure Reason* are valid or not cannot depend on anything we know about the details of Kant's life, nor can the value of *Madame Bovary* as a work of fiction depend on what we think of Flaubert himself. I have no difficulty in accepting the view urged by Richard Rorty and others that the assessment of *Being and Time* as a work of philosophy must be kept quite distinct from the question of whether Heidegger himself was a coward and a liar with regard to his Nazi associations, just as I can happily concede the point recently urged upon me that the evaluation of *Principia Mathematica* can have nothing to do with the fact that Russell was horribly insensitive to his first wife, Alys.

Yet to concede all this is not to strip biography of its purpose; it is simply to accept what is in any case obvious: that biography is irrelevant to the assessment of the greatness of a work, whether it be philosophy, fiction, poetry, or whatever. Were the understanding of a person's thought restricted to its evaluation, the conclusion would have to be that biography is the futile and even pernicious activity that many believe it to be. It seems to me, however, that there is an important sense in which to understand what somebody says is to do something other than to evaluate it. To take a reductively simple example: suppose you are in a room with someone and you hear them say, "There is a mouse under my chair." Whether this is said with a tone of delight or fear has nothing to do with evaluating its truth, and yet, if you do not hear the delight or fear in the voice, there is an important sense in which you have not understood what is being said. Or again, suppose you are talking to someone and they say, "Bill Clinton is a liar and a cheat who has made his wife's life a misery." Whether this is true or not has nothing to do with who says it, but, if you later discover that the person you were talking to was President Clinton's daughter, you would be missing something if you did not attach a new significance to it. The task of a biography, I think, is to enrich understanding in these two ways: by attending, so to speak, to the tone of voice in which a writer expresses himself or herself and by accumulating personal facts that will allow us to see what is said in a different light.

My biography of Wittgenstein was motivated in the first place by my feeling that his tone of voice was being misheard in much of the secondary literature written on him. Wittgenstein's tone – so manifestly different from that in which most analytic philosophy is written – is one of the most striking things about his work. To read anything by him is to see immediately that the spirit and personality expressed is greatly at odds with the spirit that informs, say, the work of Russell, Ryle, Quine, and Ayer. Wittgenstein himself attached enormous importance to this. He was deeply concerned that the spirit of his work might be misunderstood and deeply conscious, too, of the difficulty in preventing such a misunderstanding. In the various prefaces he wrote to his later work, he tried again and again to ensure that his readers would read him, so to speak, under the right aspect. In an early draft of the preface for *Philosophical Remarks,* for example, he insisted that he was indifferent to whether or not his work would be understood by "the typical western scientist," since "he will not in any case understand the spirit in which I write."[1] In an unpublished version of the preface to *Philosophical Investigations* he declared that it was with some reluctance that he delivered the book to the public since, "It will fall into hands which are not for the most part those in which I like to imagine it." May it soon, he urged, "be completely forgotten by the philosophical journalists and so be preserved for a better sort of reader."[2]

Despite these statements, of course, the spirit in which Wittgenstein's work was written has been, by and large, neglected in the vast amounts of philosophical commentary devoted to it. This is not to say that it has been ignored altogether. The situation when I began my book was, roughly speaking, this: two almost entirely separate bodies of literature on Wittgenstein were developing – one that discussed his ethical, cultural, and spiritual attitudes as revealed in the various memoirs of him, his personal correspondence, and the records of his conversation published by his friends, and another that discussed the themes of his philosophical work. My overriding aim was to show that there was no reason why these two aspects of Wittgenstein should be discussed in isolation from each other, that one could look at his work, no less than his private conversation, as an expression of his most fundamental attitudes. By seeing the connections between his spiritual and cultural concerns and his philosophical work, one might perhaps be able to read the latter in the spirit in which it was intended.

As I conceive it, biography is a peculiarly Wittgensteinian genre, in that the kind of understanding to which it aspires is precisely the kind of understanding upon which Wittgenstein lays great emphasis in *Philosophical Investigations,* namely, "the understanding that consists in seeing connections." In Wittgenstein's later work, this is explicitly contrasted with *theoretical* understanding, and this is precisely one of the most important respects in which he believed himself to be swimming against the tide of what he called "the spirit which informs the vast stream of European and American civilization." Whereas that spirit seeks to construct theories, Wittgenstein seeks merely to *see* clearly. Thus, the form Wittgenstein's later work takes is not to advance a thesis and then to defend it against possible objections, but rather to say, "Look at things this way." Biography, I believe, is a nontheoretical activity in the same kind of way. The insights it has to offer have to be shown rather than stated. Like Wittgenstein's later philosophy, it is descriptive rather than explanatory and this means that its elucidatory value is perpetually liable to remain elusive and misunderstood.

Drawing out connections is a perilous business because it can often appear as if one is making assertoric statements, claims to truth, to the effect that there *is* such and such a connection, and then there can arise the question, "Well, is there, in reality, such a connection or not?" Think, for example, of seeing a likeness between two faces, say those of a mother and her baby. Some people can see it and others can't, and sometimes it can help to say to those who can't things like, "Look at the nose, look at the shape of the eyes," and so forth. Yet, if a dispute breaks out about whether this likeness is real or only imagined, how is it to be resolved? Is there a *fact* here that one can appeal to? Can one say, "Look, there either is a likeness here or there isn't." One can point to one face and then to the other, but can one point to the connection between the two? One can draw one face and then the other, but can one draw the similarity between them?

Seeing connections provides at once the most familiar form of understanding and the most elusive. What eludes us, in particular, are direct statements of *what,* exactly, is understood. Stanley Cavell tells an illuminating story of his days as a student at Berkeley, when he attended Ernst Bloch's music theory class. Bloch, he recalls, "would play something simple, at the piano, for instance a Bach four-part chorale, with one note altered by a half a step from Bach's rendering; then he would play the Bach unaltered. Perhaps he would turn to us, fix us with a stare, then turn back to the piano and repeat, as if for himself, the two versions. The drama mounted, then broke open with a monologue which I reconstruct along these lines: 'You hear that? You hear the difference?' . . . He went on: 'My version is perfectly correct; but the Bach, the Bach is perfect; late sunlight burning the edges of a cloud. Of course I do not say you must hear this. Not at all. No. But,' the head lowered a little, the eyes looked up at us, the tempo slowed ominously, 'if you do not hear it, do not say to yourself you are a musician. There are many honourable trades. Shoe-making for example.' "[3]

Understanding a person is like understanding a piece of music; it is not a matter of accepting the truth of some statement or theory but of seeing the connections – and of course the differences – between the various things people do and say. Faced with someone who cannot see these connections, we cannot say that they are making a mistake, only that they are missing something, that they are suffering, as it were, from a kind of blindness, what Wittgenstein called "aspect-blindness."

Toward the end of *Philosophical Investigations,* Wittgenstein raises the question of whether there is such a thing as "expert judgment" about mental states, about, for example, the genuineness of expressions of feeling. He answers by saying that, yes indeed, "there are those whose judgment is 'better' and those whose judgment is 'worse.' "[4] More correct prognoses, he says, "will generally issue from the judgments of those with better knowledge of mankind." Can one learn this knowledge? "Yes: some can. Not, however, by taking a course in it, but through *experience* – can someone else be a man's teacher in this? Certainly. From time to time he gives him the right *tip* – this is what 'learning' and 'teaching' are like here. What one acquires here is not a technique; one learns correct judgments. There are also rules, but they do not form a system, and only experienced people can apply them right. Unlike calculating rules." It is certainly possible, he adds, to be convinced by *evidence* that someone is in such-and-such a state of mind, that, for instance, he is not pretending. "But 'evidence' here includes 'imponderable evidence' ":

Imponderable evidence includes subtleties of glance, of gesture, of tone. I may recognize a genuine loving look, distinguish it from a pretended one (and here there can, of course, be a "ponderable" confirmation of my judgment). But I may be quite incapable of describing the difference. And this is not because the languages I know have no words for it.[5]

In the manuscript published as *Last Writings on the Philosophy of Psychology,* Wittgenstein tried to elaborate further what he means by "imponderable evidence" and ends up comparing the man who understands people, who can tell the difference between real and feigned expressions of emotions, with an art connoisseur who, though able to distinguish a real from a fake painting, is unable to explain his reasons to a panel of nonexperts. He can, however, says Wittgenstein "give intimations to another connoisseur, and the latter will understand them."[6] The other connoisseur will understand these intimations because, having a similar breadth of experience and knowledge, he will be able to *see* what the first is talking about, just as musicians will be able to *hear* what Ernst Bloch was intimating to his class about the difference between the two pieces of music he played.

There are those who will say that this is all nonsense and that, just as Wittgenstein *is* – despite his protestations to the contrary – putting forward a *theory* of meaning in *Philosophical Investigations,* so a biographer who claims insight into the mind of his subject is, whether he or she acknowledges it or not, operating with a *theory* of human psychology. To those I would say this: read a truly great biography, such as Boswell's life of Johnson or Richard Ellmann's life of Oscar Wilde, and then compare it with the biographies of Jean-Paul Sartre and then you will see the difference between revealing character through *description* and trying to *explain* it through theorizing.

Sartre's biographies are philosophical in a bad sense. Reading them, one is reminded of Virginia Woolf's complaint about the novels of Arnold Bennett. Quoting a passage from Bennett's novel, *Hilda Lessways,* in which Bennett introduces his central character with a long and tedious description of the row of houses in which she lives, Woolf complains that we cannot, in all this, hear Hilda's voice, but "can only hear Mr. Bennett's voice telling us facts about rents and freeholds and copyholds and fines." Bennett, she says, "is trying to hypnotize us into the belief that, because he has made a house, there must be a person living there."[7] Similarly, in Sartre's *Baudelaire,* it is not the poet's voice we hear, but Sartre's own telling us his theories of narcissism, consciousness, being and nonbeing.

At the time of writing *Baudelaire,* Sartre had a theory that we are each of us entirely responsible for the kind of life we lead, and, in particular, that our lives are shaped by a decisive original choice that determines the kind of person we will be. His central interest in describing the events of Baudelaire's life, one feels, is to demonstrate the truth of this theory. Thus, when Baudelaire's mother remarries, Sartre decides that *this* is the moment when Baudelaire decided to be the kind of self-absorbed character he became. "The sudden break and the grief it caused," writes Sartre, "forced him [Baudelaire] into a personal existence without any warning or preparation. One moment he was still enveloped in the communal religious life of the couple consisting of his mother and himself; the next, life had gone out like a tide leaving him high and dry":

The justification for his existence had disappeared; he made the mortifying discovery that he was a single person, that his life had been given him for nothing. His rage at being driven out was coloured by a profound sense of having fallen from grace. When later on he thought of this moment, he wrote "Sense of solitude from childhood. In spite of the family – and above all when surrounded by children my own age – I had a sense of being destined to eternal solitude." He already thought of his isolation as a *destiny*. That meant that he did not accept it passively. On the contrary, he embraced it with fury, shut himself up in it and, since he was condemned to it, hoped that at any rate his condemnation was final. This brings us to the point at which Baudelaire chose the sort of person he would be – that irrevocable choice by which each of us decides in a particular situation what he will be and what he is. When he found himself abandoned and rejected, Baudelaire chose solitude deliberately as an act of self-assertion, so that his solitude should not be something inflicted on him by other people.[8]

This passage may or may not contain insights into Baudelaire's character, but think how much more convincing it would have been if the short quotation from Baudelaire himself, instead of being embedded in a lot of Sartrean theorising, had been placed alongside other remarks by Baudelaire and put into context with some pertinent facts about, and perhaps even some quotations from, his mother. For as it stands we do not *see* Baudelaire reacting as Sartre tells us he did. We do not, for example, see him make the choice to be solitary that Sartre imputes to him. Indeed, the one quotation that Sartre produces in this connection might easily be taken to imply that Baudelaire did *not* experience his solitude as a choice, but rather as something that was foisted upon him by fate. Nor do we hear Baudelaire's rage at being abandoned and rejected. What we hear is Sartre's confidence that this is what Baudelaire felt.

Faced with Satre's attempts to *explain* Baudelaire's character, one is reminded of Wittgenstein's furious reaction to Sir James Frazer's attempts to explain magical rituals as if they were early forms of science, as if the savage who sticks a pin in an effigy of his enemy does so because he has formed the mistaken scientific hypothesis that this will cause physical injury to his opponent. It would be better, more elucidatory, Wittgenstein thought, to describe this ritual alongside some of our own – such as beating a pillow when we are upset with a loved one – so as to build up something akin to a Galtonian composite photograph, in which we can see the connections between what we find it natural to do and what was done in earlier cultures. Such a "perspicuous presentation" would allow us a view of ritual that is clear, precisely because it is not obscured by theory. "For us," Wittgenstein writes, "the conception of a perspicuous presentation is fundamental . . . [it] makes possible that understanding which consists just in the fact that we 'see the connections'."[9]

Sartre's biography of Baudelaire is often criticized for its attempt to, so to speak, get inside Baudelaire's mind. He speaks of its being "easy enough to describe Baudelaire's inner life" and then proceeds to devote several pages to an account of Baudelaire's indecisive struggle between *being* and *existence,* between, that is, living as an autonomous, free agent and merely existing as an object determined by outside forces and other people.[10] "Because [Baudelaire] wanted at the same time to be and to exist," writes Sartre, "because he continuously fled from existence to being and from being to existence, he was nothing but a gaping wound."[11] I find this account intriguing, and even, in a certain sense, plausible, but I want to see the "imponderable evidence" upon which these judgments are based, so that I can see this struggle for myself. It is not just that, without the evidence, I have only Sartre's word for it that this struggle was taking place (though that certainly comes into it); it is that the best, most convincing account of that struggle would be a description of its external manifestations, the things that Baudelaire did and said that reveal it. If, in a movie, you want your audience to understand that a character is angry, the best way to do it is to show him behaving angrily, not to have a narrator or another character saying, "Gosh, he's really angry now." Similarly, in a biography you have the opportunity, indeed the duty, of revealing your subject's character by describing his actions. I was once taken to task for being "too lenient" with Wittgenstein by not criticizing his appalling treatment of the young children he taught at elementary school. Yet, it seemed to me, and still seems to me, that, if you describe someone beating a schoolgirl until she bleeds because she is unable to grasp logic, it adds nothing to the description to follow it with a comment such as, "That wasn't very nice, was it?"

The problem with Sartre's biography of Baudelaire is not that he tries to reveal Baudelaire's inner life, but that he tries to say what ought to be shown. Wittgenstein's dictum that an inner process stands in need of outward criteria is often taken to imply a general suspicion about the notion of an inner life, but it seems to me that this is a crass misunderstanding. Wittgenstein, of all people, knew that we have an inner life, that we have thoughts that we do not share with other people and desires that we deny even to ourselves. He knew what it was to have an inner struggle between inclination and duty, and a split between what we say and what we mean. His thoroughgoing attempts to be a decent person almost invariably took the form of attacking his own inclinations to give other people a false impression of himself. The most important link between his philosophy and his life, indeed, is provided by his sense that he couldn't be a decent philosopher, couldn't think clearly, until he had "settled accounts with himself," until he had, as he put it, "dismantled the pride" that stood in the way of both clear thinking and honest, decent living. The confessions that he made in 1937, at a time when he was writing what he thought would be the final version of *Philosophical Investigations*, all took the form of owning up to deceptions. All of the deceptions were, he made clear, prompted by vanity, by his wish to appear better than he was. This impulse to come clean, to confess, was also what lay behind his expressed wish to write an autobiography. He wanted to remove the obstacles that lay between him and clarity. For, as he once said to Russell, "Perhaps you regard this thinking about myself as a waste of time – but how can I be a logician before I'm a human being! *Far* the most important thing is to settle accounts with myself!"[12] To think clearly and to dismantle one's pride were, for Wittgenstein, essentially linked, and to dismantle one's pride it was necessary to reveal that which, through vanity, one would prefer to remain secret. "Nothing is hidden" is, for Wittgenstein, an ethical as well as a logical remark.

Yet it is important that "nothing is hidden" stands as a descriptive rather than a prescriptive remark. It is not that Wittgenstein thought one *ought* to reveal the less admirable aspects of one's character, but that he was convinced that, to a sufficiently perceptive observer, they *would* be revealed, whether one wanted them to be or not. A lack of integrity, for example, would infect one's style of writing, or the clarity of one's thought. It may even be revealed in one's face. There is such a thing as an inner life, but it will invariably have outward manifestations, and, to one with the necessary experience and wisdom to interpret the "imponderable evidence," *nothing* is hidden. In *The Brothers Karamazov*, Dostoyevsky describes the figure of Father Zossima, of whom, he writes, it was said by many people that "by permitting everyone for so many years to come and bare their hearts and beg for his advice and healing words, he had absorbed so many secrets, sorrows, and avowals into his soul that in the end he had acquired so fine a perception that he could tell at a glance from the face of a stranger what he had come for, what he wanted and what kind of torment racked his conscience."[13] Discussing this passage with his friend, Maurice Drury, Wittgenstein remarked that "there really have been people like that, who could see directly into the souls of other people and advise them."[14] An inner process stands in need of outward criteria, but this does not mean that they are manifest to *everybody*. To see deeply into a person's inner life requires a rare attentiveness to and understanding of its outward manifestations. We can hear anxiety in a tone of voice, see fear on a person's face, recognize insincerity in a person's prose style. Yet the depth and sensitivity with which we do so varies with our experience, our understanding, and the extent to which, like Father Zossima, we are willing to absorb the secrets, sorrows, and avowals of others.

The first requisite for a successful biography, then, is a willingness to be deeply absorbed in the inner life of another person, and this is where Sartre falls down. It is not Baudelaire or Genet or Flaubert that he finds fascinating, but his own theories of philosophical psychology. To write a really great biography, a certain self-effacement is required. The paradigm here is Boswell's life of Johnson. Boswell finds *everything* about Johnson fascinating, and though there is no theorizing in his biography and very little reasoned reflection, he succeeds in capturing the "imponderable evidence" upon which any judgment of Johnson's character must be based. Even Virginia Woolf, who was sceptical about the entire genre of biography and inclined to believe it to be an impossible task to understand the inner life of another, acknowledged that Boswell had succeeded in conveying the spirit of Dr. Johnson, largely through allowing us to hear Johnson's own voice. When we hear Johnson say things like "No, Sir; stark insensibility!", Woolf says, then we feel we know what kind of man he was.[15] The example is interesting, I think, as an illustration of "imponderable evidence." Why is this exclamation so revealing of Johnson's spirit? It is difficult, if not impossible, to say. If pressed, I would reach for some phrase like "touchingly bombastic" to describe it, but, in the end, it is imponderable. If somebody did *not* find that a whole personality was expressed in that phrase, all one could do is say, a la Ernst Bloch: "If you do not hear it, do not say to yourself you are a biographer. There are many honourable trades."

Having said what I think is the point and the appropriate method of philosophical biography, and pointed to the extent to which Wittgenstein's later work provides an intellectual framework for the genre, I want to end with some troubled and inconclusive reflections about my unfinished biography of Bertrand Russell. I have been critical of Sartre's attempts at biography, but there is at least one remark of his that rings a loud bell with me. In talking about the unity of Baudelaire's life, Sartre says, "Every event reflects back to us the undecomposable whole that he was from the first day until the last."[16] There are, of course, very great dangers in taking this view, the chief of which is falsifying a life by imposing upon its chaotic multiplicity an artificial uniformity. Montaigne was alive to this when he wrote in his *Essays*: "There is some justification for basing a judgment of a man on the most ordinary acts of his life, but in view of the natural instability of our conduct and opinions, it has often seemed to me that even good authors are wrong to insist on fashioning a consistent and solid fabric out of us."[17] "In all antiquity," Montaigne writes, "it is hard to pick out a dozen men who set their lives to a certain and consistent course."

The thought that has been troubling me is this: in revealing the unity of Wittgenstein's emotional and spiritual concerns and his philosophical preoccupations, in describing his life and work in a seamless narrative, have I done anything other than demonstrate that Wittgenstein was one of those very rare individuals for whom one *could* do such a thing? After all, Wittgenstein was, from the biographer's point of view, conveniently monomaniacal. *Everything* in his life was subordinated to the twin search – the single search, as I would claim – for philosophical clarity and ethical *Anständigkeit* (decency). Convenient, too, was his tendency to strip his life down to its bare essentials: he never owned a house or got married, he had little money, few possessions and a rather small circle of friends. Furthermore, he published just one book and one article in his lifetime, and devoted himself during the last twenty years of his life to just one task: that of putting his later philosophy into a satisfactory book. Russell, on the other hand, married four times, had countless lovers, published sixty books and over two thousand articles, was involved in many complicated public activities and corresponded with an almost unbelievably large number of people: friends, relatives, colleagues, and members of the general public. The Russell Archive in Canada estimates that it has over forty thousand letters by Russell. Future generations, I am convinced, will refuse to believe that the name "Bertrand Russell" denotes an individual, but will rather conclude that it is the name of a committee.

Faced with this multiplicity, diversity, and sheer bulk, the question arises: is the search for connections, for unity, not simply futile and bound to lead to falsification? My anxieties on this score are compounded by the reviews of the first volume of my biography of Russell, many of which, to my extreme discomfort, focused not on Russell, but on me. What my book revealed, many thought, was not Russell's inner life but my own, and, in particular, my passionate dislike of Bertrand Russell. I have said that self-effacement is a requirement in a good biography. Of course, I do not mean that an author is ever invisible. From Boswell's life of Johnson we learn quite a lot about Boswell himself, and we know, of course, that the portrait of Johnson has been fashioned by Boswell, in accordance with his own understanding of Johnson's character. Yet so convincing is the portrait that we do not take it to be *about* Boswell's thoughts on Johnson, but about Johnson himself. Similarly, few took my biography of Wittgenstein to be *about* me even though it was clear that the portrait of Wittgenstein presented in it had been painted by me. How did I inadvertently manage to paint myself into my portrait of Russell when I had successfully left myself out of my painting of Wittgenstein?

One possible answer to this is that, in my search for unity in Russell's life, I have imposed too restrictive a framework on his multifaceted life, squeezing out some aspects of his character that others regard as essential. I see Russell's life as dominated by his fears of madness and of loneliness. Unlike Sartre, I do not simply assert this, but show these fears being expressed in countless letters, remarks, and autobiographical writings and describe their consequences in various actions. In concentrating on these things, however, I have left out others, and some people have demanded to know why I have not included episodes revealing Russell to be kind, generous, witty, funny, and happy. The answer to that touches on Wittgenstein's question about whether there is such a thing as expert judgment about the sincerity of a person's expressions of emotion. For the truth is that I suspect Russell's expressions of happiness to be, often at any rate, insincere, while I regard his frequently expressed fears of madness, his misanthropy, and his feelings of solitude to be entirely sincere. After one has spent eight years reading several thousand documents revealing his private thoughts and feelings, one, in Wittgenstein's phrase, "develops a nose" for these things.

As has been forcefully and painfully pointed out to me, however, these are *my* judgments and it is open to other people, with perhaps claims equal to my own of possessing such a "nose," to make other judgments. I can, and would, claim that more aspects of Russell's life and work fit into my picture than into the alternatives, but, with a bit of straining, almost anything can be made to fit. I have known people, for example, determined to maintain their picture of Russell as an essentially happy, kind, and loving man, to deny that his repeatedly brutal treatment of those closest to him is the expression of fear and hatred, as I contend, and instead regard it as the perfectly reasonable response of an eminently rational man to the actions of stupid, selfish, and dishonest people. That this drama of rejection and recrimination was played out time and time again in four marriages, countless love affairs, and a tangled web of unhappy familial relationships, leading to much heartbreak and several nervous breakdowns, is dismissed by them as a sign only of Russell's bad luck in being surrounded by so many mentally unstable people. Here we see the limitations of appealing to "the understanding that consists in seeing connections." I can say, "Look at it like this and you will see that everything fits," but if I am met with, "No, look at this like this and you will see that it all fits together in quite a different way," then the opportunities for reasoned debate look rather slender.

Another possible answer to the question of how I managed to put myself in my picture of Russell when I avoided doing so in my picture of Wittgenstein is suggested by a remark of Douglas Collins in his book, *Sartre as Biographer.* "The understanding of another person," Collins writes, "is inseparable from the understanding, and even the provisional acceptance of his values."[18] Is it that I understand and accept Wittgenstein's values but not those of Russell? I don't think so. If I were asked to summarize in a sentence the difference between their respective values, I would say that Wittgenstein sought to improve himself, while Russell sought to improve the world, and that therefore Wittgenstein's values were essentially religious and Russell's essentially political. Am I closer to Wittgenstein than to Russell in this dichotomy? No, if anything, I am closer to Russell.

I confess that I do not really understand why, in the case of Russell, I have slipped off the frame and onto the picture. I mention it only to draw attention to one of the many perils of the undertaking of writing a philosophical biography. The purpose of such a biography, as I have said, is to understand a philosopher and thereby to shed deeper light on their thought. If I have been understood as expounding *my* thought in my biography of Russell, then something has gone wrong. A similar peril besets the Wittgensteinian conception of philosophy. Wittgenstein once began a series of lectures by announcing that everything he was about to say, if it was making a claim to truth at all, was trivially true and that, if anyone disagreed with anything he said, he would drop it immediately. When, however, Turing began an objection by saying, "I don't agree," Wittgenstein responded not by dropping what he had said, but rather by recasting Turing's objection. "Turing doesn't object to anything I say," he claimed. "He agrees with every word. He objects to the idea he thinks underlies it."[19]

The reason it was important to Wittgenstein that there could be no substantial disagreement on any philosophical point is not because he thought that everything he said philosophically was true, but rather that, in so far as it was philosophical, it was not – indeed, could not possibly be – making a truth claim at all. I would claim something similar for biography. In so far as truth claims are made in a biography they are, or ought to be, trivially demonstrable by citing the appropriate document or other piece of evidence. In so far as the biography is genuinely insightful, however, it is not making a truth claim and therefore disagreement is impossible. What then do I say to my critics? Following Wittgenstein I could claim that they are wrong even in thinking that they disagree with me. If they saw things clearly, they would see that they don't really object to anything I say. They agree with every word.

If my critics retort that they find this unsatisfying, all I can say is that I do, too. The most that can be said in my defense is that if this sense of unease points to a fundamental flaw in my conception of philosophical biography, it points equally to a fundamental flaw in Wittgenstein's later conception of philosophy.

NOTES

1. Ludwig Wittgenstein, *Culture and Value,* ed G. H. von Wright trans. P. Winch (Chicago) University of Chicago Press, 1980); rev. 2d ed. [Oxford Basil Blackwell, 1998]), p. 7/9.
2. Ibid., p. 66/75.
3. Stanley Cavell, *A Pitch of Philosophy: Autobiographical Exercises* (Cambridge, MA: Harvard University Press, 1994), pp. 49–50.
4. Ludwig Wittgenstein, *Philosophical Investigations,* ed. G. E. M. Anscombe and R. Rhees (Oxford: Basil Blackwell, 1953), p. 227.
5. Ibid., p. 228.

6. Ludwig Wittgenstein, *Last Writings on the Philosophy of Psychology,* Vol. 1, ed. G. H. von Wright and Heikki Nyman; trans. C. G. Luckhardt and Maximilian A. E. Aue (Oxford: Basil Blackwell, 1992), §927.
7. Virginia Woolf, *A Woman's Essays* (London: Penguin, 1992), p. 80.
8. Jean-Paul Sartre, *Baudelaire* (London: Hamish Hamilton, 1949), pp. 17–18.
9. "Remarks on Frazer's *Golden Bough,*" in Ludwig Wittgenstein, *Philosophical Occasions, 1912–1951,* ed. James Klagge and Alfred Nordmann (Indianapolis, IN: Hackett, 1993), p. 133.
10. Sartre, op. cit., p. 76.
11. Ibid., p. 77.
12. Ludwig Wittgenstein, *Ludwig Wittgenstein, Cambridge Letters: Correspondence with Russell, Keynes, Moore, Ramsey and Sraffa,* ed. Brian McGuinness and G. H. von Wright (Oxford: Basil Blackwell, 1995), p. 58.
13. Fyodor Dostoevsky, *The Brothers Karamazov* (London: Penguin, 1982). Part I, Book I, Chapter 5 ("Elders"), p. 30.
14. M. Drury, "Conversations with Wittgenstein," in *Recollections of Wittgenstein,* ed. R. Rhees (Oxford: Oxford University Press, 1984), p. 108.
15. Virgina Woolf, *Collected Essays, v. 4* (London: The Hogarth Press, 1967) p. 230.
16. Sartre, op. cit., p. 245.
17. Michel Montaigne, "Of the Inconsistency of Our Actions," in *Essays* (Stanford, CA: Stanford University Press, 1958), p. 220.
18. Douglas Collins, *Sartre as Biographer* (Cambridge, MA: Harvard University Press, 1980), p. 79.
19. *Wittgenstein's Lectures on the Foundations of Mathematics:Cambridge, 1939,* (Ithaca, NY: Cornell University Press, 1976), p. 67.

Philosophy and Biography*

JAMES CONANT

> The biographies and autobiographies, ... lives of great men, ... that stand cheek by jowl with the novels and poems, are we to refuse to read them because they are not "art"? Or shall we read them, but read them in a different way, with a different aim? ... How far, we must ask ourselves, is a book influenced by its writer's life – how far is it safe to let the man interpret the writer? How far shall we resist or give way to the sympathies and antipathies that the man himself rouses in us – so sensitive are words, so receptive of the character of the author? These are questions that press upon us when we read lives and letters, and we must answer them for ourselves.
>
> *– Virginia Woolf*[1]

How about the biographies and autobiographies – in short, the lives – of great *philosophers* (those many books that stand in our libraries and bookstores cheek by jowl with the volumes of their philosophy), are we to read them or not; and, if so, how? Let's call this "the first question." It is a very general question.

And how about the possibility of a certain genre of biography (or autobiography) – which I will call *philosophical biography* – a mode of representation of the life of an individual philosopher that aspires to facilitate the understanding of that individual qua philosopher? A philosophical biography (or autobiography) aspires to confer through the genre of biography (or autobiography) – that is through the depiction of a life – a sort of understanding that itself has a claim to being termed *philosophical.* Is such a genre of biography so much as possible? Let's call this "the second question." It is a fairly specific question.

It is difficult to get a hearing for the second question. The possibility of its being heard, let alone addressed, tends to be drowned out by the din of controversy surrounding various specifications of the first question, such as the following: Are we to refuse to read biographies and autobiographies of

* A version of this paper was given at a symposium on "Philosophy and Biography" on May 18, 1999, at the University of Athens, organized by Vasso Kindi.

philosophers because they are not "philosophy"? Or shall we read them, but read them in a different way, with a different aim? If so, *how* differently? Are we to read them with the aim of learning some "background" that will help us to a better understanding of the philosophical writings of the person whose writings they are? Or are we to read them with an interest in the person of the philosopher that is only permissible if kept clearly distinct from an interest in his or her philosophical work proper? How far shall we resist or give way to the sympathies and antipathies that the philosopher himself or herself (as revealed, say, through biography or autobiography) rouses in us? To what extent do the sympathies and antipathies thus roused bear on an estimate (not only of the person, but) of the philosophical work itself? Can the words that comprise the philosophical work be expressive of the character of the author in a way that makes an assessment of that character integral to an assessment of that work? Or is an estimate of the person of the philosopher always irrelevant to an understanding of his or her philosophical work?

I take these to be important and difficult questions. In what follows I will have something to say about each of them. Like the first question, however, I do not think any of them admits of a general answer; I will, accordingly, not attempt anything of the sort here. Insofar as they do admit of answers, they are the sorts of questions we must each answer for ourselves and on a case-by-case basis. The trouble is that it is easy to fall into the confusion of thinking that questions such as these do admit of a general answer, thus obstructing our view of the second question.

The aim of this paper is to lend credence to two suggestions: first, that the answer to the second question should be affirmative, that is, that philosophical biography (in the sense of the term specified above) *is* possible, not that it is *always* possible (i.e., possible for all philosophers, regardless of the character of their work), nor that it is sometimes *indispensable* (i.e., that there are philosophers whose work cannot be understood without the aid of this genre), but merely that is *possible*; and second, the suggestion that, where it is possible, it can also sometimes be a good thing.

A Deadlock

Nowadays there seem to be two standard ways to understand the relation between philosophy and biography: the first contends that biography holds *the secret* to understanding the work of a philosopher, the second that the understanding of a philosopher's life is *irrelevant* to an understanding of his work. I will call these *reductivism* and *compartmentalism,* respectively. The reductivist and the compartmentalist have this much in common: each thinks that the first question – Are we to read these books or not; and, if so, how? – admits of a general answer.

The reductivist thinks that if we learn enough about a philosopher's life, we will see why he wrote what he did and thereby discover the real meaning of his work. There are many models for how to write a reductivist biography. There is (what we might call) *the psychoanalytic model,* in which one looks for the real causes and hidden meanings latent in an author's work by pointing to the symptoms of pathology therein and then weaves them into a narrative of the aetiology of the broader pathological symptoms that marked his life as a whole. There is also (what we might call) *the Marxist model,* in which one looks for the real causes and hidden meanings latent in an author's work by pointing to the way in which his life is shaped by the ideological false consciousness of the class into which he is born, and examining how that consciousness gradually evolves (and perhaps breaks up) as he struggles to come to terms with the contradictions inherent in a capitalist form of social organization. There are many other such models of reductivist biography. (I do not mean to suggest that psychoanalytic theory, on the one hand, or Marxist theory, on the other, cannot shed a great deal of light on why an individual acts or thinks as he or she does; but only to suggest that, when such theories are employed *reductively* in the practice of writing biography, the resulting brew is inevitably a travesty of both biography and psychoanalysis or Marxism.)

The mark of such reductivist varieties of biography is that they seek to understand and evaluate an author's work by locating his work in a broader set of *causal* forces acting upon him. The work comes to be viewed as an *effect* of those forces, and evaluation of the work is grounded in features of the author's life that are *external* to his work. Compartmentalism is best seen, I think, as arising out of a kind of recoil from these evils of reductivism. Part of the reason that compartmentalism is the dominant point of view in serious intellectual circles today is because we have so few good examples of the practice of intellectual biography. Most biographies, where they are not utterly superficial and without pretense to confer intellectual understanding, tend to slide, to some degree, into reductivism. The compartmentalist rightly senses first that there is something wrong with restricting one's view of an author's life to a causal analysis of how he came to think and act as he did (e.g., "Wittgenstein was obsessed with issues of purity because of his childhood toilet training"), and second that there is something wrong with evaluating an author's work in terms of criteria drawn from wholly outside that work (e.g., "You only have to consider the way Russell treated his many wives and lovers to see that *Principia Mathematica* cannot be the work of a great mind"). This leads the compartmentalist to conclude that an understanding of the life is utterly irrelevant to an understanding of the work.

The compartmentalist therefore has (at least) two sound reasons for resisting reductivism: so as not to mistake a story about the external causes that might have led a philosopher to say certain things for an internal understanding of the work itself; and so as not to base an evaluation of a philosopher's work solely on an evaluation of the man. I will call the conjunction of these two sound reasons for resisting reductivism "the truth in compartmentalism." The question that I want to explore in a moment is the following: can we hold on to the truth in compartmentalism while rejecting the main thesis of compartmentalism?

The compartmentalist concludes that everything that is relevant to an understanding of a philosopher's work is to be found in the pages he wrote. To look beyond the pages he wrote to anything of a more "personal" nature, whether said to a friend, or written in a diary or in private correspondence, is to look to something that is not part of the work, and thus without bearing on the task of seeking insight into what is happening on the pages of the philosopher's work. The compartmentalist can allow that we may have our reasons for being curious about the lives of great men and women, and that there is nothing wrong, in and of itself, with the practice of reading and writing about the lives of such men and women; and he can allow that there is much that we can seek to understand about why these lives come to assume the sorts of shapes that they do. Nonetheless the compartmentalist thinks that we should not confuse the task of understanding these lives and what happens in them with the utterly distinct task of learning to understand the philosophical works written by the individuals who happened to live those lives. Each of these activities – biography and philosophy – is fine in its place, says the compartmentalist, but they should be kept wholly apart and should never be confused with one another. These two activities should take place in separate compartments of *our* intellectual lives and what goes on in each of these compartments should be kept from spilling over into the other.

Contemporary thinking about the topic of philosophical biography thus tends to find itself in the following deadlock: we are offered a forced choice between reductivism and compartmentalism – an understanding of an author's work is to be found *wholly outside* his work (in the external events of his life) or an understanding of the work is to be sought by attending solely to what lies *wholly within* the work (and the life is held not to be part of the work).

An Example of an Ancient Philosopher: Socrates

With a view to easing this deadlock, it might help to consider Socrates. Precisely because he did not *write* anything, the example of Socrates forces us to clarify our thinking about the crudely drawn distinction between "life" and "work" that informs the debate between reductivists and compartmentalists. Socrates's life is his work and his work is his life. He strived to live –

and to provide an example of what it means to live – a certain kind of life: the life of one who loves wisdom, a practitioner of *philo-sophia*. There is no understanding of his philosophy apart from an understanding of the sort of life he sought to live.

What the example of Socrates makes immediately evident is that, at least in the case of this philosopher, we need a nonreductive conception of philosophical biography: a way of understanding the relation between philosophy and life that preserves the truth in compartmentalism without its compartmentalization of philosophy and life. We need a way of understanding a philosopher's life that allows us to see that life (not as an effect of forces wholly external to his philosophy, but rather) as something that is internally related to his philosophy – as an *expression* of his philosophy. When and how Socrates challenges the charge (of corrupting the youth of Athens) brought against him, when and how he accepts the verdict of the court against him, when and how he refuses the opportunity to flee from prison, when and how he behaves in his final moment when he drinks the hemlock and lies down to die: these are all expressions of his philosophy. No understanding of what Socrates thought philosophy was is possible apart from an appreciation of how philosophy is meant to find expression in a life such as *this* – that is, in a life such as the one that Socrates himself sought to live.

A compartmentalist might reply by protesting: "Yes, but Socrates is a very special case just because he did not write anything: there is no place to look for his philosophy but in his life; but other philosophers, however, do write things and, in such cases, we must separate the task of understanding what they wrote from the task of understanding how they lived."

What is odd about this reply might be put as follows: it seeks to marginalize the fountainhead of Western philosophy. When Aristotle asks his rhetorical question "What more accurate standard or measure of good things do we have than the Sage?" he is the first of a long line of philosophers to bear implicit witness to the way in which the figure of Socrates leaves its mark on the whole of ancient philosophy.[2] If one turns to the great schools of Hellenistic philosophy – the Skeptics, the Stoics, the Epicureans, the Neo-Platonists – they all sought to practice (what we might call) a broadly "Socratic" conception of philosophy; that is, they all sought to encourage the pursuit of a kind of life – the life of the Sage – for which, for all their differences, they all took Socrates to offer a (more or less adequate) model. Philosophy was not something you simply learned – say, by reading certain books and taking an examination on them – it was something you practised. Yes, of course, it consisted, among other things, of long stretches of argument; but those arguments were an integral part of a set of (what Pierre Hadot has called) "spiritual exercises" through the employment of which one sought to transform oneself. (This is perhaps particularly clear in the case of the ancient skeptics. You will have misunderstood the role of any particular argument, as deployed within the practice of the ancient skeptics, if you think the skeptic wants you, in the end, to prefer that argument over the equipollent argument for the opposite conclusion.) The spiritual disciplines internal to each of the Hellenistic schools of philosophy seek to promote a certain kind of existential *telos* – for the Skeptics, the telos is *ataraxia*; for the Neo-Platonists, it is ecstatic union with the cosmos, and so forth – and the telos in question is not a merely theoretical (as opposed to practical) matter: it is a matter of successfully giving a certain sort of shape to one's self and this is achieved in part by giving a certain sort of shape to one's life.

A nostalgia for this aspect of ancient philosophy, along with the correlative contrast between ancient and modern philosophy, is a theme common to the writings of Kierkegaard and Nietzsche. A contemporary scholar of ancient philosophy who has picked up their theme, and laid particular emphasis on its importance for a proper understanding of the ancients' conception of philosophy, is the French historian Pierre Hadot. During the Hellenistic and Roman eras, philosophy was, Hadot tells us, "a way of life":

This is not only to say that it was a specific type of moral conduct. . . . Rather it means that philosophy was a mode of existing-in-the-world, which had to be practised at each instant, and the goal of which was to transform the whole of the individual's life. For the ancients, the mere word *philo-sophia* – the love of wisdom – was enough to express this conception of philosophy. . . . Philosophy was a method of spiritual progress which demanded a radical conversion and transformation of the individual's way of being. . . . Thus, philosophy was a way of life, both in its exercise and effort to achieve wisdom and in its goal, wisdom itself. For real wisdom does not merely cause us to know: it makes us "be" in a different way.[3]

On this conception of philosophy, a philosopher's life is the definitive expression of his philosophy. For such a philosopher, his writings (i.e., that which we are tempted to identify as his "work") are a mere means to facilitate the achievement of that work on the self that is (properly identified as) a philosopher's work. This has implications for the sorts of roles that writings that aim to depict the life of the philosopher are able to assume in ground-level philosophical practice. It also helps to explain the frequent deployment of anecdotes regarding the lives of philosophers in ancient Greek and Roman texts. Anecdotes about philosophers wedded to this or that philosophical teaching often seem to be adduced by the ancients as an instrument not only for describing but also for *evaluating,* the teaching in question.[4] Arnoldo Momigliano, in *The Development of Greek Biography,* writes:

Anecdotes served to characterize modes of life, of thought, of style. If Phanias of Eresus in his book on the Socratics said that Aristippus was the first of the Socratics to pay for tuition and to make money by teaching, the story must have been meant to characterize, or perhaps to discredit, the hedonistic inclinations of Aristippus. Books of this type on philosophic schools, though probably first written in the Peripatos, soon became the common patrimony of Hellenistic culture.[5]

Momigliano distinguishes, quite properly, this ancient practice of liberally deploying anecdotes from the ancient practice of biography proper (i.e., the practice of constructing a narrative of an individual's life from birth to death). Nevertheless, he argues that the two practices had this much in common: both were "used by philosophers at large as a weapon against hostile schools."[6] Arnold Davidson (commenting on the implications of Hadot's thesis that philosophy for the ancients was a way of life) develops the point:

The significance of philosophy as a way of life can be seen in the importance given to biographies in ancient philosophical work. . . . [A] philosophical biography was not predominantly a narrative intended to allow one to understand an author and his doctrines; it was not just a report of what the author said and believed. Rather, "it was, in the first place, a tool of philosophical battle", since one could defend or condemn a philosophy by way of the characteristics of the mode of life of those who supported it.[7]

The role of biography in the practice of ancient philosophy was not limited to this purely negative polemical function. It served an important positive function as well: to provide a representation of the philosophical life. The tradition of philosophical biography, so conceived, was initiated by Plato's and Xenophon's respective accounts of the life of Socrates. The influence of this mode of representing a life was not confined to the representation of the lives of philosophers. In ancient Greek and Roman times, all biography contained an element of philosophical biography. The life that the ancient art of biography seeks to depict, whatever else it may be, will be the embodiment of a conception of philosophy. Biography, so conceived, is an account of the life of the individual – whether it be the life of a poet, statesman, general, or saint – qua hero. What such an account aims to highlight is that which is *exemplary* in such a life.[8] This life, for the ancients, is not, and could not be, independent of what philosophy is. (Thus, for example, Plutarch's depiction of the life of, say, a statesman will aim to show how *philosophia* finds expression in *that* life).

If historians such as Hadot and Momigliano are right about the role that depictions of the lives of philosophers play in the ancients' understanding of the practice of philosophy, then the problem that the compartmentalist so evidently faces in the case of Socrates – whose writing cannot be understood apart from his life because he wrote nothing – confronts him no less pointedly in the shape of the whole of ancient philosophy. For, if they are right, then, at least for much of the corpus of ancient philosophy, the only understanding of those writings available independently of an understanding of the lives its authors aspired to lead is an anachronistic one.[9]

To this a compartmentalist might reply: "O.K. Perhaps you have a point about ancient philosophy. Perhaps philosophy was *once* about living a certain sort of life – and you are right that there is, in such a case, perhaps no separating an understanding of the life that a particular philosophy enjoins its practitioners to lead from an understanding of the philosophy itself. But my objection is to biographies of *modern* philosophers. The relation between one's life and one's philosophy is no longer *for us* what it was for the ancients. We, contemporary philosophers, no longer look to the *Sage* for an accurate standard or measure of anything. Nowadays, we look only to the well-reasoned philosophical *theory*; and one does not need to be a sage to put forward exemplary instances of such theory – all one needs to be is a good philosopher."

The compartmentalist has a point here. His point does not secure his thesis; but it forces one to reflect on what has become of the ancient conception of philosophy in the course of the development of philosophy in the modern era. To put the point simply, there is certainly this much of a difference between ancient and modern philosophy: what Kierkegaard and Nietzsche claim was generally true of ancient philosophy is by no means generally true of modern philosophy. Hence the possibility of their interest in the *difference* between ancient and modern philosophy. (But why were these two *philosophers* so interested in this difference? Their interest was not confined to the scholarly ambitions of the historian of ideas but was itself philosophically motivated. This interest was premised precisely on a refusal to accept the difference in question as a difference in kind with regard to the possibilities for philosophy in the modern era.) What is sound in the compartmentalist's "point" above is perhaps best formulated as two separate points: (1) the relation between philosophy and life is no longer as perspicuous as it once was, and (2) there is no longer, in contemporary philosophy, any such thing as *the* relation between philosophy and life – there are as many species of this relation as there are conceptions of philosophy, and, across these conceptions, widely varying degrees and kinds of intimacy obtain among the relata.

An Example of a Modern Philosopher: Wittgenstein

Wittgenstein is a useful example of a modern philosopher who shows that the separation that the compartmentalist seeks to effect between ancient and modern philosophy has, at the very least, its exceptions. In a manner strikingly reminiscent of ancient accounts of a philosopher's thought, many recent accounts of Wittgenstein's philosophy adduce a wealth of anecdotes and biographical details regarding Wittgenstein's life. Wittgenstein, like Socrates or Pythagoras, seems to many of his expositors to call for this sort of treatment. This is surely not merely because Wittgenstein lived in a manner that caused anecdotes about him to proliferate, but because the authors of such accounts believe that the anecdotes and details in question illuminate something about Wittgenstein qua philosopher. Yes, he was an odd fellow who lived an unconventional life; and, yes, of course, this provides colorful material for the occasional entertaining digression. Yet the authors of the accounts of Wittgenstein's philosophy at issue here do not take themselves to be *digressing* when adducing the material in question; they tend to see an intimate if elusive connection between the extraordinariness of Wittgenstein's life and the difficulty of his thought.[10] It is doubtful that most of them would imagine that they are able to see such a connection if they did not take themselves to be encouraged to look for one by something in Wittgenstein's philosophical writings. By what?

Consider the following five passages from Wittgenstein:

1. You cannot write anything about yourself that is more truthful than you yourself are.[11]
2. Nothing is so difficult as not deceiving oneself.[12]
3. If anyone is *unwilling* to descend into himself . . . he will remain superficial in his writing.[13]
4. Working in philosophy . . . is really more a working on oneself.[14]
5. That man will be revolutionary who can revolutionize himself.[15]

Numerous remarks similar to these can be found scattered throughout Wittgenstein's writings.[16] Such a remark, when one comes upon it in the middle of an extended Wittgensteinian philosophical investigation – on, for example, whether it is possible for me to give myself a private ostensive definition, or for another person to have my pains, or for there to be only one occasion on which someone obeys a rule, etcetera – is apt to strike one as a nonsequitur. Why do such remarks crop up in the midst of Wittgenstein's philosophical investigations, apparently changing the topic and interrupting the course of the investigation?

There are various ways one might answer this question. The reductivist and compartmentalist will each favor a certain direction of answer to this question. Reductivists of a certain stripe might want to insist that the real sources of Wittgenstein's philosophical preoccupations come to the surface in remarks such as these: it is through a prior and independent understanding of what prompts Wittgenstein to break out into remarks such as these that one finds the wellsprings of his philosophy. The reductivist thereby seeks an understanding of such remarks in a prior understanding of his life. He thus takes himself to be able to arrive at a key to understanding Wittgenstein's philosophy via a route that enables him to understand such remarks prior to understanding the rest of Wittgenstein's corpus. This inevitably prompts a certain stripe of compartmentalist to insist that these remarks (not only do not provide a key to understanding Wittgenstein, but) do not really belong to Wittgenstein's philosophical corpus at all: he used his notebooks to record all sorts of observations and a good editor of his philosophical manuscripts would have sound grounds for culling such remarks from a final published edition of his (properly) *philosophical* writings. (Such a compartmentalist would concede that it is, of course, still fine to collect and publish such jottings separately, as long as one does not fall into the confusion of thinking they are part and parcel of the philosophy proper.[17]) Thus this stripe of compartmentalist seeks to understand Wittgenstein's philosophy independently of any understanding of such remarks.[18]

In a previous paper, I had occasion to quote these same five remarks from Wittgenstein.[19] D. Z. Phillips, in a reply to my paper, observed that Wittgenstein, in each of these five passages, should be understood as "referring to difficulties in *doing philosophy,* difficulties in giving the problems the kind of attention philosophy asks of us."[20] I agree with this.[21] And if this is right, it helps to explain why these remarks are not nonsequiturs, and how it is that they touch on a dimension of difficulty that is pervasively, if often only tacitly, in play in Wittgenstein's investigations.[22] We can put Phillips's point this way: when such a remark occurs in the midst of one of Wittgenstein's investigations, it does not introduce an abrupt change of topic; it interrupts the investigation in order to step back for a moment and comment on a difficulty in doing philosophy that one runs up against in such investigations. Thus one will not understand what such remarks are about, unless one understands why they occur in the sorts of contexts in which they characteristically do.[23]

Phillips goes on to remark that the sort of difficulties that are at issue in the five passages from Wittgenstein quoted above will be "missed if one equates the difficulties with *personal* difficulties."[24] This is surely right if by *"personal* difficulties" Phillips means *merely* personal (as opposed to philosophical) difficulties. Yet it is equally wrong if by this Phillips means "philosophical, and therefore *in no way* personal, difficulties."[25] Erecting an opposition here between mutually exclusive categories of "the personal" and "the philosophical" will block the way to understanding why Wittgenstein thinks that work in philosophy (properly conducted) is a kind of working on oneself, and why he thinks that one cannot be any more honest in one's philosophical thinking than one can be with oneself, and why he thinks that the greatness of a philosophical work is expressive of the greatness of the particular human being who is its author. Phillips is certainly right that the wrong sort of insistence on the (idea that the sorts of *difficulty* with which Wittgenstein, in his philosophical work, is concerned are) "personal" can lead to disastrous misinterpretations of Wittgenstein's work.[26] Yet too sharp a recoil from such misinterpretations – with its complementary insistence upon too sharp a separation between (merely) personal and (properly) philosophical difficulty – is equally obstructive of an understanding of Wittgenstein's conception of the nature of the difficulty of philosophy.

Wittgenstein's remark "nothing is so difficult as not deceiving oneself" is neither more nor less a remark about a particular difficulty that arises in philosophy than it is a remark about a general ethical difficulty. For Wittgenstein's thought here is that one's ability to avoid self-deception in philosophy can be neither more nor less than one's ability to avoid it outside philosophy. (Wittgenstein concludes a meditation on the effects that the all but inevitable tendency to "lie to oneself" has on one's writing with the remark, "If you are unwilling to know what you are, your writing is a form of deceit."[27]) If you are unwilling to descend into yourself, then you will remain superficial in your thinking and writing generally, and a fortiori you will remain superficial in your efforts to write philosophy. Hence Wittgenstein writes Malcolm, "You can't think decently if you don't want to hurt yourself."[28] The issue here – as in each of the five remarks from Wittgenstein quoted above – is at once personal and philosophical.

"If anyone is *unwilling* to descend into himself . . . he will remain superficial in his writing." Wittgenstein is equally committed to the converse of this remark: if someone remains superficial in his thinking or writing this can (where it is not a function of immaturity or ineptitude) be a reflection of the character of the person whose thinking and writing it is. It is, for Wittgenstein, not only possible to discern aspects of a person's character in the character of their philosophizing, but essential to the formation of any true estimate of their philosophy that one be able to do so. The exercise of such discernment is never far below the surface in the judgments Wittgenstein himself offers of the philosophical work of others.[29] Yet this means that the line between "the personal" and "the philosophical" cannot be as sharp, for Wittgenstein, as Phillips imagines it to be. To put the point more positively and in a more Wittgensteinian idiom: the spirit of a person shows itself in the spirit of his philosophy, which in turn shows itself in the way he philosophizes.

The numerous remarks about other thinkers sprinkled throughout Wittgenstein's notebooks and recorded conversations furnish vivid documentation of the manifold sorts of ways in which Wittgenstein himself exercises such discernment. When Wittgenstein says of Frank Ramsey: that his "incapacity for genuine enthusiasm or (what is really the same thing) reverence came to disgust me more and more," he is commenting on something about Ramsey's sensibility that reflects itself in, but certainly not only in, the character of his response to philosophical ideas.[30] What is at issue here is a kind of limitation of sensibility that is neither merely personal nor merely philosophical, but rather equally – and, in Wittgenstein's eyes, equally fatefully – both. When Maurice Drury tells Wittgenstein, "I always enjoy reading William James. He is such a human person," Wittgenstein responds: "Yes, that is what makes him a good philosopher; he was a real human being."[31] That James is "a real human being" is something Wittgenstein takes himself to be able to discern as a reader of James's philosophical writings. The estimate he forms in this regard of James qua person is not – and, for Wittgenstein, cannot be – utterly independent of his estimate of James qua philosopher. When Wittgenstein remarks about A. J. Ayer: "He has something to say but he is incredibly shallow," this is, in the first instance, of course, a remark about the shallowness of Ayer's philosophizing.[32] Still it is not *merely* a remark about the quality of Ayer's efforts at philosophizing or wholly without bearing on an estimate of the shallowness or depth of the sensibility of the person whose philosophizing it is.[33] Similarly, when Wittgenstein says about the anthropologist James Frazer: that he "is much more savage than most of this savages," this is a comment on both the man and his thought.[34] It is a comment on something that shows itself in Frazer's writing about the forms of life he studies – where part of what shows itself pertains to the sorts of possibilities of thought and life that are (and are not) closed to Frazer himself.

"You cannot write anything about yourself that is more truthful than you yourself are." That is simultaneously a remark about a personal and a philosophical difficulty. (If you cannot write anything that is more truthful than you yourself are, then you cannot write anything *in philosophy* that is more truthful than you yourself are.) For Wittgenstein, the two difficulties are inseparable – they are aspects of a single difficulty.[35] One can, if one will, take the words "perspicuity" and "clarity" to stand for things Wittgenstein struggles to attain in philosophy. And one can, with equal justification, take the words "honesty" and "*Anständigkeit*" to stand for things Wittgenstein thinks everyone should struggle to attain in life. If you do not think of yourself as ever practicing philosophy, then you may take yourself only to have reason to think of yourself as caught up in the second of these two kinds of struggle.[36] If you evidently do practice philosophy, but most decidedly not in the spirit of Wittgenstein, then these two struggles may strike you as utterly independent of one another. (Though, it is worth remembering, they did not seem so to philosophers as different from one another as Socrates, Augustine, and Nietzsche.) Yet if you wish to think of yourself as practicing philosophy in anything like the spirit of Wittgenstein, then these two struggles must become for you – as they did for Wittgenstein – twin aspects of a single struggle, each partially constitutive of the other.

Ray Monk puts it well when he says, " 'Nothing is hidden' is, for Wittgenstein, an ethical as well as a logical remark."[37] Thus when Wittgenstein writes to his sister, "Call me a truth-seeker and I will be satisfied," he specifies the character of his striving in terms of something that for him is equally a philosophical and an ethical ideal.[38] All philosophical thinking and writing accordingly has, for Wittgenstein, its ethical aspect. Wittgenstein thought that what (and, more importantly, *how*) we think is revelatory of who we are (and how we live), and that learning to think better (and, above all, to *change* the ways in which one thinks) is an important means to becoming a better – what Wittgenstein calls a "real" – human being.[39] So, even though Wittgenstein, in one sense, "has no ethics" (if "ethics" names a branch of philosophy with its own proprietary subject matter), in another sense, his thinking and writing, on every page of his work, takes place under the pressure of an ethical demand.[40] If as a biographer (or reader of biography) one turns to examine his life, and has the eyes to see (which requires that one have some under-standing of his philosophy), one will discover the pressure of such a demand equally pervasively manifest in the conduct of his life and in his understand-ing of the relation between his philosophy and his life.

Such a philosopher will naturally attract biographers. If those biographers have reductivist proclivities, their biographical narratives will necessarily give a distorted picture not only of the life but also of the thought. They will give a distorted picture of the life of a philosopher such as Wittgenstein because there is no understanding the life of such a man apart from an understanding of his thought.[41] They will give a distorted picture of his thought because there is no understanding the thought of any interesting philosopher – and certainly not this one – as a straightforward function of his life, especially when the requisite understanding of the life is taken to be unproblematically available independently of an understanding of the thought.[42]

All of this naturally feeds the compartmentalist's anxieties and leads to his overreaction. I take it to be an overreaction because the compartmentalist's thesis goes well beyond the perfectly sensible claim that (*pace* reductivist biographers of Wittgenstein) it is both possible and important to attain an understanding of Wittgenstein's philosophy independently of making a study of his life. The compartmentalist insists that attention to a thinker's life cannot possibly shed any light on his thought. Thus the compartmentalist ends up attempting to enforce a veto on that genre of biography – (which I have been calling) philosophical biography – in which the biographer seeks to illuminate aspects of a philosopher's thought through an attention to his life. And, in the case of a philosopher such as Wittgenstein, whose thought embodies an understanding of what it is to lead the philosophical life, which is in turn reflected in how he lived, such a veto deprives us of a non-negligible resource for better understanding (that unity comprising both) the philosopher and his philosophy.

In the case of a philosopher such as Wittgenstein, the compartmentalist would deprive us of a genre of writing about the philosopher that, if it is done well, can be a good thing. The problem is that it almost never is done well, thus fuelling the suspicion that there is no possible thing of the relevant sort to do well.

Two Examples of Philosophical Biography

One time-honored way of demonstrating the possibility of something is to demonstrate its actuality. It is in this spirit that I conclude by considering two actual examples of philosophical biography: Ray Monk's biographies of Wittgenstein[43] and Russell.[44]

Ray Monk's biography of Wittgenstein not only shows that Wittgenstein's conception of philosophy is broadly "Socratic" (in the sense elucidated above), but it shows it in a way that only (that genre of writing known as) biography can – that is, by literally *showing* it: by presenting us with a picture of Wittgenstein's life. As anyone who reads Monk's biography is put in a position to see: Wittgenstein neither wanted to, nor thought he could, separate the task of becoming the sort of human being he wanted to be from the task of becoming the sort of philosopher he wanted to be. Indeed, it would be missing the point of Monk's biography to think that its gist could be summarized as follows: there were two different things Wittgenstein wanted to do – become a certain kind of person and become a certain kind of philosopher – but he thought that these two pursuits somehow presupposed one another or were in some way entangled in one another. These were not "two different things Wittgenstein wanted to do." There is only one "thing" here – the kind of living that is here in question and the kind of thinking that is here in question were, for Wittgenstein, two different aspects of a single unitary pursuit – which Wittgenstein called, as did the ancients, "philosophy."[45]

The compartmentalist might now venture the following reply: "O.K. I see that there are certain modern philosophers who should be exempted from my veto on trying to understand the work of a philosopher in tandem with trying to seek an understanding of how and why they lived as they did. There are philosophers, such as Wittgenstein, whose conception of philosophy and whose conception of how one should live are so deeply integrated that biography becomes a useful tool for illuminating the spirit in which such individuals seek to do philosophy and thus attaining a proper view of what philosophy is for philosophers of this funny sort. But, among modern philosophers, these philosophers are the exception. For most modern philosophers – for a typical analytic philosopher like Bertrand Russell – philosophy is one thing and life is another."

The example conveniently adduced here by the compartmentalist allows me to move straight to the following observation: Ray Monk's recent biography of Russell shows not only that this reply works almost as poorly in the case of Russell as it does in that of Wittgenstein, but also that the line that the compartmentalist seeks here to draw (between two kinds of philosophers) is in fact very difficult to draw – it is a difference in degree and not in kind.

It is the rare person whose motivations to philosophy are completely out of touch with the original ancient – we might call them "Socratic" – motivations to philosophy. It is even more rarely the case that such motivations are wholly absent from the work or life of a truly great philosopher (that is, a philosopher whose biography we might have some interest in reading).[46] There is certainly something right about the thought that among modern – unlike among ancient – philosophers there is a great deal of variety in the ways in, and the degrees to, which such a Socratic moment is legible in the life and the work, and in the ways in, and degrees to, which life and work do or do not form a genuine unity. Monk's two very different biographies illustrate two very different ways in which such a Socratic moment can be legible in the life and work of a twentieth-century philosopher, as well as two very different ways in, and degrees to, which life and work may cohere with one another.

Monk's biography of Russell shows how deeply divided a person Russell is and how those divisions shape and are given shape by the movement of his philosophical thought. Russell is, of course, famous for being a philosopher who changed his mind a lot. But what Monk's biography makes almost painfully vivid is that Russell not only changed his mind with alarming frequency when it came to his first-order philosophical convictions – about topics such as the existence of abstract entities, the nature of perception, the structure of judgment, or the analysis of matter – but that he was equally fickle in his second-order convictions about the nature, purpose, and value of philosophy as such. This shows itself, above all, in the breathtaking fluctuations in Russell's understanding of his own motivations to philosophy. Is this irrelevant to an understanding of his philosophy? Before addressing that question, perhaps a brief sample of the evidence is in order.

At times, Russell looks upon his work in mathematical logic as possibly the most exalted form of human occupation:

Pure mathematics is one of the highest forms of art; it has a sublimity quite special to itself, an immense dignity derived from the fact that its world is exempt from change and time. . . . [M]athematics is the only thing we know of that is capable of perfection; in thinking about it we become God. This alone is enough to put it on a pinnacle above all other studies.[47]

Russell's conception, however, of what it is that confers supreme value on this activity fluctuates between two poles – a quaintly contemplative, vaguely neoplatonist one and a highly modern, defiantly disenchanted one. These might be termed the *warm conception* and the *cold conception*, respectively, of the significance of mathematics. On the warm conception (which finds eloquent expression in the above quotation), the ennobling aspect of mathematics lies in the eternal character of its objects (a "world exempt from change and time"). Contemplation of such objects liberates the soul, allowing it to ascend to the heights. Other forms of knowledge accordingly pale in comparison with the sort of knowledge afforded by mathematics and those branches of philosophy properly associated with it:

I hold all knowledge that is concerned with things that actually exist – all that is commonly called Science – to be of very slight value compared to that knowledge which, like philosophy and mathematics, is concerned with ideal and eternal objects, and is freed from this miserable world which God has made.[48]

On the warm conception, (what Russell calls) "technical philosophy" represents the purest and noblest strain of philosophy because it, above all other disciplines, seeks to cut mathematical reality at its joints, revealing its true structure and nature. This contemplative conception of the importance of mathematics is, in turn, tied to a further yearning – a yearning for a world which will not disappoint:

The contemplation of what is non-human, the discovery that our minds are capable of dealing with material not created by them; above all, the realisation that beauty belongs to the outer world as to the inner, are the chief means of overcoming the terrible sense of impotence, of weakness, of exile amid hostile powers, which is too apt to result from acknowledging the all-but omnipotence of alien forces.... [M]athematics takes us still further from what is human, into the realm of absolute necessity, to which not only the actual world, but every possible world, must conform; and even here it builds a habitation eternally standing, where our ideals are fully satisfied and our best hopes are not thwarted.[49]

But, at other times, nothing strikes Russell as more deluded than such thoughts (thoughts such as that we could be "freed from this miserable world" or that our ideals could be "fully satisfied" and our best hopes remain "unthwarted"); and this triggers the recoil to the cold conception of the value of philosophy. In this mood, the thoughts expressed in the above passage are apt to strike Russell as of a piece with the illusions of the traditional religions – indeed, such thoughts are themselves species of religious illusion – and the goal of philosophy should be to free us from all such illusion: to enable us to look things hard in the face and see them as they really are.

On the cold conception, technical philosophy is, again, taken to represent the purest strain of philosophy; only now it is because, in the quest to see things as they really are, mathematics is the helpmeet of philosophy precisely because it is so "cold and passionless."[50] Russell's eulogies to coldness are no less fervent or picturesque than his odes to warmth (to "the immense dignity" of a world "exempt from time and change"); with the paradoxical result that in these eulogies the spirit of dispassionateness often appears in the guise of a passion: "Philosophy is a cold mistress – one can only reach her heart with cold steel in the hand of passion."[51] Thus the aim remains one of seeking to avoid disappointment, but the strategy changes (from seeking a safe haven for one's hopes) to seeking to free oneself of illusion through the practice of dispassionate analysis.[52]

At still other times, Russell declares himself able, in turn, to see through the pretensions of the cold conception of the value of mathematics, unmasking it, too, as only a more subtle and rarified species of romanticism, one still in search of that "shiver of feeling," which a more thoroughgoing gospel of coldness would renounce but, at the cost of losing all its appeal. For the cold conception, too, seeks to ennoble the study of mathematics by subliming the object of its study, thereby elevating the Self who studies. As Russell astutely observes: "[T]he reflection that such beauty is cold and inhuman is already romanticism – it gives a shiver of feeling in which Self has its share."[53] This observation also contains a clue to understanding the possibility of the sorts of syntheses of features of the cold and the warm conceptions one also finds in Russell's writings – such as the following: although the world of time and change in which all human endeavour must transpire is squalid and bleak and to be acknowledged as such, Man is at least vouchsafed the small consolation of being able to contemplate the beauty of a better and higher realm, in which Man cannot live, but upon which he may at least gaze. On this hybrid conception, technical philosophy acquires its value by providing a (very temporary) *refuge* from the world in which we live.

These fluctuations within Russell's view of what confers value on technical philosophy are reenacted in an even sharper register in the fluctuations in his view of whether technical philosophy as such really has value at all and, if not, what does. One source of the occasional ambivalence in Russell's attitudes toward technical philosophy is a fear of the dehumanizing effect of such philosophy on the philosopher:

Abstract work, if one wishes to do it well, must be allowed to destroy one's humanity; one raises a monument which is at the same time a tomb, in which, voluntarily, one slowly inters oneself.[54]

This passage still leaves room for the view that such self-destruction is itself a form of heroism: one sacrifices oneself but in the service of a greater good – the Truth. Yet the tone sometimes turns bitter, and the fear of disillusionment takes on additional bite in the form of a fear of retrospective disappointment: "I feel as if one would only discover on one's death-bed what one ought to have lived for, and realise too late that one's life has been wasted."[55] This occasional horror of the dehumanizing barrenness of technical work has its opposite pole in an intermittent attraction to alluringly momentous moral and political causes and, most strikingly, to religious modes of thought. Russell is famous for his fierce attacks on Christianity, but what is less well known is that he is also the author of passages such as the following:

Religion is the passionate determination that human life is to be capable of importance. . . . To assert religion is to believe that virtue is momentous, that human greatness is truly great, and that it is possible for man to achieve an existence which shall have significance.[56]

Here the very possibility of believing that one is able to achieve an existence that has even a modicum of significance is tied to a sort of hope that it is the special office of religion to confer. Rather than mathematics, here it is religion that holds out the means of conferring value on this sordid and miserable world, of satisfying our deepest desires and not leaving our best hopes thwarted: "The things that make religion are the great things; they are what make life infinite and not petty."[57] What religion, in numerous remarks such as these, is represented as able to confer is strikingly reminiscent of the solace that mathematics (on the warm conception) is represented as able to afford; only now a new wrinkle is added – the solace comes not by fleeing the world of "human sordidness"[58] (as mathematics enables us to) for a timeless inhuman world, but by escaping the sordidness and petty selfishness of everyday existence via a route *toward* humanity, with the aim not only of coming closer to others but of bringing humanity as a whole together:

What we *know* is that things come into our lives sometimes which are so immeasurably better than the things of every day, that it *seems* as though they were sent from another world, and could not come out of ourselves. . . . Religion, it seems to me, ought to make us know and remember these immeasurably better things, and live habitually in the thought of them. . . . I have hitherto only seen the greatest things at rare times of stress or exultation. . . . When [that vision] . . . is strong, the kind of philosophical work I do seems not worth doing, and so when I have to do this work that vision fades. . . . What the vision seems to show me is that we can live in a deeper region than the region of little every-day cares and desires – where beauty is a revelation of something beyond, where it becomes possible to love all men.[59]

This is not a mood Russell is ever able to sustain for long – at least not in this otherworldly key. Yet there is an underlying attitude – we might call it one of *utopianism* – to which Russell recurs throughout his life, which fuels his enthusiasm for various (sometimes astonishingly harebrained) political schemes, and which cyclically both eclipses and is alternately eclipsed by his enthusiasm for technical philosophy. Yet, whether it be in connection with his relatively enduring stretches of enthusiasm for technical philosophy or his comparatively ephemeral fits of enthusiasm for (some watered-down form of) religion, or some other project of utopian renewal, Russell never fails at some point to succumb to the feeling "that some element of delusion is involved in giving so much passion to any humanly attainable object."[60] The effect of such recurrent disillusionment is that "irony creeps into the very springs of one's being."[61]

Consequently, "the revelation of something beyond, where it becomes possible to love all men" finds its counterpoint in another vision:

In this vision, sorrow is the ultimate truth of life, everything else is oblivion or delusion. Then even love seems to me merely an opiate – it makes us forget that we draw our breath in pain and that thought is the gateway to despair.[62]

The defense against the pain such disillusionment brings is a ruthlessly disenchanted view of the cosmos and one's place in it. Thus the pair of complementary conceptions that form the poles of Russell's thought about the significance of technical philosophy are parallelled by similar poles in Russell's conceptions of the value of philosophy as such. We might term these Russell's *utopian conception* and *disenchanted conception* of philosophy (and of the character of the reality it discloses), respectively. Here, too, we come upon striking hybrids at certain phases in Russell's thought. Even in his ultradisenchanted mode, Russell's tone is able to take on, if not a utopian, at least an edifying aspect. He accomplishes this by first assuming the mantle of a staunch defender of the scientific outlook and then characterizing the requirements of a strictly scientific attitude in ways that appear to have straightforward ethical implications. Paradoxically, on a first look, however, the nature of reality as disclosed by science appears to be merely ethically neutral:

The kernel of the scientific outlook is the refusal to regard our own desires and tastes and interests as affording a key to the understanding of the world. . . . The scientific mind involves a sweeping away of all other desires in the interests of the desire to know. . . . Until we have learnt to think of . . . [the universe] in ethically neutral terms, we have not arrived at a scientific attitude in philosophy.[63]

This (apparently) ethically colourless view of the nature of things is sometimes able to take on an astonishingly vibrant aspect. In certain writings, Russell manages to convert a description of the universe as consisting of nothing more than mere clouds of particles in motion into a prelude for an edifying discourse – one that climaxes in the rousing tones of a gospel of salvation. This tendency is already manifest in as early an essay as "A Free Man's Worship" (written in 1902).[64] The essay starts with observations such as that "the world which Science presents for our belief" is "purposeless" and "void of meaning" – observations that Science has allegedly established to such a degree that today "no philosophy which rejects them can hope to stand."[65] We must acknowledge the truth of these observations not only for reasons of intellectual honesty, but in order to protect ourselves from false hope and crushing disappointment: "Only within the scaffolding of these truths, only on the firm foundation of unyielding despair, can the soul's habitation be safely built."[66] The essay rapidly moves from thus insinuating that what Science reveals is (not just ethically neutral, but) ethically dismal to apparently asserting it: the world as revealed by Science is positively "inhospitable" to human hopes and values; Science reveals an *"opposition* of fact and ideal."[67] This sets up the question "How, in such an alien and inhuman world, can so powerless a creature as Man preserve his aspirations untarnished?"[68] In its answer to this question, the voice of sober-minded scientifically-informed common sense rapidly gives way to that of someone who has looked deep into the abyss, lived to tell about it, and now returns to show the rest of us how to become skeptical heros undaunted by the task of living in a meaningless cosmos.[69] Though when he enters this postscientific sermonizing vein his cadences are sometimes dishearteningly hard to distinguish from those of as comparatively inconsequential a philosopher as, say, Albert Camus, of all Russell's many personae, this is probably the one that remains best known outside professional philosophical circles.

The preceding brief summary of Russell's intellectual pendulum-swings should suffice to make the following question urgent: How do all these attitudes (expressed in the quotations from Russell that figure in the preceding summary) fit into a single philosophical trajectory? One way of answering this question is by trying to understand another: how do these attitudes all fit into a single life? One can imagine different directions of answer to the former question (how do they fit into a single philosophical trajectory?) that might emerge through a consideration of the latter (how do they all fit into a single life?). To these different directions of answer correspond different sorts of intelligibility that philosophical biography can confer. At one extreme, one might come to see more clearly how a single overarching philosophical conception does indeed run through apparently discordant attitudes, harmonizing them into a single coherent unity: when one sees how the attitudes all fit together within the life, one sees better how they fit together philosophically. At the other extreme, one might come to see more clearly how there is no underlying unity in philosophical conception to bring this variety of attitudes into concord, yet one may still be brought to appreciate how this particular constellation of tensions and oscillations in philosophical conception fits into a single *humanly* (as opposed to *logically*) intelligible pattern: when one sees how the attitudes all fit into a life, one sees better how (although they do not form a coherent philosophical whole) they nonetheless represent an intelligible set of human responses to a certain set of intellectual needs and pressures. Monk's biography of Wittgenstein aims to confer the first of these two sorts of intelligibility on the material it lays before its reader; and his biography of Russell aims to confer the second of these two sorts of intelligibility on the material it lays before its reader.

With the aid of the narrative Monk painstakingly pieces together, we not only follow Russell through his convulsive changes of heart, but we witness how these changes are coordinated with – how they both trigger and are triggered by – such things as the fluctuations in his relationship with figures such as G. E. Moore, Joseph Conrad, and Wittgenstein; his falling into and out of the grip of the conviction that he has found the love of his life; his contributions as a pamphleteer for diverse social and moral causes; his sojourns in the Soviet Union, the United States, and China; his gruelling soapbox tours on behalf of a variety of political movements; his work as a founder of a school and an agitator for educational reform; his efforts to coauthor treatises with collaborators as different from one another in sensibility and outlook as A. N. Whitehead, D. H. Lawrence, and Dora Black; and so forth. Once Russell's contributions to philosophy are woven together by Monk into a single continuous biographical narrative – a narrative in which each of the elements of this whirl of seemingly disjointed pursuits finds its place – it becomes possible to see the whirl not merely as a frenzy of activity, most of which is extracurricular to Russell's work as a philosopher. Many elements of the whirl become legible as expressions of Russell's fluctuating philosophical aspirations, and of the restless oscillation between the poles of yearning and disenchantment that characterize both his philosophy and his life as a whole.

What emerges vividly in Monk's pair of attempts to write philosophical biography is that the sort of illumination (of the work of an individual philosopher) that the genre of philosophical biography most naturally finds itself struggling to confer pertains, for the most part, not to particular details of philosophical doctrine or method, but rather to the character – what Wittgenstein calls the *spirit* – of a philosopher's work as a whole. Thus the most significant change of aspect (in our view of a philosopher's work) effected by a successful philosophical biography is unlikely to be *local* in character. That is, it is unlikely to be such that we will be able to exhibit our understanding – of that which we have been helped by means of philosophical biography better to understand (about a given philosopher's work) – by adducing detachable bits of (the philosopher's) philosophy that we are (now better) able to expound. If there is an important relationship between what philosophical biography shows and how it shows it, then we should not be surprised to learn that the sorts of change of aspect that philosophical biography permits to dawn in our perception of a philosopher's work are not ones easily brought into view by an alternative genre of writing. In particular, the sort of change of aspect in question will not admit expression via a mode of exposition of a philosopher's thought proper to the exposition of features of his thought graspable independently of their relation to the character of his thought as a whole.

The proper expression of such changes of aspect in our perception of a philosopher's work will possess the same paradoxical combination of features that Wittgenstein observes are characteristic of the sorts of change of aspect investigated in *Philosophical Investigations,* Part II, section xi: the expression of the change of aspect in question must be "the expression of a *new* perception and at the same time of the perception's being *unchanged.*" Further, as Wittgenstein seeks to show, this is connected to its being the sort of change in view that requires either that "light dawns gradually over the whole" or not at all.[70] Thus our estimate of a particular philosopher who forms the subject of a given biography may be augmented or diminished by reading the biography in question; but, if the biography in question is a (successful instance of the genre) philosophical biography, it is likely that the resulting change of aspect will be such that the philosopher's work will appear, as it were, to wax or wane as a whole.

Contrary to what the compartmentalist urges, what strikes one as one reads first Monk's biography of Wittgenstein and then his biography of Russell, is not how Wittgenstein's life is relevant to an understanding of his work, whereas Russell's life is not relevant to an understanding of his work, but rather how differently relevant the life is to an understanding of the work in each case. In Wittgenstein's case, seeing the philosophy in the light cast by Monk's biography helps us to see the rigor and depth and purity that characterizes Wittgenstein's work as a whole and, more importantly, perhaps to see more clearly what *sort* of rigor and depth and purity it is that Wittgenstein strove for in his thinking and living. In Russell's case, seeing the philosophy in the light cast by Monk's biography helps us to see ways in which Russell's work as a whole is, in some respects, a tragic failure – the ways in which, and the reasons why, Russell was unable to think his projects through to a satisfactory conclusion, so that his entire intellectual life was marked by his restlessly moving from one project of great promise to the next, often failing to carry through on them.

Thus, in Wittgenstein's case, we can be led to see better the resolute singlemindedness of purpose that runs throughout his work – what it means to say, and why it is right to say, that "nothing is hidden" is, for Wittgenstein, an ethical as well as a logical remark, and how it comes to pass that Wittgenstein finds himself addressing remarks such as the following to his friends: "I am not a religious person, but I cannot help seeing every problem from a religious point of view."[71] In Russell's case, we are led to see the awkward furtiveness in the ways in which Russell struggles to integrate – or at least to rationalize the connection between – his theoretical and practical (his logical and ethical) motivations to philosophy, and how the shape of these struggles correlates with the cyclical pattern in the fluctuations in Russell's second-order views about the value of philosophy, and how it comes to pass that Russell finds himself addressing remarks such as the following to his friends: "I have developed a certain nausea for the subtleties and distinctions that make up good philosophy; I should like to write things of human interest, like bad philosophers, only without being bad. But perhaps it is the badness that is interesting."[72] One is helped by Monk to see the extraordinary resoluteness of Wittgenstein's philosophical thinking by seeing how various aspects of Wittgenstein's life are themselves expressions of that same insistence to achieve a sort of honesty with himself that he took to be a necessary condition of his being able to think things through philosophically. And one is helped by Monk to see the irresoluteness that characterizes Russell's broader philosophical trajectory – the way he shirks the problems that most haunt his central intellectual projects – by seeing the ways in which Russell's entire life, both in and out of philosophy, his tremendous individual accomplishments notwithstanding, is marked by ambivalence and irresoluteness.

Though there is much to admire in the Russell who comes to light in the pages of Monk's biography of him and much not to admire in the Wittgenstein who comes to light in the pages of Monk's biography of him, the following generalization is surely sound: most readers will find the resulting changes of aspect induced in their respective perceptions of Wittgenstein's and Russell's philosophical work to be such that the former will appear as a consequence to wax as a whole, while the latter will appear to wane. This difference in character in what Monk's biographies appear to disclose of Wittgenstein and Russell respectively has the inevitable consequence that Wittgenstein's admirers will, on the whole, tend to admire Monk's biography of Wittgenstein more than most of Wittgenstein's detractors will, and that roughly the opposite will tend to be the case with regard to the reception of Monk's biography of Russell amongst admirers and detractors of Russell. This inevitably leaves Monk open to the charge of a certain bias of sympathy in the one case and antipathy in the other.[73]

If Monk succeeds in his quest to write the sort of biography he claims to aspire to write, then neither of these charges should be upheld. He aspires to confine himself to *showing* us the lives through a well-documented narrative of the thoughts and actions of the individuals themselves. If he is faithful to this aspiration, then all this pair of biographies could be said to be doing is simply confronting members of these respective circles of admirers and detractors with what there is to notice about the reciprocal interaction of the life and work of each of these two philosophers. The reader would thus find himself or herself confronted with each of these two individuals themselves – the ways in which each of their respective philosophical sensibilities emerges and finds expression in the course of shaping, and being shaped by, these interactions. Whether Monk does remain faithful to this aspiration (in each of his two very different efforts to write philosophical biography) is at best a delicate question, and no doubt one that different readers will decide differently (and perhaps differently with regard to each of his two efforts).[74]

Even if one judges Monk to have remained faithful to this aspiration (in either of his two efforts), this still leaves it undecided whether one should judge the result to be of *philosophical* interest. Whether one thinks being thus confronted with the entwinement of a philosopher's life in his thought, and vice versa, is of philosophical interest will depend in part upon whether one thinks (the genre I have been calling) philosophical biography has any useful role to play in deepening our understanding of the work of particular philosophers. This is a question each of us must answer for him- or herself, on a case-by-case basis. How we answer this question will, of course, depend on our view, in each case, of the biography in question (on how successful we take it to be qua philosophical biography) and the philosopher in question (that is, on what *sort* of philosopher we take him or her to be); but, more significantly, it will depend on our conception of philosophy – on what we think philosophy now is and what we think it ought to be – and on the ways in which that conception may be either confirmed or challenged by a philosophical biography. These are not matters that someone else can decide for us.

Whatever one thinks of Monk's work – whether one thinks that it succeeds as philosophical biography or not – one ought to concede that it shows that one can at least *aspire* to write a philosophically illuminating biography of a philosopher without lapsing into reductivism. The reductivist biographer tries to show us the secret of a philosopher's work by locating the key to understanding his work outside of his work – in his life rather than his work. This is not what Monk does. Monk's mode of biography, in helping us to see the rigor and depth and purity that characterizes Wittgenstein's struggles generally, aims to help us to see Wittgenstein's work afresh: to see the rigor and depth and purity that are there *in* the work. What we are supposed to be thus helped to see is accordingly there to be seen in the work without the help of Monk's biography. But it can be hard to see.[75]

Similarly, the ways in which, and the reasons why, Russell's work are tragically flawed in the respects that Monk's biography aims to reveal are ways and reasons that are internal to Russell's work itself. What Monk aims to do is to allow us to see that work as a whole more clearly and perspicuously than we were previously able to. Philosophical biography, if it succeeds, can play a role in enabling us to see in the work of a philosopher what we might otherwise miss. Though philosophical biography attempts a depiction of philosophy in vivo (rather than, as it were, in vitro), it is still the *philosophy* (and not just the philosopher) that it seeks to bring into view. Monk, unlike the reductivist biographer, does not take "the real meaning" of Wittgenstein's or Russell's texts to be of a sort that must remain hidden to us as long as we fail to situate those texts in the wider contexts of their respective biographies. He does not seek to explain or evaluate the work of either of these philosophers by privileging what is legible in their lives over what is legible in their work – offering a reading of the texts of their lives that, in effect, pretends that it can serve as a substitute for the hard work of reading the texts that they wrote. He seeks rather to show how an attention to Wittgenstein's life or Russell's life can furnish a background against which one can more clearly discern what is already written, and there to be read, in the texts that Wittgenstein and Russell each wrote.

In the previous paragraph, when I speak of what Monk "aims" and "seeks" to do, I am crediting Monk with aiming to write philosophical biography (in the sense defined at the outset of this paper); but it is one thing to claim that Monk's work aspires to belong to this particular genre of writing and another thing to claim that it is a successful instance of the genre to which it thereby aspires to belong. By any discriminating person's lights, most attempts at philosophical biography must be judged failures. Many people who set out to do something like what Monk aspires to do – to write a biography that illuminates the work of a philosopher – wind up, I think, more or less inadvertently sliding into writing some more reductivist form of biography; because in order to construct a narrative that offers the appearance of illuminating the work through attention to the life, they slide into trafficking in the forms of pseudo-illumination that reductivist narratives confer. If one judges Monk to have succeeded in his aim then one will have judged him to have succeeded in doing something difficult. There is an art to writing such biographies; and, like any art worth practicing, it is hard to excel at. As with all such arts, people will differ widely in their assessments of whether the efforts of a given practitioner of the art are to be judged a success and, if so, how much of a success. My aim here is not to *settle* an argument concerning the relative success of Monk's particular pair of attempts to practice the art of philosophical biography, but only to show that this argument itself is a sensible one and its outcome not be decided on a priori grounds. My aim in this paper has been to exhibit the coherence of taking sides in such arguments by showing that the attempt itself – the genre of philosophical biography, as such – is in no way incoherent.

Other Honorable Trades: Shoemaking, for Example

Monk has himself written illuminatingly about his own conception of philosophical biography and, in particular, about the role played within that conception of the sort of understanding that consists in being able to see (and allow others to see) connections. In the course of explicating what it means to have the eye to notice such connections, he finds occasion to quote an anecdote from Stanley Cavell. The anecdote is from Cavell's days as a student at Berkeley when he attended Ernest Bloch's music theory class. Cavell's original reason for adducing the anecdote, in his book *A Pitch of Philosophy,* is as a parable of philosophical instruction. The parable occurs as part of an extended exploration of the twin themes of having an ear for music and cultivating one's voice qua singer – an exploration within which these twin themes function as figures, respectively, for what it is to have an ear for philosophy and what it is to find one's voice qua philosopher. Here's the anecdote:

He [Bloch] would play something simple, at the piano, for instance a Bach four-part chorale, with one note altered by a half step from Bach's rendering; then he would play the Bach unaltered. Perhaps he would turn to us, fix us with a stare, then turn back to the piano and repeat, as if for himself, the two versions. The drama mounted, then broke open with a monologue which I reconstruct along these lines: "You hear that? You hear the difference?" . . . He went on: "My version is perfectly correct; but the Bach, the Bach is perfect; late sunlight burning the edges of a cloud. Of course I do not say you must hear this. Not at all. No. But." The head lowered a little, the eyes looked up at us, the tempo slowed ominously: "If you do not hear it, do not say to yourself that you are a musician. There are many honourable trades. Shoemaking, for example."[76]

Monk himself adduces this anecdote in the service of exploring the analogy between understanding a person and understanding a piece of music. He is not so immodest as to indicate the respect in which the anecdote might have served equally aptly as a parable for the entire enterprise of philosophical biography itself. For in order to write a biography of the sort to which Monk aspires, you need a finely tuned sense of when and how a philosopher's personality expresses itself in his work and when and how his philosophy achieves expression in his life. Not everyone has the ear to catch each of these manifestations of a philosopher's vision as it expresses itself in the other. When the practitioners of philosophical biography are tone-deaf to what they need to hear, the sounds they produce are no less hard on the ears than those produced by tone-deaf musicians. What the widespread availability of bad biographies of philosophers shows is that in order to write philosophical biography, you need to have (not only considerable knowledge of both a philosopher's work and his life, but also) the ability to notice connections and hear resonances that not everyone will have the eye or the ear to pick up. Not everyone presently writing biographies of philosophers should obviously be doing what they are doing. To quote Ray Monk quoting Stanley Cavell quoting Ernest Bloch: there are many other honorable trades – shoemaking, for example.

Taking my lead from my epigraph from Virginia Woolf, I have indicated that the question "Should one allow a (philosophical) biography to assist one in understanding a philosopher?" is a question each person must answer on his or her own when faced with a concrete pair of examples – that is, when faced with both a philosopher and a (philosophical?) biography of that philosopher. An additional, relatively straightforward reason why this must be so is to be found in the fact that the sort of understanding that philosophical biography aspires to confer is not a sort that everyone necessarily seeks of a philosopher's work, and especially not necessarily when reaching for a biography. The quest for this sort of understanding may seem to defeat the pleasure of reading biography. What many people want most out of a biography is not to have light shed on elusive aspects of the work of a difficult philosopher; most readers, when they pick up a biography, just want to read an entertaining and edifying story about the life of a great person. Moreover, even if one takes oneself to have a use for the sort of understanding that philosophical biography (as I have here sought to define it) aims to confer, regardless of how successful an instance of the genre one takes up – as with all forms of understanding properly termed "philosophical" – such understanding can only come if earned.

Thus, even if one deems a philosophical biography successful, not everyone who reads such a book will come away with the variety of understanding it aspires to confer merely as a consequence of having attentively turned its pages – the more so if the reader turns the pages eager to see how it will all turn out, consuming it like an adventure story, without looking for connections that are left to the reader to draw himself. For it is a hallmark of good philosophical biography that a great deal of work be left to the reader. (Wittgenstein's remark about how philosophy ought to be written applies equally here: "Anything your reader can do for himself leave to him."[77]) Hence a reader may come away without any sense of gratitude; he may well feel, with justification, after reading even an exemplary philosophical biography of, say, Wittgenstein, that he is in no better position than before to see *who* Wittgenstein was and *why* he wrote what he did, let alone why he wrote *as* he did. That is only to say that philosophical biography is not for everyone: the sorts of connection that this genre of prose-writing seeks to bring to the fore, even when brought to light, will not seem salient to certain readers. In such cases, the changes of aspect in our perception of a philosopher's work that philosophical biography seeks to bring about will fail to dawn. There are however, many worthwhile ways to spend your time other than reading philosophical biography.[78]

NOTES

1. "How Should One Read a Book?," in *The Collected Essays of Virginia Woolf, Volume II* (New York: Harcourt, Brace & World, 1967), pp. 3, 5.
2. Aristotle, *Protrepticus,* fragment 5, in *Aristotelis Fragmenta Selecta,* ed. W. D. Ross (Oxford: Oxford University Press, 1955), p. 33.

3. Pierre Hadot, *Philosophy as a Way of Life,* ed. Arnold Davidson (Chicago: University of Chicago Press, 1995), p. 265.
4. The question of exactly what role such anecdotes are meant to play in ancient philosophical writings is a complex and delicate one. This much seems clear: if one thinks that a consideration of the manner in which a philosopher lives can contribute in some way to an assessment of the cogency of his philosophical doctrines, then this will have implications for what one takes to be the role and standing of (what we would tend to consider merely) *ad hominem* forms of argument. Nonetheless, it is difficult for a modern reader not to be struck by the abundance of (what is apt to strike one as) apparently irrelevant biographical detail in ancient philosophers' discussions of each others' views. As an amusing yet representative sample, consider the manner in which Aristotle introduces his discussion of the political doctrines of Hippodamus:

   Hippodamus the son of Euryphon, a citizen of Miletus, was the first man without practical experience of politics who attempted to handle the theme of the best form of constitution. He was a man who invented the planning of towns in separate quarters, and laid out the Peiraeus with regular roads. In his general life, too, [apart from these innovations] he was led into some eccentricity by a desire to attract attention; and this made a number of people feel that he lived in too studied and artificial a manner. He wore his hair long and expensively adorned: he had flowing robes, expensively decorated, made from a cheap but warm material, which he wore in summer time as well as in winter. (*Politics,* 2.1267b22; tr. E. Barker [Oxford: Oxford University Press, 1946], p. 68)

   Can the observation that a philosopher lives "in too studied and artificial a manner" shed light on the character of his philosophy?
5. Arnoldo Momigliano, *The Development of Greek Biography* (Cambridge, MA: Harvard University Press, 1971), p. 71.
6. Ibid., p. 84.
7. Arnold Davidson, "Editor's Introduction," ibid., p. 30. The embedded quotation is from Giuseppe Cambiano.
8. Momigliano argues that, precisely because the model of how to live furnished by such representations embodies an ideal, the practice of philosophical biography among the ancients must be distinguished from that of history:

   The Socratics were infuriating in their own time. They are still infuriating in our time. They are never so infuriating as when approached from the point of view of biography. We like biography to be true or false, honest or dishonest. Who can use such terminology for Plato's *Phaedo* or *Apology,* or even for Xenophon's *Memorabilia? . . .* [T]he fact we have to face is that biography acquired a new meaning when the Socratics moved to the zone between truth and fiction which is so bewildering to the professional historian. We shall not understand what biography was in the fourth century if we do not recognize that it came to occupy an ambiguous position between fact and imagination. Let us be in no doubt. With a man like Plato, and even with a smaller but by no means simpler man like Xenophon, this is a consciously chosen ambiguity. The Socratics experimented in biography, and the experiments were directed towards capturing the potentialities rather than the realities of individual lives. Socrates, the main subject of their considerations . . . was not so much the real Socrates as the potential Socrates. He was not a dead man whose life could be recounted. He was the guide to territories as yet unexplored. . . . The Greeks and the Romans realized that writing about the life of a fellow man is not quite the same as writing history. . . . By keeping biography separate from history the Greeks and the Romans were able to appreciate what constitutes a poet, a philosopher, a martyr, a saint. (Momigliano, op. cit., pp. 46–7, 104)

9. I do not mean to be claiming here (or anywhere, for that matter) that one cannot understand ancient philosophy (or any other kind of philosophy) without recourse to philosophical biography, but only that one has not understood what philosophy is for the ancients if one fails to understand that there is a distinctively philosophical role for the practice of biography to play in the practice of ancient philosophy. Hence the point here is not that one must be familiar (through biographical accounts or other forms of documentary evidence) with the concrete details of some particular individual ancient skeptic's, stoic's, or epicurean's life in order to understand what ancient Skepticism, Stoicism, or Epicureanism is. The point is simply that one must have some general understanding of the way of life of the skeptic, stoic, or epicurean in order to understand what ancient Skepticism, Stoicism, or Epicureanism is. Hence I say: one must have some understanding of the lives that the authors of skeptical, stoic or epicurean texts *aspired* to lead in order to understand these texts. One way of acquiring such an understanding is, while reading such texts, through imaginatively entering into the conception of how one ought to live that the texts themselves presuppose.

10. The case of Saul Kripke can serve as a useful contrast here. There are many anecdotes about Kripke circulating in contemporary philosophical circles, but no one is tempted to adduce any of them in the context of explicating Kripke's philosophical writings.

11. Ludwig Wittgenstein, *Culture and Value,* ed. G. H. von Wright; tr. P. Winch (Chicago: University of Chicago Press, 1980; rev. 2d ed. [Oxford: Basil Blackwell, 1998]), p. 33/38.

12. Ibid., p. 34/39.

13. Rush Rhees, ed., *Recollections of Wittgenstein,* rev. ed. (Oxford: Oxford University Press, 1984), p. 193.

14. Wittgenstein, *Culture and Value,* p. 16/24.

15. Ibid., p. 45/51.

16. "These passages," someone might complain, "are mostly taken from a single work: *Culture and Value* – the work that Wittgenstein devotes exclusively to topics in ethics, aesthetics, and religion!" This is not true. Wittgenstein never wrote (nor ever planned to write) such a work. The passages in *Culture and Value* are drawn from all over Wittgenstein's *Nachlass.* (See the Revised Edition (1998) of *Culture and Value,* op. cit., with annotations by Alois Pichler indicating the manuscript sources of the remarks.) The passages from *Culture and Value* that are quoted here (like many such passages) occur, in their original place in Wittgenstein's manuscripts, in the midst of investigations of questions such as, what is it to follow a rule?, to name an object?, or to understand the meaning of a word?, etc.

17. In the opening sentence of his editor's preface to the volume, G. H. von Wright appears to be prepared to claim that the remarks he has chosen to bring together in *Culture and Value* are remarks of Wittgenstein's "which *do not belong directly with his philosophical works* although they are scattered amongst the philosophical texts" [my emphasis] (ibid., p. i/ix). A subsidiary aim of the present essay is to cast doubt on (the italicized portion of) this description of these remarks.

18. Some of the paragraphs that follow are drawn from my "On Going the Bloody

Hard Way in Philosophy" (in *The Possibilities of Sense,* ed. John Whittaker (New York: Macmillan, forthcoming)), where the topic is treated at greater length.

19. "On Putting Two and Two Together," in *The Grammar of Religious Belief,* ed. D. Z. Phillips (New York: St. Martins Press, 1995), pp. 248–331.

20. D. Z. Phillips, *Philosophy's Cool Place* (Ithaca NY: Cornell University Press, 1999), p. 46.

21. Phillips seems to assume that I would disagree with this. (I presume this is because he, mostly rightly, takes himself to disagree with so much of what I say elsewhere in my paper.)

22. Having read thus far, the reader may have formed the impression that the topic of this section of the paper is one that could be summarized under the heading "Wittgenstein's remarks about ethics." Is that my topic? *Are* these remarks about ethics? It depends upon what you think "ethics" is. Stanley Cavell remarks upon the "pervasiveness of something that may express itself as a moral or religious demand in the *Investigations,*" and goes on to observe that "the demand is not the subject of a *separate* study within it, call it Ethics" (*This New Yet Unapproachable America* [Albuquerque: Living Batch Press, 1989], p. 40). I take the five remarks from Wittgenstein quoted above to be attempts to articulate (aspects of) that demand.

23. To put a somewhat more polemical edge on the point: one cannot understand many of the remarks that occur in a text such as *Culture and Value* by engaging in a close reading of that "work" alone and neglecting Wittgenstein's investigations of the sorts of questions with which the bulk of his work is concerned (questions such as is it possible for me to give myself a private ostensive definition?, or for another person to have my pains?, or for there to be only one occasion on which someone obeys a rule?, etc.) – neglecting, that is, what he thought philosophy is.

24. Phillips, *Philosophy's Cool Place,* p. 46.

25. This does appear to be what Phillips means. The most he seems to be prepared to concede by way of a connection between "the personal" and "the philosophical" is an *analogy* "between working on philosophical problems and working on moral problems" (ibid., p. 46). Phillips is unwilling to allow for any connection more intimate than this because it seems important to him to be able to maintain that "Wittgenstein . . . is not saying, as Conant thinks, that a shoddiness in how we speak is, at the same time, a shoddiness in how we live" (ibid.).

26. Many of these misinterpretations have been occasioned by picking up from the wrong end Wittgenstein's oft-repeated analogy between philosophy and therapy.

27. Rush Rhees, ed. *Recollections of Wittgenstein,* op. cit., p. 174. In this connection, see also the remark about the relation between cheating others and cheating oneself in "Notes for the 'Philosophical Lecture'," in Ludwig Wittgenstein, *Philosophical Occasions, 1912–1951;* ed. J. Klagge and A. Nordmann (Indianapolis, IN: Hackett, 1993), p. 450.

28. Ludwig Wittgenstein to Norman Malcolm, 16.11.44 in Norman Malcolm, *Ludwig Wittgenstein: A Memoir* (Oxford: Oxford University Press, 1984).

29. Such discernment is essential to the capacity for distinguishing (genuine) *philosophy* from what Wittgenstein was fond of calling (mere) *cleverness* – a distinction that underlies a great many of Wittgenstein's judgments of the work of other "philosophers."

30. Ludwig Wittgenstein, *Denkbewegungen: Tagebücher 1930–1932, 1936–1937,* ed. Ilse Somavilla (Innsbruck, Austria: Haymon Verlag, 1997), 27.4.[19]30, p. 7.

31. M. Drury, "Some Notes on Conversations with Wittgenstein," in R. Rhees, ed. *Recollections of Wittgenstein,* p. 1.
32. Ibid., p. 159.
33. See, in this regard, Ray Monk's review of Ben Rogers's *A. J. Ayer: A Life,* in *The Sunday Times,* 13 June, 1999, Book Section, p. 12.
34. "Remarks on Frazer's *Golden Bough,"* in Ludwig Wittgenstein, *Philosophical Occasions, 1912–1951,* p. 131.
35. A related double-faced "difficulty" that surfaces repeatedly in Wittgenstein's notebooks as an urgent topic for him is the danger of *pride* (or *vanity*). Consider the following remark: "The edifice of your pride has to be dismantled. And that is terribly hard work" (*Culture and Value,* p. 26/30). Phillips's mutually exclusive opposition between the personal and the philosophical gets in the way of an understanding of this remark. The question, "Is 'dismantling the edifice of one's pride' a personal or a philosophical difficulty?" is, by Wittgenstein's lights, misconceived from the start. In one of the possible prefaces he drafts for a possible book, Wittgenstein writes:

> I would like to say "This book is written to the glory of God", but nowadays that would be chicanery, that is, it would not be rightly understood. It means the book is written in good will, and in so far as it is not so written, but out of vanity, etc., the author would wish to see it condemned. *He cannot free it of these impurities further than he himself is free of them.* [my emphasis] (*Philosophical Remarks,* ed. R. Rhees, trans. R. Hargreaves and R. White; [Oxford: Basil Blackwell, 1975], Preface)

36. Though it is a mistake to assume, as some commentators do, that Wittgenstein thinks that there can be a kind of person – call him an "ordinary" person or a "nonphilosopher" – who is in full possession of his intellectual faculties and yet utterly free from philosophical perplexity, and hence from the need for philosophy and the forms of perspicuity and clarity which it aims to confer.
37. Ray Monk, "Philosophical Biography: The Very Idea," in the present volume, p. 10.
38. The remark occurs in a letter to his sister: Ludwig Wittgenstein to Helene Salzer (née Wittgenstein), in M. Nedo and M. Ranchetti, eds., *Ludwig Wittgenstein, Sein Leben in Bildern und Texten* (Frankfurt am Main: Suhrkamp, 1983), p. 292.
39. Wittgenstein therefore does not only think that the limitations of a person qua person limit his possibilities of imagination and reflection qua philosopher; he also thinks that the activity of philosophy itself represents a possible means of overcoming such limitation in oneself – hence both the promise and the danger of philosophy. Throughout Wittgenstein's life, an important ground of his motivation to philosophy (to, that is, what he hopes philosophy, at its best, can be), and of his fear of philosophy (of, that is, what he knows philosophy, at its worst, can do to a person), is the thought that in developing his or her philosophical sensibility, a person is thereby (for better or worse) profoundly shaping him- or herself as a person.
40. I take it that the term "ethics" in Wittgenstein's vocabulary no more names an independent subject matter or separable area of philosophy than does the term "logic" (or "grammar"). For Wittgenstein, logic and ethics are each, and each differently, concerned with a pervasive dimension of human thought and action.
41. In his review of W. W. Bartley's biography of Wittgenstein, Rush Rhees puts it well: "Unless you know what his [Wittgenstein's] work means to him and what he tries hardest to bring into his work – and unless you know what other features

of his living and his relations to other people he counts important – you cannot say whether some . . . desire or 'practice' is significant or rather insignificant in his character and his life" (*The Human World* 14 [February, 1974], p. 73).

42. Those who imagine, for example, that Wittgenstein's homoeroticism ("the love that dare not speak its name") is the key to understanding everything else in his life, including his philosophical preoccupations ("no wonder he's interested in what cannot be said but only shown!"), invariably end up offering a shallow and skewed representation of his philosophical thought. I discuss how this happens in the biographical representations of the relation between Wittgenstein's philosophy and his sexuality offered by W. W. Bartley and Bruce Duffy in my "Throwing Away The Top of the Ladder," *The Yale Review* 79 (3): 328–64.

43. Ray Monk, *Ludwig Wittgenstein: The Duty of Genius* (London: Jonathan Cape, 1990); Ray Monk,

44. *Bertrand Russell: The Spirit of Solitude* (London: Jonathan Cape, 1996). Thus far only the first volume of the Russell biography has appeared.

45. Wittgenstein, both early and late, employs the words "philosopher," "philosophy," and "philosophical" in (among others) the following two distinct senses: to denote that which he seeks to combat through his practice (e.g., "the philosopher is someone who is prone to . . ."; "the crucial trick in the philosophical conjuring game is the one which . . .", and so forth) and to denote that practice itself (e.g., "philosophy is the battle against the bewitchment of our intelligence . . ."; "there is not *a* philosophical method, though there are indeed methods, like different therapies"; "my aim in philosophy is to . . .", and so forth). For Wittgenstein, each of these two opposed senses of the word "philosophy" has equal claim to inherit the ancient sense of the word. I mean here to refer only to his use of "philosophy" in the second of these two senses.

46. This is not to say that the extreme opposite end of the spectrum is entirely unoccupied. Quine is perhaps the clearest example of an important contemporary analytic philosopher who resolutely eschews any (what I am here calling) "Socratic" motivation to philosophy; see, for example, his essay "Has Philosophy Lost Contact with People?" in *Theories and Things*, Cambridge, MA: Harvard University Press, 1981), *passim* but especially p. 193. It is a not uninteresting fact, though, that when such a philosopher undertakes to write an autobiography, the result is likely to be not only a singularly boring book, but one that is, in any conventional sense, a remarkably unilluminating autobiography. Or more precisely: if it is illuminating, it will be so mainly in ways utterly independent of the author's design and mainly through the character of the void it discloses, that is, through the enormity of that which is absent from its pages and the pervasiveness of its absence. Both Quine's and A. J. Ayer's autobiographies are examples of books that possess this sort of unintended sublimity: even at those moments where one expects to catch a glimmer of involuntarily disclosed human depth, one glimpses only surfaces all the way down.

    Does that mean that, with regard to philosophers who occupy this opposite end of the spectrum, there is nothing about their work for (the genre I am here calling) philosophical biography to illuminate? Can one only write (as it were, mere) *biographies* (as opposed to *philosophical* biographies) of such philosophers? That depends upon whether there is an interesting relation between that which is necessarily absent from the representation of the lives of such philosophers and that which is present (if only elusively so) in their philosophical thought, and, if so, whether the following two conditions are additionally satisfied by this relation:

first, that it illuminates something important about the character of the philosophical thought as such; and second, that what is thus illuminated can be brought to
light with particular clarity or poignancy by means of the genre of philosophical
biography. To put the point less delicately: it depends upon whether there is a
philosophically interesting reciprocal relation between the poverty of the life (the
magnitude of its accomplishments notwithstanding) and the poverty of the
thought (its significance as a contribution to philosophy notwithstanding). I am
inclined to think that there is indeed something here for philosophical biography
to disclose, but that it takes tremendous talent and tact (not to mention courage)
to do it well. Lest this be taken as an invitation, I ought also to add that I take
this particular species of philosophical biography to belong to that category of
activities (like shooting an apple off your son's head) that, however spectacular if
successful, are far better left unattempted by those of us who possess a merely
average prospect of success.

The topic of an internal relation between the poverty of the life of a philosopher
and the poverty of his philosophy is arguably the central topic of J. S. Mill's
Autobiography (as well as other of his writings, such as his essay on Bentham).
It is a matter of some interest, in the light of the topic of this paper, that Mill
should at some point have felt the need to resort to the genre of autobiography in
order to do justice to the grounds of his most profound dissatisfactions with
Benthamism. The point of the conclusion of the preceding paragraph might be
put as follows: it takes a different order of delicacy and tact to do by means of
biography what Mill there attempts (by means of autobiography).

47. Monk, *Bertrand Russell: The Spirit of Solitude*, p. 142.
48. Monk, ibid., p. 147.
49. From "The Study of Mathematics," in *The Collected Papers of Bertrand Russell*,
    Vol. 6, ed. John G. Slater (London: Routledge, 1983), p. 88.
50. Monk, *Bertrand Russell: The Spirit of Solitude*, p. 142.
51. Bertrand Russell to Ottoline Morrell, 24.5.12, in ibid., p. 262.
52. There come to be, later on, of course, additional reasons for the demise of the
    warm conception of mathematics – ones that are strictly internal to the develop-
    ment of Russell's first-order views in technical philosophy – most of which are
    connected, in one way or another, with Russell's eventual conversion to Wittgen-
    stein's conception of logical truth (as mere tautology). That conversion spells the
    demise in Russell's thinking of the idea that philosophy of logic constitutes an
    inquiry into fundamental features of reality. From this point on, Russell becomes
    able to look for warmth only outside technical philosophy.
53. Bertrand Russell to Helen Thomas, 10.6.02, in *The Selected Letters of Bertrand
    Russell*, Vol. 1, ed. N. Griffin (Boston: Houghton Mifflin, 1992).
54. Bertrand Russell to Lucy Donnelly, 23.5.02, in Monk, *Bertrand Russell: The
    Spirit of Solitude*, p. 150.
55. Bertrand Russell to Goldsworthy Lowes Dickenson, 13.2.13, in ibid., p. 292.
56. From "Pilgrimage of Life," in *The Collected Papers of Bertrand Russell*, Vol. 12
    (London: Routledge, 1985), pp. 53–4.
57. Bertrand Russell to Ottoline Morrell, 1.1.12, in Monk, *Bertrand Russell: The
    Spirit of Solitude*, p. 244.
58. Monk, ibid., p. 142.
59. Bertrand Russell to Ottoline Morrell, 3.1.12, in ibid., pp. 244–5.
60. Bertrand Russell to Goldsworthy Lowes Dickenson, 13.2.13, in ibid., p. 292.
61. Ibid.

62. Bertrand Russell to Ottoline Morrell, 3.1.12, ibid., p. 245.
63. "Science as an Element in Culture," in *The Collected Papers of Bertrand Russell,* Vol. 12 (London: Routledge, 1985), pp. 395–6.
64. Originally published in the *Independent Review,* 1903; reprinted in *Mysticism and Logic* (London: Longmans, Green and Co., 1919), pp. 46–57 (all references to this essay will be to this edition).
65. Ibid., pp. 47–8.
66. Ibid., p. 48.
67. Ibid., p. 51.
68. Ibid., p. 48.
69. Here is a taste of what the answer sounds like:

> Brief and powerless is Man's life; on him and all his race the slow, sure doom falls pitiless and dark. Blind to good and evil, reckless of destruction, omnipotent matter rolls on its relentless way; for Man, condemned today to lose his dearest, tomorrow himself to pass through the gate of darkness, it remains only to cherish, ere yet the blow falls, the lofty thoughts that ennoble his little day; disdaining the coward terrors of the slave of Fate, to worship at the shrine that his own hands have built; undismayed by the empire of chance, to preserve his mind free from the wanton tyranny that rules his outward life; proudly defiant of the irresistible forces that tolerate, for a moment, his knowledge and his condemnation, to sustain alone, a weary but unyielding Atlas, the world that his own ideals have fashioned despite the trampling march of unconscious power. (Ibid., pp. 56–7)

> In "A Free Man's Worship," in the task of facing up to the coldness of the physical universe (the omnipotence of matter, the imperiousness of chance, and the like), Man's capacity "to burn for eternal things" is adduced as a crucial support: "this is emancipation, and this is the free man's worship" (ibid., p. 55). As Russell's attachment to a warm conception of mathematical reality cools and his ontology accordingly dwindles – so that the reality that Science discloses increasingly coincides with the whole of reality – the contemplation of beauty that was to be a free man's worship gradually yields to a gospel of a resolutely disenchanted prometheanism. The only posture that remains open to an intellectually honest free man is "to defy with Promethean constancy a hostile universe" (ibid., p. 51).

70. Ludwig Wittgenstein, *Philosophical Investigations,* ed. G. E. M. Anscombe and R. Rhees, trans. G. E. M. Anscombe (Oxford: Basil Blackwell, 1953), p. 196.
71. Rhees, ed., *Recollections of Wittgenstein,* p. 94.
72. Bertrand Russell to Lucy Donnelly, 21.1.12, in Monk, *Bertrand Russell: The Spirit of Solitude,* p. 296.
73. I would argue that it is constitutive of the enterprise of philosophical biography that a successful philosophical biography must remain open to (at least) one of these two charges. If, in the light of the biography, the philosopher's work appears neither to wax nor wane as a whole, then the biography will have failed as philosophical biography.
74. If one suspects a bias (whether it be one of sympathy or antipathy), one may imagine one detects its influence not only in the manner of the *presentation* of facts, but in the manner of their *selection* as well. Since no biographer worth his salt fails to exercise considerable restraint in the selection of detail as well as considerable discrimination in the arrangement of same, the charge of having misjudged the salience of particular details (through their manner of either inclu-

sion or omission) will inevitably remain a live one among unsympathetic readers.

75. One, of course, might not need such help; and, as I will suggest in a moment, even if one does need it, one might not be able to receive it.

76. Stanley Cavell, *A Pitch of Philosophy* (Cambridge. MA: Harvard University Press, 1994), pp. 49–50. The anecdote is quoted by Monk in his contribution to this volume, pp. 5–6.

77. Wittgenstein, *Culture and Value,* p. 77/88.

78. This paper is indebted to conversations that took place in and around the symposium in Athens with Aristides Baltas, Vasso Kindi, Ray Monk, and Lisa Van Alstyne; to comments by Jim Klagge; and to conversations over the years with Stanley Cavell and Arnold Davidson.

Wittgenstein

Wittgenstein and the Mind's Eye

KELLY HAMILTON

The significant verb in this description of drawings is *show.*
> – Eugene Ferguson, *Engineering and the Mind's Eye*

A proposition *shows* its sense.
> – 4.022

Propositions *show* the logical form of reality. They display it.
> – 4.121

What *can* be shown, *cannot* be said.
> – 4.1212
> – Ludwig Wittgenstein, *Tractatus Logico-Philosophicus*

[The hinged railings] are stood upright as is made clear and obvious in the illustration because I cannot so well set it forth in words as I see it in my mind's eye. But the picture will show it.
> – Guido da Vigevano, 1335, in Eugene Ferguson,
> *Engineering and the Mind's Eye*

On what kind of knowledge is engineering design based? How does an engineer solve problems, communicate ideas, and create designs? The engineer's ability to visualize an invention, to solve design problems by creatively altering configurations of its elements, calls for a kind of constructive, spatial, synthetic thinking that is also crucial for a certain type of scientific imagination. Before he studied philosophy under Bertrand Russell at Cambridge, Ludwig Wittgenstein's education was technical and scientific. His formal training and postgraduate research prior to approaching Russell to study logic were directed toward shaping the mind of a sophisticated research engineer. The visual thinking involved in the mathematical drawings of engineering design trains the mind's eye to picture how the elements of a structure function in combination with one another. This kind of visual thinking plays a critical role in the *Bild* theory of language in the *Tractatus Logico-Philosophicus* (hereafter *Tractatus*). I will argue that Wittgenstein's practice as a design engineer informed his conception of the *Bild* theory of language in the *Tractatus,* and that understanding the character of his scientific training gives us deeper insight into the doctrine of what can only be shown and not said.

Drawings embody the engineer's knowledge, and engineering design draws on a wealth of training, skill, and intuition. "Engineering drawings are expressed in a graphic language, the grammar and syntax of which are learned through use; it also has idioms that only initiates will recognize" (Ferguson 1992, p. 3). In *A History of Engineering Drawing,* Peter Booker expands on this thought:

In its narrowest sense engineering drawing is a language used for communication. However, languages in general are not only useful for communication; they play an inherent part in our very thinking, for we tend to think in terms of the languages that we know. Drawing is of this nature, and he who can draw can think of, and deal with, many things and problems which another man can not. Between thinking and communication, in the form of geometry, drawing has another function; . . . it is . . . a primary tool of design (p. xv).

In this account of the historical development of the engineering drawing language, Booker's "main theme" is "the representation of three-dimensional objects on a two-dimensional surface," and this was the purpose of descriptive geometry as Wittgenstein knew it (Booker 1963, p. xv). Wittgenstein would ask himself in his *Notebooks,* "What is the ground of our – certainly well founded – confidence that we shall be able to express any sense we like in our two-dimensional script?" (Wittgenstein 1961a, p. 6e).[1] Working through the implications of this question with confidence was crucial to the *Bild* theory of language in the *Tractatus.* In his engineering training in descriptive geometry, he had a powerful exemplar of the solution to this problem.

In the course of answering this question, he developed a law of projection to translate between what he referred to as "pictorial forms" of different media. He came to see his *Bilder* in a "projective relation" to reality.[2] "A picture can depict any reality whose form it has" (Wittgenstein 1961b, 2.171). For "a picture is a model of reality" (2.12), and "a proposition is a picture of reality" (4.01). In its projective relation to the world, "a proposition is a model of reality as we imagine it" (4.01). "We use the perceptible sign of a proposition (spoken or written, etc.) as a projection of a possible situation. The method of projection is to think of the sense of the proposition" (3.11). Thinking about a state of affairs means picturing it to ourselves. "A proposition is a propositional sign in its projective relation to the world" (ibid., 3.12).

Wittgenstein's method of projection calls for the visual thinking of the engineer and the descriptive geometer. If you think of the sense of the proposition, you will see it in its projective relation to reality. To use language and understand its relation to the world, we need to think in a certain manner. The visual thinking of the engineer involves seeing projective relations in the mind's eye. It is an important contribution of Wittgenstein's engineering training to his early philosophy. Pepper White wrote in his autobiographical account of his engineering training at MIT that

The first professor I met told me that it didn't really matter what I learned there, but that MIT would teach me "how to think." . . . I learned how to model physical systems, how to design, how to invent. . . . This book is about the changes that take place in engineers as they learn to think (1991, p. xv).

Wittgenstein earned his engineering certification at the MIT of imperial Germany, the Technische Hochschule at Charlottenberg in Berlin, when Germany was emerging as the industrial giant of Europe.[3] The reputation of German engineering education was built on its combination of practical background in experimental research and graphic methods, and strong theoretical training.

What changes would have taken place in the mind of Ludwig Wittgenstein as he learned to think like an engineer? As Eugene Ferguson notes,

Many features and qualities of the objects that a technologist thinks about cannot be reduced to unambiguous verbal descriptions; therefore, they are dealt with in the mind by a visual, nonverbal process. The mind's eye is a well-developed organ that not only reviews the contents of a visual memory but also forms such new or modified images as the mind's thoughts require. As one thinks about a machine, reasoning through successive steps in a dynamic process, one can turn it over in one's mind. The engineering designer, who brings elements together in new combinations, is able to assemble and manipulate in his or her mind devices that as yet do not exist (1992, p. xi).

This "visual, nonverbal process" will be crucial to the logic of our language in the *Bild* theory, for not everything can be expressed verbally. "A proposition *shows* its sense (Wittgenstein 1961b, 4.022). "Propositions *show* the logical form of reality. They display it" (4.121). "What *can* be shown, *cannot* be said" (4.1212).

The model present in Wittgenstein's mind from his training in geometrical drawing would fundamentally mark his confidence that we can capture three-dimensional reality in our two-dimensional script. His claim that "man possesses the ability to construct languages capable of expressing every sense, without having any idea how each word has meaning or what its meaning is – just as people speak without knowing how the individual sounds are produced" (4.002) is taken as a given, which the theory of the *Tractatus* must account for adequately in order to succeed. In the picture of the physical world implicit in his scientific training, Wittgenstein had a model whose ontology the *Tractatus* also had to satisfy in order to be complete. I have argued elsewhere that this model of reality reflected the Helmholtzian ontology of Heinrich Hertz's *The Principles of Mechanics*.[4] The graphical qualities

of his ontology, reflected in what Joachim Schulte refers to as his preference
"for a 'palpable,' 'graphic' presentation of logic," were informed by habits in
visual thinking instilled by his engineering education and training in descriptive geometry (1992, p. 55). He shared these habits with Heinrich Hertz,
whose influence on his work is well acknowledged. It would be when the
questions from all of his different problems were satisfied in the structure of
his *Bild* theory that he would feel that this convergence justified his feeling
that he had found "on all essential points, the final solution of the problems"
(Wittgenstein 1961b, p. 5).

Thus I want to consider fundamental theories of the *Tractatus* from a
different perspective, one that will connect the *Bild* theory to his world view
as an engineer. I will present those parts of his work that bear directly on the
relationship between the visual thinking of the engineer and the theories of
the *Tractatus*. My argument here will be solely concerned with establishing
what influence Wittgenstein's cast of mind as an engineer had on his conception of the relation between language and the world in the *Tractatus*.

The Training of Russell's "German Engineer"

Russell's "German engineer" was admitted as a member of Trinity College in
February of 1912, after unofficially attending Russell's lectures in logic during the previous term.[5] By the end of the spring, Russell felt that Wittgenstein
had learned all that he could teach him and gone further. In the Cambridge
philosophical community, it was clear that he was Russell's designated heir.
It would be Wittgenstein's task to resolve the paradox of the *Principles of
Mathematics*.

Russell was extremely impressed by his mathematical mindset. He wrote
Ottoline Morrell in December of 1912:

... I believe a certain sort of mathematicians have [*sic*] far more philosophical capacity than most people who take up philosophy. Hitherto the people attracted to philosophy have been mostly those who loved the big generalizations, which were all wrong,
so that few people with exact minds have taken up the subject. It has long been one
of my dreams to found a great school of mathematically minded philosophers, ...
Wittgenstein of course is exactly my dream (Monk 1990, p. 75).

For a twenty-three-year-old who was technically still an undergraduate reading philosophy at Cambridge, with one year of formal background in logic,
this was a remarkable accomplishment. When she visited England, Russell
told Wittgenstein's sister Hermine that they expected her brother to take the
next big step in philosophy. What training had prepared him for this?

Wittgenstein received an unusual education for someone of his social
background. His formal schooling began at the Oberrrealschule in Linz in
Upper Austria when he was fourteen years old. The normal course of studies

for university-bound students was to attend the prestigious *Gymnasium*, but the emphasis there was on the classics, particularly Greek. His father, Karl Wittgenstein, was a wealthy self-made industrialist who had been trained as an engineer and had little patience with traditional German education. He would have been pleased to encourage his son's practical interests.

The decision to send Ludwig to an Oberrealschule reflected the family perception that his talents naturally led him in a practical direction.

... He had also in a more literal sense the abilities of the future engineer. ... At the age of ten his technical interests were so far advanced that he made a model with wood and wire of the house sewing-machine, a model that actually sewed a few stitches (McGuinness 1988, p. 45).

A picture survives of an earnest little boy bent over his sewing machine, and another of him at work on a lathe. He retained this love of machines, as well as a practical ability in experimental research, throughout his life.[6]

Examining Wittgenstein's schedule of courses reveals that he was enrolled in a mathematical drawing or descriptive geometry (*darstellende Geometrie*) class during every term of his secondary and undergraduate education (*Programm* 1906, pp. 87 and 88).[7] During his last semester in Berlin, his training in descriptive geometry changed only to the extent that he learned graphical statics, which is a specialized area of engineering drawing, instead (figs. 1 and 2).[8] His formal study in technical engineering drawing would train him in the modes of visual thinking typical of the engineer and further develop the concrete cast of mind reflected in his early interest in machine construction and design. At the Oberrealschule, he attended two mathematics courses, *Mathematik* and *Elemente der darstellenden Geometrie,* every year for all three years.[9] Thus, from the beginning, Wittgenstein consistently studied descriptive geometry at the same time that he learned the rest of his mathematics and science. His mathematical background was intensive for a contemporary secondary level education. He devoted much more time in class hours to mathematics than to any other subject. Also, his mathematics would have been more oriented toward application in physics than Gymnasium mathematics.

After graduating from the Oberrealschule in Linz, Wittgenstein, as previously mentioned, received his engineering certification from one of the finest engineering schools on the continent, the Technische Hochschule in Charlottenberg.[10] His professors were among the best in their field, and many of them were powerful and influential men, both in industry and academics. The Berlin that Wittgenstein knew was progressive in a way the Habsburg Empire was not.[11] It had the best research facilities, the best educational institutions, and the leading professors. In Wittgenstein's field, recent academic debates had strongly emphasized the need for practical hands-on instruction that was

I. Jahreskurs für alle Studierenden der Abteilung

Lauf. Nr	Unterrichts-Gegenstände	Dozent	Winter-Halbjahr		Saal	Sommer-Halbjahr		Saal
1	Einleitung in den Maschinenbau	E.Reichel	Fr Mi Do	10-12 3-6 3-6	V. U. „	E.-B. 50 E.-B. 23, 30, 32, 33, 34, 46, 47	Fr Mi Do	10-12 4-7 4-7	V: U. „	E.-B 50 E.-B. 23, 30, 32, 33, 34, 46, 47
2	Mechanische Technologie I und Eisenhüttenkunde	Heyn	Di	10-12	V.	E.-B. 50	Di	10-12	V.	E.-B. 50
3	Experimental-Physik	Rubens	Di Fr	2-4 2-4	V. „	Phys.Hörs. „	Di Fr	2-4 2-4	V. „	Phys. Hörs. „
4	Übungen im physikalischen Laboratorium (Physikalische Messungen) (Halbjahrskursus W. od. S.*)	Grunmach Rubens	wöchentl.4St. Zeit n.Verabredung		U.	Physikal. Laborat.	wöchtl. 4 St.*), Zeit n.Verabredung		U.	Physikal. Laborat.
5	Einführung in die Elektrotechnik	W.Wedding					Mi Sb	7-9. 7-9	V. „	141 „
6	Übungen zur Einführung in die Elektrotechnik	W.Wedding					wöchentl.4St. Zeit nach Verabredung		U.	Elektrot. Laborat.
7	Mechanik I	Meyer	Mi Sb Di	10-12 10-12 4-6	V. „ U.	241 „ „	Mi Sb Do	9-11 11-1 10-1	V. „ U.	241 „ E.-B. 50 u. (Fest.-Lab.)
		Leist	Mi Sb Di	8-10 10½-12½ 4-6	V. „ U.	259 „ „	Di Do Sb	4-6 10-12 11-1	V. „ U.	259 „ „
8	Höhere Mathematik	Hettner	Di Do Fr Mo	8-10 8-10 8-10 4-6	V. „ „ U.	221 „ „ -	Di Do Fr Mo	8-10 8-10 8-10 4-6	V. „ „ U.	221 „ „ -
		Lampe	Di Do Fr Mo	8-10 8-10 8-10 4-6	V. „ „ U.	120 „ „ „	Di Do Fr Mo	8-10 8-10 8-10 4-6	V. „ „ U.	120 - „ „
9	Darstellende Geometrie	Hertzer	Mo Sb Mo	8-10 8-10 10-2	V. „ U.	259 „ E.-B. 34, 46. 47	Mo Sb Mo	8-10 9-11 10-2	V. „ U.	259 „ E.-B. 34, 46. 47
		Jolles	Mo Sb Mo	8-10 8-10 10-2	V. „ U.	221 „ E.-B. 29, 30. 32. 33	Mo Sb Mo	8-10 9-11 10-2	V. „ U.	221 „ E.-B. 29, 30. 32. 33
10	Einführung in die Experimental-Chemie (Halbjahrskurs W.od.S)	Staven-hagen	Do	6-8	V.	158	Fr	6-8	V.	158
	Abriß der Experimental-Chemie (Halbjahrskurs W. od. S.)	Erdmann	Do	6-8	V.	Lab. 121	Do	6-8	V.	Lab. 121
11	Allg.Volkswirtschaftslehre I u. II	Paasche	Fr	6-8	‚.	E.-B. 50	Fr	6-8	V.	E.-B. 50

Figure 1. Schedule of Courses 1906–1907.

II. Jahreskurs für **Maschinen**-Ingenieure und **Verkehrs**-Maschineningenieure

Unterrichts-Gegenstände	Dozent	Winter-Halbjahr		Saal	Sommer-Halbjahr		Saal
Maschinenelemente	Kammerer	Di 8-10	V.	E.-B. 50	Mo 2-6	U.	E.-B. 45, 56,
		Fr 8-10	„	„	Do 2-6	„	57, 59, 60
		Mo 2-6	U.	E.-B. 45, 56,			
		Do 2-6	„	57, 59, 60			
Mechanische Technologie II und Materialienkunde	Heyn	Mo 8-10	V.	E.-B. 50	Mo 8-10	V.	E.-B. 50
		Di 6-8	„	„	Di 6-8	„	„
		Do 8-10	U.	„	Do 8-10	U.	„
				u. E.-B.17, 21, 22	oder		u. E.-B.17, 21, 22
					Mi 9-11		
Wärmetechnik	Josse	Mi 8-10	V.	E.-B. 50	Di 10-12	V.	241
Übungen I im Maschinen-Laboratorium (Jahreskurs)	Josse	alle 14T. 5 St. Zeit nach Verabredung	U.	Masch.-Lab.	alle 14T. 5 St. Zeit nach Verabredung	U.	Masch. Lab.
Mechanik II	Meyer	Mo 10-12	V.	241			
		Di 10-12	„	241 u.			
		Fr 3-5	U.	Fest.-Lab.			
	Leist	Di 10-12	V.	221			
		Fr 3-5	„	259			
		Mo 5-7	U.	„			
Graphische Statik	Jolles	Mi 10-12	V.	E.-B. 50			
		Mi 12-2	U.	E.-B. 56, 57, 59, 60			
	Kötter	Mi 10-12	V.	120			
		Mi 8-10 oder 12-2	U. „	341			
Hebemaschinen	Kammerer				Di vorm. 7-9	V.	E.-B. 50
					Mi „ 7-9	„	„
Arbeitsmaschinen	Riedler				Fr 8-10	V.	241
					Sb 8-10	„	„
Elektromechanik	Slaby	Fr 10-12	V.	141	Mo 10-12	V.	141
		Sb 10-12	„	„	Sb 10-12	„	„
Übungen I im Elektrotechnischen Laboratorium	W. Wedding				wöchentl. 4 St Zeit nach Verabredung	U.	Elektro Labora.
Volkswirtschaftspolitik I u. II	Paasche	Sb 8-10	V.	158	Do vorm. 7-8	V.	120
					Fr „ 7-8	„	„

Figure 2. Schedule of Courses 1907–1908.

visually oriented and theoretically sophisticated. All of these facets of fin de siècle Berlin would affect the quality and character of Wittgenstein's engineering training.

In the nineteenth century, important technical institutes had been formed in Germany, and the Technische Hochschule in Charlottenberg was the largest and most impressive. It was a leader in its field, and, like the Physicalische Technische Reichanstalt, it was emulated and envied by its foreign competition. It was on the steps of the great hall at Charlottenberg, dressed in the uniform of an officer of the engineering corps, that the emperor announced his decision to grant the right to bestow the doctorate to the technical institutes in 1899, praising the institute for its contribution to the empire.

The successful new technical schools, however, had to struggle for recognition within the state educational system, and the elevation of their inferior position was fiercely resisted by the classically oriented *Gymnasien.* The great interests at stake are mirrored in the long fight of the German Technische Hochschulen for the right to grant doctoral degrees. The universities, including many science professors, opposed the concession on the grounds that it would cheapen the degree intellectually and socially.[12]

During the *Schulkrieg,* the name used to refer to "the war over the schools" in late nineteenth-century Germany, many professionals would strenuously resist extending the qualifications for prospective university students in their fields to include graduates of nonclassical schools, specifically citing the loss of social esteem that the profession as a whole would suffer. There were three sorts of reformers who initiated the *Schulkrieg,* and accomplished the change in educational policy: "engineers, science docents at the universities and the institutes of technology, and Oberlehrer at the Realanstalten. All sought to expand the privileges reserved for classically-educated professionals" (Pyenson 1983, p. 27). Wittgenstein's professors were among the leaders in the reform movement.[13]

Rektor Alois Riedler, professor of mechanical engineering at the Technische Hochschule in Berlin since 1888, was a vociferous advocate of the necessity and importance of technological education. His debate with Felix Klein over the direction that reform should take was highly acrimonious and well-publicized. The question brought about a revolution from below, as teachers in the *Realanstalten* and technologists fought for recognition and stature commensurate with their importance.

Riedler also drove "the reorientation in mechanical engineering education toward a greater concern for application, research laboratories, and experimentation." He "was indeed instrumental in the wholesale adoption of mechanical engineering research and teaching laboratories by the *technische Hochschulen* after 1895" (Gispen 1989, p. 152).[14] The drive toward practical orientation that came to dominate the Technische Hochschule under Riedler's influence in the 1890s began in the 1870s. He strongly advocated increasing the role of experimental training in the curriculum, particularly after attending the Chicago World's Fair in 1893.

Materials-testing laboratories took hold in Germany. The use of laboratories and experimentation was linked to materials-testing becoming important for industrial purposes. "The many innovations in iron and steel technology in those years continued to yield an array of potential applications and new construction materials. Before these could find commercial application, their qualities had to be clearly known" (Gispen 1989, p. 154). Old laboratories were upgraded, and new ones were expanded. Their use was extended to educational purposes as well. Wittgenstein's formal engineering training required hours of intensive, hands-on work in some of the finest examples of these new institutions.

At the 1895 meeting of the German Engineering Association, the Verein Deutscher Ingenieure (VDI), a highly influential and widely supported resolution was passed calling for large-scale laboratories and laboratory instruction. Two of the changes that were part of the implementation of the new approach addressed the criticism of study at the technical institutes as being too abstract. Both of these moves within engineering education would have a serious influence on Wittgenstein's scientific training. Gispen comments on this change:

It is important to summarize two of its major aspects: (1) de-emphasis of calculus in favor of less precise but much more pragmatic graphic methods and (2) the adoption of laboratories for research and training in conjunction with a tremendous expansion of drafting instruction (Gispen 1989, p. 153).

This change was connected to the debates concerning the teaching of pure and applied mathematics that were a particularly heated part of the *Schulkrieg*. As a result, there was a revolutionary increase in the use of graphic methods of instruction, indicator and vector diagrams, and statistical techniques.

Wittgenstein's Berlin

Engineering training had undergone a refashioning to become what it would be during Wittgenstein's training – experimental, hands-on instruction emphasizing models, draughting, and design. In the 1890s there was important progress:

Riedler's address on mechanical engineering laboratories and . . . the wholesale adoption of his program. The new laboratories not only exposed all students to extensive practical training but also permanently transformed mechanical engineering education. From a stepchild of the natural sciences it matured into an autonomous professional discipline with its own particular subject matter and methodology. The fundamental principles of its method were model building, scientific experiment and measurement (Gispen 1989, p. 156).

This training would develop a constructive, visually oriented cast of mind. It would foster qualities of mind traditionally important to engineering thinking.

This was deliberately built into the curriculum, along with an insistence on the importance of engineering drawing and design.

Closely related to the new trend was a heavy emphasis on drafting and design. Once again Riedler was instrumental in bringing about the change. Students were made to spend long hours in the drafting rooms of the *technische Hochschulen* learning how to become practical designers and do the work of ordinary draughtsmen, in order to develop their powers of spatial conceptualization and shed erroneous notions about the easy road to success through technical education (Gispen 1989, p. 156).

In 1903, *Engineering* published a paper on "The Education of Engineers: The Education of Engineers in America, Germany and Switzerland" by Professor W. E. Dalby.[15] The section on Germany focuses on the Konigliche Technische Hochschule zu Berlin, and the comments in the "Remarks on the Engineering Course" are important for our argument.

The most striking feature of the course is the relatively large amount of time devoted to machine construction. (Under this head is included machine drawing, graphic statics, descriptive geometry, and the lectures connected with the various forms of machines, in which exercises in the drawing-office are given.) This department is under the direction of Professor Riedler. Not less striking is the method of teaching the subject. Professor Riedler carries on a large engineering practice in the building, employing between twenty and thirty draughtsmen for the purpose. The majority of these men take part in teaching the subject, so that mechanical drawing and machine design are taught by practical draughtsmen engaged for the greater part of their time in actual designing. No better method than this could be devised, because, to all intents and purposes, the students are working under actual drawing-office conditions. There are a large number of rooms devoted to the teaching of mechanical drawing, and the engineering department in the main building of the school and in the recently-erected wing consists mainly of a succession of drawing offices (Dalby 1903, p. 601).

In Riedler's *Das Maschinen-Zeichnen. Begründung und Veranschaulichung der sachlich notwendigen zeichnerischen Darstellungen und ihres Zusammenhanges mit der Praktischen Ausführung* (1896), one can see the vigor with which he pursued reforms, and the strength of his conviction that machine drawing was essential to engineering education.

For Wittgenstein, the effect of this focus on powers of spatial conceptualization can be clearly seen in the development of the picture theory of language in the *Tractatus*. His course work thus reflected the heavy emphasis on mathematical drawing and hands-on use of models and laboratory exercises typical of fin de siècle German engineering training, as well as the advantages of being in one of the leading scientific capitals in the world. For the average engineering student, laboratory experiments consumed 58 percent of work time during the first, 67 percent the second, and 80 percent the third year of school. The curriculum of the technical institutes was designed to encourage hands-on, practical expertise among its graduates.

Examining Wittgenstein's actual schedule of courses, we see the embodiment of the transformed engineering curriculum.[16] In Berlin, Wittgenstein would have attended two mathematics courses, I. u. II. *Höhere Mathematik (Differential-und Integral-rechnung, Analytische Geometrie) mit Ubungen* and I. u. II. *Darstellende Geometrie,* for his first two semesters (*Programm 1906*, p. 61). As usual, mathematics made up the majority of class hours during Wittgenstein's course work, and there were exercise sessions in both mathematics courses. Students spent long hours in the drafting rooms of the Technische Hochschule in order to develop their powers of spatial conceptualization. The cumulative impact of the changes showed perhaps most dramatically in the shifting distribution between lectures and classroom hours on the one hand, and applied and laboratory training (including drafting and design exercise) on the other. "In Berlin, laboratory and drafting hours went from roughly 35 percent of the total time devoted to instruction in 1881–2 to 45 percent in 1886–7, 48 percent in 1888–9 and 1895–6, and over 70 percent in 1898–9" (Gispen 1989, p. 156).

In the first course listed in Wittgenstein's schedule for the *Winter-Halbjahr* 1906–1907, *Einleitung in den Maschinenbau* with Professor Reichel, of the eight weekly class hours, six would be spent in practical exercises. There was a two-hour lecture on Fridays, with the bulk of coursework being accomplished in the three hours of exercises on Wednesday and Thursday. This course familiarized students with the principles of machine building and the basic component parts of machines.[17] Professor Reichel was a practicing engineer who accompanied Rektor Alois Riedler on his fact-finding trip to America. The goal of such a course would be to gain familiarity with machine construction, which would enable an engineer to see in his "mind's eye" the standard parts of machines in various configurations and have a feel for their inner workings. Its success would, among other things, explain Wittgenstein's later apparently "uncanny" ability to fix industrial machines during his teaching years in the tiny countryside villages of Austria in the 1920s.

The next course listed was *Einfuhring in die Electrotechnik* with Professor Wedding. It began in the second semester and consisted of four hours of lecture and four hours of laboratory instruction per week. Professor Wedding's textbook, *Anleitung zu den Arbeiten im Elektrotechnischen Laboratorium der Technische Hochschule Berlin,* gives us the opportunity to examine closely what laboratory instruction at the Technische Hochschule would have been like (Wedding 1903). Work in this course consisted of four courses with eighty-eight exercises, and Wittgenstein would have been in the first two courses of the sequence. The goals of the first course were to teach students the application of the fundamental laws, the use of simple technical measuring equipment of a variety of constructions, and their practical application to the investigation of batteries, simple light measurements, and some simple, workable machine measurements. Wedding noted that the performance of these tasks – and he literally meant performance, for the students did the experiments establishing the laws that they were learning as they were being instructed – would not be sufficient for mechanical engineers. For them, it was absolutely necessary to obtain theoretical knowledge of both direct and alternating currents.

Through practical application of the laws and formulas as they learned them, the goal of the course was to give students knowledge that they could use to go further in their later, independent practice. The exercises involved instructions for individual or group practice. Drawings of the apparatus used accompany the instructions, and the mathematical formulas were developed and established as the experiments were performed. Students were encouraged to repeat the exercises and to write down their results clearly and immediately. The course, in other words, was in practice precisely what one would expect for the practical laboratory application combined with concern for acquisition of theoretical knowledge typical of German engineering training.[18]

The German fin de siècle turn to graphic, visual methods can particularly be seen in Wittgenstein's last mathematics course, *Graphische Statik,* taught by Professor Jolles. In the 1860s, Karl Culmann of the Zurich Polytechnique developed a system that was widely adopted and could "calculate the stresses in trusses for roofs and bridges graphically with justifiable confidence."[19] This visual mathematical technique has "qualitative" advantages, which Ferguson describes as "presenting in the calculations a sense of 'what's going on' – a 'feel' – and permitting the engineer to build in the mind's eye a vision of the forces in a complex structure."[20]

Engineers and Visual Thought

In a standard college textbook on engineering graphics, Eugene Paré begins his chapter on the mechanics of drafting with a general observation that is instructive for the purposes of our argument.

The engineer or scientist is expected to be thoroughly familiar with the technique of reading a multiview drawing. Since the scientist or engineer often guides others in the intricacies of the manufacture of a machine or the erection of a structure or testing apparatus, he must be trained to transform in his imagination the drawing depicted on the flat surface of the drawing paper into the actual three-dimensional object. Just as the reading and writing of the language of words is essential to general education, interpreting the language of drawings is essential to complete education in the technical professions (Paré 1959, p. 7).

The interpretation of engineering drawing as an alternative language, which shapes thought, communicates ideas, and functions to allow the designer to express ideas that he could not adequately realize verbally, is strikingly constant throughout the literature on engineering drawing.

The more familiar one becomes with the traditions of engineering education, the more one becomes aware how crucially important visual thought is, and has been, in the engineering profession. Ferguson argues that "pyramids, cathedrals, and rockets exist not because of geometry, theory of structures, or thermodynamics, but because they were first pictures – literally visions – in the minds of those who conceived them" (1992, p. xi). He comments further:

Visual thinking is necessary in engineering. A major portion of engineering information is recorded and transmitted in a visual language that is in effect the *lingua franca* of engineers in the modern world. It is the language that permits "readers" of technologically explicit and detailed drawings to visualize the forms, the proportions and the interrelationships of the elements that make up the object depicted (1992, p. 41).

Visual thinking has pervaded the design process, and it has been integral to the engineer's ability to solve his basic problems.

The connection this immediately brings to mind with the artistic imagination has been confirmed by scholars concerned with design. David Pye notes that one who "is capable of invention as an artist is commonly capable also of useful invention." While Leonardo da Vinci is perhaps the most famous example of the combination of artistic and practical talents that Pye feels "are really different expressions of one potentiality," there are many such examples in the history of technology (Pye 1978, p. 65). Brook Hindle has investigated the connection between the artistic tendencies and engineering accomplishments of some of the great American inventors. Describing the process of engineering design, he observed:

Designing a machine is a creative process. Scientific laws and experimental, analytical data had increasingly to be fed into the process, to become a part of the design along with physical components, linkages and arrangements. The composition can be achieved only by an exercise in spatial thinking (Hindle 1981, p. 133).

The role of spatial thinking, seeing the form or configuration of a structure in space, is crucial for understanding the possibilities of the structure being designed.

Hindle has documented the artistic training and aspirations of Samuel Morse and Robert Fulton, but he did not present these men as unique in combining artistic training and engineering achievement. There were many others, and Morse and Fulton were simply among "the most successful." Discussing Morse's invention of the telegraph, Hindle developed this thought:

The primary strength he brought to the telegraph was an excellent design capability based upon a mind practiced in *forming and re-forming multiple elements into varying complexes* (emphasis mine). This sort of synthetic-spatial thinking is required in its most unalloyed form in painting or in sculpture where analytic, logical, verbal or arithmetic thinking plays almost no role. Synthetic-spatial thinking is, of course, involved in most intellectual activity including science, but in technology it has to be central (1981, p. 93).[21]

This reinforces Edwin Layton's argument that, historically, design has been the essential component of engineering knowledge. Layton observes that "design involves a structure or pattern, a particular combination of details or component parts, and it is precisely the gestalt or pattern that is of the essence for the designer" (Layton 1974, p. 37).[22] As Morse put it himself, "painting and her sister *arts of design* rely upon *form* displayed in *space*" (Hindle 1981, p. 136). "Form displayed in space" is an excellent way to characterize the structure of a state of affairs in the *Tractatus*. Pictorial form mirrors the structure of objects standing in relation to one another in logical space, which is what constitutes a state of affairs, in a picture.

Engineers learn to think through drawings. They use a variety of sketches that represent the basic steps involved in producing a machine or structure. First, the engineer clarifies the vision in his mind into tentative drawings as the decisions that solve the design problems are made. The large, open questions are largely resolved at this point. There is almost always no one best way to solve engineering design problems; more usually there are a variety of possibilities, some better than others. As Ferguson notes, "engineering design is surprisingly open-ended" (1992, p. 23). The process of clarification and exploration of ideas proceeds until the finished precise drawings, complete with specifications to guide the construction of the finished product, are made. From these blueprints, workmen construct the structures pictured in the engineer's drawings. Both sets of drawings communicate more or less precise information, and both types are necessary in engineering design.[23]

Another standard form of communicating engineering ideas is the talking sketch. Engineers can develop and communicate ideas through what appear to be doodlings. A sociologist studying designing first-hand in industrial design departments quotes a young designer concerning her surprise at the form that communication took in the shop. Designers don't "just sit down and talk," she said. "Everybody draws sketches to each other." Watching this, Kathryn Henderson observed designers actually taking the pencil from one another as they discussed their design and drawing on the same sketches (Ferguson 1992, p. 97). Another form of conceptualization, the thinking sketch, illuminates the graphical methodology of Wittgenstein's *Notebooks,* written for private consumption. His philosophical comments are interlaced with thinking sketches, some of which he will use in the published version of the *Tractatus.* Such sketches figure in philosophical discussions in his letters as well.[24] He uses a variety of models for visualizing relationships. These sketches help him think through ideas that he returns to worry again, and again, and again, coming at them from new perspectives to see everything that he can in them.

In some ways this seems to be related to the engineer's ability to visualize his problem in certain types of thought experiments. Ferguson recounts a story told him by a colleague, James Althouse, about how visualizing a problem in an informal social setting at lunch, joking and kicking ideas around, solved an engineering problem and earned him a patent. The problem was that "commercially available liquid-level controllers were unreliable when used to maintain a constant level in a highly agitated truck-mounted tank that discharged a high volume of liquid into a well while being refilled from a stationary reservoir." Someone said that it was like trying to keep a bucket with a hole in the bottom full without splashing with an open-ended water hose turned on full blast. Someone else responded that if you kink the hose you could regulate it by feel. The comeback to that was that they should train giant gorillas to kink a four inch high pressure hose and watch the tank level. Everyone laughed.

It made Althouse think, though, and he remembered once using a filled bucket to hold a kink in a hose until he could go back and shut off the faucet. The problem was that if the bucket wasn't full it wouldn't hold the kink. He realized that all he had to do was "to counter-spring the weight of the tank so we could use a conventional valve. Sketched that afternoon, I got a relatively uncontested patent on the device." What intrigued him was whether or not he would ever have had the idea if kidding around at lunch had gone in a different direction (Ferguson 1992, pp. 32–34). This story immediately called to mind for me, as a historian and philosopher of science, the case of Newton's famous rotating buckets. Here the scientific problem is embedded in the visualization of the situation – if you can't see it with understanding in your mind's eye, you won't understand the problem, and if you can see it you can think through the principles involved.

The *Bild* Theory

In the first set of propositions in the *Tractatus,* Wittgenstein presents an ontology that describes the basic structures of the world as we know it according to his theory. He starts by asserting that "the world is all that is the case" (1), then specifies that this means that "the world is the totality of facts, not of things" (1.1). His definition of states of affairs tells us what that crucial distinction means. In proposition 2 he states that "what is the case – a fact – is the existence of states of affairs." This is spelled out in the comment that "a state of affairs (a state of things) is a combination of objects (things)" (2.01). Thus, it is not things by themselves, objects standing alone and unrelated to each other, that constitute the world, but things (objects) as they exist in combination, as they are related to one another in states of affairs. Existing states of affairs make up what is the case, or the world as we know it.

It is important to understand how objects are related to one another in states of affairs, for the theory of objects in the *Tractatus* is still a matter of discussion and controversy. In 2.011 he writes, "it is essential to things that they should be possible constituents of states of affairs," then shortly afterwards adds that "if things can occur in states of affairs, this possibility must be in them from the beginning" (2.0121). What makes it possible for things to come together, to combine, in states of affairs? He notes that "if I know an object I also know all its possible occurrences in states of affairs. (Every one of these possibilities must be part of the nature of the object). A new possibility cannot be discovered later" (2.0123). "If I am to know an object, . . . I must know all its internal properties" (2.01231).

He continues, "if all objects are given, then at the same time all *possible* states of affairs are also given" (2.0124). Thus all possible states of affairs are determined by the internal properties of the objects that constitute them. How an object is capable of combining with other objects determines the possibility of various states of affairs. "Each thing is, as it were, in a space of possible states of affairs" (2.013).

In order to know an object, then, one must know all its internal properties. If the internal properties are known, all of its possibilities for occurring in combinations with other objects in states of affairs are known. Objects, therefore, "contain the possibility of all situations" (2.014), and "the possibility of its occurring in states of affairs is the form of an object" (2.0141). "Objects make up the substance of the world" (2.021), and in doing so they ground the determinacy of sense. "If the world had no substance, then whether a proposition had sense would depend on whether another proposition was true" (2.0211). "In that case we could not sketch any picture of the world (true or false)" (2.0212).

What is important for us to realize here is expressed in the following series of propositions:

2.026   There must be objects, if the world is to have an unalterable form.

2.027   Objects, the unalterable, and the subsistent are one and the same.

2.0271   Objects are what is unalterable and subsistent; their configuration is what
           is changing and unstable.

2.0272   The configuration of objects produces states of affairs.

2.03   In a state of affairs objects fit into one another like the links of a chain.

2.031   In a state of affairs objects stand in a determinate relation to one another.

2.032   The determinate way in which objects are connected in a state of affairs
           is the structure of the state of affairs.

2.033   Form is the possibility of structure.

2.034   The structure of a fact consists of structures of states of affairs.

Objects are simple and unalterable; they are the unalterable form of the world. The form created by the configuration of objects combined with one another can be the structure of a state of affairs. The structure of the state of affairs that is actually realized is not precisely the same as the logical form, however. Form is only the possibility of structure. The only way to determine what actual structure is instantiated in the world is to check to see which one of all the possible combinations of objects did, in fact, occur.

After dealing with the properties of objects and their possibilities of combining in states of affairs, Wittgenstein asserts that "we picture facts to ourselves" (2.1). 2.11 develops that thought as "a picture presents a situation in logical space, the existence and non-existence of states of affairs." Furthermore, he states that "a picture is a model of reality" (2.12) and tells us how that works. "In a picture objects have the elements of the picture corresponding to them" (2.13). Obviously, elements in a picture stand in certain places in the picture, and they are presented as standing in a definite spatial configuration. Thus, as objects are the constituent elements of states of affairs, their configuration, or how they stand in relation to one another, should be reflected in the configuration of the corresponding elements of the picture. Wittgenstein makes this explicit, pointing out that "in a picture the elements of the picture are the representatives of objects" (2.131), and developing his meaning by observing that "what constitutes a picture is that its elements are related to one another in a determinate way" (2.14).

This is how he thought through the idea in the *Notebooks*:

20.10.14
   The proposition must enable us to see the logical structure of the situation that makes it true or false. (As a picture must shew the spatial relation in which the things represented in it must stand if the picture is correct (true).)

The form of the picture might be called that in which the picture MUST agree with reality (in order to be capable of portraying at all). [cf. 2.17 and 2.18.]

The first thing that the theory of logical portrayal by means of language gives us is a piece of information about the nature of the truth-relation.

The theory of logical portrayal by means of language says – quite generally: In order for it to be possible for a proposition to be true or false – agree with reality or not – for this to be possible something in the proposition must be *identical* with reality [cf. 2.18.] (1961a, p. 15e).

This is made even clearer by 2.15: "The fact that the elements of a picture are related to one another in a determinate way represents that things are related to one another in the same way. Let us call this connexion of its elements the *structure* of the picture, and let us call the possibility of this *structure* the *pictorial form* of the picture" (emphasis mine).

Returning to Wittgenstein's engineering training, using models of working parts of machines to teach machine construction to engineers was standard. Many major scientific societies developed collections of such models.

Of particular interest was a series of models called Polhem's "mechanical alphabet." These were models of mechanical movements described . . . as necessary for a "mechanicus" to know and keep in mind as he designed complex machines. . . . Polhem saw the five "powers" of Hero of Alexandria – the lever, the wedge, the screw, the pulley and the winch – as the vowels of his mechanical alphabet. "Not a word can be written that does not contain a vowel," he averred; "neither can any machine limb be put into motion without being dependent on one of these" (Ferguson 1992, p. 137).[25] (Fig. 3)

This alphabet of objects, whose configurations produced a variety of working inventions, gave the engineer working knowledge of the basic component parts of machines and the principles underlying the forms of machines. This allowed an engineer to visualize these elements recombined into new configurations.

Using a variety of such models was very important to Wittgenstein's coursework, and professors from the Technische Hochschule, like Franz Reuleaux, made important contributions to such pedagogical techniques.

Reuleaux, German author of the 1875 treatise that established the kinematics of machinery as an engineering subject, designed a set of nearly 300 models of gears, cam, linkages, crank mechanisms, and many other "mechanical movements" as a supplement to his textbook. Reuleaux's models, sturdily constructed of iron and brass, were sold to engineering schools in Europe and the United States (Ferguson 1992, p. 143).[26] (fig. 4)

As noted earlier, Wittgenstein's professors helped pioneer the hands-on, model-and graphics-oriented approach to engineering training established in German technical institutes by the turn of the century.

In terms of Wittgenstein's *Bild* theory, I am asking you to imagine, to visualize in your mind's eye, individual machine parts. Then see what com-

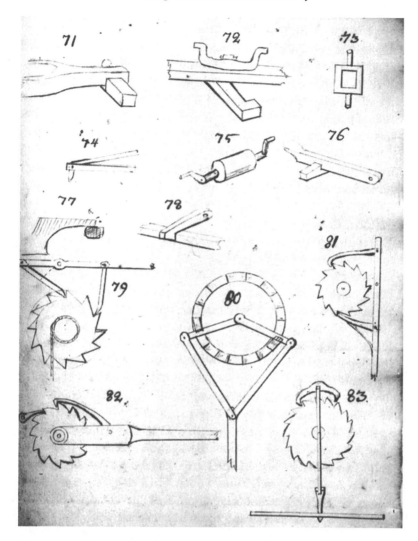

Figure 3. Example of Polhem's mechanical alphabet as recorded by Carl Cronstedt in a 1729 notebook. Reprinted from Ferguson, *Engineering and the Mind's Eye,* 141.

binatorial possibilities exist between them. Obviously, the forms of the parts determine how they can stand in relation to one another in a machine that will work. Obviously, again, there are many possible, yet predetermined (as only certain combinations are possible), structures that can exist. The forms of the parts (objects) determine the possibilities of many different structures

Figure 4. Reuleaux model. Reprinted from Ferguson, *Engineering and the Mind's Eye,* 147.

of machines (possible states of affairs). The actual combination of parts (configuration of objects) realized depends on which of those possibilities was instantiated in the construction of the machine.

This illuminates the distinction between the logical form and the structure of a state of affairs. "Form is the possibility of structure." The structure of the state of affairs is the form as it was made concrete in an actually existing state of affairs. This takes us further, actually into the truth value of a proposition, for there is only one way to know what actual structure is embedded in the state of affairs. That method is to compare our *Bild,* our proposition, to reality, to see if we have a match. If we do, the proposition is true; if not, it is false.

The engineer can "see" the structure of a projected machine; he can actually think through in his mind's eye how the principles will work in a nonverbal fashion. I am arguing that this is one way the engineering mindset, with its implicit reliance on visual thinking, shaped Wittgenstein's understanding of the nature of language and thought in the *Tractatus.* What is important to keep in mind here is that the ability to see basic, simple elements in their various possible configurations would have been second nature to Wittgenstein given his engineering training. Seeing the *Bild* theory from this perspective is unusually concrete, but this makes sense. For "that utterly simple thing, which we have to formulate here, is not a likeness of the truth, but the truth itself in its entirety. (Our problems are not abstract, but perhaps the most concrete that there are)." (5.5563)

Descriptive Geometry

In histories of engineering drawing, the Renaissance is often pointed to as a turning point in the ability to communicate visually. New methods of drawing combined with the new printing technology to greatly extend the range of engineering possibilities. The designer uses a body of engineering knowledge of great depth and breadth, which has a long history. An example Ferguson gives is the technology of the auto engine. Except for the electrical elements, all of the mechanical components were already known when Leonardo da Vinci was alive, and he filled his notebooks with copies of them. Engineers invent using familiar, standard components arranged in different configurations, and much design is based on intimate understanding of a standard body of knowledge concerning the possible mechanical components in different combinations.

The notebooks of Renaissance engineers were an important source of transmission of this knowledge. Leonardo da Vinci's notebooks may be the most famous example, but he drew on a body of knowledge disseminated by a network of engineers who already combined originality with copywork in their investigations of engineering problems (fig. 5). The Renaissance saw great advances in the ability to standardize and communicate such technical information. The art of printing, developed in the West in the fifteenth century, produced a watershed in the dissemination of visual as well as verbal information.

The ability of printed books to duplicate exactly in hundreds of copies not only text but also drawings and diagrams was of revolutionary significance in science and

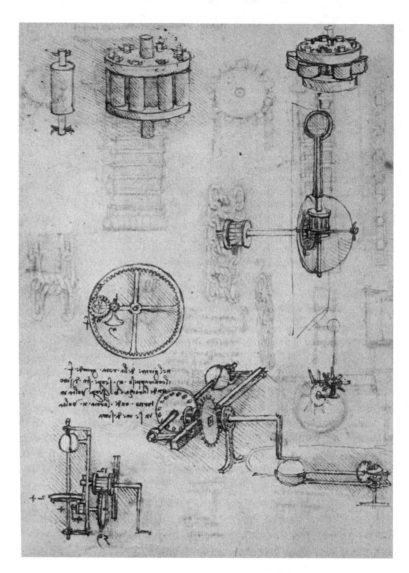

Figure 5. "Thinking sketches from Leonardo da Vinci, c. 1500. Engineers use thinking sketches to clarify visions in their minds' eyes. This page of Leonardo's notebooks reflects two different trains of thought. The two studies at the top are studies to reduce friction in [lantern] gear teeth. Other sketches probe ways to arrange epicyclic gear trains to give proper movement to the moon (spheres in lower views) in an astronomical clock." Reprinted from Ferguson, *Engineering and the Mind's Eye,* 99.

technology, where visual information is quite as necessary as verbal. Copper-plate engravings, numerous by the latter part of the sixteenth century, permitted finely detailed drawings to be reproduced in large numbers (Ferguson 1992, p. 76).

William M. Ivins, Jr., curator of prints at the Metropolitan Museum of Art, argues that "the importance of being able exactly to repeat pictorial statements is undoubtedly greater for science, technology, and general information than it is for art" (1953, p. 2).

This Renaissance invention of the technology necessary for "exact repetition of pictorial statements has had incalculable effects upon knowledge and thought, upon science and technology, of every kind" (Ivins 1953, p. 3). According to Ferguson,

The most significant graphic invention of the Renaissance was *pictorial perspective* (also called *linear perspective*), which produced a qualitative change in the ease with which a visual image in one mind could be conveyed to another mind. Since their invention in the fifteenth century, perspective drawings have provided a uniform convention for pictorial representations of three-dimensional objects (1992, p. 77).

The fundamental principle of pictorial perspective can be seen in the Renaissance portrayal of Alberti's window. An artist looks through a fixed eyepiece and records the outline of his subject on a transparent screen. The eyepiece and the transparent screen locate and define a visual pyramid of light rays converging from base to apex (fig. 6).

Perspective drawing conveys precise visual information, and geometrical drawing has been developed into a powerful tool for science and technology.

When William Blake, in a hostile image, depicted Newton with dividers in his hand and a geometrical drawing at his feet he created a symbol of modern thought that was full of insight. The new science and the new engineering both depended on an ability to construct such graphic models of reality: science of what is; engineering of what could be (Baynes and Pugh 1981, p. 6).

Another example is Albrecht Dürer's drawing of three views of a head and a foot, for "with these drawings, Dürer taught artists (and eventually modern engineers) how to describe three-dimensional objects exactly on flat paper" (Ferguson 1992, p. 83). New methods of drawing combined with the new technology to greatly extend the range of engineering possibilities (fig. 7 and fig. 11).[27]

The mathematical discipline associated with this drawing was developed by Gaspard Monge in the eighteenth century. August Comte described the discipline as follows:

The study of Descriptive Geometry possesses an important philosophical peculiarity, quite independent of its high industrial utility. This is the advantage which it so preeminently offers in habituating the mind to consider very complicated geometrical combinations in space, and to follow with precision their continual correspondence with the figures which are actually traced – of thus exercising to the utmost, in the

Figure 6. Alberti's window. Reprinted, from Ferguson, *Engineering and the Mind's Eye,* 80.

most certain and precise manner, that important faculty of the human mind which is properly called 'imagination,' and which consists, in its elementary and positive acceptation, in representing to ourselves, clearly and easily, a vast and variable collection of ideal objects, as if they were really before us (Willson 1909, p. 104).

Some familiarity with the principles and methods of descriptive geometry is necessary to understand how its manner of representing bodies in space is reflected in the doctrines of the *Tractatus.* Even technical terms from the discipline will be translated directly into Wittgenstein's philosophy.

Wittgenstein's technical term for the activity creating the relation between thought, language and reality is the method of projection. It is accomplished by "thinking" the sense of the *Bild,* with its sense being understood as how its elements are configured, how they stand in relation to one another. "We use the perceptible sign of a proposition (spoken or written, etc.) as a projection of a possible situation. The method of projection is to think of the sense

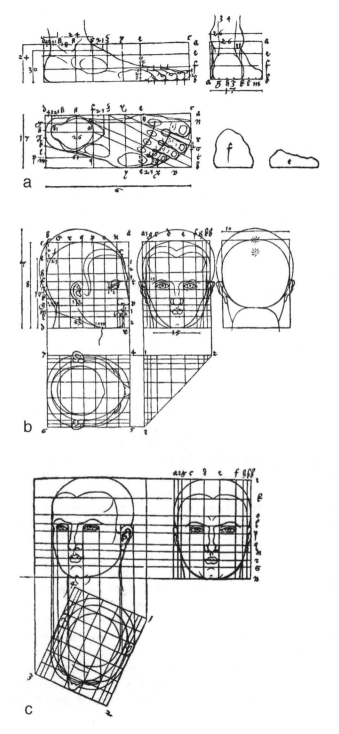

Figure 7. Dürer's foot (7a) and head (7b, c). Reprinted from Ferguson, *Engineering and the Mind's Eye,* 90–91.

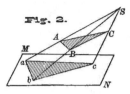

Figure 8. A figure, as *ABC* (Fig. 2) is projected on a plane, *MN,* by drawing projectors, *SA, SB, SC,* through its vertices and prolonging them, if necessary, to meet the plane. The figure *abc,* formed by joining the points in which the projectors intersect the plane, is then the projection of the first, or *original* figure. The plane upon which the projection is made is the *plane of projection.* Reprinted from Willson, *Theoretical and Practical Graphics: An Educational Course on the Theory and Practical Applications of Descriptive Geometry and Mechanical Drawing,* 7.

of the proposition" (3.11). "I call the sign with which we express a thought a propositional sign. And a proposition is a propositional sign in its projective relation to the world" (3.12).

In this brief presentation of descriptive geometry, we will make use of contemporary engineering textbooks. In *Theoretical and Practical Graphics,* Willson observes that "the mathematical properties of geometrical figures, as also the propositions and problems involving them, are divided into two classes, *metrical* and *descriptive* (or *positional*)." In the second class, we find only those properties dependent upon *relative position.* Properties of figures that remain unaltered by projection are called projective, and, while many descriptive properties are projective, few metrical properties are. Basically, "descriptive geometry is the geometry in which figures are represented and their properties investigated and demonstrated by means of projection" (Willson 1909, p. 2).[28]

Willson comments that projection is one of the most valuable and interesting methods of investigating and demonstrating the mathematical properties of figures. He begins by defining the figures treated in graphic science. "Geometrically considered, any combination of points, lines and surfaces is called a *figure.* A figure lying wholly in one plane is called a *plane figure*; otherwise a *space figure.*" In the method of projection, figures are considered connected with a center of projection. Assuming a center of projection, *S,* and a point in space, *A,* the straight line joining *S* with *A* is a projecting line (also called a ray, or projector), and its intersection, *a,* with any line or plane is its projection on that line or plane. "The word 'projection' is used not only to indicate the method of representation but also the representation itself" (1909, p. 1). The plane upon which the projection is made is the plane of projection (fig. 8). In descriptive geometry we are concerned with projection

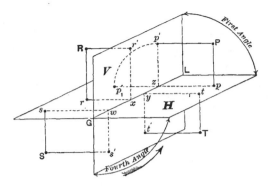

Figure 9. Figure accompanying the explanation of "FUNDAMENTAL PRINCIPLES" concerning orthographic projection in Article 284. Reprinted in public domain from Willson, *Theoretical and Practical Graphics: Educational Course on the Theory and Practical Applications of Descriptive Geometry and Mechanical Drawing*, 105.

on a plane, more accurately with projection of the points comprising a three-dimensional body (space figure) onto two planes at right angles to one another. These two planes orient the position of the body in space with precision.

Linus Faunce gives another definition in his textbook, *Descriptive Geometry*.

Descriptive Geometry is the art of representing a definite body in space upon two planes, at right angles with each other, by lines falling perpendicularly to the planes from all the points of the intersection of every two contiguous sides of the body, and from all points of its contour, and of solving all graphical problems involving three dimensions (1888, p. 3).

In figure 9, the basic elements of orthographic projection upon mutually perpendicular planes are represented. Note that "*the orthographic projection of a point on a plane* is the foot of the perpendicular from the point to the plane" (Willson 1909, p. 105). Thus, the perpendiculars Pp' and Pp give the projections of the point P on the two planes of projection; one, H, horizontal, the other, V, vertical. The projection on H is the plan, or horizontal projection, and the projection on V is the elevation or vertical projection. V and H intersect in a line called the ground line, marked GL in figure 9. They make four angles delimiting four quadrants. The observer is considered to be in the first angle, which is above H and in front of V. This is the first quadrant. In back of V, but above H is the second quadrant, Q_2. The third quadrant, Q_3 is below Q_2, and the fourth quadrant, Q_4 is below Q_1.[29]

The complexity of the drawings increases dramatically as the student advances in the subject. What is important for the *Tractatus,* however, is the concrete character of the manner in which points on the surfaces of figures, represented in a mathematical space where relative position is determined with absolute accuracy, are connected to real world figures.[30] When the subject of these drawings is a sophisticated invention that can fail, or a working bridge, the realism of these elegant pictures is immediately obvious. A faulty invention won't work. Wittgenstein once drew sketches for a machine based on a principle that had occurred to his father when he was a young boy. The principle was faulty, and the machine would not have been able to move. When force is added, as in the drawings of graphical statics, it is even more concrete. Mistakes might mean that someday a bridge could collapse with your car on it.

The Logic of Depiction

For Wittgenstein, our ability to represent the world in language depends on the logic of depiction, for "the possibility of all imagery, of all our pictorial modes of expression, is contained in the logic of depiction" (4.015). Again, is it likely that the relationships between words in a sentence, the way they stand in relation to each other, are how he sees language modeling reality? He says "the essence of a propositional sign is very clearly seen if we imagine one composed of spatial objects (such as tables, chairs, and books) instead of written signs. Then the spatial arrangement of these things will express the sense of the proposition" (3.1431). For "in a proposition a thought can be expressed in such a way that elements of the propositional sign correspond to the objects of the thought" (3.2), and "the configuration of objects in a situation corresponds to the configuration of simple signs in the propositional sign" (3.21). Why simple signs? "The simple signs in a proposition are called names" (3.202), and "in a proposition a name is a representative of an object" (3.22). In other words, names are simple signs, representing objects, that are simple in principle and stand in a determinate relation to one another in a state of affairs represented in a proposition.

The determinate order of names in the proposition mirrors the determinate order of objects in states of affairs. For Wittgenstein, our ability to analyze complex propositions into their constituent elementary propositions is crucial to the determinacy of sense and the logic of our language. "In a proposition a thought can be expressed in such a way that elements of the propositional sign correspond to the objects of the thought" (3.2). "I call such elements 'simple signs', and such a proposition 'completely analyzed' " (3.201). "The simple signs employed in propositions are called names" (3.202), and "a name means an object. The object is its meaning" (3.203). "The configuration

Figure 10. Leonardo's ratchet shown assembled and exploded.

of objects in a situation corresponds to the configuration of simple signs in the propositional sign" (3.21).

Considering another variety of engineering drawings gives us further insight. In exploded drawings, the elements of the machine are shown as separated pieces in order to clarify how they come together in the machine (fig. 10). The mechanism can be analyzed into its simplest component parts. "It is obvious that the analysis of propositions must bring us to elementary propositions which consist of names in immediate combination" (4.221); thus, "a proposition has one and only one complete analysis" (3.25).

In 4.0311 he repeats the idea of spatial objects standing in relation to each other. "One name stands for one thing, another for another thing, and they are combined with one another. In this way, the whole group – like a tableau vivant – presents a state of affairs." Names in propositions present states of affairs in a tableau vivant? Names as signs for objects, objects as concrete as real tables, chairs, and books, standing in relation to one another, for, after all, "logic is interested only in reality. And thus in sentences only in so far as they are pictures of reality" (1961a, p. 9e).

4.031   In a proposition a situation is, as it were, constructed by way of experiment.

Instead of, "this proposition has such and such a sense," we can simply say, "This proposition represents such and such a situation."

This is the "logic of our language."

We can construct pictures of situations that do not exist, that do not represent real situations in the world. In the *Notebooks,* he remarked, "A picture can represent relations that do not exist! How is that possible?" (1961a, p. 8e). He answered as follows:

2.22   What a picture represents it represents independently of its truth or falsity, by means of its pictorial form.

2.221   What a picture represents is its sense.

2.222   The agreement or disagreement of its sense with reality constitutes its truth or falsity.

2.223   In order to tell whether a picture is true or false we must compare it with reality.

For "reality is compared with propositions" (4.05), and "a proposition can be true or false only in virtue of being a picture of reality" (4.06).

How do we compare it to reality? Picturing the engineering drawings that we have been studying, how the elements of a machine, or the points on a figure in space are represented with lines of projection, consider the following propositions:

That is how a picture is attached to reality; it reaches right out to it. It is laid against reality like a measure. Only the end-points of the graduating lines actually *touch* the object that is to be measured. So a picture, conceived in this way, also includes the pictorial relationship, which makes it into a picture. The pictorial relationship consists of the correlations of the picture's elements with things. These correlations are, as it were, the feelers of the picture's elements, with which the picture touches reality (2.1511–2.1515).

How literally does he mean this? If he means what he has said about the method of projection, then these feelers do in some sense "touch" reality. They are like the projective rays of the descriptive geometer.

He goes on to say that "a logical picture of facts is a thought" (3), and "a state of affairs is thinkable: what this means is that we can picture it to ourselves" (3.001). "The totality of true thoughts is a picture of the world" (3.01). "In a proposition a thought finds an expression that can be perceived by the senses" (3.1). Again, "we use the perceptible sign of a proposition (spoken or written, etc.) as a projection of a possible situation. The method of projection is to think of the sense of the proposition" (3.11). Thinking about a state of affairs means picturing it to ourselves. "A proposition is a propositional sign in its projective relation to the world" (3.12).

Therefore, the form of the proposition makes its sense, its ability to represent a state of affairs, possible. "A picture can depict any reality whose form it has" (2.171). It depicts by means of a projective relation to the world. One can almost see Alberti's window. Its form, as we have seen, depends on the determinate relations in which its elements stand to each other. He reiterates this thought and develops it.

3.14   What constitutes a propositional sign is that in it its elements (the words) stand in a determinate relation to one another.
A propositional sign is a fact.

3.141   A proposition is not a blend of words. (Just as a theme in music is not a blend of notes).
A proposition is articulate.

The form created by the relationships among the elements carries the sense; the pictorial form articulates a sense. "It is only in so far as a proposition is logically articulated that it is a picture of a situation" (4.032). "Only facts can express a sense, a set of names cannot" (3.142).

The reference to *Bilder* in music is significant, and he will use the example of music tellingly to illustrate his "law of projection." The important argument presented from propositions 4.01 to 4.022 should now fall clearly into place.

4.01   A proposition is a picture of reality.
A proposition is a model of reality as we imagine it.

4.011   At first sight a proposition – one set out on the printed page, for example – does not seem to be a picture of the reality with which it is concerned. But neither do written notes seem at first to be a picture of a piece of music, nor our phonetic notation (the alphabet) to be a picture of our speech.
And yet these sign languages prove to be pictures, even in the ordinary sense, of what they represent.

4.012   It is obvious that a proposition of the form *"aRb"* strikes us as a picture. In this case the sign is obviously a likeness of what is signified.

4.013   And if we penetrate to the essence of this pictorial character, we see that it is *not* impaired by *apparent irregularities* (such as the use of # and ♭ in musical notation).
For even these irregularities depict what they are intended to express; only they do it in a different way.

4.014   A gramophone record, the musical idea, the written notes, and the sound waves, all stand to one another in the same internal relation of depicting that holds between language and the world.
They are all constructed according to a common logical pattern. (Like the two youths in the fairy tale, their two horses, and their lilies. They are all in a certain sense, one.)

4.0141   There is a general rule by means of which the musician can obtain the symphony from the score, and which makes it possible to derive the symphony from the groove on the gramophone record, and, using the first rule, to derive the score again. That is what constitutes the inner similarity between these things which seem to be constructed in such entirely different ways. And that rule is the law of projection which projects the symphony into the language of musical notation. It is the rule for translating this language into the language of gramophone records.

4.015   The possibility of all imagery, of all our pictorial modes of projection, is contained in the logic of depiction.

The law of projection thus enables us to translate from the musical idea, to the written notes, to the groove on the gramophone record; and it can do that because what is projected is the logical form, the internal pattern of depicting.[31]

As in projective geometry, the relations of the elements are not changed by being projected. Again, the inner structure, a structure based on fixed relationships among the elements (and the elements are different in the different media), carries the identity through the pictorial mode of projection. It has that projective relation because of our thinking it, picturing it to ourselves. The form of the proposition makes its sense, its ability to represent a state of affairs, possible. "A picture can depict any reality whose form it has" (2.171). It depicts by means of a projective relation to the world.

4.016   In order to understand the essential nature of a proposition, we should consider hieroglyphic script, which depicts the facts it describes.
              And alphabetic script developed out of it without losing what was essential to depiction . . .

4.021   A proposition is a picture of reality: for if I understand a proposition, I know the situation that it represents. And I understand the proposition without having had its sense explained to me.

4.022   A proposition *shows* its sense.
              A proposition *shows* how things stand *if* it is true. And it *says that* they do so stand.

What Can Only Be Shown and Not Said

As Wittgenstein notes after stating that what a picture must have in common with reality in order to depict it is its pictorial form, "a picture cannot, however, depict its pictorial form: it displays it" (2.172).

4.12   Propositions can represent the whole of reality, but they cannot represent what they must have in common with reality in order to be able to represent it – logical form.

4.121   Propositions cannot represent logical form: it is mirrored in them.
              What finds its reflection in language, language cannot represent.

> What expresses *itself* in language, *we* cannot express by means of language.
> Propositions *show* the logical form of reality.
> They display it.

What propositions can display, but not express verbally, is something that can only be shown and not said. One can visualize relations that cannot be verbalized. Richard Feynman, Nobel laureate in physics and creator of Feynman diagrams, described his first realization of this fact.

> One time, we were discussing something – we must have been eleven or twelve at the time – and I said, "But thinking is nothing but talking to yourself inside."
> "Oh Yeah?" Bernie said. "Do you know the crazy shape of a crankshaft in a car?"
> "Yeah, what of it?"
> "Good. Now tell me: how did you describe it when you were talking to yourself?"
> So I learned from Bernie that thoughts can be visual as well as verbal (Feynman 1988, p. 54).

In the Preface to the *Tractatus,* Wittgenstein says that the "aim of the book is to draw a limit to thought or rather, not to thought, but to the expression of thoughts." This depends on understanding the logic of our language, for the problems of philosophy are caused by misunderstanding the logic of language. It will only be within language that the limit can be drawn. As in the structure of Hertz's reaxiomatization of mechanics, one shows the limits of expression from within the formalism. What cannot be expressed in language in the manner laid out in the *Bild* theory as we have just presented it cannot be talked about. For example, one can literally not say anything about ethics, for "it is impossible for there to be propositions of ethics" (6.42). "Ethics cannot be put into words" (6.421). Above all, one must bite the bullet. "What we can not speak about we must pass over in silence" (7). After that last proposition he says nothing more.[32]

The pristine clarity of the "crystalline" world of the *Tractatus* thus leaves one empty, for it turns out that the important part is what cannot be said. What is the case (what can be expressed in language) is radically contingent; it is accidental. Value cannot be accidental, hence value is not in this world. Fact and value are absolutely distinct. One can make statements concerning matters of fact in our language, but one cannot make statements concerning value. So in the enigmatic and controversial last several pages of the *Tractatus,* Wittgenstein touches on mysticism, ethics, and the meaning of the world in ways that are surprisingly different from the body of the text.

If the text is not understood as a whole, however, its point will be lost. This is clearly Wittgenstein's understanding in the famous passage in his letter to Ludwig Ficker.

> *The book's point is an ethical one.* I once meant to include in the preface a sentence which is not in fact there now, but which I will write out for you here, because it will

perhaps be a key to the work for you. What I meant to write, then, was this: My work consists of two parts: the one presented here plus all that I have *not* written. And *it is precisely this second part that is the important one.* My book draws limits to the sphere of the ethical from the inside as it were, and I am convinced that this is the ONLY rigorous way of drawing those limits (Janik and Toulmin 1973, p. 192).[33]

The most important part is what was not said.

6.522   There are, indeed, things that cannot be put into words. They *make themselves manifest.* They are what is mystical.

6.53   The correct method in philosophy would really be the following: to say nothing except what can be said, i.e. propositions of natural science – i.e. something that has nothing to do with philosophy – and then, whenever someone else wanted to say something metaphysical, to demonstrate to him that he had failed to give a meaning to certain signs in his propositions. Although it would not be satisfying to the other person – he would not have the feeling that we were teaching him philosophy – *this* method would be the only strictly correct one.

6.54   My propositions serve as elucidations in the following way: anyone who understands me eventually recognizes them as nonsensical, when he has used them – as steps – to climb up beyond them. (He must, so to speak, throw away the ladder after he has climbed up it.)
          He must transcend these propositions, and then he will see the world aright.

7   What we cannot speak about we must pass over in silence.

Wittgenstein's engineering training provided him with powerful metaphors for understanding our modes of representing the world. One of its most important goals was to develop and deepen a fundamental human intellectual faculty, our ability to represent and explore the world in our mind's eye. In the *Bild* theory of language, Wittgenstein's conception of the modeling activities involved in our ways of knowing and representing mirrored the ways in which engineers envision their "objects."[34] For Wittgenstein, the abstract, isomorphic models of the *Tractatus* embodied the important relationships among their elements, and thinking projectively enabled us to represent by means of language. The insights that arose from his experience of engineering ways of knowing provided him with a key to understanding a range of issues that moved beyond his engineering training. They were crucial to his comprehensive claims for the *Bild* theory of language. What he learned in his engineering education was not limited to a particular style of representation. It embodied principles that provided him a deeply interconnected understanding of the principles behind all of our modes of representation.[35]

In the language of projective geometry, it also provided him with a technical vocabulary that captured the principles behind "the deep structures of all languages." Miss Anscombe has commented on his use of this language:

Wittgenstein's use of "projection" is a metaphorical extension of the mathematical use, which may be explained thus: "The drawing of straight lines through every point of a given figure, so as to produce a new figure each point of which corresponds to a point of the original figure." The new figure is also said to be a *projection of* the original one, which is *projected into* it (Anscombe 1959, p. 69).

I would like to underline the importance of that powerful insight and further spell out its importance. I believe that it extends directly into the heart of the *Tractatus*.

A fruitful metaphor is precise, suggestive, and extends our imaginative powers to broaden the explanatory character of its model. Ernan McMullin has described the role of the metaphor at the heart of the model associated with a successful scientific theory as "the only way that complex things forever somewhat out of reach *can* be known" (McMullin 1976, p. 429). A good metaphor challenges a thinker "to explore, to transfer knowledge-elements from one part of his experience to another." In a scientific theory,

it is to be found primarily in the model associated with the theory, a postulated explanatory structure whose elements are capable of further imaginative development. And the possible lines of development are suggested by the model itself. . . . The epistemic appraisal of the model will have to take into account how successfully the model has guided research so far, what sorts of extensions and modifications have taken place, and how much they owe to the imaginative resources of the undeveloped original. . . . The bond between the original and what comes of the original in consequence of an active period of development is such that an appraisal of one is an appraisal of the other: a good model, after a fruitful career, has developed into the basis for a highly corroborated theory (McMullin 1976, p. 427).

A metaphor that captures a powerful insight "allows the imagination to work, and guides it in certain directions. It is not a merely vague or indefinite object of thought. It directs the mind, not coercively but tentatively, by analogies and hints. The mind's response to it will be highly individual. . . . It will be a search, not a resting in any one place" (McMullin 1976, p. 427). Certainly, this is an excellent description of the workings of Wittgenstein's mind as recorded in the *Notebooks*.

Just as certainly, when he finished the *Tractatus*, Wittgenstein felt that he had found the final solution to the problems concerning philosophical misunderstandings of the "logic of our language." In doing so he brought together a variety of bodies of knowledge – music, mathematics, natural science, and language, with important roots in his past. Indeed, it could be argued from the structure of his argument in the *Tractatus* that its success in Wittgenstein's eyes, and thus his confidence that "the truth of the thoughts that are here communicated seems to me to be unassailable and definitive," was crucially dependent on the consilience of the many different forms of representation that were explained by his *Bild* theory.

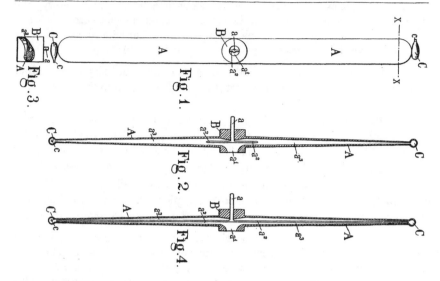

Figure 11. Wittgenstein's "Complete Specification" for his patent application for "Improvements in Propellers Applicable for Aerial Machines."

In the Preface, Wittgenstein wrote that "the book deals with the problems of philosophy, and shows, I believe, that the reason why these problems are posed is that the logic of our language is misunderstood." He felt that he had resolved the problems with the logic of our language and concluded that "the *truth* of the thoughts that are here communicated seems to me unassailable and definitive. I therefore believe myself to have found, on all essential points, the final solution of the problems" (1961b, p. 5). This was an impossibly strong claim. Why did he feel that it was true? I believe that it was because the *Bild* theory of the *Tractatus* accommodated so many of the important elements of his intellectual life; it brought them together in a structured understanding that fit. It mapped onto the ontology of his engineering *bildliche Darstellungen* and the Helmholtzian physics of Hertz's *Principles of Mechanics*. From his perspective, it accounted for music, mathematics, logic, ethics, aesthetics, representation in language, and scientific knowledge. It solved the problems he inherited from Frege as it resolved the paradox of the *Principles of Mathematics*.[36] It also satisfied the personal ethical imperatives of "the man with the gospels," who repeatedly risked his life as an Austrian soldier on the brutal eastern front during World War I.

It would thus only be when the essential questions from all of his different concerns were satisfied by his *Bild* theory that he would feel that this convergence justified his feeling that he had found "on all essential points, the final solution of the problems." In order for it to be successful *all* of the ways in which he thought had to be explained by the *Bild* theory. It is in this sense that I want to argue that Wittgenstein's engineering training profoundly affected his philosophy. Professor G. H. von Wright, Wittgenstein's friend and literary executor, told Allan Janik that it was important to remember "firstly, that he was a Viennese and, secondly, that he was an engineer with a thorough knowledge of physics" (Janik and Toulmin 1973, p. 28). This insight was at the heart of *Wittgenstein's Vienna*. In this paper, I have explored one important aspect of the manner in which Wittgenstein came to his logical work under Bertrand Russell with a world view and a set of problems embedded in his background as a "Viennese engineer."

WORKS CITED

Anscombe, G. E. M. 1959. *An Introduction to Wittgenstein's Tractatus.* London: Hutchinson University Library.

Baird, Davis, R. I. G. Hughes, and Alfred Nordmann. 1998. *Heinrich Hertz: Classical Physicist, Modern Philosopher.* Dordrecht: Kluwer Academic Publishers.

Baynes, Ken and Francis Pugh. 1981. *The Art of the Engineer.* Woodstock, New York: Overlook Press.

Booker, Peter. 1963. *A History of Engineering Drawing.* London: Chatto and Windus.

Bucciarelli, Louis L. 1994. *Designing Engineers.* Cambridge, MA.: MIT Press.

Cahan, David. 1989. *An Institute for an Empire.* Cambridge: Cambridge University Press.

Dalby, W. E. 1903. "The Education of Engineers: The Education of Engineers in America, Germany and Switzerland," *Engineering* 75: 600–603.

Faunce, Linus. 1888. *Descriptive Geometry.* Boston: Ginn & Company.

Ferguson, Eugene S. 1992. *Engineering and the Mind's Eye.* Cambridge, MA.: MIT Press.

Feynman, Richard. 1988. *What Do You Care What Other People Think?* New York: W. W. Norton.

Gispen, Kees. 1989. *New Profession, Old Order: Engineers and German Society, 1815–1914.* Cambridge: Cambridge University Press.

Hankins, Thomas L. and Robert J. Silverman. 1995. *Instruments and the Imagination.* Princeton: Princeton University Press.

Hindle, Brooke. 1981. *Emulation and Invention.* New York: New York University Press.

Ivins, William M., Jr. 1953. *Prints and Visual Communication.* Cambridge, MA.: Harvard University Press.

Janik, Allan and Stephen Toulmin. 1973. *Wittgenstein's Vienna.* New York: Simon and Schuster.

Layton, Edwin T., Jr. 1974. "Technology as Knowledge." *Technology and Culture* 15: 31–41.

Locke, Robert R. 1984. *The End of the Practical Man: Entrepreneurship and Higher Education in Germany, France and Great Britain, 1800–1940.* London: Jai Press.

McGuinness, Brian. 1988. *Wittgenstein: A Life.* Berkeley: University of California Press.

McMullin, Ernan. 1976. "The Fertility of Theory and the Unit of Appraisal in Science." *Boston Studies in the Philosophy of Science* 39: 395–432.

Monk, Ray. 1990. *Ludwig Wittgenstein: The Duty of Genius.* London: Jonathan Cape.

Monk, Ray. 1996. *Bertrand Russell: The Spirit of Solitude 1872–1921.* New York: Free Press.

Paré, Eugene. 1959. *Engineering Drawing.* New York: Henry Holt.

Pye, David. 1978. *The Nature and Aesthetics of Design.* London: Herbert Press.

Pyenson, Lewis. 1983. *Neohumanism and the Persistence of Pure Mathematics in Wilhelmian Germany.* Philadelphia: American Philosophical Society.

Riedler, Alois. 1896. *Das Maschinen-Zeichnen.* Berlin: Springer Verlag.

Schulte, Joachim. 1992. *Wittgenstein: An Introduction.* Albany: State University of New York Press.

Stern, David G. 1995. *Wittgenstein on Mind and Language.* Oxford: Oxford University Press.

Wedding, W. 1903. *Anleitung zu den Arbeiten im Elektrotechnischen Laboratorium der Technischen Hochschule Berlin.* Berlin: Leonhard Simon.

White, Pepper. 1991. *The Idea Factory: Learning to Think at MIT.* New York: Dutton.

Willson, Frederick Newton. 1909. *Theoretical and Practical Graphics: An Educational Course on the Theory and Practical Applications of Descriptive Geometry and Mechanical Drawing.* Princeton: Graphics Press.

Wittgenstein, Ludwig. 1961a. *Notebooks 1914–1916.* Edited by G. E. M. Anscombe and G. H. von Wright. Oxford: Basil Blackwell.

1961b. *Tractatus Logico-Philosophicus.* Translated by D. F. Pears and B. F. McGuinness. London: Routledge.

1974. *Letters to Russell, Keynes and Moore.* Edited by G. H. von Wright. Oxford: Basil Blackwell.

NOTES

1. Wittgenstein's *Notebooks 1914–1916* record the development of his thinking as he worked through the major ideas of the *Tractatus* during his military service in World War I. The *Tractatus* is famous for its terse, aphoristic style. As Russell commented in a letter to Ottoline Morrell written on May 27, 1912, Wittgenstein did not present arguments for his philosophical ideas. "I told him he ought not simply to *state* what he thinks true, but to give arguments for it, . . . I am seriously afraid that no one will see the point of anything he writes, because he won't recommend it by arguments addressed to a different point of view" (Monk 1996, p. 264). The *Notebooks* are helpful in this regard, but they must be used cautiously. There is development in Wittgenstein's thought between the *Notebooks* and the *Tractatus.* Thus, there are philosophical differences as well as continuities.

This is helpful in itself at times, as it can clarify his problems in thinking through philosophical issues.

2. As David Stern notes, "Wittgenstein used the German word *'Bild'* to talk about the model, a term usually translated as 'picture'; as a result, the theory of meaning it inspired is generally known as the picture theory. While both words cover such things as images, film frames, drawings, and paintings, the idea of a three-dimensional model is more readily conveyed by the German *'Bild'* than the English 'picture.' So while I will follow established usage and [will] not talk of Wittgenstein's 'model theory of meaning,' it is important not to be misled: the theory involves generalizing from what models, pictures, and the like are supposed to have in common, and treats two-dimensional pictures as just one kind of *Bild.*" (1995, pp. 35–36). Similarly, keeping this three-dimensional sense of the German word *"Bild"* in mind will be important for understanding the translation of the German *"Bild"* as the English "picture" in the propositions cited in the following argument.

3. "Ultimately, the professionalization of engineering identified the engineering societies as the qualifying agencies, and they agreed that 'design' was the key requirement. Typically, certification identifies the engineer as 'qualified to design' " (Hindle 1981, p. 137).

4. In *"Darstellungen* in *The Principles of Mechanics* and the *Tractatus*: The Representation of Objects in Relation in Hertz and Wittgenstein," a paper presented at the History of Science Society meeting in November 1996. For a complete bibliography of the scholarship concerning Heinrich Hertz, including the substantial literature on Hertz and Wittgenstein, see the bibliography compiled by Alfred Nordmann (Baird, Hughes and Nordmann 1998, pp. 281–305).

5. Russell described his first meeting with Wittgenstein as follows: ". . . an unknown German appeared, speaking very little English but refusing to speak German. He turned out to be a man who had learned engineering at Charlottenberg, but during his course had acquired, by himself, a passion for the philosophy of mathematics & has now come to Cambridge on purpose to hear me." Russell frequently referred to Wittgenstein as his "German engineer" when he first knew him (Monk 1990, pp. 38–39).

6. "He liked to think with the machine – to understand every detail of its functioning – and this accounts both for his interest in the older and more perspicuous types of mechanism . . . and for his success in repairing mechanisms that had gone wrong. Always it was achieved by the most careful observation of the machine from every side and deep and concentrated reflection until he had internalized the principle of the machine. It was thus that he had observed the distrustful sempstress in the Alleegasse and it was thus that he would examine the searchlight or boiler or whatever it was, sometimes rather to the irritation of onlookers, only intervening . . . when the course to be followed was absolutely clear to him" (McGuinness 1988, p. 45).

7. The information pertaining to his secondary school courses comes from the registrar's records at the Bundes Realgymnasium in Linz, Austria, which lists the individual courses and grades received. The information pertaining to his undergraduate coursework is from the published schedules of courses at the Technische Hochschule: the *Programm für das Studienjahr 1906–1907* and the *Programm für das Studienjahr 1907–1908,* which are reproduced in figures 1 and 2.

8. In an overview of the various branches of the graphical sciences, Frederick

Newton Willson defined projective geometry as follows. *"Projective Geometry (Geometry of Position).* While in its most general sense this science includes all projections, yet in its ordinary acceptation it may be defined as that branch of mathematics in which – *with the center of projection considered as a mathematical point at a finite distance from the line or plane of projection* – the projective properties of figures are established and investigated. Its chief practical application is in *Graphical Statics,* in which the stresses in bridge and roof trusses or other engineering constructions are determined graphically, by means of diagrams" (Willson 1909, p. 2). Willson was Professor of Descriptive Geometry, Stereotomy, and Technical Drawing in the John C. Greene School of Sciences at Princeton University. I shall use this contemporary textbook for my presentation of the principles of mathematical drawing.

9. Investigation of the *Leistungen in den Einzelnen Unterrichtsgegenständen* section of Wittgenstein's records at the Oberrealschule (now the Bundes Realgymnasium, Fadingerstrasse 4, Linz, Austria) for the years 1903–1906 reveals that his grades at the Oberrealschule were generally not strong. His grades there are not necessarily reflective of his talents or interests in any absolute sense, however. His marks for application (*Fleiß*) were *befriedigend* (adequate or satisfactory) for all three years, and he was for the most part very unhappy at the Oberrealschule. It should be kept in mind that he would necessarily have mastered the material to pass the examination that allowed students to move on to the next level at the end of the year.

10. The scientific community in Berlin was in a unique position due to what David Cahan has described as the Berlin triangle. The presence of the Physicalische Technische Reichanstalt (the finest institute for precision measurement in physics in the world), Helmholtz's physics institute at the University of Berlin, and the Technische Hochschule, created a concentration of talent that proved to be very important to Wittgenstein's training (Cahan 1989).

11. It is understandable why a powerful entrepreneur and industrialist with an engineering background like Karl Wittgenstein would send his son to Charlottenberg for his engineering training. In the Habsburg Empire, a powerful and successful industrialist like Wittgenstein was an outsider. In fin de siècle Berlin, Werner von Siemens could influence the highest government circles to create the Physicalische Technische Reichanstalt. There was active government interest in technological research, and the economic advantages that would accrue from it. Many of the leading German advocates of modernization and educational reform had visited America, and they were as enthusiastic as Karl Wittgenstein about its technological and economic advances. Engineers and captains of industry interacted in powerful ways towards practical ends. Berlin was a prominent center of high-powered research in Central Europe, and the capital of the most technologically advanced nation on the continent. It was an education of which Karl Wittgenstein would have approved.

12. The German engineers, for all of their success, suffered under a distinct disadvantage. In France, for example, the *Polytechniciens* and *Centraliens* graduated students from the best families, with *lycée* educations, and they entered the highest reaches of government; however, "neither the engineer nor his schools ever acquired the status in Imperial Germany that they had in Third Republican France. Although William II called on ' . . . the best families . . . to send their sons . . . into technology,' the engineers remained not quite respectable. The VDI, . . . repeatedly called for the elimination of, . . . the *Prestigedifferenz* existing between 'higher civil servants, judges, professors, medical doctors, and theologians, on the

one side, and the technician-engineers on the other.' From an educational perspective this *Prestigedifferenz* reflected the deep-seated prejudice of the classically educated *Gymnasium* student against the practically oriented engineer" (Locke 1984, p. 35). The right to grant the degree would admit the upstart technical schools to equality with the agencies of culture and the preservers of *Bildung,* the graduates of the *Gymnasium* and the university, and diminish teaching and research funds previously reserved for the universities.

13. One of them was Adolf Slaby, who would have been Wittgenstein's professor for the *Electromechanik* course taught during his last *Winter-Halbjahr* at the Technische Hochschule. He was an early investigator of wireless telegraphy who knew the emperor personally. He was also one of the three *Realgymnasium* graduates named to the Prussian House of Lords in 1898, when the Kaiser extended the university's privilege of sitting in the House of Lords to representatives of the Technical Institutes (Pyenson 1983, p. 69).

14. See Alois Riedler, *Zur Frage der Ingenieur Erziehung* (Berlin, 1895).

15. Read before the Institution of Mechanical Engineers, the paper was invited by the president and was based on reports dealing "with facts and object-lessons industriously gathered by travel and expert investigation" by a "member competent to analyse the facts ascertained" (Dalby 1903, p. 600).

16. While the records of Wittgenstein's secondary education at the Oberrealschule still exist, his records at the Technische Hochschule were destroyed. The fortunes of war have played a crucial role in our knowledge of Wittgenstein's education. In November of 1943, during particularly heavy bombings of Berlin, the buildings of the Technische Hochschule were severely damaged. No personal records relating to Wittgenstein's academic work survived. An immatriculation book containing the signatures of the incoming students still existed, but the information concerning his course of studies appeared to be lost. During my dissertation research in Berlin, however, I discovered that the morning of the day the Technische Hochschule was bombed an unknown gentleman walked out of the main building carrying three bound volumes of the student programs for the years 1906–1909. Wittgenstein attended the Technische Hochschule for three academic semesters, registering on October 23, 1906 and receiving his *Abgangzeugnis* on May 5, 1908. These programs contain complete information concerning the curriculum for mechanical engineers, and thanks to them it is now possible to reconstruct Wittgenstein's scientific and mathematical training in detail. I would like to thank the archivist of the Technical University, Herr Gerhard von Knobelsdorff, for his aid during my dissertation detective work, and in particular for his generosity in allowing me to make complete copies of the schedules of courses. I would also like to thank the University of Notre Dame for the support of the Zahm Travel Grant that enabled me to locate Wittgenstein's schedule of courses. The bound schedules are contained in the *Programm für das Studienjahr 1906–1907* and the *Programm für das Studienjahr 1907–1908,* printed in Berlin by Denter and Nicolas.

17. Wittgenstein would have attended a further course in *Maschinenelemente* with Professor Kammerer in his third *Halbjahr.*

18. Detailed information concerning Wittgenstein's course of studies (including information relating to his professors and their research, classroom techniques and textbooks, as well as the social and professional historical context of his training) will be included in my biography of Wittgenstein's scientific years, *Herr Ingenieur Ludwig Wittgenstein: The Scientific Training of Russell's German Engineer* (in progress).

19. "Under the assumption of an equilibrium of forces at every joint in a truss (a basic requirement of any stationary structure), a graphical construction called a *force polygon* made it possible to predict relative forces in the members for a given loading of the structure. Forces might be read directly from the force polygon, being proportional to the length of the lines in the polygon" (Ferguson 1992, p. 150).

20. Ferguson relates a story written to him by a colleague, Elwin C. Robison, who resisted his supervisor's suggestion that he use graphical statics to analyze a roof truss. "The technique caught my imagination and I spent an hour going through an example in the text. With only this sketchy background I resisted [the supervisor's] request that I analyze the truss graphically – besides, why would somebody be satisfied with a three-place graphical analysis when my calculator has 13 internal places. At his insistence I grudgingly complied, probably muttering something under my breath about his fear of technology. However, as I referred back to the textbook and reviewed the technique, I realized that it provided a built-in check of the analysis through the closure of the diagram, and that the magnitudes of forces are visible at a glance. Compression and tension were clearly distinguished as I worked my way up and down the diagram, and it didn't take long to realize that the three-place accuracy of graphical analysis is far more precise than what you're going to get in the field when the trusses are set in place" (Ferguson 1992, p. 150).

21. "His great strength remained a quality of mind that permitted him to manipulate mental images of three-dimensional telegraph components as well as complete telegraphic systems, altering them at will and projecting various possibilities for change and development. Although he had used this mode of thinking in his art, his telegraph in no way depended upon his art. Conspicuous success in each, however, absolutely required conspicuous ability in spatial thinking" (Hindle 1981, p. 107).

22. American engineers in the twentieth century have assumed that the ability to design is what characterizes the engineer. This idea frames "membership criteria for the professional grades of engineering societies, a matter which engineers take with deadly seriousness. The professional engineer is usually considered the creative practitioner, the 'real' engineer. In the definition of such a person, the 'ability to design' has been almost universally acknowledged as the crucial test" (Layton 1974, p. 37). Particularly in his seminal article, "Technology as Knowledge," Layton was one of the earliest and most influential figures in the ongoing discussions of technology as knowledge. An introduction to this literature can be found in the classic study of aeronautical engineering knowledge by Walter Vincenti, *What Engineers Know and How They Know It: Analytical Studies from Aeronautical Engineering* (Baltimore: Johns Hopkins University Press, 1990).

23. "The drawings have two principal purposes. First, they show designers how their ideas look on paper. Second, if complete, they show workers all the information needed to produce the object. The information that the drawings convey is overwhelmingly visual: not verbal. . . . Such drawings, resulting from nonverbal thinking and possessing the ability to transfer visual information across space and time, are so constantly present in offices and shops that their crucial role as intermediaries of engineering thought is easily overlooked" (Ferguson 1992, p. 5).

24. There are many instances of visual thinking in Wittgenstein's published and unpublished works. He uses thinking sketches at crucial points in his *Notebooks* as he thinks through the basic principles of the *Tractatus*. An example that is

important for our argument is his drawing of two stick figures fencing to represent the proposition: "A is fencing with B." He continues this thought in the following manner:

> The proposition in picture-writing can be true and false. It has a sense independent of its truth or falsehood. It must be possible to demonstrate everything essential by considering this case.
>
> It can be said that, while we are not certain of being able to turn all situations into pictures on paper, still we are certain that we can portray all logical properties of situations in a two-dimensional script (1961a, p. 7e).

Another such example is the thinking sketch in his letter of November or December 1913 to Bertrand Russell from Skjolden (1961a, Appendix III).

I will cite two more examples from the *Tractatus,* but Wittgenstein scholars will be familiar with many others. In 6.1203 he draws a series of signs to illustrate how "to recognize an expression as a tautology." He finishes with a sign showing that "the truth of the whole proposition is correlated with all the truth-combinations of its argument, and its falsity with none of the truth-combinations." Perhaps the famous instances of visual thinking in the *Tractatus* are the truth tables. In 4.31 he notes that "we can represent truth-possibilities by schemata of the following kind (T means true, F means false; the rows of the Ts and Fs under the row of elementary propositions symbolize their truth-possibilities in a way that can easily be understood) . . ." and presents his first truth table.

25. "Polhem . . . identified and rendered in the form of wooden models a number of mechanical actions that formed the components of most mechanisms: . . . His intention was to fill the minds of students with visual and tactile images of the components of mechanisms so that they could manipulate them mentally as they designed machines" (Hindle 1981, p. 134).

26. The Technische Hochschule's *Kinematische (Reuleaux) Sammlung* was located at Nr. 239 Hauptgebäude. There were twenty-four such *Sammlungen* listed in the *Program für das Studienjahr 1907–1908* of the Konigliche Technische Hochschule zu Berlin. The *Sammlung für Maschinen Aufnahmen* was in the care of Professor Reichel, Wittgenstein's Professor for the *Einleitung in den Maschinenbau* course. The *Sammlung für Maschinen-Ingenieurwesen* was in the care of Professor Kammerer, who would have been Wittgenstein's professor in the *Maschinenelemente* course in his third *Halbjahr.* Professor Dalby noted that "there are various collections of apparatus forming small museums in connection with the various departments. The most celebrated of these is the collection of Professor Reuleaux's kinematic models" (1903, p. 601).

27. Patent No. 27,087: "Improvements in Propellers Applicable for Aerial Machines" – Date of Application 22nd Nov., 1910, Complete Specification Left 21st June, 1911, Accepted 17th August, 1911." The specification for the patent application reads as follows:

> I, Ludwig Wittgenstein, of Palatine Road, West Didsbury, Manchester, County of Lancaster, late of Wilmslow Road, Fallowfield, City of Manchester, Research Engineering Student, do hereby declare the nature of this invention and in what manner the same is to be performed, to be particularly described and ascertained in and by the following statement:
>
> This invention relates to propellers for aeroplanes, helicopters, dirigible balloons, or other forms of aerial machines.
>
> It consists essentially of a radially armed motor each arm carrying a combustion chamber,

and the exhaust nozzle at its extremity and each arm formed as, or fitted with, a propeller blade.

The invention will be fully described with reference to the accompanying drawings forming part of the specification.

Fig. 1 Side Elevation.

Fig. 2 Longitudinal Elevation.

Fig. 3 Section on line *x–x*.

Fig. 4 Longitudinal section through a modification of the invention.

28. In his "Introduction" to the *Tractatus,* Russell comments that Wittgenstein "compares linguistic expression to projection in geometry. A geometrical figure may be projected in many ways: each of these corresponds to a different language, but the projective properties of the original figure remain unchanged whichever of these ways may be adopted. These projective properties correspond to that which in his theory the proposition and the fact must have in common, if the proposition is to assert the fact" (Wittgenstein 1961b, p. xi).

29. An amusing story concerning how concretely a literally minded student could take this representation is provided by one of the famous teachers of engineering drawing in the early twentieth century, Thomas French. In an article in the *Proceedings of the Society for the Promotion of Engineering Drawing,* he described walking in on his students doing their exercises in descriptive geometry, only to see a very serious, but not terribly bright student, sitting underneath the table. Asked what he was doing there, the student replied quite seriously that he was working in the fourth quadrant.

30. We have looked briefly at the character of descriptive geometry and seen quite concretely how a three-dimensional object could be "represented in our two-dimensional script." Ferguson also discusses the "cluster of powerful graphic ideas" that came together to form "the visual basis of most mathematical calculations in modern engineering. Napierian logarithms and Cartesian coordinate geometry, followed later by graphic statics and nomography, enabled engineers to visualize their calculations in ways that they could not with numbers alone" (1992, p. 143).

31. In *Instruments and the Imagination,* Thomas Hankins and Robert Silverman investigate the development of graphical methods in science, and particularly in the use of instruments. When discussing the importance of these methods for the new sciences of acoustics and experimental physiology, they describe Chladni's sand figures as the "start of a sustained tradition in which the visual representation of sound became a ubiquitous feature in acoustical research" (1995, p. 130). They note that "the gifted British natural philosopher, Rosetta stone sleuth, and undulatory optical theorist Thomas Young embraced the pictorial approach to the study of sound" (1995, p. 132), and that "the British physicist Charles Wheatstone came from a family of musical instrument makers . . . (and) created images of vibration with an instrument." They comment further that "while Young and Wheatstone did not expressly identify their 'graphs' as languages, their acoustic techniques coincided with and informed their studies in language, speech and vision. Young began his career with an attempt to understand the physiology of vision and the nature of vowel sounds. . . . Wheatstone also studied cryptography and invented communication devices including the telegraph. Their creation of instruments to give visual representations of sound was part of a much broader investigation into the nature of language, speech, vision and hearing. It is worth noting that if one

wants to measure the quantitative features of sound, one must employ a visual image. The ear detects pitch, loudness and timbre, but not the frequency, amplitude and shape of sound waves. Recording instruments give us this information by representing the sound visually" (1995, p. 133). These connections recall Drury's description of the innovative apparatus Wittgenstein improved for Dr. Grant at Guy's Hospital during the World War II. "Dr. Grant had asked him to investigate the relationship between breathing (depth and rate) and pulse (volume and rate). Wittgenstein had so arranged things that he could act as his own subject and obtain the necessary tracings on a revolving drum. He made several improvements in the original apparatus, so much so that Dr. Grant had said that he wished Wittgenstein had been a physiologist and not a philosopher" (Monk 1990, p. 453).

32. 6.41   The sense of the world must lie outside the world. In the world everything is as it is, and everything happens as it does happen: *in* it no value exists – and if it did exist, it would have no value.

       If there is any value that does have value, it must lie outside the whole sphere of what happens and is the case. For all that happens and is the case is accidental.

       What makes it non-accidental cannot lie *within* the world, since if it did it would itself be accidental.

       It must lie outside the world.

    6.42   So too it is impossible for there to be propositions of ethics. Propositions can express nothing that is higher.

    6.421   It is clear that ethics cannot be put into words. Ethics is transcendental.

       (Ethics and aesthetics are one and the same.)

33. While this letter is undated, Monk feels that it was "almost certainly" written in November 1919 (Monk 1990, p. 604).

34. As Louis L. Bucciarelli argues, for participants in the design process: "It is the object as they see and work with it that patterns their thought and practice, not just when they must engage the physics of the device but throughout the entire design process, permeating all exchange and discourse within the subculture of the firm. This way of thinking is so prevalent within contemporary design that I have given it a label – 'object-world thinking' " (Bucciarelli 1994, p. 4).

35. In my book, *Wittgenstein and the Mind's Eye: Visual Thinking and Modeling in the Tractatus Logico-Philosophicus* (in progress), I explore the role of visual thinking and modeling across the range of disciplines practiced by Wittgenstein. Not only engineers think visually in three dimensions, and Wittgenstein was a man of wide-ranging interests and talents. Visualization is also an important feature of much scientific thinking.

36. It satisfied the engineer who came into philosophy from an interest in the foundations of mathematics; and the little boy who grew up in the Wittgenstein palais listening to Brahms in a musical household, seeing Klimt teach his sisters to paint, and reading Kraus, Goethe, Nestroy, and the other classics central to his Viennese upbringing. Small wonder that, on its completion, he left philosophy to become a school teacher, and, on his return to consideration of philosophical problems, read poetry to the rather turned-off members of the Vienna Circle.

Deep Disquietudes:
Reflections on Wittgenstein as Antiphilosopher

LOUIS SASS

Introduction[1]

Wittgenstein once said that he would prefer a change in the way people live to a continuation of his philosophical work by others, a change that would render superfluous all the issues and questions of his philosophizing: "You must change the way you live and . . . what is problematic will disappear" (CV 27/31, cf. 61/70). He suggested that, like "the sickness of a time," it was possible for "the sickness of philosophical problems to get cured only through a changed mode of thought and of life."[2] On another occasion he asked, "What is the good of philosophy if it does not make me a better human being?"[3]

As these statements indicate, Wittgenstein was by no means concerned with only the *logic* of philosophical perplexity and illusion. Indeed, in his later work, he often seems less interested in assessing specific philosophical theories than in diagnosing an entire attitude or mode of living that he saw as accompanying the philosophizing stance in general. This attitude or mode of living, I will argue, involves a predilection for detached contemplation, abstraction, and reifying introspection – for a sense of separation from body, self, community, and world. It is one with which Wittgenstein, like many members of modern Western society, especially intellectuals, was personally all too familiar.

In previous work, I adopted a Wittgensteinian perspective to offer a critique of some of the central concepts of psychiatry (especially delusion) and to develop a more adequate understanding of the subtleties of certain kinds of mental disorder.[4] Here I wish to take Wittgenstein and his thought as the *object* of analysis. I hope to illuminate Wittgenstein's complex, at times bewildering, intellectual project by drawing out strands that have broad existential, psychological, and cultural implications, and by connecting these with his personality and cultural milieu. My aim is to clarify some of the psychological resonance and ambiguities – and, perhaps, motivations – of his central philosophical ideas or attitudes, and also something of the basis of their relevance and widespread appeal in this modernist or postmodernist age. I shall attempt to show how Wittgenstein's philosophical positions and meta-philosophical attitudes (especially in his early philosophy) can be understood in light of his personality, as having interesting affinities with his own shifting experience of, and ways of coping with, his own deepest propensities. To move in this direction is to pursue the idea famously stated in Nietzsche's *Beyond Good and Evil,* the notion that every great philosophy is, in fact, "a confession on the part of its author and a kind of involuntary and unconscious memoir."[5] This is an idea to which Wittgenstein himself was not unsympathetic: "It is sometimes said that a man's philosophy is a matter of temperament, and there is something in this," he wrote in 1931 (CV 20/17).[6]

As several biographers and commentators have noted, Wittgenstein's interest in philosophy was from the outset highly intense and, in some mysterious way, profoundly personal. His interest in philosophy began not with a search for certitude but with a desire to escape "painful contradictions." Perhaps the first time he was drawn to philosophy was when he encountered the Theory of Types in Bertrand Russell's book, *The Principles of Mathematics,* in 1908, at age nineteen.[7] Indeed, issues surrounding the Theory of Types seem to have been the paradigm case of the kind of painful contradiction by which Wittgenstein was vexed and from which he sought release – not necessarily through solving the problem but through dissolving it in some way. In his biography of the young Wittgenstein, Brian McGuinness remarks on the mystery of why Wittgenstein should have been drawn so intensely, and in so personal a way, to such abstract questions of logic and mathematics. Wittgenstein "was a musician," writes McGuinness,

he read passionately works of literature that 'said something to him' – something, that is, about human life. He brooded over his own defects and difficulties. He was a fierce critic of failings, especially those of honesty, in others. He came to write a book whose main point (he said himself) was an ethical one. What had the foundations of mathematics [i.e., Frege's and Russell's difficulties with the paradoxes] in common with propensities like these? The question is the expression of a confused feeling that not quite everything fits (McG 77).

The present essay is an attempt to answer this question from a psychological or psycho-philosophical standpoint and, in particular, to dissipate some of the sense of confusion of which McGuinness speaks. I will discuss Wittgenstein's general urge toward genius, a central theme of the biography by Ray Monk, but will focus in greater detail on more intimate but necessarily more speculative connections between Wittgenstein's psychological constitution or existential stance, his aesthetic and ethical attitudes, and the specific philosophical issues and moves that preoccupied him.[8] These latter include Russell's Theory of Types as well as Wittgenstein's own distinction between "saying" and "showing," which he once described as "the cardinal problem of philosophy" (M 164).

The difficulty of understanding Wittgenstein was nicely captured by Wittgenstein himself in a remark recalled by his sister Hermine. Hermine describes Ludwig's reaction when she expressed her inability to comprehend why he, with his incomparable philosophical mind, would rather work as a gardener's assistant or elementary school teacher than as a professor of philosophy: "Ludwig replied with an analogy that reduced me to silence. He said, 'You remind me of somebody who is looking out through a closed window and cannot explain to himself the strange movements of a passer-by. He cannot tell what sort of storm is raging out there or that this person might only be managing with difficulty to stay on his feet.' Then I understood the state of mind he was in."[9] Understanding something of Wittgenstein's personality and existential concerns may help us to grasp the atmosphere of Wittgenstein's thinking and thereby to comprehend something of the strange movements of his antiphilosophizing – with its continual invocation, and its continual warding off, of the seductions of philosophy. It may also help to explain what has been called the confessional nature of Wittgenstein's style of philosophical writing, with its deeply practical and negative nature, its concern with sensibility and personal change rather than reasoning or dogma. For "in confessing," as Stanley Cavell points out, "you do not explain or justify, but describe how it is with you."[10]

Wittgenstein, as a person, was familiar with many of the temptations and sources of illusion that he criticized in the philosophical tradition – with the temptations of both solipsism and skepticism, with those of introversion, detachment, and abstraction. As shall be seen, he felt very acutely the conflict between contrary wishes – yearnings to exist both inside and outside his own perspective, to be fully absorbed into the world or cultural surround, yet also to adopt a free-floating or synoptic standpoint outside space and time, language, or any particular set of cultural forms. Though he certainly experienced his philosophical preoccupations and torments with rare intensity, the themes themselves are of broad intellectual and existential relevance. They could, in fact, be said to be paradigmatic of the orientation of the post-Cartesian or post-Kantian soul.

The key features of this orientation are introversion and a sense of isolation, a tendency to feel alienated from the world and from others and to suffer a sense of inner dividedness. There is often an intense self-consciousness, a sense of looking on at the self and its encompassing context as if from a remove. Such persons tend to identify with what the philosopher Thomas Nagel has called the "objective self": they attempt to "climb outside" the finite mind and body and to adopt a "view from nowhere" in which life, the world, and one's own self can be viewed from the outside and *sub specie aeternitatus*.[11] The work of various scholars – including Georg Simmel, Norbert Elias, Michel Foucault, and Anthony Giddens – suggests that these and related characteristics have become increasingly prominent since the Enlightenment and Industrial Revolution – a time of growing reflexivity, pluralism, and individualism, with attendant crises of legitimacy, knowledge, and identity. As I argued in *Madness and Modernism,* these characteristics, if considered in psychological terms, are best described as having a distinctly schizoid or (to use older terms) a schizothymic, dystonic, or isolative flavor.[12]

The term "schizoid" is easily misunderstood. We need, first, to distinguish it sharply from "schizophrenic." "Schizoid" does not imply a psychotic condition but, rather, a general style of character or personality that may be found to any degree and can be present in well-functioning and reasonably healthy persons. It is a style dominated by a certain hypersensitivity and vulnerability and by detachment from both self and world. "Schizothymic" was used by Ernst Kretschmer in 1921 to refer to a normal temperament akin to the abnormal "schizoid."[13] The term "dystonic" has sometimes been preferred by those who wish to downplay any association with schizophrenia.[14] Both the latter terms have largely fallen out of use, however, while "schizoid' has come to be employed in a more inclusive and not necessarily pathologizing way (see, for example, the writings of W. R. D. Fairbairn, Harry Guntrip, and Anthony Storr).[15]

In exploring the schizoid or schizothymic aspects of Wittgenstein's personality and outlook, I shall be trying to capture qualitative characteristics rather than to gauge degrees of pathology or health. The primary implicit contrast is *not,* then, with the normal or healthy condition (whatever that may be) but, rather, with other distinctive types of personality or styles of character, such as the paranoid, narcissistic, borderline, histrionic, or impulsive types. Although we are using the language of personality *disorder,* there is a sense in which all human beings tend, more or less, to fall into or at least to approach one or another (or perhaps several) of these categories.[16]

I do not mean to deny the abnormal, at times pathological, features of Wittgenstein's personality. We are speaking, after all, of a person who had three brothers who apparently committed suicide, who thought often of committing suicide himself (McG 10, 26, 157, 254, 294), and who often feared that he himself would go mad, a concern that his closest friends took seriously indeed. "I often believe that I am on the straight road to insanity," Wittgenstein told a friend in 1948 (M 523). A diary entry from 1937 conveys his persistent sense of being on the brink:

I feel as if my intellect was in a very labile equilibrium; so as if a comparatively minor jolt could bring it to snap over. It is like when one sometimes feels close to crying, feels the approaching crying fit. One should then try to breathe quite calmly, regularly and deeply until the fit dissipates. And if God wills I will succeed (D 159, 31.1.37).

In a letter written in 1913, Bertrand Russell described an exchange he had with Wittgenstein: "I said he was mad and he said God preserve me from sanity. (God certainly will.)" (M 91).[17]

To be preoccupied with the question of pathology or pathologizing would, however, be to miss almost entirely the point of this essay. As I use it here, the term "schizoid" describes not a mental disorder, but rather a particular style of being involving certain temperamental or emotional propensities and a distinct set of characteristic conflicts, concerns, and styles of psychological defense. Although I will show that Wittgenstein's temperament and existential stance have a certain schizoid flavor, equally significant is the degree to which he was also at odds with this defining aspect of his being. Many such individuals are highly self-critical and self-aware; Wittgenstein was unusual in the degree to which his criticism focused precisely on his own schizoid tendencies themselves. Indeed, we might say that Wittgenstein, in some ways the greatest anti-intellectual intellectual of the twentieth century, is also the most antischizoid of schizoids – a person who both epitomizes and attacks the forms of inwardness and separation that are the lot of the modern human being.[18]

Wittgenstein is the author of two rather different philosophical positions – represented in his books *Tractatus Logico-Philosophicus* and *Philosophical Investigations*; and these largely reflect or express two very different attitudes toward the schizoid aspects of his mode of being. There is certainly a stark contrast between Wittgenstein's characteristic personal concerns in the earlier and later periods. In his wartime notebooks of 1914–1916, Wittgenstein seems preoccupied with securing the purity, solidity, and separateness of a kind of inner-self – not only as a way of overcoming fears of death, deprivation, and injury (all understandable enough given his situation as a soldier near the front line of battle), but also as a bulwark against temptations toward inauthenticity and against any tendency to give in to bodily needs or desires.

Later his concerns seem to shift. No longer is he so preoccupied with attempting to detach himself from the dangers or temptations presented by the external world, but, instead, with a threatening sense of inner division or deadness and of profound isolation from fellow human beings. Rather than providing a sense of invulnerability, separation from the body, for instance, has come to seem pathetic, even shameful, a condition of vacuity and deadness: "It is humiliating to have to appear like an empty tube which is simply inflated by a mind," he writes in his notebooks in 1931 (CV 11/13).[19] "In my soul there is winter (*now*) like all around me," Wittgenstein wrote in February 1937. "Everything is snowed in, nothing greens and blossoms." He describes an extinguishing of a light such that "mere existence" seemed to him "completely empty, *barren*. . . . One has then died alive . . . this is the real death" (D 196,199, 22.2.37). This transformation or shift of attitudes is not, however, the entire story: for (as shall be seen concerning the early Wittgenstein) on the more abstract or reflexive plane of metaphilosophy, Wittgenstein's schizoid *and* his antischizoid inclinations are simultaneously in play in *both* his earlier and his later periods.

Wittgenstein demonstrated a remarkable ambivalence regarding the very enterprise of philosophizing. Although he insisted, at times, on his great respect for philosophy, he more often described it as a source of "deep disquietudes," of vague mental "uneasiness," "mental cramps," and even "torments," and as an illness in need of cure (PI § 111, § 133, P 173–5).[20] He could describe the metaphysical writing of the past as "among the noblest of human endeavours," yet would also ask, debunkingly, "What would my bedmaker say of this kind of abstract talk?"[21] In this ambivalence about philosophy, Wittgenstein was invoking a key human dilemma: the question whether thinking should be considered the most vibrant expression or the most profound depletion of the vitality of the human condition.[22] Though always torn between these views, Wittgenstein did move in his later work rather closer to the second, more negative position, attacking the intellectualism of the Western philosophical tradition and seeking to root human existence in the exigencies of practical and social life, even, at times, in the most creaturely, instinctual part of human nature. "I want to regard man here as an animal," he wrote just a few weeks before his death, "as a primitive being to which one grants instinct but not ratiocination. As a creature in a primitive state. . . . Language did not emerge from some kind of ratiocination."[23]

To situate Wittgenstein's philosophical and metaphilosophical concerns in the context of his schizoid traits need not be seen as a reductionistic move. It is obvious that a philosophical theory, argument, or perspective must ultimately be judged independently of any psychological analysis of its origins or personal motivations. I do think, however, that such an analysis can have some significant implications for the hermeneutical stance with which we approach Wittgenstein's thought. It can, for example, make us more able to discern certain ambiguities, paradoxes, and tensions that one might otherwise overlook or deny. It may also help us to recognize certain tendencies toward exaggeration or onesidedness in Wittgenstein's thought. (Neither exaggeration nor inconsistency need, however, be seen as decisive flaws that destroy or even seriously compromise the value of a body of philosophical thought. An extreme position can shed more light than a more balanced one, and inconsistency, even contradiction, may sometimes be the price of addressing certain kinds of philosophical problems.)[24]

To point out certain schizoid or schizothymic aspects is certainly not meant to imply any lack of validity or relevance in Wittgenstein's thought or writings. I agree with those who see Wittgenstein as the most important philosopher of the twentieth century; I myself have been profoundly influenced by him. Further, as readers of my own *Madness and Modernism* and *The Paradoxes of Delusion* will know, I am not working with a model that contrasts a sane or normal condition marked by rationality and insight with some general notion of psychopathology understood as error, absence of volition, or lack of self-consciousness. The schizoid condition may, in fact, make one more sensitive to, and liable to have keener insight into, certain potentials of human existence than are other individuals.[25] The tension between an external view-from-nowhere and the sense of engagement in a more spontaneous, nonreflective kind of experience is, after all, a very real and potentially profound aspect of human existence. It is an insurmountable tension, and one that is especially prominent in the generation of philosophical problems, as Thomas Nagel has noted. To appreciate it fully is to recognize that pursuing an overly unified conceptualization of life and the world can sometimes be futile and even misleading; we may simply be "stuck with the clash of standpoints."[26] Although pervasive in human life, and present in some residual way for most human beings, the internal-external tension is much less salient for people with, say, predominantly hysterical, obsessive-compulsive, narcissistic, paranoid, or impulsive character styles than it is for schizoid or schizothymic individuals. Some people, writes Nagel, are "more susceptible to this problem than others, and even those who are susceptible to it vary over time in the degree to which it grips them."[27]

Clearly, then, I will not be arguing that the philosophical moves of this great thinker are but a shadow play, epiphenomenal reflections of some unseen, real events happening elsewhere and out of sight. My project is not, in fact, an attempt to explain the philosophy in light of the personality so much as to flesh out our understanding of each domain in the light of the other. One might say that the psychological and the philosophical are, in a sense, simultaneous expressions of the same issues, which are themselves rooted in human nature as this is refracted through a particular kind of personality and cultural formation. Through studying these affinities, we can better grasp how certain very general, abstract, even intellectual concerns – concerns bound up with issues of knowing and being – can nevertheless be experienced with a kind of vividness, concreteness, and emotional immediacy by a certain type of individual. I hope to do justice to the complexities and quiddities of Wittgenstein's thought while at the same time viewing him as a representative figure, one who, for all his uniqueness, can usefully be seen as emblematic of modern philosophy and of modernist culture more generally.

Any attempt to correlate the life and thought of a major philosopher is likely to be difficult, of course, but several features of Wittgenstein's thinking and writing make such an attempt particularly hazardous. First there is the difficulty of identifying or recognizing precisely who is speaking in his texts. Understanding Wittgenstein requires that one read with an ear cocked to the dramatic ironies and other complexities that make up the ebb and flow of his argument. This means recognizing that we are confronted not with a textbook or treatise so much as with a series of conversational dialogues in which it can be difficult to discern the location, or even the existence, of a settled point of view attributable to Wittgenstein. What at first may seem the assertion of a philosophical view often turns out to be the provision of a target or a stalking horse for his criticism. A remark from 1951 is apropos: "But see, I write one sentence, and then I write another – just the opposite. And which shall stand?"[28]

Wittgenstein's own acutely critical self-awareness can make one feel that there is nothing to which he is not himself already reacting, nothing of which he is not already aware. With no other philosopher is an interpreter as likely to feel that his every move has already been anticipated.[29] This makes it especially important to go beyond what Jean Starobinski has called the "principle of emanation or reflection," which would treat a work, such as Wittgenstein's *Tractatus,* as some kind of direct reflection or causal outcome of spontaneous inner tendencies or other psychological factors operating below the level of conscious awareness or control. One must obviously appreciate as well how the author himself may have already responded to and transcended some central elements of his psychic constitution, but this does not undermine the potential relevance of a psychological understanding. Indeed, as Starobinski notes, it may be "necessary to know the *man* and his empirical existence in order to know what the work is opposing or its coefficient of negativity."[30]

I do not claim, then, to have discovered a perspective on Wittgenstein's thinking of which he himself was wholly unaware. I prefer to think of myself as fleshing out the existential and psychological ramifications that, though not exactly unconscious, were nevertheless too pervasive and foundational to have been in the focus of Wittgenstein's attention or awareness. The psychological approach adopted here is primarily indebted to the phenomenological tradition, but also to psychiatric and psychodynamic schools that focus on temperament and characterological style rather than on childhood origins. The purpose of a phenomenological analysis is to render explicit something latent. What is latent, however, is not a repressed content so much as a mode of intentionality, the existential orientation or grasp of consciousness whereby the author himself takes stock and considers his place in the world. Like Starobinski in his book on Rousseau, I hope to capture both the variety of Wittgenstein's tendencies and the unity of his intentions, and to do so by clarifying, at a psychological level, not the historical causes, but what might be termed the fundamental style or organizing structure of Wittgenstein's awareness and general sensibility. This is one way of taking up the challenge Wittgenstein himself poses in the following line: "The movement of thought in my philosophizing should be reproducible in the history of my mind, of its moral concepts and in the understanding of my situation" (D 125, 7.11.31).

If successful, such a perspective should add to our understanding of Wittgenstein's life as well as to the appreciation of his texts, helping us pursue a variety of questions. What, specifically, are the existential implications of Wittgenstein's philosophical thoughts? What sort of existence do they encourage – and what do they condemn? How might his philosophical preoccupations be connected with his personality or sensibility, and with his deeply felt aesthetic preferences and ethical intuitions? How, in light of these questions, might we understand the development of his philosophical thoughts, which are characterized by radical reversal as well as by certain deep-lying continuities? And, finally, what light might all of this shed on Wittgenstein's ambivalent and shifting attitudes toward philosophy in general and, more particularly, toward his own brand of philosophizing or antiphilosophizing?

These are complex questions. They have no single or simple answers. Here I offer one possible "perspicuous representation" of the relationship between a philosopher's life and his thought, hopefully producing "just that understanding which consists in 'seeing connections' " (P 175).[31]

Schizothymic Temperament and Schizoid Personality

The concept of schizoid personality dates back to the beginning of the twentieth century and has been described in various ways.[32] Three classical conceptualizations are complementary and, taken together, offer a rich and complex portrait. These are the temperamental approach of the early 20th-century psychiatrist, Ernst Kretschmer, the existential-phenomenological account offered in R. D. Laing's *The Divided Self,* and the psychoanalytic accounts of the British object-relations theorists, W. R. D. Fairbairn and Harry Guntrip. These are to be distinguished from the narrower, deficit-oriented conceptualization offered in the recent diagnostic manuals of the American Psychiatric Association.

Ernst Kretschmer viewed schizoid or schizothymic individuals as being characterized by a tendency to combine two opposite tendencies that he conceived as being the extremes of a single temperamental dimension involving sensitivity to the environment, especially to other human beings. (Recall that "schizoid" refers to the more pronounced manifestation of these tendencies, "schizothymic" to the milder forms.) At one extreme is hypersensitivity, typically characterized by timorousness, a sense of vulnerability to intense stimuli, and a propensity for defensive withdrawal; at the other is anaesthesia, characterized by indifference, coldness, and condescension toward others. Kretschmer believed both tendencies to be latently present in each individual of the schizoid or schizothymic type. Thus, behind an affectless exterior, we may find, "in the innermost sanctuary, a tender personality-nucleus with the most vulnerable nervous sensitivity, which has withdrawn into itself, and lies there contorted." The point is exemplified by this self-description from August Strindberg: "I am hard as ice, and yet so full of feeling that I am almost sentimental."[33]

Kretschmer's account is complicated and dialectical, allowing for various subtypes and considerable variability within a single schizoid or schizothymic person. At a given moment, such an individual will usually appear to be either hypersensitive or anaesthetic, either hyperaesthetic or cold, but there is frequently a propensity to shift between these opposites, with each being dominant at least for a time. Following Kretschmer's lead, Eugen Bleuler contrasted the schizoid or schizothymic with what he called the "syntonic" type, which involves a more relaxed and spontaneous mode of being and a tendency toward harmony both within the self and in relationship with the outer and social world.[34]

Kretschmer's reflections on the relationship between temperament and creativity, especially in the genius, are of special relevance here. In a discussion of scholarly personality types, he notes the preponderance of schizoid and schizothymic personalities among "philosophers, systematizers, and metaphysicians," persons with a predilection for "formalism" and a "taste for the intangible and unreal." He mentions two interpenetrating groups: "accurate, clear logicians and system-builders of the Kantian type," and "emotional, romantic metaphysicians like Schelling." Despite differences, these two schizothymic intellectual dispositions are closely related: "Even in the exact epistemological critics of the Kantian type," writes Kretschmer, "we find marked metaphysical leanings, . . . a seeking after a priori, supernatural, religio-moral postulates. . . . One is always being surprised by coming across the well-known 'mystical corner' in the background of the emotional life of even the most accurate thinkers [of the schizothymic type], a corner which one will seek for in vain in the exquisitely observant [syntonic] empiricist like Alexander Humboldt."[35]

According to the existential-phenomenological account presented in R. D. Laing's *The Divided Self,* the predominant characteristic of schizoid persons is to be split in two main ways: they experience themselves as not at home in the world or with others, and they feel divided within themselves, whether as a mind divorced from the body or as two selves interacting as if at a distance.[36] The sense of self and the mind-body relationship are strongly reminiscent of a Cartesian philosophical position. Thus such persons locate their true sense of being in a private, mental domain, a realm of pure thought, a kind of *cogito* that is felt to be more real or more vital than the body or external world. There is a tendency to feel somehow awkward, at odds with, at a distance from, or otherwise not at one with one's self, one's body, or with the customs and practices of one's society. There is also a particular proclivity for experiences of derealization and depersonalization, whereby the world, other people, or the self comes to seem devoid of the normal sense of reality or emotional resonance.

Like Kretschmer, the psychoanalyst W. R. D. Fairbairn stresses the extreme sensitivity and sense of vulnerability of such persons; and, like R. D. Laing (whom he influenced), Fairbairn describes a characteristic "splitting of the ego," a process of intrapsychic defense that results in a sense of being a purely mental self or subject separated from both the body and the external world, as well as in feelings of "intensive self-consciousness and a sense of looking on at oneself."[37] Such persons frequently "experience an acute aware-ness of their surrounding environment, an emotional attunedness to others, and yet a sense of unavailability of feelings."[38] The psychoanalyst Harry Guntrip, a follower of Fairbairn, speaks of a persistent sense of "noninvolve-ment and observation at a distance without any feeling," a tendency to expe-rience one's life from a "free-floating" position, as if one were a press reporter at a social gathering or an observer from another planet.[39]

Such psychological processes can have advantages as well as disadvan-tages. The splitting serves as a most powerful defense, seeming to protect a fragile inner core of selfhood from any conceivable harm. No injury to the body, no worldly deprivation or adversity, at the limit not even death itself, can be of any relevance, given that such events will seem to occur in a purely external, physical universe quite separate from the precious, inner realm of the mind. The feeling of detached self-consciousness, of looking on at oneself and one's situation as if from somewhere far above, can contribute to a characteristic sense of emotional detachment, intellectual superiority, and even godlike omniscience, leading, in extreme cases, not just to hyperintellec-tualism but to feelings of solipsistic omnipotence. To the schizoid individual, people who lack this propensity for self-consciousness may seem to be some-how less than fully human.[40] Yet along with its self-protective and self-flattering effects, the schizoid's splitting also has debilitating, devitalizing, and anxiety-provoking effects. Separation from the body and external world may confer a sense of safety, but it can also lead to intense suffering as a result of being out of touch with or cut off from one's emotions, shut out and shut down, apart and strange, or artificial, and to forms of depression charac-terized by a deadening sense of emptiness, futility, or loneliness. Such per-sons are especially vulnerable to feelings of alienation, arbitrariness, and the absurd, and to conflicts of perspective that can undermine commitment and upset the coherence of their attitudes.[41] Some such persons, however, may also have a particular sensitivity for and insight into what, at least from a philosophical perspective, may seem to be the central dilemmas of human knowledge and existence.[42]

Fairbairn and Guntrip describe the schizoid's intense social ambivalence as leading to a couple of characteristic ploys or modes of psychological defense. One of these is the "in-and-out program": a tendency to oscillate between contact and isolation, finding neither peace nor security nor a sense of ontological groundedness in either state and therefore always yearning for the opposite one. Since the sense of interpersonal vulnerability naturally makes it difficult to share one's more private thoughts and feelings in a straightforward fashion, it often evokes another characteristic move: what Fairbairn calls the substitution of *showing* for *giving* – the replacement of a full human encounter by a kind of psychic exhibitionism that refuses fully to acknowledge the presence of the other.[43]

Wittgenstein as Schizoid Personality

Anyone familiar with Wittgenstein's biography, his more personal jottings, or the various memoirs by his acquaintances and friends, should have little difficulty recognizing the lineaments of a schizothymic or even schizoid temperament. Throughout his life, Wittgenstein gave the impression of separateness from his surroundings or of alienation from those around him (McG 234; M 16). The publisher Ludwig von Ficker, who encountered Wittgenstein at age 25, described him as presenting "a picture of stirring loneliness at the first glance" (M 107). Wittgenstein's writings are replete with descriptions of a pervasive sense of estrangement, from others and from the environment more generally. "Even though I am with quite friendly people (or just because of it?)," he wrote in 1930, "I feel constantly disturbed – even though they do not actively disturb me – and cannot come to myself. That's an awful state. Every word I hear them speak disturbs me. . . . In my room I feel not alone but exiled" (D 47, 9.10.30). "I must live in a more rarified atmosphere and belong there," he wrote the next year, "and should resist the temptation of wanting to live in the thick layer of air with the others, who are allowed to do so" (D 87, 6.5.31).[44]

In 1946 Wittgenstein spoke of living in an "environment . . . cheaply wrapped in cellophane and isolated from everything great" (CV 50/57), and, toward the end of his life, of feeling himself to be "an alien in the world" (M 516) – a feeling that, no doubt, owed something to the sense of being different inherent in being both a homosexual and a Jew.[45] In 1914 he described his proclivity for what seems an extreme experience of depersonalization: "We tend to take the speech of a Chinese for inarticulate gurgling. Someone who understands Chinese will recognize *language* in what he hears. Similarly I often cannot discern the *humanity* in a man" (CV 1/3).[46]

Wittgenstein was certainly capable of great coldness, condescension, and even contempt. He describes "a phenomenon that is extraordinarily characteristic of me: Unless their appearance or demeanor makes a special impression on me, I consider people lesser than myself: that is, I would be inclined to use the word 'ordinary' about them" (D 152, 28.1.37). At times he felt profound disgust for average people ("I suffer much from the human, or rather inhuman, beings with whom I live"); their pettiness, greed, affectation, and general lack of honor was so overwhelming as to make them seem virtually subhuman – like "loathsome worms" or "one-quarter animal" (M 228, 212, also 89). Even Wittgenstein's best friends were likely to feel the force of his severity and ruthless judgments, which could turn suddenly upon them if they said or did something that Wittgenstein considered inauthentic, fatuous, or weak. Yet it was with himself that Wittgenstein was at his most severe. Bertrand Russell once described a withering self-criticism in which Wittgenstein was "always analyzing, pulling things up by the roots" (M 80). At least from his earliest years in philosophy, this tendency toward self-criticism would bring Wittgenstein to the brink of suicide or madness: he seemed as obsessed or perturbed by his own character flaws as he was by problems of logic or philosophy with which these flaws seemed, somehow, to be linked. A famous anecdote from Russell describes a visit in which Wittgenstein paced "up and down . . . like a wild beast for three hours in agitated silence." When Russell asked "Are you thinking about logic or your sins?" Wittgenstein answered, "Both," then continued to pace (M 64).

Along with what Wittgenstein himself described as a characteristic "cold-heartedness" in himself (Monk speaks of "emotional solipsism" [M 380, 428]) went an extreme vulnerability, hypersensitivity, and neediness that is consistent with Kretschmer's description of the hyperaesthetic side of the schizoid temperament. Throughout his life Wittgenstein seemed acutely aware of what he described as "the fundamental insecurity of life," and recognized that "I am easily hurt and afraid of being hurt." "It is terrible how easily I am overcome by anxiety (*die Sorge*)," he wrote in 1937 (M 506, 504, 374).[47] In a diary entry from 1931, Wittgenstein describes his thoughts as like a tender inner-self that is unprepared for brutal contact with the world:

My thoughts rarely come into the world unmutilated. Either some part of them gets *twisted* at birth or broken off. Or the thought is a premature birth altogether and not yet viable in the language of words. Then a small foetus of a sentence is born that still lacks the most important limbs (D 98, 13.5.31).

It seems that Ludwig was a highly sensitive youth, and, surprisingly enough given his adult personality, abnormally anxious to please (M 4, McG 49–50).[48] After meeting Wittgenstein for the first time, Ficker remarked on the combination of discomfort and neediness that is so characteristic of many schizoid individuals: "Though there was something awkward in [Wittgenstein's] manner of speech, he seemed possessed by a deep need for communication" (McG 206).

Wittgenstein did not, however, find it easy to be in touch with his feelings, or to communicate them to others. In an anguished diary entry from 1930, he describes an inner blockage or paralysis:

Often I feel that there is something in me like a lump which, were it to melt, would let me cry or I would then find the right words (or perhaps even a melody). But this something (is it the heart?) in my case feels like leather and cannot melt. Or is it just that I am too cowardly to let the temperature rise sufficiently? (D 3–4, 26.4.30)

Here we see, in particularly clear fashion, a central irony of the schizoid condition. The blockage may protect him from painful emotion, but at the cost of making him feel deadened and out-of-touch. The attempt to escape one kind of suffering leads to another that is still more intense.[49]

Wittgenstein seems to have had a recurrent, almost instinctive need for withdrawal, a yearning for solitude and distant places where, it seemed, he might somehow find peace or some kind of redemption as well as escape from the possibility of theatricality or inauthenticity inherent in social life: "I thank God that I came to Norway into the loneliness!" (D 187, 20.2.37). But once there – for instance, alone in a hut he had built in a remote Norwegian fjord – Wittgenstein could feel terribly lonely, almost, in fact, unable to function without the saving balm of a few affectionate words in a note from a friend. Hence normal human beings were, as he put it in 1919, "a balm to me, and a torment at the same time" (M 181).[50] In 1942 he wrote of "the fear of complete isolation that threatens me now." "My unhappiness is so complex that it is difficult to describe, but probably the main thing is still *loneliness*" (M 442).[51]

Early Writings: The View from Inside

Wittgenstein's early writings, especially the *Tractatus Logico-Philosophicus,* are famously enigmatic, but there can be little doubt that they constantly flirt with a position congruent with the schizoid sensibility. Somewhat like Descartes, but perhaps in a more radical way, Wittgenstein was inclined to assume a sharp distinction between consciousness and its objects, then to place the human body, including the subject's own body, squarely on the side of the latter. "The human body . . . my body in particular, is a part of the world among others, among beasts, plants, stones, etc. etc." "A stone, the body of a beast, the body of man, my body, all stand on the same level," he wrote in 1916 in the wartime notebooks that were to serve as preliminary studies for the *Tractatus* (NB 82, 84). Similar ideas found their way into the *Tractatus,* where Wittgenstein describes the "philosophical I" as a "metaphysical subject" who is "not a part of the world" (5.641). He imagines a book entitled "The World as I Found It" in which everything that could be observed would be described. In such a book, there would be no description of the subject or the "I", but reports on the body would take their place alongside reports of all other external or objectifiable things (TLP 5.631; NB 50).

Wittgenstein was strongly drawn toward solipsism in this period. This is apparent from various remarks toward the end of the *Tractatus*: "The world is my world." "The I occurs in philosophy through the fact that 'the world is my world' " (TLP 5.62, 5.641) – as well as, more colorfully, in his overtly Schopenhauerian wartime jottings: "As my idea is the world, in the same way my will is the world-will." "What has history to do with me? Mine is the first and only world!" (NB 85, 82).

These are provocative but cryptic statements. There has been considerable debate about what, precisely, they may mean, and how these dark, portentous utterances might link up with the more sober doctrines of logic and semantics that preoccupied Wittgenstein during the period leading up to and including the composition of the *Tractatus*. The combination may well seem strange. The *Tractatus,* after all, is a treatise (or perhaps we should say an antitreatise) of mathematical logic and semantics that teaches (or seems to teach)[52] *both* that: "What can be said at all can be said clearly" (4.116) *and* that: "There is indeed the inexpressible. This *shows* itself; it is the mystical" (6.522). There may be no contradiction between these two facets of the *Tractatus,* but there is certainly a tension – a tension between the logical and the mystical that Bertrand Russell, for one, found both enigmatic and dismaying (M 182–3). This duality in the *Tractatus* does seem to exemplify the "connection between systematic exactitude and mystical unreality" that, according to Kretschmer, is common in schizothymic thinkers but absent in, and often incomprehensible to, scholars of a more worldly and empirical disposition (i.e., of the syntonic type).[53]

Wittgenstein himself said of the *Tractatus,* "the book's point is an *ethical* one" – using "ethics" in an exceptionally broad sense, one inclusive of aesthetics and that he defined some years later as "the enquiry into what is valuable, or, into what is really important," the enquiry "into the meaning of life, or into what makes life worth living, or into the right way of living" (E 38). What position, if any, the *Tractatus* can be said to espouse is very much a matter for debate, as recent arguments offered by Cora Diamond and James Conant make clear.[54] In the *Notebooks,* however, we can see how close Wittgenstein came to advocating a certain kind of schizoid ideal, a life based on separation from the body, others, and the external physical universe, and on retreat to an inner and purely cerebral realm, devoid of all passion, yearning, and pain.

During World War I, Wittgenstein was often scared, hungry, and uncomfortable, but what seems to have particularly galled and appalled him at this time was finding himself reduced to his creaturely nature, at the mercy of all the demands or trepidations of the flesh: "From time to time I become an *animal*," he wrote in his diary, ". . . eating, drinking, and sleeping . . . at the mercy of my appetites and aversions. Then an authentic life is unthinkable" (M 146). In August 1916, while serving in dangerous circumstances as a soldier at the front, he was inclined to see "the life of knowledge" as offering the only hope for happiness and for "ward[ing] off the misery of the world" (NB 81). During the war, Wittgenstein repeatedly returned to the idea that the body belonged to the external world and that its welfare should therefore be a matter of indifference to him. He would repeat the following litany: "Don't be dependent on the external world and then you have no fear of what happens in it" (M 116, also 51–3).

To "make myself independent of fate": this was Wittgenstein's ambition. Achieving such a goal requires recognition and renunciation – recognition that, as he put it, the world "is independent of our will" (NB 74), and renunciation of all desire and all wish for control: "What do I know about God and the purpose of life?" asked Wittgenstein. "I know that this world exists. That I am placed in it like my eye in its visual field. . . . I cannot bend the happenings of the world to my will: I am completely powerless. I can only make myself independent of the world – and so in a certain sense master it – by renouncing any influence on happenings" (NB 72–3; M 141). Attaining independence means living "without fear or hope." It means recognizing that "in a certain sense . . . not wanting is the only good" (NB 76–7). The influence of Wittgenstein's reading of Arthur Schopenhauer and Otto Weininger is patent in these pages. We hear echoes both of Schopenhauer's Buddhistic world-denial and of the denigration of unconsciousness, instinct, and the desire for merger to be found in Weiningers's *Sex and Character,* a book that glorifies masculinity as a condition of self-awareness, intellectual clarity, utter self-sufficiency, and freedom from physical fear and desire. "Man has no object outside himself; lives for nothing else; he is far removed from being the slave of his wishes . . . he stands far above social ethics; he is alone," writes Weininger in extolling the "splendid supremacy" of the person courageous enough to "acquiesce in his loneliness."[55]

This yearning for complete security through detachment, for a kind of security unavailable to any creaturely being living *within* the world, was an enduring preoccupation for Wittgenstein. In his "Lecture on Ethics" of 1929, he speaks of "the experience of feeling *absolutely* safe. I mean the state of mind in which one is inclined to say 'I am safe, nothing can injure me whatever happens.' " He explains that, for him, this had always been one of the instances *par excellence* of an experience that gives meaning to the concept of absolute or ethical value (E 41).

In other entries in his wartime notebooks, Wittgenstein states that "the solution of the problem of life" is "to be seen in the disappearance of this problem," then goes on to equate this disappearance with a life that escapes from time. Such a person avoids all the anxieties of the human condition until even death itself dissolves into illusion: "A man who is happy must have no fear. Not even in face of death. Only a man who lives not in time but in the present is happy. For life in the present there is no death. Death is not an event in life. It is not a fact of the world" (NB 74–5). This banishing of death seems to be a direct corollary of the solipsistic realization that if one's own death can be considered unreal, this is because it cannot, by definition, be experienced – a point made clear in the following lines from the *Tractatus*:

As in death, too, the world does not change, but ceases.
Death is not an event in life. Death is not lived through. . . .
Our life is endless in the way that our visual field is without limit (TLP 6.431, 6.4311).

Later Writings

It can be difficult to attain a comprehensive grasp of the work of the later Wittgenstein, who is famous for his fragmentary and dialogic style, his persistently questioning and negative stance, and the wide-ranging nature of his concerns, covering topics in the philosophy of language, mind, and mathematics, in logic and epistemology, in ethics and aesthetics, as well as questions of metaphilosophy. There are, however, certain unifying themes. At least as a first approach, these might be characterized in negative terms: as a rejection of any vision of human nature or consciousness that would treat inner, private, or mental events as being more fundamental, definitive, or immediate than is human activity, social existence, or the world of common-sense reality, and as a profound (even if somewhat self-contradictory) suspicion of self-conscious reflection and abstraction as routes to an understanding of human life.

The first point is clear enough in Wittgenstein's critique of solipsism, in his rejection of sense-data phenomenalism,[56] and in his famous argument against the very possibility of a private language – a language whose words would "refer to what can only be known to the person speaking; to his immediate private sensations," and which another person would therefore not be able to understand (PI § 243). In related arguments, Wittgenstein considers the status of first-person sentences concerning sensations, emotions, and other psychological phenomena (e.g., "I am in pain" or "I have [a] toothache"; PI § 244). He argues that, in most instances, these should not be viewed as descriptions of mental states. They are more like expressions or avowals, akin to such natural reactions as wincing or crying, and having the social and practical role of eliciting human response rather than the private or cognitive one of characterizing inner events. The *Philosophical Investiga-*

tions also contains more general meditations on psychological concepts such as "understanding," "expecting," "intending," "reading," and "thinking." In each case, Wittgenstein concludes that the use of these concepts (whether in first- or third-person) is not linked to some essential and definitive inner process but, rather, to certain patterns of behavior and practical contexts. We speak of someone as "understanding" a given order or piece of advice if he shows in his actions that he knows how to go on; we speak of him as "thinking" if he acts in certain meaningful and appropriate ways (PI §§ 316, 327, 332, 339).[57]

In other works from his later period, Wittgenstein gives more attention to issues of philosophical psychology and the general status of human knowledge, including knowledge of the external world and other minds. Wittgenstein wants to block the notion, implicit in many philosophies, that we are somehow at a distance from our own bodies, from other human beings, or from the ambient world. We don't *know* our body's posture; it is something we inhabit, something we *are*.[58] Nor is it necessary to intuit, infer, or project a soul or sense of awareness into the other, or a sense of reality onto the objects about us. These are things we see directly; we don't *believe* in them so much as take them for granted, as the foundation or framework on the basis of which, or within which, other, more particular events can be experienced. Wittgenstein's inclination is to block any propensity for thought to turn away from the public or practical world and toward a realm of inner and private experience. He is opposed to any conception of human experience that would suggest we are somehow removed from our bodies, thoughts, or sensations, or that we have only an indirect, inferential relationship to other persons or the external world.

In his later work Wittgenstein offers a famous semantic perspective that roots all meaning in "language games" and "forms of life," the shared understandings and practices and the practical contexts of human activity and social life. Wittgenstein was inclined to view this perspective as undermining or even denying the very possibility of entertaining solipsism or skepticism, or of pursuing most forms of philosophical generalization and abstraction. Thus he states that he is bringing words back from their metaphysical to their everyday uses, rooting them again in the language games that are their original homes and from which, presumably, they derive all possibility of significance (PI § 115). "If the words 'language', 'world', have a use," he writes, "it must be as humble a one as that of the words 'table', 'lamp', 'door' " (PI § 97).

Related transformations occur at the level of Wittgenstein's philosophical style, which comes, at least in certain obvious ways, to be almost antithetical to the *Tractatus* – in style, tone, aspirations, and ideals. Instead of numbered sentences logically ordered, we now get a series of fragments that Wittgenstein describes as no more than remarks in an album, "sketches of landscapes which were made in the course of . . . long and involved [philosophical] journeyings" (PI, Preface). Instead of an equation of meaning with clarity or semantic exactitude, we have a return to the "rough ground" of language games, forms of life, and family resemblances, and a general defense of the necessity of vagueness. Instead of the wish to say everything once and for all, in a burst of incontrovertible but self-immolating clarity (the *Tractatus*), we get an acceptance of the continuing need for a more humble kind of therapeutic philosophizing, a necessary housekeeping operation whose work can never finally be done.

In summary, then, we can see that Wittgenstein did, at one level, go through a significant change in his attitude toward the schizoid tendencies that seem to have been at the core of his being. The *Notebooks* and other evidence strongly suggest that, at least at first, he attempted to exploit these tendencies, to live them out to the fullest extent possible while berating himself for any failure to live up to what could be considered rather schizoid ideals – ideals of autonomy, personal integrity, utter equanimity in the face of danger and deprivation, and indifference to appearance and the opinion of others.[59] From this Wittgenstein moved to a position in which, on the philosophical plane as well as on that of personal existence, he seems more concerned about the errors or dangers of detachment, in which he struggles to cure himself of the temptations of the schizoid position and to reinsert himself into society and reconnect with the world. The transition is not, of course, perfectly smooth; one can find, both early and late, many exceptions to the general trend. Still, whereas in 1929 Wittgenstein could still describe his ideal as "a certain coolness," by the end of his life we more often find statements like the following: "Wisdom is passionless [whereas] faith by contrast is what Kierke-gaard calls *a passion*." It "merely *conceals* life from you . . . like cold grey ash . . . covering up the glowing embers" (CV 56/64, cf. 2/4).

Much more could certainly be said about the contrast between the earlier and later philosophies, but I think the general point should be clear enough by now. Indeed, much of what I have been saying will, I suspect, be fairly obvious to anyone familiar with the general lines of Wittgenstein's life or thought. Matters become somewhat more complicated, however – and more interesting – if we turn to another, more reflexive or "meta-" set of Wittgen-stein's philosophical concerns; that is, if we now focus less on the actual doctrines or general orientations that he espouses or encourages than on his attitudes toward the very legitimacy of philosophizing itself, including his own. To understand the psychological resonance and relevance of the latter set of issues, it is necessary to consider a different aspect of the schizoid stance.

What now become central are not Cartesian issues and themes – the sense of inwardness involved in identifying with a mental core set apart from body, the emotions, and the external and material world – but, rather, the sense of removal and remoteness that derives from adopting the position of an external observer who exists somewhere outside both the self and the entirety of its world. Such an observer presumes to be able to adopt a totalizing or transcendental stance in which it is possible to know, describe, or somehow intuit the knowable world as a whole in its most fundamental relationship with the human mind. These issues have a more Kantian or post-Kantian flavor, for they pertain to the issue of limits, to questions about the nature and the knowability of the boundaries of possible experience or of sensible discourse itself. Such issues were, in fact, central throughout the entire course of Wittgenstein's philosophical career. By considering them, it is possible to show that Wittgenstein, both early and late, was always driven *both* to express and simultaneously to deny his schizoid inclinations. In this paper, however, I will focus on the earlier period.

The View from Outside

Before proceeding, it is useful to recall several features of a schizoid orientation that were mentioned above: first, what has been called the "in-and-out" program, and second, the tendency to look on at oneself and one's existence from a distant or external standpoint. A third feature, the propensity for showing or exhibiting rather than giving, will become relevant in the final section of this paper.

Psychologists have generally described the in-and-out program in interpersonal terms. One can, however, think of this program in a more inclusive way: as a matter of moving back and forth between, first, a position of engagement or immersion not just in the social encounter but, one might say, in existence in general, and, second, a position of detachment or removal – the latter being a state in which one has the sense of floating outside the entirety of one's being, consciousness, or world, and of taking all of this, everything that one is or experiences or within which one normally moves, as the target of objectifying experience in the present moment. Perhaps any philosopher, at least any philosopher working in the wake of Kant's Copernican revolution in human self-awareness, must inevitably be concerned with, or implicated in, this duality or dilemma. For Wittgenstein, however, it seems to have had a special, indeed at times an excruciating, salience.

Wittgenstein's propensity for this kind of detachment is not difficult to demonstrate. In a notebook entry from October 1916 (NB 83), he writes:

The good life is the world seen *sub specie aeternitatis*. This is the connexion between art and ethics. The usual way of looking at things sees objects as it were from the midst of them, the view *sub specie aeternitatis* from outside. In such a way that they have the whole world as background. Is this it perhaps – in this view the object is seen *together with* space and time instead of *in* space and time."

In the *Tractatus,* he speaks of contemplating the world "as a limited whole" (TLP 6.45).

Wittgenstein made an analogous point in 1930: ". . . there is a way of capturing the world *sub specie aeterni* other than through the work of the artist. Thought has such a way – so I believe – it is as though it flies above the world and leaves it as it is – observing it from above, in flight" (CV 5/7). In another line from 1930, Wittgenstein describes a somewhat related propensity, the predilection, which was present throughout his life, for a detached, synoptic, or "possibilitarian" perspective: "For me . . . clarity, perspicuity are valuable in themselves. I am not interested in constructing a building, so much as in having a perspicuous view of the foundations of possible buildings" (CV 7/9).[60]

One should also recall Wittgenstein's reference, in his 1929 "Lecture on Ethics," to two experiences that stood for him as paradigms of the sense of ultimate value: first, the sense of wonder, by which he meant the sense of amazement at the very existence of the world itself rather than of any particular object in it, and second, the sense of safety, of feeling absolutely safe regardless of what happens to one. As Wittgenstein himself explains in the ethics lecture, both experiences assume a capacity that would seem to be impossible or even nonsensical: a capacity to separate oneself from the entirety of the world, to "*go beyond* the world and that is to say beyond significant language" by taking the world's existence not as the presupposed background but as the hypothetical target of an objectifying form of awareness. Wittgenstein describes this as a "running against the walls of our cage [that] is perfectly, absolutely hopeless" and "does not add to our knowledge in any sense." For, he says, "it is nonsense to say that I wonder at the existence of the world, because I cannot imagine it not existing." Nevertheless, he says, this "is a document of a tendency in the human mind which I personally cannot help respecting deeply and I would not for my life ridicule it" (E 42, 44).

Clarity, absolute safety, a sense of awe: these are among Wittgenstein's most central values – and as we see, he associated each of them with a certain capacity for distancing from the world or from oneself. Yet despite Wittgenstein's respect as well as predilection for this kind of distancing, there is no person who is more acutely aware than he of the potentially misleading as well as devitalizing effects of such removal, no person who yearns more deeply for the condition of engagement that is its antithesis and its antidote. This should be clear enough in what I have already said about Wittgenstein's later philosophy – a philosophy that one critic, Ernest Gellner, has compared to an attempt to restrict thought and discourse to the condition of a traditional *Gemeinschaft* community, whose members would be relatively devoid of abstraction, of self-critical or cosmopolitan meta-awareness, or of the capacity for skeptical deliberation on fundamental questions.[61] A similar sense of revulsion at the position of the removed onlooker is, however, equally central to the early philosophy, where, as we shall see in the final section, it gets expressed in a curious and paradoxical manner.

Gellner is out of sympathy with Wittgenstein's later work and, it seems to me, rather deaf to its fundamental spirit. His reference to *"Gemeinschaft"* does, however, call attention to an important strain: the antipathy Wittgenstein always felt toward the modern condition of cultural fragmentation and self-consciousness, in which basic cultural presuppositions come under scrutiny and can no longer serve as the taken-for-granted foundation of spontaneous thought and action. In a draft of the preface to his *Philosophical Remarks,* Wittgenstein describes his antipathy to the dominant trends of European and American "civilization" and contrasts this with a true "culture," in which each member has "a place where he can work in the spirit of the whole" (CV 6/8–9).

The distinction between culture and civilization is the central theme of *The Decline of the West* by Oswald Spengler, one of the handful of authors whom Wittgenstein repeatedly cited as a major influence and a writer whose thinking Wittgenstein described as "completely in touch with what I have often thought myself" (D 17, 6.5.30). Spengler contrasts *Kultur* and *Zivilisation* as "the living body of a soul" versus "the mummy of it." In his view, a crucial caesura in European history occurred around 1800. On one side of this frontier, Spengler sees "life in fullness and sureness of itself, formed by growth from within [i.e., culture] . . . on the other, the autumnal, artificial, rootless life of our great cities under forms fashioned by the intellect [civilization]." For what Spengler calls "the Gothic and Doric men, Ionic and Baroque men" of the earlier era, "the whole vast form world of art, religion, custom, state, knowledge, social life was easy. They could carry it and actualize it without 'knowing' it." For culture, writes Spengler, is "the self-evident." He remarks on the typical modern feelings of "strangeness" with regard to these cultural forms, "the idea that they are a burden from which creative freedom requires to be relieved," and the "fatal imposition of thought upon the inscrutable quality of creativeness." All these, he says, are "symptoms of a soul that is beginning to tire. Only the sick man feels his limbs."[62] In such a condition, we might say (paraphrasing Wittgenstein), life does not fit into a mold and hence what is problematic cannot disappear (CV 27/31).

In a conversation on these issues recollected by O. K. Bouwsma, Wittgenstein spoke of changes in the kind of human beings we are in the modern world: "There was a time when our lives were furnished rather simply, a house, a place, tools so many, a beast, and a circle of people. In this simplicity and this stability one grew attached to a limited environment. This gave a life a certain quality – roots."[63] This simplicity and stability is in sharp contrast with the present era, a time in which, to quote from Wittgenstein's personal notes, "ordinary common sense no longer suffices to meet the strange demands life makes." We live now in a time when "skill at playing the game is no longer enough [and] the question that keeps coming up is: can this game be played at all now and what would be the right game to play" (CV 27/31).

In a diary passage from 1930, Wittgenstein seems to be describing the fate of people such as himself: "In the metropolitan civilization the spirit can only huddle in some corner. And yet it is for instance not atavist and superfluous but hovers above the ashes of culture as an (eternal) witness – as if an avenger of the deity. As if it were awaiting a new incarnation (in a new culture)" (D 46, 8.10.30).

Philosophy

Now, it is hardly surprising that a philosopher with views like these might be highly ambivalent about the worth and legitimacy of philosophy itself, about many of the great figures of the past, and, perhaps especially, about his own work. For if culture is the self-evident, then philosophy – at least *modern* philosophy – would seem to be its enemy. Philosophy, it is said, originates with wonder;[64] modern philosophy, however, clearly begins with doubt – with a will-to-knowledge that undermines the sense of easy certitude and natural self-evidence. Wittgenstein, in fact, actually *defined* philosophy in this way: as a bringing to explicit awareness of what would normally stay in the background – a matter of focusing on "aspects . . . hidden because of their simplicity and familiarity," of examining "the real foundations of his inquiry [which normally] do not strike a man at all" (PI § 129).[65] Indeed, he doubted that anyone who lacked this capacity for getting outside normal presuppositions could really be called a philosopher at all.[66] It is easy to see how philosophizing, so understood, might have contributed to, yet also been inspired by, the discomfort Wittgenstein was alluding to when he described himself as sitting "astride life like a bad rider on a horse" (CV 36/42; & cf. D 234, 6.4.37). Whereas religion and myth, at least as they function in a true culture, provide orientation and confidence, philosophical problems, according to Wittgenstein, cause "vague mental uneasiness" or "mental cramp" (NM 43); he likens philosophical views and questioning to a kind of illness in need of therapy.[67]

It is understandable that Wittgenstein was especially ambivalent about his own philosophical tendencies. He was, in fact, caught in something of a dilemma: philosophizing, for him, was a disturbing activity and yet, at the same time, also the most energizing and reassuring one. When bereft of inspiration, philosophical inspiration, Wittgenstein was plunged into despair (M 75). "I feel well only when I am in a certain sense inspired. And then again I fear the collapse of this inspiration" (D 10, 29.4.30). "Don't leave me, mind! I.e., might the weak spirit-fed flame of my mind not expire!" (D 122, 7.11.31). Philosophy, he said, was the only work "that's given me real satisfaction" or "really bucks me up" (M 455), and he once described doing logic as giving him the feeling of being "sheltered again, at home again, in the warmth again, that is what my heart yearns for" (D 51, 16.10.30).[68] At times, however, Wittgenstein was prone to experience his own philosophical impulse not as vitalizing or comforting but as a sign or source of deterioration. Perhaps this is what was surfacing when, around 1933, he spoke of himself as "already philosophizing with toothless gums" (CV 23/27).[69] Norman Malcolm has described the intense self-disgust that Wittgenstein would feel after lecturing in the late 1930s: his words, he said, sometimes felt like corpses to him, and afterwards he would desperately rush off to sit in the front row at the movies, drowning himself in the "shower-bath" of the Fred Astaire and Ginger Rogers musicals or American westerns which he preferred (NM 23, 26).

Here we might recall Wittgenstein's preoccupation with genius, an issue emphasized in Ray Monk's biography: Wittgenstein's sense, from an early age, that life is not worth living or, more accurately, that one is not worthy of living it, unless one is a genius. The notion of the genius was a central theme of the romantic and post-romantic era, and had become a major preoccupation in the German-speaking world by the turn of the century. In Otto Weininger's *Sex and Character,* which Wittgenstein acknowledged as a major influence on his intellectual development, the condition of the genius is presented as a kind of ethical and aesthetic imperative – a necessity for any human being self-respectful enough to want to transcend mere animality and fulfill the human essence. Weininger believed, in fact, that the only honorable alternative to striving toward genius would be to kill oneself – an act he carried out himself in 1903.

One of Wittgenstein's first images of genius was that of seeing his brother Hans playing the piano, in a state of complete absorption; and this, Ray Monk tells us, remained for Wittgenstein a kind of paradigm of what it must be like to be possessed of genius (M 13). As a child he had been woken one night at three in the morning by music and, venturing downstairs, found his brother at the piano playing one of his own – Hans's – compositions. Hans was sweating, in a state of utter, manic concentration – completely oblivious to the fact of being observed. Wittgenstein was drawn to the idea that one should be a creature of impulse (M 45). He also believed that genius involves creation of some kind. The paradigm cases of true genius, for him, were such composers as Mozart and Beethoven, whom he called the true "sons of god" (M 13), and works that expressed "veneration," which he associated with "genuine enthusiasm" (D 7, 27.4.30).

Yet Wittgenstein's strongest impulse, his own genius, if indeed that is the appropriate term, was for philosophizing, and philosophizing of a peculiarly negative sort. If genius is to be defined as creation and absorption – absorption in the *service* of creation – then one has to recognize the problematic status of Wittgenstein's own work, which both early and later in his career has a distinctively negative flavor. After all, it derives in large measure from a distantiated contemplation and critique of the philosophical discourse of others. The main goal of Wittgenstein's thinking may be the discouragement of philosophizing itself ("Philosophy is a tool which is useful only against philosophers and against the philosopher in us"), but, in some respects at least, it traffics in *further* alienation, merely recapitulating the condition of philosophy in a higher degree.[70]

Wittgenstein's own antiphilosophizing is, after all, grounded not in absorption but in a kind of alienated critical self-consciousness – or perhaps we should speak of absorption *in* a kind of alienated critical self-consciousness. The purpose, in any case, is deconstruction, discouragement, perhaps therapy, certainly not the construction of an alternative philosophical edifice. Wittgenstein writes, "The philosopher is not a citizen of any community of ideas. That is what makes him into a philosopher."[71] This would, however, seem to be doubly true of the *Wittgensteinian* philosopher: alienated not only from the language of household, workshop, and marketplace, but from normal philosophical conversation as well. Perhaps this is part of what Wittgenstein had in mind when he wrote: "It's only by thinking even more crazily than philosophers do that you can solve their problems" (CV 75/86).

Can we speak, then, of inspiration and genius in the case of Witttgenstein? Yes, of course – by the usual standards of importance, originality, and sheer brilliance; but not, perhaps, from Wittgenstein's *own* distinctly post-romantic viewpoint. For if we consider Wittgenstein's talent, it is surely less akin to the "genuine enthusiasm" of a Mozart or a Beethoven than to the intellectual and self-critical impulses that Nietzsche ascribes to "Socrates" in *The Birth of Tragedy*. Nietzsche describes Socrates, whom he begrudgingly admires, as a "monstrosity," the "*non*-mystic, in whom the logical side has become overdeveloped." In (Nietzsche's) Socrates, consciousness, conceived as "dissuader and critic," as a "great Cyclops eye which never glowed with divine inspiration," replaces instinct as the dominant motivating force. If Socrates hears an inspiring quasidivine voice, it is surely a "purely inhibitory agent" that "always spoke to *dissuade*."[72] This, perhaps, can help us understand the deeply critical feelings Wittgenstein sometimes had about his own philosophizing – his sense that he was so negative ("I destroy, I destroy, I destroy"

[CV 21/19 – written by Wittgenstein in English]) and his inclination, at times, to urge his own students to give up philosophy and take up some more useful profession such as medicine or auto mechanics.[73] He was inclined to think that he himself lacked some fundamental spark necessary for true originality, whether in philosophy or in other domains that he considered more vibrant:

I often think that the highest accomplishment I wish to achieve would be to compose a melody. Or it mystifies me that in the desire for this, none ever occurred to me. But then I must tell myself that it is quite impossible that one will ever occur to me, because for that I am missing something essential or *the* essential (D 9, 28.4.30).

I really only think reproductively. I don't believe I have ever *invented* a line of thinking (CV 18–19/16.)[74]

Wittgenstein's philosophizing is imbued with this self-critical, indeed meta-self-critical, tendency. It is this that gives his thought a certain tragic tone, an almost incomparable depth, and a curious wavering ambivalence – both about its own worth and that of many of its major targets. This great master of distancing is unable to resist the meta-move yet, at the same time, quite unable to glorify it. Indeed, he is often disgusted by his own tendencies toward pride in his intellect as well as toward endless critique.[75]

How little respect I have at bottom for my own achievement shows itself for me in that I would acknowledge or esteem only with great reservation a person of whom I had reason to believe that he is in some other discipline what I am in philosophy (D 136, 28.1.32).

An understanding of this ambivalence is relevant to one major controversy in current Wittgenstein interpretation. Both parties to the dispute are fully aware that Wittgenstein (or at least the later Wittgenstein) is not in the business of offering positive theses about the nature of knowledge, language, truth, or the mind, but they disagree about the *kind* of antiphilosopher Wittgenstein was. For Richard Rorty, Wittgenstein is a thoroughgoing *anti*philosopher who shows philosophy, of a metaphysical or transcendental kind, to be a mere source of error and illusion of which human beings need to be cured, thereby ultimately dissolving – this of course is only a utopian ideal – the very need for Wittgensteinian critique. Stanley Cavell takes a different view. He believes that even though Wittgenstein could describe himself as destroying mere "houses of cards" (PI § 118), he actually had a deep and enduring respect for the philosophical impulse, for the potential in human consciousness that Cavell terms "skepticism."[76] Cavell appears to believe that a comprehensive rejection of philosophy would be merely puerile or sophomoric, something unworthy of Wittgenstein. For Cavell's Wittgenstein, philosophical speculation and doubt are to be seen as an inevitable and invaluable expression, as well as a deepening, of the tragic dimension of human existence, which includes the capacities for doubt and alienation.[77]

My own intuitions are closer to Cavell than to Rorty on this issue; but to appreciate what I have called Wittgenstein's ambivalence is to recognize that this is ultimately a false choice – that Rorty and Cavell may each have captured an important strain of Wittgenstein's sometimes ambivalent and sometimes wavering views. What must be recognized is that Wittgenstein was an antiphilosopher as well as something of an anti-*anti*philosopher. In what may have been different moods, one or the other of these attitudes tended to be expressed, and sometimes they emerge at once.[78] To negate a negation will sometimes amount to an affirmation; Wittgenstein's anti-*anti*philosophical impulse did not, however, bring him full circle: it did not make him a philosopher of a more traditional kind. It did, however, make him gaze at times with respect, envy, and even some sense of inferiority at the philosophers who engaged in what they at least consider(ed) to be a constructive and worthwhile enterprise.

Wittgenstein spoke more than once of the hollowness of those, like himself, who largely debunk and criticize the sincere efforts of other philosophers more earnestly engaged in the pursuit of truth. "Don't criticize what serious people have written seriously, for you don't know what you are criticizing," he wrote in his diary in 1937 (D 226, 26.3.37). Bouwsma recounts a conversation in which Wittgenstein spoke disparagingly of his own work and approach: "It's not important but if anyone is interested I'm good at it and I may help. I don't recommend it. It's for people who cannot leave it alone." In this same conversation, Wittgenstein went on to scorn his own distanced negativity: "Very well, these other philosophers made mistakes, in earnest, but what now are you doing in earnest? There you are crowing over the mistakes of earnest men. So you will never make an important mistake, for nothing is important to you. Wonderful! Crow!"[79]

In a famous, and famously enigmatic, passage in the *Investigations,* Wittgenstein states that the "real discovery" would be "the one that makes me capable of stopping doing philosophy when I want to" (PI § 133). There has been much discussion of how one should interpret this remarkably ambiguous passage, and in particular how thoroughly antiphilosophical a position Wittgenstein may be espousing.[80] To my knowledge, however, no one has suggested an *anti*-antiphilosophical reading, namely, that the discovery of which Wittgenstein speaks might above all dissolve his *own* form of philosophizing, perhaps even leaving traditional metaphysics relatively undisturbed. He speaks, after all, of "giv[ing] philosophy peace, so that it is no longer tormented by questions which bring *itself* [i.e., philosophy itself] in question" (PI § 133).[81] The questioning that most brings philosophy into question is, of course, that of Wittgenstein himself – and Wittgenstein was very aware of how such questioning may mislead us both in intellectual and existential matters.[82]

There is obviously a strong antiacademic impulse in Wittgenstein's thought, and, beyond this, some truly anti-intellectual strains that cannot be denied.[83] In my opinion, some of the subtlest readers of Wittgenstein have not been willing to acknowledge, or at least to take seriously enough, the degree to which Wittgenstein did, at times, adopt a position that is truly against all philosophizing, including even *anti*philosophy – a position verging on the anti-intellectual in which he felt disgust not only for the other denizens of what he once called the "influenza area" that is philosophy (NM 79), but perhaps especially for himself and his antiphilosophizing, with its condition of double remove.[84] This blindspot in Wittgenstein interpretation is not difficult to understand, given the power of professional identifications and the existential commitments necessary for sustained action. It is, after all, a rare human being (and probably an even rarer *productive* human being) who is capable of this degree of self-criticism, which verged for Wittgenstein on self-loathing.[85] And, I dare say, it may be especially rare among intellectuals and others among us who are wont to philosophize – we being, perforce, people who need to be fairly immune to the sense of ridiculousness that overcomes the average person when he seeks to pronounce upon foundational matters or ultimate things. Perhaps it is also not surprising that when we do feel this encroaching sense, we generally do our best to fend it off as quickly as we can.

I do not agree, then, that there is necessarily something sophomoric about this anti-intellectual attitude – though it certainly does set Wittgenstein apart from nearly all of his exegetes. Indeed, it seems to me that it was precisely this willingness to question (or perhaps one should say, this inability *not* to question), and at other moments to question the questioning impulse itself, that makes Wittgenstein's thought so deeply exciting yet also so ultimately unassimilable to academic philosophy.[86]

I think, in any case, that a grasp of these issues, particularly of Wittgenstein's ambivalence regarding a totalizing or self-critical, external perspective, can shed considerable light on the nature of his specific philosophical concerns and counter-philosophical yearnings throughout the course of his intellectual career. If philosophy is alienation, as Wittgenstein was inclined to think, then the metaposition inherent in antiphilosophy has a necessarily shifting status depending on whether it is seen as a rejection or a furthering of this alienated condition.[87] As we shall see, a grasp of these issues can help to explain why he felt so strongly about certain questions and what particular replies or solutions may have meant to him on a more personal, as well as ethical and aesthetic, plane. It may also help to explain why certain equivocations and ambiguities may have had to remain unresolved.

Recall Wittgenstein's suggestion that "the movement of thought in my philosophizing" should be discoverable as well in "the history of my mind, of its moral concepts and in the understanding of my situation" (D 125). For the rest of this paper, I shall attempt to trace some of the interwoven concerns, existential as well as intellectual, that eventuated in his writing of the *Tractatus*.

Wittgenstein's *Tractatus* and the Theory of Types

In the introduction I mentioned the intensely personal way in which Wittgenstein reacted to philosophical problems, noting that his interest began not with a search for certitude, but with a desire to escape certain "painful contradictions." To describe his own conception of philosophy's role, he frequently invoked a line from the physicist Heinrich Hertz: "When these painful contradictions are removed," certain abstract questions will not have been answered, but "our minds, no longer vexed, will cease to ask illegitimate questions" (M 26). One might also recall Brian McGuinness's (p. 77) remarks on the mysterious nature of the connection between Wittgenstein's psychological and aesthetic predilections and his interest in the most abstract questions of logic and mathematics.

But what *were* the questions that first came to fascinate the young Ludwig Wittgenstein? What was the intellectual situation by which he was gripped – so much so that, according to his sister Hermine, he was in a "constant, indescribable, almost pathological state of agitation?"[88]

Wittgenstein, it seems, was first drawn to philosophy at age 19 when he encountered Bertrand Russell's Theory of Types (M 30). It is natural for thinkers to feel strongly about ideas and to be deeply invested in solving intellectual problems; Wittgenstein's reaction to the Theory of Types seems, however, to have been unusually personal and intense. On one occasion, after becoming preoccupied with problems in the Theory of Types, Wittgenstein returned from a vacation in what Russell called "a shocking state – always gloomy, pacing up and down, waking out of a dream when one speaks to him," and told Russell that logic was driving him mad (M 76). On a vacation in Norway a few months later, Wittgenstein was moody and unapproachable, and explained, according to his friend David Pinsent, that it was "some very serious difficulty with the 'Theory of Types' that has depressed him. . . . He is morbidly afraid he may die before he has put the Theory of Types to rights" (M 87).[89]

The more technical details of the Theory of Types need not concern us here. We must, however, introduce the main philosophical issues before we can return to our psycho-philosophical explorations.

The Theory of Types is Russell's response to a problem that Russell had discovered in both Frege's and his own attempt to show that mathematics is an extension of logic. The key point to understand is that Russell was responding to a problem that involved a paradox of the reflexive, a paradox that arises from self-reference, specifically, from allowing the possibility of classifying classes. From this latter possibility there arises the question of whether a class can be a member of itself – a notion that gives rise to a paradox, namely, that inherent in asking whether the class of classes that are *not* members of themselves is a member of *it*self. It turns out that, whichever answer one gives, the situation is impossible: the class in question can neither *be* nor can it *not be* a member of itself. Russell illustrated the point with the paradox of the barber who shaves all and only the men in town who do not shave themselves: to the question, does he shave himself?, both the answer yes and the answer no turn out to be self-contradictory. A similar point emerges in the simpler case of the Liar's Paradox, Epimenides' paradox of the Cretan who says all Cretans are liars; and, simpler still, in the assertion, "This statement is false."[90]

To eliminate the possibility of paradoxes of this sort, Russell developed his Theory of Types, which asserts a strict hierarchy of levels and metalevels and enjoins one from saying of one level what can be said of another. According to the Theory of Types, the statement, "The class of all chairs is not a chair," is really meaningless because, as the theory states, one cannot predicate of a logical type what does not belong to it, but rather to a higher or lower one. The point of this division into types is to avoid the threatening paradoxes that Russell termed "reflexive fallacies."[91]

Earlier I described this problem, a problem involving a reflexive fallacy, as the paradigm case of the kind of painful contradiction by which Wittgenstein was vexed and from which he sought release, not by solving the problem but by dissolving or otherwise eliminating it. Wittgenstein, however, found Russell's solution, the Theory of Types, to be vitiated by the very condition it was meant to resolve, namely, by an illegitimate attempt at reflexive self-reference. The Theory of Types is, after all, a theory – and one that turns out to be by no means self-evident or noncontroversial; and it is a theory that attempts to assert generalizations about logic, in this case about the logic of classes. As such, in Wittgenstein's view, it is an attempt to *assert* what can only be *shown*.

According to the view of linguistic meaning put forward in Wittgenstein's *Tractatus* (I say "put forward" because the question of whether he actually embraced it is under debate),[92] all meaningful sentences (propositional signs) are ones that "picture" facts – these latter being, in essence, contingent concatenations of simple objects. To put things in a nutshell, one might say that the logico-semantic thesis given central place in the *Tractatus* is, roughly speaking, the claim that all meaningful sentences are sentences of the following kind: "The cat is on the mat." In the *Tractatus* Wittgenstein writes, "Everything we can describe at all could also be otherwise" (TLP 5.634).

Since sentences about meaning or logic – and to this Wittgenstein adds ethics, aesthetics, and all the rest of philosophy – are not of this kind, that is, they are not about states of affairs that might have been otherwise, it follows that all such sentences are, strictly speaking, meaningless.

Consider the following proposition asserted by the Theory of Types: "The sentence 'a class of tables is not a table' is meaningless." According to the *Tractatus,* this proposition is *itself* meaningless, since the proposition at issue states a truth that could not possibly have been otherwise; it follows from this that the Theory of Types is *itself* meaningless. In Wittgenstein's view, one cannot stand above language and use a metalanguage in which one describes the logic or functioning of what is imagined to be a sort of first-order language. To do so would require one to be outside, that is, *not* to adopt the logic *by* which the language described operates – and this is impossible: the mind cannot think and language cannot express the illogical; hence one cannot speak about (or "say") the nature of logic. "No proposition can say anything about itself, because the propositional sign cannot be contained in itself (that is the 'whole theory of types')" (TLP 3.332).

This concern with the impossibility of certain kinds of self-reference or self-representation was a persistent one for Wittgenstein. In a passage from around 1929, he writes, "I cannot use language to get outside language."[93] In a conversation with Bouwsma some thirty years after the *Tractatus* was written, Wittgenstein said, "Now it's as though everything on the map represents something, but representing is not represented on the map."[94]

What cannot be said can, however, be *shown* – or so Wittgenstein suggests. Thus a "picture . . . cannot represent its form of representation; it shows it forth" (TLP 2.172). Indeed, according to this key distinction introduced in the *Tractatus,* the very functioning of language *shows* in some implicit way such "truths" as that meaningful sentences picture contingent concatenations (Wittgenstein's own point in the *Tractatus*) or that one cannot meaningfully speak across metalevels of logical classes (the point Russell attempted to convey with his Theory of Types). Although logical form cannot be stated *in* language, it is manifest in language. It is in fact the very form of language itself: "Logical so-called propositions *show* the logical properties of language and therefore of the universe, but *say* nothing," as Wittgenstein puts it in notes he dictated to G. E. Moore in 1914 (NB 108, M 102). To understand a word like "table" or "class" is, ipso facto, already to know that a table is not a class or that a class *of* tables is not itself a table. A theory of types is thus both impossible and unnecessary – impossible because one cannot get *outside* logic to describe it; unnecessary because everything the theory wants to say is in fact *shown* in the sentences themselves. Yet for Wittgenstein, it seems, it was not merely *fruitless* to attempt to say what could only be shown; it was actually *destructive,* perhaps in some subtle ontological way. This, at least, seems to be suggested in the following lines from one of Wittgenstein's letters to Paul Engelmann: "And this is how it is: if only you do not try to utter what is unutterable then *nothing* gets lost. But the unutterable will be – unutterably – *contained* in what has been uttered."[95]

Wittgenstein, it seems, preferred an approach to grasping the logical structure of human knowledge or language in which, if you will, it is recognized that nothing of a philosophical nature need or could (without contradiction and self-vitiation) be said *about* anything else, since everything of a constitutive or foundational nature would be self-evident, beyond need for comment, beyond all possibility of controversy; in a universe in which conceptual elements inherently contain within themselves, as essential, self-evident features, their possibilities of combining or not combining with other such elements. As an analogy, one might think of a plug and a socket, objects that cannot even be conceived without simultaneously recognizing their specific combinatory possibilities. The functionalist, Bauhaus-style house Wittgenstein designed for his sister Gretl in Vienna seems to express – or perhaps we should say, to *show* – this logico-aesthetic vision with particular clarity.

The logical universe Wittgenstein describes is, then, a universe that is entirely self-contained and that exists, in some sense, entirely on one level, without higher or lower, or more or less foundational, features, and, most important, without any metalevels of self-justification, detached self-consciousness, or self-reference. It is a universe that, in a certain sense, simply *is*; in which any type of distancing, higher-level, philosophical saying or knowing has vanished – and, we might say, the glow of pure being has taken its place.

Now, as the reader familiar with the *Tractatus* well knows, there is something of a problem here. The *Tractatus,* after all, is itself a philosophical work – or so it would appear. Even a sentence of the following type, "All meaningful sentences are of the type, 'The cat is on the mat,' " is not, by its own asserted criteria, a meaningful sentence, for *it* does not picture a contingent concatenation but rather attempts to state a necessary (and therefore unsayable) truth. This implies that the *Tractatus* (like the Theory of Types, which it criticizes) must itself consist, in large measure, of nonsense. Wittgenstein did not, of course, flinch from drawing this conclusion. He states it in rather Zenlike fashion at the end of the *Tractatus*:

My propositions are elucidatory in this way: he who understands me finally recognizes them as senseless, when he has climbed out through them, on them, over them. (He must so to speak throw away the ladder, after he has climbed up on it.) (TLP 6.54)

This is followed by the self-erasing, final line of the *Tractatus,* Wittgenstein's valediction forbidding metastatement: "Whereof one cannot speak, thereof one must be silent."

I need hardly remind the reader of the tremendous importance these issues had for Wittgenstein – who went so far as to say that he considered the distinction between saying and showing to be the cardinal problem of philosophy (M 164); and of the intensely personal way in which he reacted to this problem in logic and the philosophy of mathematics, a problem that vexed and tormented him and that he associated with sin and the possibility of going mad. Bearing this in mind, let's try to get an overall sense of the problematic at issue.

"Reflexive Fallacies"

We begin with a paradox of the reflexive, a paradox – the one Russell discovered in Frege's system – that derives from a condition of self-reference (which presupposes the possibility of self-distancing). To this we have an attempted solution, Russell's Theory of Types, which in Wittgenstein's view is illegitimate because of its own illegitimate attempt to adopt a metastance, a position of self-referentiality. Further, to this Wittgenstein addresses his own work, the *Tractatus,* which makes (or at least *appears* to make) a metastatement concerning the impossibility of Russell's own attempt at metastatement, but which ends by acknowledging, by means of yet another (apparent) metastatement (namely, the Zenlike framing sentences at the *Tractatus*'s conclusion) its own impossibility *as* metastatement, and which, all the while, seems to hold out, as a kind of utopian dream, the counterpossibility of a condition uncontaminated by all this recursive metastatement or metaremoval, namely, the notion of showing.

To understand the intense personal relevance for Wittgenstein, one might think of the hierarchy of logical types as an analogue for the nature of self-consciousness, with higher logical types corresponding to higher and more inclusive forms of self-consciousness.[96] The possibility of metastatement in philosophy would then be an analogue for the existential stance of the schizoid person who gravitates toward a kind of detached self-consciousness that allows, or *seems* to allow, an encompassing awareness of one's own entire self and situation. The philosophers John McDowell and Cora Diamond have characterized Wittgenstein's project in a way that brings this out: they speak of his preoccupation with the question of whether it is possible to adopt "the view from sideways on" (McDowell), or with the problematic, perhaps impossible, nature of any attempt to "step outside" our ordinary practices in order "to justify the answers we give when we are inside our ordinary practice" (Diamond).[97]

There is an intriguing line in the *Investigations* in which Wittgenstein critically characterizes the point of view of the *Tractatus,* a line that captures the contradictory way in which he experienced these issues of metastatement and self-detachment: "There is no outside; outside you cannot breathe" (PI § 103). Here we have, on one hand, the logical level, where Wittgenstein would exclude the very possibility of removal from oneself ("there *is* no outside"), and, on the other, the psychological level, the description of an all too possible existential condition that he would dearly like to deny or to ward off ("*outside* you cannot breathe").[98]

Wittgenstein was inclined to view the condition of detached meta-awareness as arrogant and misleading, and even as having contaminating or deleterious effects. Although this critical attitude emerges in many ways, its existential and psychological dimensions are perhaps easiest to identify in Wittgenstein's response to issues of art and morality. Recall that Wittgenstein considered aesthetics to be part of "ethics," which he defined, broadly and idiosyncratically, as "the enquiry into the meaning of life, or into what makes life worth living, or into the right way of living" (E 38).

In the arts, Wittgenstein shows a clear preference for what the art historian Michael Fried has called an aesthetic of absorption over one of theatricality – that is, for states of being that avoid any kind of (theatrical) self-display, any consciousness of being an object of awareness for an audience or the sense of dependence or of inner division (into watcher and watched) that this would imply.[99] Wittgenstein shows a closely related preference for an eschewal of explicit moralizing or direct address to an audience in favor of more implicit and self-contained modes of communication or expression. Such preferences came to prominence in the romantic era, for instance, in Wordsworth's and Rousseau's veneration of the "sentiment of being" and in the general shift from an ethic of "sincerity" to the more self-expressive and self-contained ethic of "authenticity" that is described in Lionel Trilling's book on the topic.[100] To be aware of oneself as the object of another's gaze, or even to refer beyond oneself, is to be outside oneself, and this can be experienced not only as a loss of personal integrity, but also as a decline in the sense of vitality and existence. These preferences were central to the symbolist poetry and painting of the late 19th century, and remained dominant in the aesthetics of high modernism.[101] At the extreme one finds yearnings for absolute self-containment and self-sufficiency – as, for instance, in a poet like Mallarmé, who disdained the referential function of words and sought instead to make language "curve back in a perpetual return upon itself, as if its discourse could have no other content than the expression of its own form, [as if] it has nothing to say but itself, nothing to do but shine in the brightness of its being."[102]

Wittgenstein was steeped in these traditions, in romanticism, certainly, but also in the early modernist movements of fin de siècle and early 20th-century-Vienna.[103] His own proclivities are apparent in his dislike of any kind of explicit moralizing and didacticism in literature and in his preference for works of art that refuse to betray the purity, authenticity, or integrity of their being through theatrical self-consciousness or by attempting to say what can only be shown. Literary works that Wittgenstein appreciated for such qualities include Tolstoy's *Hadji Murat* (McG 33) and the detective stories of Norbert Davis and other American writers of the "hard-boiled" school. "A typical American film, naïve and silly, can – for all its silliness and even *by means of* it – be instructive," he wrote. "A fatuous, self-conscious English film can teach one nothing" (CV 57/65).[104] Wittgenstein accepted an aesthetics (and an ethics) of authenticity – a view that would equate detached or theatrical self-consciousness with a diminishment of both the reality of one's existence and the distinctiveness of one's identity. "If I perform to myself, then it's this that the style expresses," wrote Wittgenstein. "And then the style cannot be my own."[105]

Wittgenstein's intense love of music is also relevant.[106] The concept of "absolute music" had come to serve as the artistic paradigm of German musical culture and, more generally, of what Carl Dallhaus has called the "art-religion" of the 19th century, in which Wittgenstein was steeped. If all art aspired to the condition of music (in Walter Pater's famous phrase), this was because music seemed uniquely able to exclude all forms of reference, didacticism, or theatricality, and thereby to be fully self-manifesting, self-sustaining, and self-contained. With its premise of unspeakability, absolute music was the exemplar of a self-representational and autonomous art that withdraws into itself, "into the depth of its own medium" (Hegel), and in which form *is* the content – the very paradigm of what Wittgenstein called "showing."[107]

Perhaps it is only natural to experience this aesthetic demand as having a certain recursive force: that is, to experience the very refusal of theatricality and inappropriate explicitness as being itself an attitude that should not (at the risk of self-vitiation) be stated in any explicit and direct way. This may explain Wittgenstein's conduct at a meeting with philosophers who were probably hoping he would explain the meaning of the *Tractatus*: he turned his back to the audience and read instead from the poetry of Rabindranath Tagore (M 243).

Similar attitudes and intuitions pervade Wittgenstein's more explicitly ethical or moral concerns. Perhaps the main object of his ethical condemnation was what he termed "vanity," a quality he associated largely with tendencies toward theatrical self-display – that is, with what he saw as the inauthenticity and lack of courage inherent in being overly concerned about the impression one makes on other people, and with the detached self-consciousness inherent in imagining oneself as a potential object of admiration for others (M 278).[108] In Wittgenstein's diaries of the 1930s, "vanity" is a central theme; he despises "vanity" yet is constantly discovering it in himself:

Everything or nearly everything I do, these [diary] entries included, is tinted by vanity and the best I can do is as it were to separate the vanity, to isolate it and do the right thing in spite of it even though it is always watching. Only sometimes it is not present (D 15, 2.5.30).

"Soiling everything with my vanity," he wrote a year later (D 85, 6.5.31).

To understand the nature of Wittgenstein's ethical concerns, it is useful to consider his struggles with the problem of confession. In the mid-1930s, Wittgenstein came to be preoccupied, even obsessed, with what he considered a number of sins he himself had committed, and he struggled to gain a sense of redemption through speaking of what he called these "very difficult and serious matters" to a number of friends and close relatives over the Christmas period of 1936–7 (M 367). To judge from Wittgenstein's diaries, however, the very *act* of confessing seems to have recapitulated the precise defect that Wittgenstein was trying to address *in* his confession; and in both cases this involved the inauthenticity of self-consciousness. He reported, in any case, that although confession initially brought him "into more settled waters . . . and to a greater seriousness," he soon came to feel as if he had "spent all that" and was in turbulent waters once again (M 372). As we shall see, Wittgenstein's acute self-consciousness, along with critical awareness *of* this self-consciousness, account for his sense of the elusive power of vanity – which, despite his efforts to know himself (indeed, partly *because* of these efforts), always seems to ambush him and gain the upper hand.

The friends and family members who witnessed Wittgenstein's confessions may well have been struck by the discrepancy between the nature and magnitude of the sins and the sense of extreme urgency Wittgenstein had about confessing them (M 367). One of the sins concerned an occasion when, on being told of the death of an American acquaintance, Wittgenstein had feigned sorrowful surprise even though he already knew of the person's death. Another sin was the fact that he had let others think he was one-quarter Jewish rather than the three quarters he actually was. The most serious sin (Wittgenstein had trouble keeping control of himself when speaking of this event) concerned his having hit a little girl during the period, several years before, when he was teaching in a village school in Austria: when the girl went to complain to the headmaster, Wittgenstein denied he had done it (M 369).

In all three of these cases, the sin to which Wittgenstein confessed was a sin of inauthenticity – of lacking the courage to be at one with himself due to being overly concerned with how he would appear in the eyes of others.[109] This was consistent with Wittgenstein's usual attitudes. According to Norman Malcolm, Wittgenstein "really *hated* all forms of affectation and insincerity" (NM 28). Wittgenstein seems, however, to have viewed himself as especially prone to these very defects, which he saw as antithetical to his attempts to be courageous or decent (*anständig*; M 278): "What others think of me always occupies me to an extraordinary extent. I am often concerned to make a good impression. I.e. I very frequently think about the impression I make on others" (M 278). "While I talk I sometimes see that I am on an ugly track: that I say more than I mean, talk to amuse the other, draw in irrelevancies in order to make an impression etc. I then strive to correct the conversation, to steer it back onto a more decent course" (D 91, 6.5.31).[110]

In his diaries of the 1930s, Wittgenstein does not mention the particular sins he confessed to family and friends. He does, however, devote considerable attention to the nature of confession itself and to the closely related issue of "vanity," and this provides insight into the inadequacy of his own acts of confessing. Wittgenstein was keenly aware of the danger of the self-consciousness inherent in vanity: although the vain person might try to be utterly candid, his self-consciousness was liable to make him experience his own confession as a performance, that is, as a further occasion for vanity – and this would necessarily deprive it of all authenticity and force.[111]

Even to confess that one "had not love etc.," for example, would be of no use, Wittgenstein points out, if it were made as "an artful ethical trick" – that is, as "something that I perform for the others, or also only for me (my *self*)" (D 124–5; 7.11.31).[112] He was therefore disturbed when he received a letter from his friend, Hänsel, in which Hänsel said that he admired Wittgenstein for having confessed something that Wittgenstein found shameful. To Wittgenstein, Hänsel's response must have seemed a temptation to vanity: "[Hänsel] writes that he admires me. What [a] trap! . . . Just as the screws are tightened, they become loose again, because what they are to squeeze together is giving way again." In the next sentence, Wittgenstein recapitulates, on another level, the point he has just been making: "I always have such joy in my own good similes; were it not such vain joy" (D 145, 21.11.36).

Vanity, Wittgenstein realizes, ruins the usual avenues of redemption: "The conscience burdened by guilt could easily confess; but the *vain person* cannot confess" (D 116, 2.11.31). He therefore calls upon himself to overcome the condition of theatrical or divided self-consciousness that is inherent in vanity: "that is what I must do, not watch the others watching me" (D, 130, 15.12.31). Such a call is inherently problematic, however, since even the attempt to acknowledge or confess the vanity inherent in one's own prior confessions (and thereby distance oneself from this vanity) is itself a temptation to *further* vanity and self-detachment: "When I say I would like to discard vanity," he observed, "it is questionable whether this wish is once again a kind of vanity. . . . In my mind I already estimate the benefit I would gain from 'discarding' vanity. As long as one is on stage, one is a performer, regardless of what one does" (D 130, 7.11.31).[113]

Wittgenstein's problems concerning confession have an interestingly recursive structure. The problems begin with the feeling of being burdened by a "sin," and, as we have seen, this original transgression (e.g., feigning surprise at the news of a death) often involves a sin of inauthenticity or vanity, that is, of performing for real or imaginary others rather than having the "courage" and "decency" to be at one with oneself. Then there is Wittgenstein's first attempt at self-redemption through confessing this "original" sin to his intimates. This however is vitiated by a *further* act of vanity, that is, by the fact that he does not dwell fully within his act of confession but, rather, finds himself outside, admiring himself *for* his confession. Then comes a meta-confession, a confession, now in the privacy of the diaries, *of* this vanity that pervades and vitiates his attempts to confess to family and friends. And then comes another level – call it a *meta*-metaconfession – whereby Wittgenstein confesses (also in his diaries) the vanity of his confessing of the vanity of his confessing of vanity.

All the levels just described are explicitly stated in the diaries, as the previous quotations show. In addition, one might argue, there is at least the hint of an awareness of the "vanity" of even this *meta*-metaconfession; and thus of the fact that no degree of self-recursion can prevent the private confessing that occurs *within* the diaries from being contaminated by the same, seemingly inescapable sin. It seems unlikely, after all, that Wittgenstein would have been able to forget that the diary entries themselves are *also* acts of confession, subject to the temptations of a vanity that, as he says, "is always watching"; and that they too may therefore be ultimately futile. This recursive spiral is reminiscent of the *Tractatus*; and like the *Tractatus,* it calls itself into question in what is at least a potentially self-undermining fashion.[114] "The ultimate ground (I mean the ultimate depth) of my vanity I won't uncover here anyway," wrote Wittgenstein in his diaries (D 88, 6.5.31).[115]

We see, then, that Wittgenstein was keenly sensitive to the paradoxes of recursion, self-reference, and infinite regress, not only in logic and semantics (as we know from the *Tractatus*) but in more existential realms as well. Vanity, as Wittgenstein understands it, is a form of self-consciousness whose recursiveness precludes rather than fosters true insight, rendering the quest for self-awareness futile: "[W]hen you bump against the limits of your own honesty it is as though your thoughts get into a whirlpool, an infinite regress: You can *say* what you like, it takes you no further" (CV 8/11).

We have explored Wittgenstein's attitudes toward self-consciousness and self-removal or detachment in the aesthetic as well as ethical realms. I want to suggest that Wittgenstein's fascination or even obsession with certain, far more abstract issues concerning logic, the foundations of mathematics, and the nature of meaning has something to do with these same concerns, that is, with the existential condition of this particularly self-critical individual, an individual who knows that self-consciousness is his primary source of error, temptation, and despair. If Wittgenstein feels so tormented by problems with Russell's Theory of Types, this is, at least in part, because it invokes, yet fails to exorcise, the demon of reflexivity that afflicts him; indeed, it actually recapitulates or exacerbates the workings of this demon – the same demon that haunts his attempts at confession and metaconfession. If we ask, then, whether Wittgenstein, contemplating the Theory of Types, is thinking about logic or his sins, the answer should indeed be: both – and not merely because he jumps from one issue to the other, but because he is, in a certain sense, contemplating both issues at the same moment and by means of the very same thoughts.

Wittgenstein's preoccupation with "vanity" and the related paradoxes of self-consciousness (such as the new forms of vanity generated by confessing one's vanity) suggests a heightened awareness of what has been called "the eternal penultimacy of consciousness," or in this case, of *self-*consciousness.[116] This is the fact that each new perspective on oneself brings, along with the legitimate insights it may offer, new and perhaps even more tortuous possibilities of ignorance, self-alienation, and self-deception.[117] Perhaps it is this realization that motivated Wittgenstein's repeated statements about the extreme difficulty, verging on impossibility, of true self-awareness ("Nothing is so difficult as not deceiving oneself." "It is . . . impossible to view one's own character from outside" [CV 34/39, 23/26]); as well as his skeptical reaction to the promise of self-knowledge through psychoanalysis: "In a way having oneself psychoanalysed is like eating from the tree of knowledge. The knowledge acquired sets us (new) ethical problems; but contributes nothing to their solution" (CV 34/40).

There seems, however, to be something intrinsic to realizing the impossibility or inefficacy of meta-awareness that prevents it from ever being fully and finally taken to heart. There is always the hope that somehow, this time, one will indeed be able to transcend the very limits that one recognizes as unsurpassable. This, perhaps, is what Wittgenstein is getting at in one intriguing passage from *Culture and Value*: "Telling someone something he does not understand is pointless, even if you add that he will not be able to understand it. (That so often happens with someone you love.)" (M 300; CV 7/10).

Showing and Saying

We have seen that Wittgenstein is profoundly critical of philosophical inclinations, particularly of any attempt at what we might call transcendental awareness – that is, of any attempt to get outside oneself and to take, as the *object* of one's knowledge, the unsurpassable limits or universal foundations of thought, experience, or language. Yet it is also the case that he is intimately identified with these same inclinations: they are, in fact, perhaps the deepest and most distinctive impulse of this individual who, as we know, was preoccupied with foundational matters and the unsayable and tended to identify these with what is most important in life.[118] We might say, in fact, that at some profound level of his self-experience, Wittgenstein *is* transcendental awareness; he *is* philosophy. Indeed, I think one could go further and view each of the philosophical positions Wittgenstein takes as being, at one level, a kind of self-object or self-representation – that is, as standing as a sort of proxy or objective correlative for his own characteristic stance or self.[119] Bearing this in mind, I shall conclude with a few words about the different possibilities for transcendental awareness or transcendental expression that are laid out in the *Tractatus*.

The first possibility, it would seem, is the *Tractatus* as it actually exists: a metastatement forbidding metastatements, delivered with a wink – which one might say is philosophy, or the schizoid self, still in its fallen condition, redeeming itself from the sin of self-consciousness, if at all, only with the self-consciousness of irony. The irony of the *Tractatus* (the book's acknowledging of its own illegitimacy) allows Wittgenstein to express both sides of his ambivalent attitude. He attacks the self-detachment characteristic of philosophy yet also expresses it – expresses it through the meta-ness of irony and also, perhaps, through the fact that the *Tractatus* does, after all, manage to say, or somehow to hint at, what supposedly cannot be said.[120]

The second possibility is the stance of showing – and this, it may have seemed to Wittgenstein, is almost a condition of grace. It is important to understand "showing" *not* as an attempt (paradoxical and perhaps ultimately incoherent) to refer to some ineffable "it,"[121] but, rather, as a kind of pure self-expression, or better, a pure and undivided *manifestation* of 'Being.' As I noted above, achieving such a state is an aspiration central to a number of aesthetic movements of the late 19th and early 20th centuries, particularly symbolism and certain strains of modernism.[122] Wittgenstein's veneration for "showing" also resonates with his preference for absorption over theatricality and for avoiding explicit moralizing in favor of a more implicit manifesting.

If we think of the transcendental concerns of Wittgenstein's *Tractatus* as standing proxy for his own self, then the notion of showing, if appropriately understood, can be seen to forge a peculiar compromise between Wittgenstein's schizoid yearnings or ambitions and his desire to overcome or repair certain schizoid potentialities.

On the one hand, the condition of showing can allow a person to feel he has overcome all need for or dependence on the other (the addressee or audience). We know that Wittgenstein, at least in his earlier period, often viewed social relationships in a jaundiced light. Other human beings were part of an external world from which one needed to separate oneself – in order to recognize the true nature of the ego, in order to achieve happiness and a sense of being "absolutely safe," and in order to evade temptations towards self-consciousness, inner division, and related forms of inauthenticity and self-betrayal.

Showing obviates the need for an other; it is like turning one's back to the audience. When something is shown, it is just there, like a feature of the universe. Though it may be seen, it is not there *to be seen,* and thus is not in an ontological sense dependent on any possible audience whether external or internal to a divided self. (Wittgenstein's fear of this kind of dependency is clear in a diary entry from 1931: "I don't want happening to me what happens to some wares. They are lying on the display table, the shoppers see them, the color or sheen catches their eye and they handle the object for a moment and then let it drop back on the table as undesired" [D 97–8, 13.5.31].) Another feature of showing is that the show-er and the shown are fully at one. Something that is shown does not exist at a remove from that which shows it. There is no possibility of imagining the one apart from the other, nor any possibility of holding that which is shown at arm's length and treating it as a mere hypothesis, an option among other possible options.

The doctrine of showing rather than saying could be seen, then, as *serving* Wittgenstein's schizoid impulses: by manifesting an utter autonomy, independence, and integrity of being as well as by placing transcendental awareness – the schizoid self – in the charmed circle of the necessary and the self-evident, where it seems to exist beyond reach of all conceivable doubt or debate.

In his striving for an undivided, self-expressive, but utterly self-contained and isolated integrity of 'Being,' Wittgenstein is aiming toward an ideal of which Weininger would have approved. ("Duty is only toward oneself," wrote Weininger. "Nothing is superior to [oneself], to the isolated, absolute unity.")[123] Wittgensten also shares an aspiration fundamental to aesthetic modernism. There it takes the form of a preference for a seemingly un-self-conscious presentness or absorption over the dividedness and display inherent in "theatricality"; for the formal self-containment and self-manifestation epitomized by "absolute music" and formalist painting; or for the integrity and autonomy of the symbol in preference to the derivative and divided nature of allegory[124] – for the symbol Yeats described as "full, sphere-like, single," or which Joyce says is apprehended "as *one* thing . . . self-bounded and self-contained . . . [in a] luminous silent stasis of esthetic pleasure."[125]

Wittgenstein's problem, however – and it is a problem that no one would have felt more acutely than he – is that he is a philosopher and not a poet, or what, for him, would be better still, a musician or composer. ("I think I summed up my attitude to philosophy when I said: philosophy ought really to be written only as a *poetic composition.* . . . I was thereby revealing myself as someone who cannot quite do what he would like to be able to do" [CV

24/28].) The *Tractatus* itself is not, of course, an instance of showing – at least not in the way that Wittgenstein means. Unlike the aesthetic symbol – "sphere-like, single," "self-bounded and self-contained" – it does *not* achieve the fullness of being inherent in the act of showing. Rather, cruel irony of ironies, it manages merely to *say* the doctrine of showing – that is, of all things, to *state* (or to appear to state) the ineffable doctrine of ineffability.[126] It is clear that, in the end, this curious amalgam of contrary impulses – of logical and mystical urges, of schizoid and antischizoid tendencies, involving what we might call post-romantic yearnings expressed in a protopostmodernist manner – could not seem satisfactory for very long. Some years later Wittgenstein would dismiss the very concern with the issue of logical paradox and self-referential contradiction as a kind of irrelevant and mystifying illusion.[127] He would write of the *Tractatus* that every sentence of the book was the expression of a disease.[128] For a time, however, it seemed to offer a promising resolution of the contradictions that so vexed him, both in philosophy and in life.

ABBREVIATIONS FOR FREQUENTLY CITED REFERENCES

Works by Wittgenstein:

CV: *Culture and Value,* ed. G. H. von Wright; trans. P. Winch. Chicago: University of Chicago Press, 1980; rev. 2d ed. Oxford: Basil Blackwell, 1998.

D: *Denkbewegungen: Tagebücher 1930–1932, 1936–1937,* ed. Ilse Somavilla. Innsbruck, Austria: Haymon Verlag, 1997. To appear in *Public and Private Occasions,* ed. J. Klagge and A. Nordmann. Rowman and Littlefield (Draft translation by Alfred Nordmann used here; quoted with permission). Original pagination is cited, along with date of diary entry.

E: "A Lecture on Ethics." In *Philosophical Occasions, 1912–1951,* ed. J. Klagge and A. Nordmann. Indianapolis and Cambridge: Hackett, 1993, pp. 37–44.

NB: *Notebooks 1914–1916,* 2d ed, ed. G. H. von Wright and G. E. M. Anscombe; trans. G. E. M. Anscombe. Chicago: University of Chicago Press, 1979.

P: "Philosophy." In *Philosophical Occasions,* pp. 160–199.

PI: *Philosophical Investigations,* trans. G. E. M. Anscombe. Oxford: Basil Blackwell, 1953.

TLP: *Tractatus Logico-Philosophicus,* with introduction by Bertrand Russell; trans. D. Pears & B. McGuinness. London: Routledge and Kegan Paul, 1961.

Biographical Works

M: Monk, Ray *Ludwig Wittgenstein: The Duty of Genius.* New York: Free Press, 1990.

McG: McGuinness, Brian *Wittgenstein: A Life: Young Ludwig, 1889–1921.* Berkeley: University of California Press, 1988.

NM: Malcolm, Norman *Ludwig Wittgenstein: A Memoir,* 2d ed. Oxford: Oxford University Press, 1984.

NOTES

1. I am indebted to a number of friends and colleagues for useful criticism or conversation concerning earlier drafts or presentations of this article, and wish to extend thanks to Rupert Read, Jeffery Geller, James Conant, James Klagge, David Schuldberg, Paul Voestermans, and James Phillips. In this essay I emphasize Wittgenstein's early philosophy; I hope to focus on his later work in a future publication.
2. Wittgenstein, *Remarks on the Foundations of Mathematics,* ed. G. H. von Wright, R. Rhees, and G. E. M. Anscombe; trans. G. E. M. Anscombe (Oxford: Basil Blackwell, 1956), pp. 57, 157.
3. "What is the good . . .": quoted in James Conant, "Throwing away the Top of the Ladder," *Yale Review,* 79: 328–64, p. 364. For a related passage, see NM 35, 93. Another relevant quotation from Wittgenstein: "Working in philosophy – like working in architecture in many respects – is really more a working on oneself" (CV 16/24; P 161). Wittgenstein seems to have felt antipathy toward philosophers who took a merely professional interest in the field (NM).
4. Louis Sass, *The Paradoxes of Delusion: Wittgenstein, Schreber, and the Schizophrenic Mind* (Ithaca, NY: Cornell University Press, 1994).
5. Friedrich Nietzsche, *Beyond Good and Evil,* trans. R. J. Hollingdale (Harmondsworth UK: Penguin Books, 1973), p. 19.
6. Thomas Nagel makes a similar suggestion: "Philosophical ideas are acutely sensitive to individual temperament, and to wishes. . . . The personal flavor and motivation of each great philosopher's version of reality is unmistakable"; Nagel, *The View from Nowhere* (New York: Oxford University Press, 1986), p. 10.
7. Wittgenstein apparently formulated a solution of his own to the paradoxes surrounding the Theory of Types before April 1909 (M 33; McG 76). It is possible that Wittgenstein was exposed to Schopenhauer even before this.
8. At the beginning of his admirable biography of Wittgenstein, Monk states that he intends to show "the unity of [Wittgenstein's] philosophical concerns with his emotional and spiritual life," thereby to explain "what his work has to do with *him*" (M xviii). Monk does illuminate a number of important connections between these two domains, such as Wittgenstein's general urge toward genius and his belief that honesty about oneself is a prerequisite for honest work in philosophy. Monk does not, however, make any real attempt to connect the personal dimension with Wittgenstein's *specific* philosophical themes; nor does he offer an explicit or elaborated psychological interpretation of Wittgenstein's personality.

Given his goals, Monk is probably wise to have eschewed both of these attempts. My own project, however, is rather different; it requires a willingness to be more speculative and also to risk sounding more tendentious than would be appropriate for a standard biographical work.

9. Hermine Wittgenstein, "My Brother Ludwig," in *Recollections of Wittgenstein*, 2d ed., ed. Rush Rhees (New York: Oxford University Press, 1984), p. 4.

10. Stanley Cavell, "The Availability of Wittgenstein's Later Philosophy," in Cavell, *Must We Mean What We Say?* (Cambridge: Cambridge University Press, 1976), p. 71.

11. Nagel, *View from Nowhere,* especially pp. 6, 11, 214, 216.

12. Louis A. Sass, *Madness and Modernism: Insanity in the Light of Modern Art, Literature, and Thought* (New York: Basic Books, 1992; Harvard paperback 1994).

13. Ernst Kretschmer, *Physique and Character*, 2d ed., trans. W. J. H. Sprott (London: Kegan Paul, Trench, Trubner & Co., 1936).

14. Erik Essen-Möller, "The concept of Schizoidia," *Monatschrift für Psychiatrie und Neurologie,* 112, 1946: 258–271, p. 261; Essen-Möller uses the term "isolative." On the "isolated" as well "schizoid" types, see Karl Menninger, *The Human Mind* (New York: Knopf, 1955).

15. W. R. D. Fairbairn, *An Object-Relations Theory of the Personality* (New York: Basic Books, 1954); Harry Guntrip, "The Schizoid Personality and the External World," in Guntrip, *Schizoid Phenomena, Object-Relations, and the Self* (New York: International Universities Press, 1969); Anthony Storr, *The Dynamics of Creation* (New York: Atheneum, 1972).

16. As listed, e.g., in axis II of: American Psychiatric Association, *Diagnostic and Statistical Manual of Mental Disorders,* 4th ed. (Washington D.C.: American Psychiatric Association, 1994).

17. "It is probably true that [Wittgenstein] lived on the border of mental illness. A fear of being driven across it followed him throughout his life," wrote Wittgenstein's friend and student Georg Henrik von Wright; von Wright, "Biographical Sketch," in Malcolm, *Wittgenstein: A Memoir* (NM), 3–20, p. 4.

Some additional quotations from Wittgenstein: "I feel that my mental health is hanging on a thin thread" (1946, M 492). "I am often afraid of madness" (1946, CV 53/61). "I think I may go nuts" (quoted in O. K. Bouwsma, *Wittgenstein: Conversations, 1949–1951* [Indianapolis, IN: Hackett, 1986], p. 9).

Some additional passages from his diaries of the 1930s: "Sometimes I think that at some point my brain won't take the strain on it and will give out. And given its strength it is frightfully strained – at least that's how it often seems to me" (D 4, 26.4.30). "I believe that my mental apparatus is built in an extraordinarily complicated and *delicate* manner and therefore more sensitive than normal. Much that wouldn't disturb a cruder mechanism disturbs it, puts it out of *action.* Just as a particle of dust can bring a fine instrument to a standstill but will not influence a cruder one" (D 50–1, 16.10.30). "I sometimes feel as if my intelligence were a glass rod which *bears pressure* and can break any moment" (D 142, 28.1.32). "You shall live so that you can withstand in the face of madness when it comes. And you shall not *flee* insanity. It is luck when it isn't there, but *flee* it you shall *not*" (D 185; 20.2.37). " 'There is no one here' – but I can go mad all by myself, too." (D 206, 24.2.37). See also D 50, 157, 159, 185.

In one passage, Wittgenstein speculates as to whether madness should be seen less as an illness than "as a sudden – more or *less* sudden – change of character," and he goes on to describe this as involving exacerbation of what might be termed schizoid propensities: "Why shouldn't a man suddenly become *much* more mistrustful towards others? Why not *much* more withdrawn? Or devoid of love? . . . Why shouldn't they – *perhaps* suddenly – become *much* more wary? And *much* more inaccessible?" (1946, CV 54/62).

18. Although there is an obvious sense in which the antischizoid aspect is a *non*schizoid feature of Wittgenstein, there is also a sense in which it can be seen as a further manifestation of his schizoid self-consciousness and self-criticism. This will become apparent below.

19. When he looked back, in 1940, on the highly rationalized, functionalist, Bauhaus-style house he had designed for his sister fourteen years earlier, Wittgenstein found it to be "an expression of great *understanding*" that was nevertheless lacking in the essential: "All great art has man's primitive drives as its groundbass. . . . But primordial life, wild life striving to erupt into the open – that is lacking. And so you could say it isn't healthy" (CV 37–8/43).

20. "Mental cramp": NM 43. Also: "Wittgenstein's lectures in 1930–33," notes recorded and paraphrased by G. E. Moore, *Mind,* 64, 1955: 1–27, p. 27; reprinted in Klagge and Nordmann, Eds., *Philosophical Occasions,* 45–114, p. 114.

21. "Noblest endeavour": see K. T. Fann, *Wittgenstein's Conception of Philosophy* (Berkeley, CA: University of California Press, 1969), p. 86. "Bedmaker": quoted in Wolfe Mays, "Recollections of Wittgenstein," in K. T. Fann, Ed., *Ludwig Wittgenstein: The Man and his Philosophy* (Atlantic Highlands, NJ: Humanities Press, 1978), p. 82. Wittgenstein also warns: "Beware of cheap grandeur when writing about philosophy!" (D 228, 30.3.37).

22. In *Volume I: Thinking* of *The Life of the Mind* (San Diego: Harcourt Brace Jovanovich, 1971), Hannah Arendt discusses both views: "[T]hinking, the quest for meaning – as opposed to the thirst for knowledge, even for knowledge for its own sake – has so often been felt to be unnatural, as though men, whenever they reflect without purpose . . . engage in an activity *contrary to the human condition.* Thinking as such . . . is, as Heidegger once observed, '*out of order*' " (p. 78). "Plato . . . remarked that the philosopher appears to those who do not do philosophy as though he were pursuing death" (p. 79). She also mentions the contrary view: ". . . the metaphor Aristotle tried out in the . . . *Metaphysics:* 'The activity of thinking [*energeia* that has its end in itself] is life.' " (p. 123).

   Wittgenstein's shifting use of the metaphor of sleep illustrates a similar ambivalence. Sometimes he describes sleep, which involves release from self-consciousness and other distractions, as a desirable state: "And being able to work is in so many ways similar to being able to fall asleep" (D 49, 16.10.30). At other times he describes it as a kind of living death: "One could imagine a person who from birth to death is always either sleeping or lives in a kind of half-sleep or daze. This is how my life relates to one that is really alive (I am just now thinking of Kierkegaard)" (D 135, 11.1.32).

23. Wittgenstein, *On Certainty,* ed. G. E. M. Anscombe and G. H. von Wright, trans. Denis Paul and G.E.M. Anscombe (New York: Harper & Row, 1972), § 475.

24. I agree with Thomas Nagel: ". . . often the pursuit of a highly unified conception of life and the world leads to philosophical mistakes – to false reductions or to the refusal to recognize part of what is real." "Certain forms of perplexity . . . seem to me to embody more insight than any of the supposed solutions to those problems" (p. 4); *View from Nowhere,* pp. 3, 4. Michel Foucault's arguments concerning the unavoidable paradoxes that are inherent in modern, post-Kantian

thought would seem to imply a similar view; see *The Order of Things* (New York: Vintage Books, 1994); discussed in Sass, *Madness and Modernism,* pp. 327–31.

Wittgenstein, too, came to be drawn to a more relaxed view of the relevance of logical contradiction. See Ray Monk's account of Wittgenstein's ridiculing of the concern for "hidden contradictions" in the foundations of mathematics, which amounts to a direct challenge to the Principle of Contradiction (M 420–1). See also *Wittgenstein's Lectures on the Foundations of Mathematics: Cambridge 1939,* ed. Cora Diamond (Harvester, 1976), pp. 206–7; quoted in penultimate note to the present article.

25. Wittgenstein sometimes suggests an association between madness and insight. Consider the following quotations from his diary: "Insanity . . . is the most severe judge (the most severe court) of whether my life is right or wrong" (D 185, 20.2.37). "But madness does *not sully* reason. Even though it does not guard it" (D 194, 21.2.37). "Respect of madness – that is really all I am saying" (D 203, 23.2.37).

On the schizoid aspect of Descartes and Kant and its relationship to their philosophical insight, see Storr, *Dynamics of Creation.* On Descartes, see also Wolfgang Blankenburg, *La Perte de L'Evidence Naturelle,* trans. Jean-Michel Azorin and Yves Tatossian (Paris: Presses Universitaires de France, 1991), p. 110. One intellectual advantage that persons of the schizoid or schizothymic type can have is that they tend to be relatively free from conventional views. On the general question of the connection between creativity and the "schizophrenia spectrum," which includes schizoid and schizophrenic individuals, see Louis Sass, "Schizophrenia, Modernism, and the 'Creative Imagination': On Creativity and Psychosis," *Creativity Research Journal,* 13, 2000–2001, pp. 55–74.

26. Nagel, *View from Nowhere,* p. 11. This somewhat relaxed view concerning contradiction or inconsistency has interesting implications for one's hermeneutic approach insofar as it complicates the question of what it means to apply the principle of charity to a given philosopher's thought. Seeking to find the most internally consistent position is not necessarily the most charitable, or potentially illuminating, approach to adopt. These issues would seem, by the way, to be central to recent controversies about the interpretation of the *Tractatus.* The approaches of both Cora Diamond and James Conant are centrally motivated by the attempt to avoid attributing any internal inconsistency to the *Tractatus,* and this strongly affects their reading and general deployment of the textual evidence. Peter Hacker and others adopt a more relaxed view. It could be argued, of course, that the early Wittgenstein was himself centrally concerned with logical consistency, and that the relaxed view is therefore less appropriate in this exegetical context; but one could also argue that the early Wittgenstein's apparently positive attitude toward "the mystical" implies a more relaxed attitude toward at least certain *kinds* of inconsistency.

See Cora Diamond, "Throwing Away the Ladder," in Diamond, *The Realistic Spirit* (Cambridge, MA: MIT Press, 1991), 179–204; Diamond, "Ethics, Imagination and the Method of Wittgenstein's *Tractatus,*" in Richard Heinrich and Helmut Vetter, Eds., *Bilder der Philosophie: Reflexionen über das Bildliche und die Phantasie* (Munich: Oldenbourg, 1991), 55–90; reprinted in Alice Crary and Rupert Read, Eds., *The New Wittgenstein* (London: Routledge, 2000), 149–73. James Conant, "Throwing Away the Top of the Ladder," *Yale Review* 79, 328–64. Conant, "The Method of the *Tractatus,*" in Erich Reck, Ed., *From Frege to Wittgenstein: Perspectives on Early Analytic Philosophy* (Oxford: Oxford University Press, in press). For a critique of their views, see P. M. S. Hacker, "Was He Trying to Whistle It?" in Crary and Read, *The New Wittgenstein,* 353–88.

27. Nagel, *View from Nowhere,* p. 214.
28. Quoted in O. K. Bouwsma, *Wittgenstein: Conversations, 1949–1951* (Indianapolis, IN: Hackett, 1986), p. 73.
29. Malcolm reports a remark of Wittgenstein's to the effect that "it was very unlikely anyone in his classes should think of something of which he had not already thought" (NM 47).
30. Starobinski, quoted in Robert J. Morrissey, "Introduction: Jean Starobinski and Otherness," in Starobinski, *Jean-Jacques Rousseau: Transparency and Otherness,* trans. Arthur Goldhammer (Chicago: University of Chicago Press), xi–xxxviii, p. xix.
31. One might distinguish three different kinds of claims about the relationship between the philosophical and the psychological planes.

The first (and weakest) kind of claim would say nothing about Wittgenstein's choice of philosophical concerns and problems or about the *way* in which he approached them or the solutions (or *dis*-solutions) he proposed. It only attempts to explain why a series of philosophical concerns (which may be entirely independently motivated) came to be experienced by him as having such intense and problematic personal relevance. The second claim would argue that the psychological dimension actually played a significant motivational role in determining Wittgenstein's "choice" of problem, that is, in channeling the direction of his intellectual interests and concerns. The third (and strongest) claim would argue that the psychological dimension actually had an impact on the particular attitudes, solutions, or style of approach that Wittgenstein adopted in *dealing* with these problems.

In this essay, I am clearly making the first sort of claim, which, I believe, is of considerable interest in itself. I wish, however, to remain somewhat tentative about the second and third kinds of claim. I do not for a moment doubt that Wittgenstein's philosophical thinking was, in large measure, independently motivated or that it requires an internalist form of interpretation and analysis. Indeed, there is much in his philosophical writings, most obviously in the intricacies of particular arguments, that I would not expect to be connected with psychological factors in any significant way. Yet it would hardly be surprising if personal concerns were to play at least some role in determining the direction, and perhaps even some aspects of the form, of his philosophical thinking. Although the affinities between the personal and the philosophical that I demonstrate in the present discussion cannot *prove* either of the two latter kinds of claim, they do at least make them more plausible.

(It is not obvious to me, by the way, that the second and third kinds of psychological explanation must necessarily be seen as competing with more purely internalist, philosophical accounts. Is it not possible to imagine a position that might best be termed "psycho-philosophical parallelism" [while admitting that such a position is no easier to explicate than is its namesake, psycho-*physical* parallelism]? For an illustration of a psycho-philosophical parallelist interpretation, see the end of the penultimate section of this article.)

Let me stress again that, even if all three claims *could* be proven, this would, in itself, say nothing at all about the validity (the internal coherence, accuracy, insightfulness, and so forth) of Wittgenstein's philosophical arguments and thoughts. A psychological analysis might, however, help to account for the presence of certain features of Wittgenstein's thought (for instance, certain exaggerations or blindspots, contradictions or inconsistencies, or other peculiarities) whose dubious or problematic nature would have to be established on other, internalist grounds.

Consider, for example, what may seem to be Wittgenstein's exaggerated emphasis on the errors of any talk about "inner" experiences, an attack intense enough to have led some commentators to view Wittgenstein as a behaviorist or as some kind of enemy of the inner life (on Wittgenstein's supposed denial of the possibility or value of the "inner life," see Iris Murdoch, *Metaphysics as a Guide to Morals* [London: Chatto and Windus, 1992], pp. 269–91). Although both of these readings of Wittgenstein's work are incorrect, in my view, they do bring out the fact that Wittgenstein did indeed have a certain animus against a focus on inner phenomena. This animosity, which may have distorted at least the emphasis of some of his philosophical arguments, may itself be understood as a manifestation of the intensity of Wittgenstein's reactions against his own (schizoid) temptations *toward* introversion. (As illustrations of how very inner-focused Wittgenstein could actually be, consider the following sentences from his diary: "In the correctly written sentence, a particle detaches from the heart or brain and arrives as a sentence on paper." "I believe that my sentences are mostly descriptions of visual images that occur to me" [D 114, 24.10.31].) Other features of Wittgenstein's thought that might be understood in similar fashion include his radical (and, some would argue, self-contradictory) antitheoretical stance, and the strong, even dichotomous nature of the contrast he drew between showing and saying.

James Klagge has made an argument of the third kind concerning the later Wittgenstein's views on the supposed incommensurability or mutual incomprehensibility of differing world views. Klagge is surprised that Wittgenstein is willing to rest content with "oversimplifications" that deny the very possibility of interpreting or extending mutually foreign concepts in such a way as to bring them into conformity with each other. He suggests that Wittgenstein's "experience of [personal] alienation was so profound that he became indelibly pessimistic and incurious about the prospects for reconciliation, in ways that influenced his philosophizing"; "When Are Ideologies Irreconcilable?" *Philosophical Investigations,* 21, 1998, 268–79, p. 278.

I have said that the psychological approach is irrelevant to deciding questions concerning the validity of a philosopher's thought. In a strict sense, this is certainly true: ultimately, such decisions do rest on an examination of the ideas themselves. Considerations of the kind I raise in this article are not, however, entirely irrelevant to the *exegesis* of the philosophy itself, for they can alter the general hermeneutical approach on the basis of which one interprets a body of philosophical thought. This, in turn, is not unrelated to judgments about validity, internal consistency, and the like. One will approach Wittgenstein's work differently, for example, depending on what one assumes in advance about the likelihood of discovering aspects that are exaggerated, overly polarized, or internally inconsistent. Will one expect that such peculiarities may well be present in Wittgenstein's thought? Or will one assume that if such peculiarities *seem* to be present, they will, on careful examination, almost certainly turn out to be only superficial appearances – indications more of the inadequacy of one's *own* understanding of Wittgenstein than of anything about the (ultimately wise and ultimately consistent) work of Wittgenstein himself? (On the implications of discovering exaggeration or inconsistency, see notes 24 and 26 above.)

It is obvious that exegetical decisions of this kind are profoundly dependent on textual evidence. It is, however, naïve to assume that an objective examination of the philosophical texts will necessarily decide such issues all by itself. Indeed, in a number of important debates concerning the nature of Wittgenstein's thought (e.g., the divergent views of Richard Rorty and Stanley Cavell [described later in this article], or of Diamond/Conant and Hacker [cited above]), there seem to be no decisive, knock-down arguments to be extracted from Wittgenstein's writings. Rather, it is a matter of how one should *construe* the texts – of how one should interpret various passages or what weight one should give to them; and (as the concept of the "hermeneutic circle" implies) this is significantly influenced by prior assumptions about what one will find, which in turn may be affected by one's understanding of the psychological or existential dimensions of Wittgenstein's general project.

32. For a detailed survey, see Sass, "The Separated Self," in *Madness and Modernism,* pp. 75–115. As I explain, the term "schizoid," as traditionally understood (e.g., by Bleuler, Kretschmer, Laing, Fairbairn, Guntrip, and many others), includes aspects of both the "schizoid" and "avoidant" personalities as described in DSM IV.

33. Kretschmer, *Physique and Character,* p. 157.

34. Kretschmer contrasted the schizothymic with what he called the "cyclothymic" temperament. Whereas the schizothymic person will tend, if psychotic, to become schizophrenic, the cyclothymic person is more prone to manic-depressive forms of psychosis. In preferring the term "syntonic," Bleuler meant to emphasize the issue of the person's relationship to the environment rather than the tendency to mood swings; Essen-Möller, "The Concept of Schizoidia."

35. Kretschmer, *Physique and Character,* pp. 245–6. Among the traits that Bleuler considered to be characteristic of normal people with schizoid tendencies are the following: "the tendency to abstraction and philosophy, the disposition to create new inventions or ideas, further a certain form of perseverance or obstinacy (inveteracy) and finally a moderate degree of coldness, a deficient power of emotional experience and contact . . . poor suggestibility and insusceptibility, difficulty in rapidly catching on to the mood of others . . . and tendency to go about one's own way"; Essen-Möller, "The Concept of Schizoidia," p. 267.

36. R. D. Laing, *The Divided Self* (Harmondsworth UK: Penguin Books, 1965), p. 17 and *passim.*

37. Fairbairn, *An Object-Relations Theory,* pp. 29, 51. The term "splitting" is used in a confusing variety of ways in psychology and psychoanalysis. The psychoanalyst Heinz Kohut distinguishes between the "horizontal splitting" inherent in keeping certain mental contents out of conscious awareness (repression) and the "vertical splitting" common in patients with borderline personality disorder, who keep conscious experiences of positive and negative attitudes separate from each other. I suggest the phrase "radial splitting" to capture the characteristically schizoid forms of splitting, all of which involve a separation between an inner-self and something more on the periphery, which can be the external world, other persons, or one's own body or social persona.

38. Otto Kernberg, *Severe Personality Disorders* (New Haven, CT: Yale University Press, 1984), p. 93.

39. Harry Guntrip, "The Schizoid Personality," p. 18.

40. In *The Book of Disquiet,* Fernando Pessoa describes a feeling highly self-conscious persons may have, namely, that persons lacking such self-consciousness

are hardly conscious at all: "I see everyone with the compassion of the only conscious being alive: poor men, poor humanity. What is it all doing here? . . . I shift my gaze away from the back of the man immediately in front of me to look at everyone else, at everyone walking down this street. . . . They are all like him . . . all of this is just one unconsciousness wearing different faces and bodies, puppets moved by strings pulled by the fingers of the same invisible being. They give every appearance of consciousness but, because they are not conscious of being conscious, they are conscious of nothing. Whether intelligent or stupid, they are all in fact equally stupid"; Pessoa, *The Book of Disquiet,* trans. Margarat Jull Costa (London: Serpent's Tail, 1991), pp. 41–2.

41. Guntrip, "The Schizoid Personality," pp. 17, 41–4. See also Nagel, *View from Nowhere,* p. 209, on difficulties in maintaining coherent attitudes.

42. See Sass, "Schizophrenia, Modernism, and 'Creative Imagination' "; Storr, *Dynamics of Creation.* On heightened insight in schizoid persons, see Masud Khan, *The Privacy of the Self* (London: Hogarth Press, 1974).

43. Guntrip, "The Schizoid Personality," pp. 36–7. Fairbairn, *Object-Relations Theory,* pp. 16–20.

44. According to his sister, Hermine, "Ludwig found it particularly difficult to fit in, for right from earliest childhood he suffered almost pathological distress in any surroundings which were uncongenial to him" ("My Brother Ludwig," p. 11). In *Wittgenstein: A Critique* (London and Boston: Routledge & Kegan Paul, 1984), pp. 20–1), J. Findlay, who knew Wittgenstein starting in 1930 and attended lectures in 1939, writes: "There are many things that can be said about the personal make-up and impact of Wittgenstein. His pervasive aestheticism certainly displayed a character that, I believe, is technically describable as 'schizoid'; there was something queer, detached, surreal, incompletely human about it."

45. Wittgenstein seems to have had a primarily homoerotic sexual orientation. Also, he came from a family of assimilated Viennese Jews who had converted to Catholicism. Both of these facts may have contributed to his sense of being secretly (or not so secretly) different – an alien in the world. In various remarks, especially during his antisemitic period, Wittgenstein portrays Jewishness in a negative light. He characterizes the Jewish sensibility as deracinated and overly abstract and as devoid of true creativity (CV 12/14, 18–19/16), which suggests he viewed it as the product of what Spengler called a "civilization" rather than a true "culture." It is impossible to know whether Wittgenstein's feelings about being a Jew actually contributed to, or simply resonated with, the schizoid sense of alienation and self-consciousness that, in my view, are the key elements of his personality and existential orientation.

Concerning the homosexuality issue, Ray Monk notes that there is, in fact, no evidence that Wittgenstein was concerned about his homoerotic impulses per se. I am inclined to agree with his assessment, namely, that "Wittgenstein was uneasy, not about homosexuality, but about sexuality itself" (M 585). One can always speculate, of course, that even if Wittgenstein never expressed overt concern about it, the "abnormality" of his sexual orientation may still have contributed to his general discomfort with the sexual side of life, and perhaps in turn to a more general social discomfort. It should be noted, however, that such discomfort is highly characteristic of persons with a schizoid or schizothymic disposition; whether homosexual or heterosexual, they are likely to feel more at home with the cerebral and self-controlled aspects of human experience.

In any case, I am primarily concerned in this article with aspects of Wittgenstein's personality that connect with his philosophical attitudes and concerns. Although Wittgenstein's sexual orientation may have played a significant causal role in contributing to his sense of alienation, I do not see any way in which his homoeroticism per se resonates with his philosophical thinking or meta-philosophical attitudes.

46. In his writings, Wittgenstein often refers to the phenomenology of depersonalization experiences, generally in a philosophical but sometimes also in an autobiographical context. For example: "The feeling of the unreality of one's surroundings. This feeling I have had once, and many have it before the onset of mental illness. Everything seems somehow not *real*; but not as if one saw things unclear or blurred; everything looks quite as usual"; *Remarks on the Philosophy of Psychology*, Vol. 1, ed. G. E. M. Anscombe and G. H. von Wright, trans. G. E. M. Anscombe (Oxford: Basil Blackwell, 1980), § 125. "There are feelings of strangeness. I stop short, look at the object or man . . . say, 'I find it all strange' " (PI § 596). See also CV: 1/3, 2/4, 4–5/6–7, 78/88.

  For interesting remarks on the link between depersonalization experiences and philosophical thought, see Andrew Apter, "Depersonalization, the Experience of Prosthesis, and Our Cosmic Insignificance: The Experimental Phenomenology of an Altered State," *Philosophical Psychology*, 1992, 5: 257–85. Apter says that autobiographical reports of depersonalization experiences are more common in Wittgenstein than in any other philosopher (p. 266). He lists many autobiographical as well as nonautobiographical references to depersonalization experience in Wittgenstein's writings.

47. Perhaps this helps to account for Wittgenstein's sympathy for Heidegger's line, "that in the face of which one has anxiety is Being-in-the-World as such" (M 283).

48. Hermine Wittgenstein, "My Brother Ludwig," p. 2. "Since I am very weak, I am extremely dependent upon the opinion of others. . . . A nice word from someone or a friendly smile have a lasting effect on me" (D 14, 2.5.30). "To be deprived of the fondness of others would be altogether impossible for me because in this sense I have far too little (*or no*) self" (D 103–4, 13.5.31). "Although I cannot *give* affection, I have a great *need* for it" (NM 51).

49. Compare the following statement by Franz Kafka: "You can hold yourself back from the suffering of the world, this is something you are free to do and is in accord with your nature, but perhaps precisely this holding back is the only suffering that you might be able to avoid" (in Laing, *The Divided Self,* p. 78). For discussion of Kafka's schizoid personality in relation to modernism, see Sass, *Madness and Modernism,* pp. 82–5.

  A diary entry a few sentences earlier than the passage about the "lump" suggests that Wittgenstein sometimes doubted whether there really was anything inside him that he was holding back: "I suffer from a kind of mental constipation. Or is that imaginary, similar to when one feels one might vomit when, in fact, there is nothing there anymore?" (D 1, 26.4.30).

50. See also a diary entry from 1930 on "the choice between complete alienation and this unpleasant experience [of not being understood] . . . why don't I withdraw altogether from the others? But that is difficult and unnatural for me" (D 52, 19.10.30).

51. On Wittgenstein's sense of being an exile, see James Klagge, "Wittgenstein in Exile," in D. Z. Phillips, Ed. *Religion and Wittgenstein's Legacy* (New York: Macmillan), in press.

52. See the work of Diamond and Conant, op. cit.
53. Kretschmer, *Physique and Character,* p. 246.
54. See Diamond and Conant, op. cit.
55. Otto Weininger, *Sex and Character* (London: William Heinemann, 1906 [reprinted 1975], p. 162. "Duty is only toward oneself," wrote Weininger (p. 160).
56. See Sass, *Paradoxes of Delusion,* p. 88.
57. "The 'inner' is a delusion," states Wittgenstein; Wittgenstein, *Last Writings on the Philosophy of Psychology: The Inner and Outer,* Vol. 2, ed. G. H. von Wright and Heikki Nyman, trans. C. G. Luckhardt and Maximilian A. E. Aue (Oxford: Basil Blackwell, 1992), p. 84.
58. This seems to be implicit in Wittgenstein's denial that there are kinaesthetic sensations; see e.g., Bouwsma, *Wittgenstein: Conversations, 1949–1951,* p. 64.
59. On Wittgenstein's emphasis on personal integrity, see M 51–2.
60. Wittgenstein also seems to have feared the loss of his synoptic capacity: "With increasing age I am becoming logically more and more myopic. My powers of viewing synoptically are diminishing. And my thought is getting shorter of breath" (D 65, 8.2.31).
61. Ernest Gellner, *Reason and Culture* (Oxford: Basil Blackwell, 1982), pp. 116–24. See also: Gellner, *Language and Solitude: Wittgenstein, Malinowski, and the Habsburg Dilemma* (Cambridge: Cambridge University Press, 1998), pp. 76–7.
62. Oswald Spengler, *The Decline of the West,* abr. Helmut Werner; trans. Charles Francis Atkinson (New York: Oxford University Press, 1991 [1918]), pp. 182–3; quotations in James F. Peterman, *Philosophy as Therapy* (Albany: S.U.N.Y. Press, 1992), p. 68.
63. Bouwsma, *Wittgenstein: Conversations, 1949–1951,* p. 39.
64. Plato, *Theaetetus,* trans. Harold North Fowler (Cambridge, MA: Harvard University Press, 1952), p. 55.
65. "What we have to mention in order to explain the significance, I mean the importance, of a concept, are often extremely general facts about nature: such facts as are hardly ever mentioned because of their great generality" (PI 56n).
66. See Wittgenstein's rather dismissive remarks about Frank Ramsey, whom he once described as a bourgeois thinker with an "ugly" mind (D 7–8, 27.4.30). "Ramsey was a bourgeois thinker. I.e. he thought with the aim of clearing up the affairs of some particular community. . . . whereas real philosophical reflection disturbed him . . ." (CV 17/24). On another occasion, Wittgenstein wrote, "you cannot help those whose entire instinct is to live in the herd which has created this language as its own proper mode of expression" (in *The Wittgenstein Reader,* ed. A Kenny [Oxford: Basil Blackwell, 1994], p. 273; also p. 185).
67. On Wittgenstein on the sharp contrast between philosophy and religion, see M 540.
68. "It is remarkable, strange, how happy it makes me to be able to write something about logic again even though my remark is not particularly inspired. But the mere ability to be with it again gives me that feeling of happiness" (N 51; 16.10.30). "It is a tremendous mercy to be allowed to think no matter how clumsily about the sentences *in* my work" (D 213, 13.3.37). See also: M 94, on experiencing his mind as "on fire." Consider also this diary entry from 1931: "I am somewhat infatuated [*verliebt*: in love] with my kind of movement of thought in philosophy. (And perhaps I should omit the word 'somewhat.'). . . . Perhaps, just as some like to hear themselves talk, I like to hear myself write?" (D 100, 13.5.31).

69. See also a line from 1937: "Somehow my thoughts are now *curdling* when I try to think about philosophy. – Is that the end of my philosophical career?" (D 241, 29.4.37).

70. Quoted in Kenny, "Wittgenstein on the Nature of Philosophy," *Wittgenstein and His Times,* p. 13 (MS 219, p. 11). "The task of philosophy is to sooth [*beruhigen*] the mind about meaningless questions" (D 65; 8.2.31).

71. Wittgenstein, *Zettel,* ed. G. E. M. Anscombe and G. H. von Wright, translated by G. E. M. Anscombe (Berkeley and Los Angeles: University of California Press, 1970), § 455.

72. Friedrich Nietzsche, *The Birth of Tragedy* (published with *Genealogy of Morals*), trans. by Francis Golffing (Garden City, NY: Doubleday, 1956), pp. 84–6.

73. Wittgenstein once spoke of resigning "the absurd job of a prof of philosophy. It is a kind of living death" (M 483).

74. Consider also this line: "A writer far more talented than I would still have only a minor talent" (CV 75/86). See also Paul Engelmann regarding the fact that "no poem ever occurred to [Wittgenstein] spontaneously," and that Wittgenstein revered spontaneity; *Letters from Ludwig Wittgenstein with a Memoir by Paul Engelmann,* trans. L. Furtmuller, ed. B. F. McGuinness (Oxford: Basil Blackwell, 1967), p. 89.

75. "There is a tendency in my life to base this life on the fact that I am much cleverer than the others. But when this *assumption* threatens to break down when I see *by* how much less I am clever than other people, only then do I become aware how wrong this foundation is in general even if the assumption is or were right" (D 56, 16.1.31).

76. See, for example, Richard Rorty, "Keeping Philosophy Pure: An Essay on Wittgenstein," and "Cavell on Skepticism," both in Rorty, *Consequences of Pragmatism* (Minneapolis: University of Minnesota Press, 1982), pp. 19–36, 176–190. See also: Stanley Cavell, *The Claim of Reason: Wittgenstein, Skepticism, Morality, and Tragedy* (Oxford: Oxford University Press, 1979); and "Declining Decline," in Cavell, *This New Yet Unapproachable America* (Albuquerque: Living Batch Press, 1989). Rorty says that Cavell, in his book on Wittgenstein, "has too much respect for what I am calling 'textbook problems' " ("Keeping philosophy pure," p. 36). Cavell writes, "according to me the *Investigations* at every point . . . finds its victory exactly in never claiming a final philosophical victory over (the temptation to) skepticism, which would mean a victory over the human." "I say this struggle with skepticism, with its threat or temptation, is endless; I mean to say that it is human, it is the human drive to transcend itself, to make itself inhuman, which should not end until, as in Nietzsche, the human is over. . . . while philosophy has no monopoly, I of course think the fate of skepticism is peculiarly tied to the fate of philosophy" ("Declining Decline," pp. 38, 57).

77. A somewhat analogous controversy exists concerning Wittgenstein's *Tractatus,* with some readers (e.g., Diamond and Conant, op. cit.) tending to interpret the book as entirely "therapeutic," while others (e.g., Hacker, op. cit.) read it as attempting to state a semantic thesis, and as thereby offering a view concerning the existence of ineffable dimensions of human existence.

78. For Wittgenstein, philosophy was, by turns, a torment, an illness, and a noble endeavor. Rarely did he adopt the relaxed attitude advocated in Pascal's maxim: "To make light of philosophy is to be a true philosopher"; Blaise Pascal, *Pensees* and *The Provincial Letters,* trans. W. F. Trotter (New York: Modern Library, 1941), p. 6. Malcolm reports that Wittgenstein "could not tolerate a facetious tone

in his classes, the tone that is characteristic of philosophical discussion among clever people who have no serious purpose" (NM 27).

79. Bouwsma, *Wittgenstein: Conversations, 1949–1951,* p. 68.
80. See, for example, Rupert Read, "The *Real* Philosophical Discovery," *Philosophical Investigations* 18, 1995, pp. 362–9.
81. "Thoughts that are at peace. That's what someone who philosophizes yearns for" (CV 43/50).
82. Stephen Hilmy notes that the "tormenting questions" criticized by the later Wittgenstein were in large measure "questions that had been raised by Wittgenstein himself and his own contemporaries (most of whom considered themselves in the forefront of the assault against traditional metaphysics)"; Hilmy, "Tormenting Questions," in Robert L. Arrington and Hans-Johann Glock, *Wittgenstein's Philosophical Investigations: Text and Context* (London: Routledge, 1991), 89–104, p. 99. Hilmy does not suggest, however, that even the later Wittgenstein's current antiphilosophical thinking might have been part of what Wittgenstein wanted to eliminate.
83. See the conversation on a moonlit night recounted by Bouwsma: "If I had planned it, I should never have made the sun at all. See! How beautiful! The sun is too bright and too hot." Later Wittgenstein said: "And if there were only the moon there would be no reading and writing" (*Wittgenstein: Conversations, 1949–1951,* p. 12). See also D 66, 13.2.31: "Reading numbs my soul."
84. See also Wittgenstein's comparison of a philosophy convention to "bubonic plague" (M 487). In 1946 Wittgenstein wrote, "Everything about the place [Cambridge] repels me. The stiffness, the artificiality, the self-satisfaction of the people. The university atmosphere nauseates me" (M 493).
85. Here it may be useful to append two quotations, one from Wittgenstein, the other a passage from the Wilhelm Busch story, *"Eduard's Traum,"* that was one of Wittgenstein's favorite quotations. "You can't think decently if you don't want to hurt yourself" (NM 94). "And, joking apart, my friends, only a man who has a heart can feel and say truly, indeed from the heart, that he is good for nothing. That done, things will sort themselves out"; in Engelmann, *Letters from Wittgenstein with a Memoir,* p. 116.
86. We might say, then, that Wittgenstein *both* despises *and,* at other moments, deeply respects the tendency Cavell has termed "skepticism." Incidentally, this controversy about Wittgenstein's overall attitude toward philosophy is a good example of an exegetical issue whose treatment can be significantly affected by the overall hermeneutic stance one adopts toward interpreting Wittgenstein, which in turn may be influenced by a psychological understanding; see note 31 above.
87. Similarly, we could think of Wittgenstein's antischizoid side both as a rejection and as an expression of his capacity for schizoid detachment – in this case for critical detachment even from detachment itself.
88. Hermine Wittgenstein, "My Brother Ludwig," p. 2.
89. When working on these problems, Ludwig was, according to his sister Hermine, in a "heightened sense of intellectual intensity which verged on the pathological"; "My Brother Ludwig," p. 3.
90. See Bertrand Russell, "Mathematical Logic as Based on the Theory of Types," in Jean van Heijenoort, Ed., *From Frege to Gödel: A Source Book in Mathematical Logic, 1879–1931* (Cambridge, MA. Harvard University Press, 1967), 150–182. Although not identical, these several paradoxes share important similarities. Rus-

sell mentions both the barber and the liar paradoxes in the afore-mentioned article, stating that the common characteristic of these semantic paradoxes is "self-reference," for example, the fact that "The remark of Epimenides must include itself in its own scope" (p. 154). On "This statement is false," see H. O. Mounce, *Wittgenstein's Tractatus: An Introduction* (Chicago: University of Chicago Press, 1981), pp. 6–7. We know that the Liar's Paradox interested Wittgenstein, since he mentioned it to his students when he taught in an Austrian village; W. W. Bartley, *Wittgenstein* (Open Court, 1985), p. 22.

91. Russell: "The division of objects into types is necessitated by the reflexive fallacies which otherwise arise"; "Mathematical Logic," p. 163.

92. See the work of Diamond and Conant, op. cit.

93. Wittgenstein, *Philosophical Remarks* (Oxford: Basil Blackwell, 1975), § 6.

94. Bouwsma, *Wittgenstein: Conversations 1949–1951*, p. 24.

95. *Letters from Wittgenstein with a Memoir*, letter of 9.4.17, pp. 7, 83. Wittgenstein has just been praising a poem by Uhland. See McG 251; M 151.

96. After working out my own analysis of the *Tractatus*, I came across Joel C. Weinsheimer's excellent and illuminating discussion of the same parallel between the Theory of Types and degrees of self-consciousness. See Weinsheimer, *Gadamer's Hermeneutics* (New Haven, CT: Yale University Press, 1985), especially pp. 45–49.

97. Quotations from Diamond, "Throwing Away the Ladder," p. 185.

98. On the relationship between philosophy and breathing, consider Wittgenstein's remark to Drury: "there is no oxygen in Cambridge for you" – spoken when he was recommending to Drury to leave the university and find a job among the working class, where there was healthier air. As for himself, said Wittgenstein: "It doesn't matter . . . I manufacture my own oxygen" (M 6, 334).

99. Michael Fried, *Absorption and Theatricality: Painting and the Beholder in the Age of Diderot* (Chicago: University of Chicago Press, 1980).

100. Lionel Trilling, *Sincerity and Authenticity* (Cambridge, MA: Harvard University Press, 1972). On Wordsworth and the sentiment of being, see pp. 91–105.

101. See: Paul de Man, "The Double Aspect of Symbolism," *Yale French Studies* 74, 3–16; Frank Kermode, *Romantic Image* (London: Fontana Books, 1971); Gerald Bruns, *Modern Poetry and the Idea of Language* (New Haven, CT: Yale University Press, 1974).

   Postmodernism, in many of its variants, involves a rejection of these romantic and modernist aspirations, and a revival of theatricality, referentiality, and the more blatant forms of explicit self-consciousness and inner division. See: Paul de Man, "The Rhetoric of Temporality," in de Man, *Blindness and Insight* (Minnesota: University of Minneapolis Press, 1983). Craig Owens, "The Allegorical Impulse: Toward a Theory of Postmodernism," in Brian Wallis, Ed., *Art After Modernism: Rethinking Representation* (New York: New Museum of Contemporary Art and David R. Godine Inc., Boston, 1984), 203–35. See also Michael Fried's antitheatrical and antipostmodernist essay, "Art and objecthood," which ends with the line, "presentness [by which Fried means the absence of theatrical self-consciousness] is grace"; in Gregory Battcock, Ed. *Minimal Art* (New York: E. P. Dutton, 1968), 116–47, p. 147.

102. Foucault, *The Order of Things*, p. 300. Foucault is describing the aesthetic orientation epitomized by the poetry of Mallarmé, in which "literature becomes progressively more differentiated from the discourse of ideas, and enclosed itself within a radical intransitivity . . . a manifestation of a language which has no

other law than that of affirming its own precipitous existence." See also Bruns, *Modern Poetry and the Idea of Language.*

103. See; M. W. Rowe, "Wittgenstein's Romantic Inheritance," *Philosophy* 69, 1994: 327–51; Allan Janik and Stephen Toulmin, *Wittgenstein's Vienna* (New York: Simon and Schuster, 1973).

104. Wittgenstein: "I once tried to read 'Resurrection' but couldn't. You see, when Tolstoy just tells a story he impresses me infinitely more than when he addresses the reader. When he turns his back to the reader then he seems to me *most* impressive . . . It seems to me his philosophy is most true when it's *latent* in the story"; quoted in NM 38.

105. Quoted in Rush Rhees, "Postscript," in Rhees, Ed. *Recollections of Wittgenstein* (Oxford: Oxford University Press, 1984), 172–209, p. 174. Wittgenstein wrote, "Style is the expression of a general human necessity" (D 28, 9.5.30). Wittgenstein also wrote (but I cannot locate the source) that only a culture – as opposed to a civilization – makes having a style truly possible.

In the diaries and elsewhere, Wittgenstein characterizes vanity as a form of self-reflection that threatens to disrupt the spontaneous movement of creative thinking (see Alfred Nordmann's essay in this volume: "The Sleepy Philosopher: How to Read Wittgenstein's Diaries") and that "destroys the *value* of a work" by emptying it out (D 205, 24.2.37).

106. "It is impossible for me to say one word in my book about all that music has meant in my life," said Wittgenstein to Drury (M 537).

107. C. Dallhaus, *The Idea of Absolute Music* (Chicago: University of Chicago Press, 1989), pp. 88, 97, 143, 152–3. Dallhaus also speaks of a "dialectic between absorption and retreat" (p. 152). I am grateful to Richard Eldridge for calling my attention to the relevance of Dallhaus's book on "absolute music."

108. Many in Wittgenstein's circles viewed the dominance of theatricality and self-display as the cause of the atrophy or decadence that Viennese culture had suffered since the middle of the 19th century. Engelmann, for example, spoke of "an arrogated base culture – a culture turned into its opposite, misused as ornament and mask" (M 56). See also Janik and Toulmin, *Wittgenstein's Vienna.*

109. One of the sins to which Wittgenstein confessed does not fit this definition. It is a straightforward instance of what Wittgenstein saw as cowardice concerning carrying some bombs across a plank during his military service in World War I (M 369).

110. I would speculate that Wittgenstein's intense dislike of what he considered "bourgeois" may be due to the typical middle-class preoccupation with appearances, which he found uncomfortably akin to his own tendency to be "weak . . . cowardly: in fear to make an unfavorable impression on others" (D 148, 27.1.37): "The thought of Marguerite's bourgeois engagement makes me nauseous. . . . Every defilement I can tolerate except the one that is bourgeois. Isn't that strange?" (D 121, 7.11.31).

111. "Today I mailed the letter with my confession to Mining," writes Wittgenstein in his diary. "Even though the confession is candid, I am still lacking the appropriate seriousness for the situation" (D 145, 24.11.36).

112. I think this is what Wittgenstein is getting at when he points out that it is perfectly possible to be lying even when one tells the truth. " 'I can lie *like this* – or also *like that* – or best of all, by telling the truth quite sincerely.' So I often say to myself" (D 114, 31.10.31).

113. In another passage Wittgenstein makes a related point about knowledge: "It is

then roughly like this: they say that they know that they don't know but take enormous pride in this discovery" (D 68, 22.2.31).

114. Below I offer a description of this parallel. Although overly literal (the correspondences need not be conceived precisely as follows), it may nevertheless help to convey the general idea.

First there is an original "sin," which is an instance of self-detachment or inauthenticity: the self-reference in Frege's system; Wittgenstein's lying to the headmaster. Then, an attempt to distance oneself from this error involving self-detachment: Russell's Theory of Types; Wittgenstein's confession to his friends. Then, the attempt to distance oneself from, and thereby overcome, the defect inherent in the just-prior attempt at self-distancing: the semantic doctrines of the *Tractatus*; Wittgenstein's self-critique, in his diaries, of the vanity inherent in his attempt to confess to his friends and family. Then, references to the inevitable inadequacy or self-vitiation inherent in the just-prior metaconfession: the *Tractatus's* explicit acknowledgment of its own transgression of the semantic rules that it itself puts forward; Wittgenstein's acknowledgment, in his diaries, of the vanity of his confessing the vanity inherent in his confessing. Beyond this there seems to be, in both texts, an implicit acknowledgment of the ultimately empty or futile character of the whole recursive enterprise, which is unable to state or in any way to reach an "ultimate ground."

115. There is something in the nature of vanity that precludes the possibility that one could truly understand it in oneself. For, as Wittgenstein points out, (adding a typically self-deprecating afterthought): "Self-knowledge and humbleness are one (These are cheap remarks.)" (D 97, 6.5.31).

116. The phrase comes from Gilbert Ryle, *The Concept of Mind* (New York: Barnes and Noble, 1949), p. 195; quoted in Weinsheimer, *Gadamer's Hermeneutics*, p. 39.

117. On this point, see Nagel, *View from Nowhere,* pp. 126–30: "But this objective self-surveillance will inevitably be incomplete, since some knower must remain behind the lens if anything is to be known. Moreover, each of us knows this . . . this blind spot is part of our objective picture of the world. . . . The incomplete view . . . faces us with the certainty that however much we expand our objective view of ourselves, something will remain beyond the possibility of explicit acceptance or rejection, because we cannot get entirely outside ourselves, even though we know that there is an outside" (pp. 127–8). See also Weinsheimer, *Gadamer's Hermeneutics,* p. 39.

118. See the line (quoted above) from the "Lecture on Ethics" in which Wittgenstein avows his deep respect for the "hopeless" and nonsensical yearning of the human mind to "go beyond the world and that is to say beyond significant language," to run "against the walls of our cage" (E 42, 44). See also Engelmann's characterization of Wittgenstein as believing that "all that really matters in human life is precisely what, in his view, we must be silent about." "When [Wittgenstein] nevertheless takes immense pains to delimit the unimportant," writes Engelmann, "it is not the coastline of that island which he is bent on surveying with such meticulous accuracy, but the boundary of the ocean"; *Letters from Wittgenstein with a Memoir,* p. 97.

119. Such a view is anticipated by statements in Weininger's *Sex and Character,* which may have influenced Wittgenstein: "Fichte was right when he stated that the existence of the ego was to be found concealed in pure logic, inasmuch as the ego is the condition of intelligible existence" (p. 158); "Logic and ethics are

fundamentally the same, they are not more than duty to oneself" (p. 159). Incidentally, the term "selfobject" comes from the psychoanalyst Heinz Kohut; I am not however using the term in quite the same way Kohut uses it.

For an explicit suggestion of Wittgenstein's identification of his inner-self with his thoughts, see the passage quoted above (in the section, "Wittgenstein as Schizoid Personality") which begins, "My thoughts rarely come into the world unmutilated" (D 98, 13.5.31).

120. As Bertrand Russell noted in his introduction to Wittgenstein's *Tractatus* (TLP 22): "Mr. Wittgenstein manages to say a good deal about what cannot be said, thus suggesting to the skeptical reader that possibly there may be some loophole through a hierarchy of languages, or by some other exit."
121. See the works by Conant and Diamond, op. cit.
122. See Paul de Man, "The Double Aspect of Symbolism," especially p. 5 regarding the claim of the post-romantic, symbolist movement to offer, through poetry, "man's only way of salvation out of an inner division which threatens his very being," which involves taking over "obligations and duties which, up to then, had been the exclusive concern of the religious life."
123. Weininger, *Sex and Character,* pp. 160, 162.
124. On presentness and absorption, see Fried, "Art and Objecthood" and *Absorption and Theatricality.* On formal self-expression, see Clement Greenberg, "Modernist Painting," in Gregory Battcock, Ed., *The New Art: A Critical Anthology* (New York: Dutton, 1966), 100–10. On symbol versus allegory, see Paul de Man, "The Rhetoric of Temporality."
125. Yeats: quoted in M. Perloff, *The Futurist Moment* (Chicago: University of Chicago Press, 1986), p. 72. James Joyce, *A Portrait of the Artist as a Young Man* (New York: Viking, 1965; [1916]), pp. 212–13.
126. According to Diamond and Conant, op. cit., the *Tractatus* gives only the *illusion* of trying to say the ineffable. On their reading, the book achieves a final, untrumpable act of ironic self-distancing, and thereby manages to undermine any aspiration toward a positive mode of transcendental expression, leaving one with silence alone.
127. See M 416, 420–1. Regarding the Liar's Paradox, Wittgenstein said the following: "It is very queer in a way that this should have puzzled anyone – much more extraordinary than you might think: that this should be the thing to worry human beings. Because the thing works like this: if a man says 'I am lying' we say that it follows that he is not lying, from which it follows that he is lying and so on. Well, so what? You can go on like that until you are black in the face. Why not? It doesn't matter." "One may say, 'This can only be explained by a theory of types.' But what is there which needs to be explained?" (*Wittgenstein's Lectures on the Foundations of Mathematics,* pp. 206–7; M 420)
128. Quoted in P. M. S. Hacker, *Insight and Illusion: Themes in the Philosophy of Wittgenstein,* rev. ed. (Oxford: Clarendon, 1986), p. 146. Malcolm reports that Wittgenstein frequently said disparaging things about the *Tractatus* to him (NM 58).

The Sleepy Philosopher:
How to Read Wittgenstein's Diaries

ALFRED NORDMANN

In the second week of November 1931, Ludwig Wittgenstein entered the following remark in his diary:

The movement of thought in my philosophy should be discernible also in the history of my mind, of its moral concepts & in the understanding of my situation (Koder Diaries [KD] 125).[1]

Wittgenstein appears to be suggesting here that one may better appreciate his philosophy if one studies the history of his mind and understands the situation in which his thoughts originate, for example, by reading his diaries. Yet, before following his invitation to turn to the diaries, we should consider the scope of his promise and just what it means for a movement of thought to be found again in the history of a mind.

This essay entertains two approaches to Wittgenstein's remark; it criticizes the first, recommends the second. On the first reading, Wittgenstein's philosophical writing poses interpretive problems in need of solution; like pieces of a puzzle his remarks need to be fitted into a coherent whole. Emboldened by Wittgenstein's remark about his movement of thought, one therefore looks to the diaries for answers to interpretive questions. Even if they do not immediately provide a key that will unlock some hidden philosophical meaning, one expects at least to find clues or missing pieces to the puzzle.

The second approach takes quite literally Wittgenstein's repeated assertion that there is nothing hidden in his philosophy, that his remarks are "clear as crystal," that philosophy does not present doctrines or theses.[2] It is thus opposed to the hermeneutic strategy of drawing on diaries, notebooks, or manuscripts in order to discover a supposedly missing text for the coherent reconstruction of some element of doctrine. Instead, the diaries ought to be viewed as self-contained texts with considerable literary merit of their own, useful for our philosophical understanding of Wittgenstein only in that they rehearse movements of thought and thereby familiarize their readers with characteristic moves that Wittgenstein performs also in the texts he prepared for publication.

At stake between the two approaches to Wittgenstein's remark is a question far too broad for comprehensive treatment in these pages: What does it mean to understand or appreciate a philosophy that is conceived not as doctrine but as activity? Therefore, instead of considering the entire range of relevant sources concerning Wittgenstein's philosophical practice, I will here limit myself to his diaries from the years 1930 to 1932 and 1936–1937 (the so-called Koder Diaries).[3]

I

Three general observations about biography and philosophy set the stage for the contest between the two approaches to Wittgenstein. In 1975, Roy Emanuel Lemoine published in the series *Janua Linguarum* a monograph entitled *The Anagogic Theory of Wittgenstein's 'Tractatus.'* It is really quite an interesting book, and it shares with other unjustly neglected studies of Wittgenstein the claim that "it departs radically from the traditional interpretations of the *Tractatus*." Lemoine offers a peculiarly disarming justification for his radical departure from tradition:

The *Tractatus* is probably the most significant philosophical document since the *Critique of Pure Reason,* from which it is in some ways derivative; but it is much harder to read. Even Wittgenstein, as he stated in his foreword, was aware that perhaps only those who had thought similar thoughts would understand him. It may be that my contribution to the study of the *Tractatus* comes from the fact that my own background is different from that of most scholars and has some similarity to Wittgenstein's. I have been both a line officer and a chaplain, and I also served in a great war.[4]

Lemoine's reasoning raises the question of access: Can we privilege it by becoming more familiar with the peculiar situation from which Wittgenstein was writing, or with Wittgenstein's peculiar character? Is it perhaps the case that Wittgenstein's philosophical texts, the *Tractatus* and the *Philosophical Investigations,* are so opaque due to his situatedness, his character, his problematics, that only external sources of experience and information can render these texts intelligible? If the answer to these questions is yes, will not a critical interpretation of Wittgenstein's writing become hopelessly intertwined with appeals to authority such as Lemoine's unimpeachable claim that he has a special affinity to Wittgenstein's thought?

A second observation introduces a possibly instructive contrast. Readers of Ray Monk's marvelous biography may well find irresistible the feeling that it helps them better understand Wittgenstein: it shows a satisfying harmony of his life, work, and thought.[5] Yet readers of Joseph Brent's equally fascinating and knowledgable biography may find that it erects an obstacle toward their understanding of Charles Sanders Peirce: It shows a disturbing disharmony between a brilliantly systematic thinker and his utterly unprincipled life.[6]

Should this difference, however, make a difference in an assessment of the two philosophers? Or does this difference reflect only the reader's aesthetic, perhaps irrational, preference for unity of form and content, life and thought?[7]

The third and final observation dramatizes this contrast considerably. All the true stories about Peirce may not provide a deeper understanding of his work, but even apocryphal or false stories about Wittgenstein do the job. Of course, an encounter with Wittgenstein's mind would have created resentment and confusion in someone like Hitler, and of course we may better understand the principles that may have governed Wittgenstein's life and thought once we try to imagine him as an enigmatic master-spy.[8] These two false stories make about as much sense as the true one in which Wittgenstein gives money to Rilke and Trakl (to what extent did he read and appreciate Trakl's poetry at all?), and all three of them make more sense than the true one in which he donates a million *Kronen* for the army to build a new cannon.[9]

While these three observations make one wary of all appeals to biography, they also alert us to the very special case of Wittgenstein. If many students, teachers, and scholars of his work are grateful for characteristic anecdotes about him, if they consider these anecdotes not primarily for their veracity but for their aesthetic or heuristic merit, there is more going on here than a sentimental fascination with the man or with the unity of his life and thought. The contrast with Charles Sanders Peirce may bring this out.

Peirce, one might argue, filled page after abundant page in the attempt to explain himself. Wittgenstein, on the contrary, worked hard to purify his thought, at the expense of rendering it cryptic. Accordingly, the argument continues, one needs to mobilize different resources for the purposes of interpretation and understanding. Wittgenstein himself sets up a similar contrast to Spengler when, on May 6, 1930, he records in his diary:

It's a shame that Spengler did not stick with his Good Thoughts & went further than what he can answer for. Greater cleanliness, however, would have made his thought more difficult to understand, but only through that also really lastingly effective. Thus is the thought that the string instruments assumed their *Definitive* Shape between 1500 and 1600 of *enormous* magnitude (& symbolism). Only most people see nothing in such a thought if one gives it to them without much ado [*drumherum*]. (KD 19f.)[10]

While "much, perhaps most of [Spengler's thought], is completely in touch with what I have often thought myself" (KD 17f.), Wittgenstein strives for greater cleanliness: instead of making indefensible claims, he presents his thoughts without much ado, even if it means that most people will see nothing in them.[11] They therefore lack a "*drumherum*," as each is surrounded by a blank line, a bit of empty space; and thus his remarks assume their enigmatic, or oracular, character that renders them lastingly effective to those who see something in them.

Thus, even if in general one is wary of appeals to biographical sources, the argument concludes, Wittgenstein's case is different. For, to the extent that each remark stands somewhat by itself and is not entirely absorbed in the progression of an overarching train of thought, each remark asks the reader to fill in the missing text, to solve its riddle, to find the "*drumherum*" that allows them to see something in the remark. Often enough it appears that Wittgenstein's biography, his letters, his diaries, his notebooks and type-scripts, personal memoirs and anecdotes can provide that missing text.

The following diary entry from 1936, for example, provides context that might facilitate a rational reconstruction of Wittgenstein's philosophical development:

A sentence can appear absurd & this absurdity of its surface engulfed by the depth which as it were lies behind it.

This can be applied to the thought concerning the resurrection of the dead & to other thoughts linked to it. – What gives it depth, however, is its use: the *life* led by those who believe it (KD 147).[12]

As in numerous related diary entries, Wittgenstein apparently tries to establish the meaningfulness of religious language that here gives rise to central notions of his later philosophy such as "meaning is use," "language game," or "form of life." Taken together with his struggle to attain religious faith, the diary thus delivers a story that is both consistent with the facts and compellingly elegant. It allows us to understand in simple terms the transition from his early to his later philosophy: Did he not effectively rule out the possibility of meaningful religious language in the *Tractatus*? Did he not even then claim that language is alright as it is? Does not ordinary language include many religious statements that would thus seem absurd, yet perfectly clear to those who use them? And did this not create a productive tension that left him conflicted in his diaries and finally issued in the *Philosophical Investigations*? By the same token, one might appeal to the empirical evidence of Wittgenstein's religious struggles to decide the disagreement between P. M. S. Hacker and Cora Diamond on whether he considered it possible that there is a *something* that we ought to be silent *about*.[13]

Even if one is generally reluctant to draw on biographical sources to reconstruct philosophical positions, there thus seems much to recommend in Wittgenstein's case the heuristic strategy of drawing on diaries, notebooks, and/or manuscripts in order to discover crucial motivations and transitions that were left unstated in the published works. Yet this argument for the use of the diaries to solve problems of interpretation implies that Wittgenstein's method of writing (hitting the nail on the head) and the proposed method of reading (recovering context) move in opposite directions, one undoing the accomplishment of the other. Wittgenstein scholars would thus find themselves in a predicament familiar to historians and sociologists of scientific knowledge: scientific writing achieves objectivity precisely in that it becomes detached from the context and circumstances of its production. When historical or parochial context is read back into scientific texts, they are effectively deconstructed. Science Studies thus unravel the scientific achievement of objectivity without being able to account for it. Defenders of science and reason will therefore often and rightfully resist such readings, questioning whether there is a hermeneutics of science at all, suggesting that the very pursuit of science is premised upon its denial.

Similarly, the biographical approach to understanding Wittgenstein takes away with one hand what it gives with the other. Overtly aiming to establish the unity of life, work, and thought, it severs the unity of style and content, failing to account for the "cleanliness" of Wittgenstein's remarks, that is, for the philosophical meaning attached to its attainment. Instead, the interpretive conflation of texts creates much textual and anecdotal ado, substituting or cementing seamless stories of intellectual development for a carefully arranged succession of critical and succinct, yet discontinuous, remarks. Although the words and practice of the later Wittgenstein have often been recruited for hermeneutic purposes, his rejection of riddles and of anything that is hidden implies a rejection of a hermeneutic stance toward his own writing, which is meant to be crystal clear.[14]

The proposed use of the diaries thus imposes a biographical hermeneutics on remarks that were meant to speak for themselves, and the supposedly charitable reconstruction of Wittgenstein's texts would begin with an implicit criticism of their composition.

II

Even though Wittgenstein's remarks were meant to be clear as crystal, this is not how they appear to his readers – and all too soon Wittgenstein became well aware of this.[15] Thus, if they are not perfectly self-explanatory, if they require interpretive reconstruction, how can that reconstruction avoid biographical hermeneutics?

Instead of treating the remark as a riddle or puzzle that needs to be solved, an encryption that needs to be decoded, as the surface trace of a deep, intentional story, possibly a life-story, one might treat it as the occasion for a thought experiment that is prompted by the remark, but not usually carried to its conclusion within it. Wittgenstein provides such a reading after isolating from its context Spengler's thought about string instruments. There is much ado surrounding that thought. It appears in a chapter on "The Meaning of Numbers" that proposes a history of musical instruments. This history explores "the deep spiritual bases of the intended tone-colors and tone-effects," namely "the wish, intensified to the point of longing, to fill a spatial infinity with sounds."[16] Wittgenstein's reading does not draw on this immediate context at all, but takes the remark, as it was isolated by him, to reenact the thought experiment that could have prompted it:

Thus is the thought that the string instruments assumed their *Definitive* Shape between 1500 and 1600 of *enormous* magnitude (& symbolism). . . . It is as if someone believed that a human being keeps on developing without limit & one told him: look, the cranial sutures of a child close at . . . years & that shows already that development comes everywhere to an end, that what is developing here is a self-contained whole which at some point will be completely present & not a sausage which can run on indefinitely (KD 20).[17]

We might read Wittgenstein's texts in just this manner: There is nothing missing in them, it is up to us to follow out the movement of thought that is initiated by any given remark.[18]

On this second approach to understanding Wittgenstein, we need not read his diaries in order to gain a better understanding of his philosophical writing. We need not read his letters either, or earlier variants and drafts of final versions. Nothing is hidden in his private writing; everything is in the open in the published manuscipts.[19] As a matter of interpretive charity and parsimony, one might thus conclude that if we need not read the diaries, then we ought not; but how should we understand on this second approach Wittgenstein's remark that the movement of thought in his philosophizing should be discernible or, literally, re-cognizable in the history of his mind and its moral concepts, in an understanding of his situation?

This remark does not speak diachronically of a temporal or causal relation; it does not suggest a historical movement where one thing leads to another and a condition or thought in his moral life prompts a reflex or response in his philosophical writing. Instead, Wittgenstein suggests that one should be able to map self-contained movements of his philosophizing synchronically across a variety of contexts or situations onto other such movements in the history of his mind and its moral concepts, in an understanding of his situation. The discovery of such correspondences shows that he makes similar moves when he philosophizes and when he leads his life. His "private" thoughts thus illuminate his "public" or philosophical reflections no more than his "public" writing prefigures his "private" movements of thought. Instead, we witness Wittgenstein performing a certain kind of work that concerns the articulation of meaning, and meaning is articulated in the course of leading a life. Yes, Wittgenstein's diaries are philosophically interesting, not however because they provide answers to riddles, but because they allow us to rehearse Wittgensteinian movements of thought – as in philosophy so in life, as in life so in philosophy.[20]

An elucidation of "movement of thought" may render more concrete how the performance of a certain kind of philosophical work is rehearsed also in the context of the diaries. It begins by revisiting a remark, the previous discussion of which had overlooked how it initiates a self-contained movement of thought. It overlooked this because it considered the remark straightforward evidence for a transitional movement between Wittgenstein's interests in religious faith, giving meaning to religious propositions, and doing so by way of the formula that "meaning is use" within a form of life:

A sentence can appear absurd & this absurdity of its surface engulfed by the depth which as it were lies behind it.
   This can be applied to the thought concerning the resurrection of the dead & to other thoughts linked to it. – What gives it depth, however, is its use: the *life* led by those who believe it (KD 147).

Should we really view this remark as part of a larger movement that leads from its reflection on the meaningfulness of religious language to general notions of philosophical grammar, language games, forms of life, and "meaning is use"? Or is a movement of thought prompted within this remark, does it go on to revolve around it, thus belonging only to the remark itself? On this latter interpretation, the movement begins with the stratified picture of sentences that have surface meanings as well as depths that are, so to speak, lurking behind them and that can well up, overwhelm, or consume the surface meanings. The movement continues with a jarring "however" introducing a decisive turn that threatens the whole picture and turns the remark upon and against itself: "What gives [the sentence] depth, however, is its use: the *life* led by those who believe it." The initial picture of meaning that lies, at some depth, behind the proposition is thus confronted with the notion that meaning is use where application or use do not lie behind the sentence at all, but rather surround or contextualize it on the surface, in the realm of overt practice. Instead of comparing one picture with the other, however, perhaps rejecting one in favor of the other, Wittgenstein leaves this contrast in an unresolved tension when he suggests that the depth is in the use which, of course, has no depth.

   Wittgenstein and his readers have yet to work themselves out of this tension and only then can return to propositions regarding the resurrection of the dead: if the meaning of such a proposition is its place in the life of those who believe it, the question of meaning may end up quite separate from the question of literal or historical truth; and one can no longer talk of a straightforward transition from a given religious belief to a philosophical proposal that serves to render it meaningful.[21]

   Thus Wittgenstein's remark merely inaugurates and does not conclude its movement of thought, and yet it does not continue in another remark either, but plays itself out from within the confines of its formulation: It provides philosophical occasion for a reflection that questions the metaphor of "depth" without rejecting the problem that prompted it.[22]

III

Wittgenstein's diaries are continuous with the typescripts in that they issue in characteristically Wittgensteinian thought-experiments. They are, however, discontinuous with the typescripts in that they attend to the very conditions that occasion these thought experiments and render them philosophically productive.

There is another occasion in his diaries where Wittgenstein refers to his "movement of thought." This time his remark bounces off other reflections on joy and vanity, on writing itself, and the preconditions for philosophical work.

I am somewhat in love with my kind of movement of thought in philosophy. (And perhaps I should omit the word "somewhat.")
This does not mean, by the way, that I am in love with my style. That I am not.
Something is serious only to the extent that it is really serious
Perhaps, just as some like to hear themselves talk, I like to hear myself write? . . .

The joy I have in my own thoughts (philosophical thoughts) is joy in my own strange life. Is that the joy of life? (KD 100f., 108)[23]

These reflections are offset by a set of remarks that censure the joy he takes in his writing. They were recorded in November 1936 after receiving a letter from Ludwig Hänsel. Wittgenstein had confessed to Hänsel a "cowardly lie" concerning his Jewish descent, but in his response Hänsel did not condemn him at all, but called him a "marvelous human being."[24] In light of Hänsel's response Wittgenstein finds himself thinking lightly about the matter of his confession and in the space of a few lines reigns himself in, lets loose, and reigns himself in again:

Just as the screws are tightened, they become loose again, because what they are to squeeze together is giving way again.

I always take joy in my own good similes; were it not such vain joy (KD 144f).[25]

Here and throughout the diaries, Wittgenstein *works* to know himself and thereby to defeat his vanity, which, he worries, will always catch up with him and regain the upper hand.[26] Also, he wonders throughout whether and when he will *work* again: write philosophy, do logic, prepare for his lectures. Accompanying all of that is Wittgenstein's ongoing concern with how and when language *works* rather than idles. The diaries show these various conceptions of "work" entangled in the problem of life and the articulation of meaning: "What gives meaning, is the *life* led by those who live by it."

What kind of life engenders the movements of thought that can perform these kinds of work?

One could imagine a person who from birth to death is always either sleeping or lives in a kind of half-sleep or daze. This is how my life compares to one that is really alive (I am just now thinking of Kierkegaard). Should such a one who lives half-asleep ever wake up for a minute, he will deem himself quite something else & he would not be disinclined to consider himself a genius.

There is a kind of space for thought in which, when falling asleep, one can sojourn further or not so far & when awakening there is a return from a greater or lesser distance.

My thoughts are so ephemeral, evaporate so fast, like dreams which must be recorded immediately after awakening if they are not to be forgotten right away.

Toward dawn today I was dreaming that I had a long philosophical discussion with others.
    In it I arrived at a sentence which upon awakening I still vaguely knew:
    "But let us talk in our mother tongue, & not believe that we must pull ourselves out of the swamp by our own hair; that was – thank God – only a dream. We are only supposed to remove misunderstandings, after all." I think, this is a *good* sentence (KD 135f., 142, 65, 235).[27]

Wittgenstein here describes movements or journeys of thought that, upon his awakening, bring with them into the light of day good sentences from far away, sentences that might well serve to characterize his mature philosophy: "Let us talk in our mother tongue."
    Wittgenstein thus associates the conditions of work, sleep, and dream. Since any discussion of their relation must invoke the name of Freud and his conception of dreamwork, Wittgenstein refers to Freud when he reflects on the circumstances under which he can work at all:

I am capable of accommodating myself to all situations. When I come into new living quarters under new circumstances I undertake as soon as possible to devise a technique to endure the various discomforts & to avoid friction: I accommodate myself to the given circumstances. And thus I accommodate myself gradually also with thinking, only this cannot be done simply through a certain degree of self-mastery & intellect. Instead this must form & arrange itself on its own. Just as one finally does fall asleep in this strained position.[28] And being able to work is in so many ways similar to being able to fall asleep. If one thinks of Freud's definition of sleep one could say that both cases concern a shift of the troops of interest. (In the one case it is merely a withdrawal, in the other a withdrawal and concentration at some location.) (KD 48f.)[29]

Something has to be right before we can fall asleep, before we can work:

What disturbs me in my sleep also disturbs me in my work. Whistling & speaking but not the sound of machines or at least *much* less (KD 55).[30]

Machines work, and on various occasions Wittgenstein compares the workings of language to that of engines or machines. The withdrawal of attention
from certain things sets the thought free, gives it motion, allows it to attain
momentum, to do its work in an unforced, uninterrupted manner where
sentences and images can occur to Wittgenstein, and language is not derailed
or idled by a kind of reflection that breaks the subtle interplay of gears and
levers.[31] This is, admittedly, a vague description of Wittgenstein's method of
thinking and writing. A long list of evidences can be offered that ranges from
his early to his late writing, from his frequent insistence that he records
thoughts and sentences as they occur to, or even invade (*einfallen*), him, to
his explicit insistence that philosophical questions can jam the engine and
interrupt the smooth, ordinary workings of the game. Various sundry entries
from the diaries can be added to this list:

In art, too, there are people who believe that they can forcibly bring about their eternal
life by doing good works & those who cast themselves in the arms of grace.

I believe that my sentences are mostly descriptions of visual images that occur to me.

I frequently copy to the wrong place Philosophical Remarks which I made earlier:
they do not *work* there! They must stand *there* where they can perform their whole
work! (KD 53f., 114, 210f.)[32]

Such a list of evidences, however, can only provide an impression of a certain
state envisioned by Wittgenstein, a state in which philosophical work can
begin. A phenomenological description of this state should be attempted, one
that designates a particular way of writing and living.

The state in which Wittgenstein can work and sleep gives occasion to his
thought experiment or movements of thought, and is supposed to do so in an
unforced manner, quasi-naturally against the backdrop of familiar linguistic
practice. It is a relaxed state in which things occur to Wittgenstein, in which
thoughts are admitted rather than forced:

I could almost see myself as an amoral nucleus to which the moral concepts of other
people stick easily.
   So that, what I am saying is eo ipso never my own, since this nucleus (I picture it
as a white dead bale) cannot talk. Instead, printed sheets stick to it. These then talk;
of course, not in their original state but mixed up with other sheets & influenced by
the position into which they are brought by the nucleus (KD 109f.).[33]

In order for Wittgenstein to "relieve" the reader of "mental cramps," his own
writing had to proceed in a seemingly effortless, mechanical, uncramped
manner.[34] To the extent that the diaries rehearse his movements of thought,
they cultivate the conditions for work and sleep, helping him from a state of
mental constipation to one of unforced exploration. This can be traced
through the diaries. Here are some of its very first entries:

I suffer from a kind of mental constipation. Or is that my imagination, similar to when one feels one might vomit when, in fact, there is nothing left? . . .

Often I feel that there is something in me like a lump which, were it to melt, would let me cry or I would then find the right words (or perhaps even a melody). But this something (is it the heart?) in my case feels like leather & cannot melt. Or is it just that I am too much a coward to let the temperature rise sufficiently?

There are people who are too weak to vomit. I am one of them (KD 1, 3f.).[35]

Later on, he describes a rather different state – not one of mental constipation, not one of warmly melting into the right words or a melody, not one of violently disruptive relief. None of these metaphors characterize the tone of his philosophical writing. Only later in the diary appear remarks that, in the judgement of his readers, may describe his philosophical procedure more aptly:

Just as one seems to know quite well one's way about a hollow tooth when the dentist is probing in it, so in the course of probing thought one learns to know & recognize every space, every crevice of a thought (KD 102).[36]

IV

The exploration of Wittgenstein's "work" in the diaries began with his observation that "being able to work is in so many ways similar to being able to fall asleep." The attempt to illuminate this in terms of Wittgenstein's peculiar experimental method has shown that – like "play" or "game" – "sleep" is no contrast to "work." If "work" is exemplified in the continuous operation of a finely calibrated machine, its antonyms are "force," "talent," "intelligence," "style," and any attempt to "forcibly bring about . . . eternal life by doing good works." The following two entries, for example, explore this opposition:

A man with more talent than I is he who wakes then, when I sleep. And I sleep a lot and therefore it is easy to have more talent than I.

There is a tendency in my life to base this life on the fact that I am much cleverer than the others. But when this assumption threatens to break down when I see how much less clever I am than other people, only then do I become aware how wrong this foundation is in general even if the assumption is or were right (KD 31, 56).[37]

Once vain assumptions of talent or cleverness make way for the sleepy philosopher, once the various sheets of paper talk among themselves, philosophical grammar becomes possible.

One kneels & looks up & folds one's hands & speaks, & says one is speaking with God, one says God sees everything I do; one says God speaks to me in my *heart*: one speaks of the eyes, the hand, the mouth of God, but not of the other parts of the body:

Learn from this the grammar of the word "God"! [I read somewhere, Luther had written that theology is the "grammar of the word of God," of the holy scripture.] (KD 202f.)[38]

This movement of thought becomes possible when attention is no longer fixed on a particular relation and only when a detached spectator, a *flaneur*, lets himself be guided, effortlessly, from one thing to another. When we relax our attention on knowledge-as-the-absence-of-doubt we become aware that the usage of "I thought I knew" is continuous with the usage of "I know."[39] Similarly, when we relax our attention on kneeling-as-humility-toward-a-someone, we become aware that "Kneeling means *that one is a slave*. (Religion might consist in this)" (KD 210).[40]

This withdrawal of attention or relaxation of attachment requires a willingness to admit and accept what occurs in the movement of thought. If the clever and talented philosopher forcibly brings about eternal life by doing the good work of spelling out some truth, Wittgenstein – the sleepy philosopher – needs to muster all his courage to admit what occurs to him in his movements of thought.

At the end of October or early November 1931 Wittgenstein notes:

"I can lie like *that* – or also like *that* – or best of all, by telling the truth quite sincerely." So I often say to myself (KD 114).[41]

Indeed, throughout these diaries Wittgenstein is worried that he might be lying even when saying the truth. It is as if he first allows a thought to occur, then judges whether he has caught himself in a moment of self-deception or self-revelation.[42] As an attempt to write his life or to attain self-knowledge, the diaries are therefore characterized by editorial comments, as are his manuscripts and typescripts.

Everything or nearly everything I do, these entries included, is tinted by vanity & the best I can do is as it were to separate, to isolate the vanity & do the right thing in spite of it even though it is always watching. I cannot chase it away. Only sometimes is it not present (KD 15f.).[43]

The problem of knowledge, self-knowledge in particular, is therefore less a problem of saying something that is true but a problem of constant vigilance and courage: "The word know or recognize is misleading, after all, for it is a deed which requires courage."[44] At the same time, the problem of vanity is not a problem of character or ethical conviction that arises prior, or in addition, to the problem of epistemology or of writing philosophy. Indeed, there is no indication that Wittgenstein thought of himself as *particularly* vain. The encroachment of vanity threatens to distort *every* pursuit of an unadulterated, pure movement of thought toward self-knowledge.[45]

It is here, finally, where some of the strands of this investigation come together – and together they suggest how the diaries can be usefully read. Wittgenstein's attempt to write his life in his diaries involves philosophical work, the same kind of work that he performs in all his writing. Vigilance against vanity, and the attempt to isolate it, requires courage and only this courage makes (self-)knowledge possible. His confessions are therefore phil-osophically significant not because a truth is stated or revealed in them, but because they help him defeat a vanity that would compromise the purity of his thought. To be a philosopher expresses itself only partially in what one says:

To be an apostle is a *life*. In part it surely expresses itself in what he says, but not in that it is true but in that he says it. Suffering for the idea defines him but here, too, it holds that the meaning of the sentence "this one is an apostle" lies in the mode of its verification. To describe an apostle is to describe a life (KD 73f.).[46]

While a philosopher is not an apostle or vice versa, the performance of a philosophical thought experiment is also a way of living; and while it does not require suffering for an idea, it requires the ability to work which, in turn, requires the courage to recognize what occurs in an unadulterated movement of thought.

Wittgenstein's private "suffering of the mind" (KD 191) thus appears not as a motivation of his philosophy, but as its rehearsal.[47] As in the case of vanity, his suffering is exemplary rather than idiosyncratic. Take, for example, an entry that at first appears to be intensely personal:

The thought occurred to me that I should fast tomorrow (on Good Friday) & I thought: I will do that. But immediately afterwards it appeared to me like a commandment, as if I *had* to do it & I resisted that. I said: "I want to do it if it comes from my heart & not because I was *commanded* to." But this then is no obedience! There is no *mortification* in doing what comes from the heart (even if it is friendly or in some sense pious). You don't *die* in this, after all. Whereas you *die* precisely in obedience towards a command, from mere obedience. This is agony but can be, is supposed to be a pious agony. That's at least how I understand it. But I myself! – I confess that I do not want to die off, even though I understand that it is the higher (KD 225f.).[48]

What Wittgenstein articulates here is not his idiosyncratic inability to will-ingly surrender to a command, but the heightened awareness of an impossi-bility. Just as vanity ineluctably watches everyone in their movements of thought, a general problem is rehearsed by Wittgenstein's attempt to will the surrender of the will: his thought experiment issues in a dead end, a perfor-mative contradiction.[49]

Conclusion

Wittgenstein wrote of a space for thought in which one can sojourn further or not so far, and when one returns from it, it is from a greater or lesser distance. The diaries and typescripts involve him in the same kind of experimental movements of thought, but in the diaries he sojourns further. We read them at our own risk, hoping that from their greater distance we will be able to return to the typescripts. The diaries do not hold answers but in interesting ways complicate our conceptions of Wittgenstein's philosophical life-work or work of life.

Were P. M. S. Hacker and Cora Diamond to turn to the Koder Diaries to determine whether, according to Wittgenstein, there is a something *about* which we are to remain silent, they would find the following remark:

Is this absolute aversion against using words here some kind of flight? A flight from a reality? I don't think so; but I don't know. Let me not shy away from any conclusion, but absolutely also not be superstitious!! *I do not want to think uncleanly!* (KD 173)[50]

Wittgenstein accordingly has a profoundly paradoxical encounter with "the higher" in what is finally the most striking moment in these diaries, a moment comparable in significance to that feeling of absolute safety in a Vienna theater:[51]

Let me confess this: After a very difficult day for me I kneeled during dinner today & prayed & suddenly said kneeling & looking up above: "There is no one here." That made me feel at ease as if I had been enlightened in an important matter.

But what it really means, I do not know yet. I feel relieved. But that does not mean, for example: I had previously been in error (KD 184).[52]

Do Wittgenstein's diaries fill in the missing text? Is there a reality that compels Wittgenstein's silence? If a reading of his philosophy as doctrine does not provide answers to such questions, perhaps we need to rehearse his movements of thought:

Now I often tell myself in doubtful times: "There is no one here." and look around (KD 198).[53]

NOTES

1. *"Die Denkbewegung in meinem Philosophieren müßte sich in der Geschichte meines Geistes, seiner Moralbegriffe & dem Verständnis meiner Lage wiederfinden lassen."*

2. Such remarks on the nature and practice of philosophy accompany the *Tractatus Logico-Philosophicus* (preface, 6.5, 4.112), as well as the *Philosophical Investigations* (Preface, 126, 128); see also Wittgenstein's *Letters to Russell, Keynes and Moore* (Ithaca: Cornell University Press, 1974), pp. 68, 76.

3. The Koder Diaries are newly listed as MS 183 in G. H. von Wright's catalogue of Wittgenstein's writings, so called because they were recently discovered to be in the possession of the family of Wittgenstein's friend, Rudolf Koder. A diplomatic and normalized edition was prepared by Ilse Somavilla and published in

1997 as Ludwig Wittgenstein, *Denkbewegungen: Tagebücher 1930–1932, 1936– 1937* (Innsbruck, Austria: Haymon Verlag), 2 volumes. An English translation is forthcoming in James C. Klagge and Alfred Nordmann, eds., *Ludwig Wittgenstein: Public and Private Occasions* (Lanham: Rowman and Littlefield). Page numbers refer to the pages of the original diaries.

4. Roy Emanuel Lemoine, *The Anagogic Theory of Wittgenstein's 'Tractatus'* (The Hague: Mouton, 1975), p. 9.

5. Ray Monk, *Ludwig Wittgenstein: The Duty of Genius* (New York: The Free Press, 1990).

6. Joseph Brent, *Charles Sanders Peirce: A Life* (Bloomington: Indiana University Press, 1993).

7. For a third example, consider a collection of essays in memory of Paul Feyerabend: John Preston, Gonzalo Munévar, and David Lamb, eds., *The Worst Enemy of Science?* (New York: Oxford University Press, 2000). The fascination of friends and antagonists alike with the life of the brilliant and lovable man quite unwittingly proffers the impression that his philosophical writing was profoundly inadequate.

8. Both suggestions appear in Kimberley Cornish, *The Jew of Linz: Wittgenstein, Hitler and Their Secret Battle for the Mind* (London: Century Books, 1998).

9. Concerning the gifts to Rilke and Trakl, see pp. 106ff. in Monk, op. cit., especially pp. 110 and 126 for Wittgenstein's attitude toward Trakl's poetry. Wittgenstein's donation to the army for construction of a cannon is reported in Hermine Wittgenstein's *Familienerinnerungen,* quoted on p. 123 of Michael Nedo, ed., *Ludwig Wittgenstein: Sein Leben in Bildern und Texten* (Frankfurt: Suhrkamp, 1983).

10. *"Es ist schade daß Spengler nicht bei seinen Guten Gedanken geblieben ist & weiter gegangen ist als er verantworten kann. Allerdings wäre durch die größere Reinlichkeit sein Gedanke schwerer zu verstehen gewesen aber auch dadurch erst wirklich nachhaltig wirksam. So ist der Gedanke daß die Streichinstrumente zwischen 15–1600 ihre* Endgültige *Gestalt angenommen haben von ungeheurer Tragweite (& Symbolik). Nur sehen die meisten Menschen wenn man ihnen so einen Gedanken ohne viel drumherum gibt nichts in ihm."*

11. *"Vieles, vielleicht das Meiste berührt sich ganz mit dem was ich selbst oft gedacht habe."*

12. *"Ein Satz kann absurd erscheinen & die Absurdität seiner Oberfläche von der Tiefe, die gleichsam hinter ihm liegt verschlungen werden. Das kann man auf den Gedanken von der Auferstehung der Toten & auf andere mit ihm verknüpfte anwenden. – Was ihm aber Tiefe gibt ist die Anwendung: das* Leben *das der führt der ihn glaubt."*

13. See the Conclusion and note 53 for the diary's contribution to that debate. A third example for biographical hermeneutics might draw on one of the few coded entries, dated January 30, 1937. It helps motivate Wittgenstein's choice in the *Philosophical Investigations* and elsewhere of the example of pain, suggesting that it originates in an epistemological dilemma: "Feel physically sick; I am extraordinarily weak & have a certain feeling of dizziness. If only I could relate myself correctly to my physical condition! Even today I am still like the small boy at the dentist's, when I would also always mix up the real pain with the fear of pain & didn't really know where one ended & the other began." (*"Fühle mich körperlich krank; ich bin ausserordentlich schwach & habe ein gewisses Schwindelgefühl. Wenn ich mich nur richtig zu meinem körperlichen Zustand stellen würde! Ich bin noch heute, wie als kleiner Bub beim Zahnarzt, wo ich auch immer*

die wirklichen Schmerzen mit der Furcht vor Schmerzen vermengt habe & nicht eigentlich wusste wo das eine aufhörte & das andere anfing") (KD 157f.).

14. See note 2 above. In the Koder Diaries, Wittgenstein remarks: "An artist is 'difficult to understand' in a good sense when the understanding reveals secrets to us, not a trick which we hadn't understood." (*"Im guten Sinne 'schwerverständlich' ist ein Künstler, wenn uns das Verständnis Geheimnisse offenbart, nicht, einen Trick, den wir nicht verstanden hatten")* (KD 162).

15. Frege's and Russell's reactions to the *Tractatus Logico-Philosophicus* represent only the most prominent instances of this.

16. Oswald Spengler. *The Decline of the West – Volume 1: Form and Actuality* (New York: Knopf, 1957), p. 62: "The string instruments assumed their definitive shape in Upper Italy between 1480 and 1530."

17. The German text quoted in note 10 above continues: *"Es ist wie wenn einer glaubte daß ein Mensch sich immer unbegrenzt weiter entwickelt & man sagte zu ihm: schau, die Kopfnähte des Kindes schließen sich mit . . . Jahren & das zeigt dir schon daß die Entwicklung überall zu einem Ende kommt was sich da entwickelt ein geschlossenes Ganzes ist das einmal vollständig da sein wird & nicht eine Wurst die beliebig lang weiterlaufen kann."*

18. Thus, that we need to make something of Wittgenstein's remarks does not imply that we can make of them whatever we please: The very austerity of his style imposes discipline on our thought experiments. I cannot fully substantiate this in the remainder of this paper, but must refer to a work-in-progress on aphorism and thought experiment in Wittgenstein's *Tractatus*.

19. Matters are a bit more complicated, to be sure, in that the body of Wittgenstein's manuscripts does not just contain earlier drafts of extant material, but entire books which he might, or should have written.

20. "As in philosophy so in life seeming analogies (to what others do or are permitted to do) lead us astray." And as in life "[m]y work (my philosophical work), too, is lacking in seriousness & love of truth." *"Wie in der Philosophie verleiten uns auch im Leben scheinbare Analogien (zu dem was der Andere tut oder tun darf). . . . Es fehlt auch meiner Arbeit (meiner philosophischen Arbeit) an Ernst & Wahrheitsliebe"* (KD 88, 145: a coded entry, see also 209, 229).

21. Compare this to a difficult passage in the diaries that concludes: "If good & evil are historical at all then the divine order of the world & its temporal beginning & center are also conceivable." (*"Wenn das Gute & Böse überhaupt etwas Geschichtliches ist dann ist auch die göttliche Weltordnung & ihr Zeitlicher Anfang & Mittelpunkt denkbar")* (KD 133).

22. The entry in Wittgenstein's diary continues as follows: "This sentence can be, for example, the expression of the highest responsibility. Just imagine, after all, that you *were* placed before the judge! What would your life look like, how would it appear *to yourself* if you stood in front of him. Quite irrespective of how it would appear to *him* & whether he is understanding or not understanding, merciful or not merciful. [Blank line, then:] 'White is also a kind of black.' " (*"Denn dieser Satz z.B. kann der Ausdruck der höchsten Verantwortung sein. Denn denke doch Du würdest vor den Richter gestellt! Wie sähe Dein Leben aus, wie erschiene es Dir selbst, wenn Du vor ihm stündest. Ganz abgesehen davon, wie es etwa ihm erscheint & ob er einsichtig, oder nicht einsichtig, gnädig, oder nicht gnädig ist.)* [Blank line, then:] *'Weiß ist auch eine Art Schwarz' ")* (KD 147). The very last sentence in quotation marks inaugurates a witty movement of thought in its own right (compare a related remark of 1942 in *Culture and Value*, p. 42 [1980

edition]/49) [1998 edition]). It reflects or dramatizes the paradoxical use of "depth" in the first part of the entry. (I do not suggest that each movement of thought is isolated from all others, only that each remark occasions its own movement that may or may not implicate or bounce off prior movements.)

23. *"Ich bin in meine Art der Gedankenbewegung beim Philosophieren etwas verliebt. (Und vielleicht sollte ich das Wort 'etwas' weglassen.)* [blank line] *Übrigens heißt das nicht, daß ich in meinen Stil verliebt bin. Das bin ich nicht.* [blank line] *Etwas ist nur so ernst, als es wirklich ernst ist* [blank line] *Vielleicht, wie sich mancher gern reden hört, höre ich mich gerne schreiben? ... Die Freude an meinen Gedanken (philosophischen Gedanken) ist die Freude an meinem eigenen seltsamen Leben. Ist das Lebensfreude?"* The last of these remarks, from 1931, can also be found in *Culture and Value* (p. 22/20).

24. The exchange appears on pp. 136f. of Ilse Somavilla, Anton Unterkircher, and Christian Paul Berger, eds., *Ludwig Hänsel – Ludwig Wittgenstein: Eine Freundschaft* (Innsbruck, Austria: Haymon Verlag, 1994). An English translation is forthcoming in James C. Klagge and Alfred Nordmann, eds., *Ludwig Wittgenstein: Public and Private Occasions* (Lanham: Rowman and Littlefield).

25. *"Die Schraubenmuttern, kaum angezogen, werden gleich wieder locker, weil, was sie zusammenpressen sollen, wieder nachgibt. Ich habe immer Freude an meinen eigenen guten Gleichnissen; möchte sie nicht eine so eitle Freude sein."*

26. See, for example, KD 15, 88, 102, 115f., 130, 136, 145, 148, 205, and 222.

27. *"Man könnte sich einen Menschen vorstellen, der von seiner Geburt bis zu seinem Tod immer entweder schliefe oder in einer Art Halbschlaf oder Dusel lebte. So verhält sich mein Leben zu dem wirklich lebendigen Menschen (ich denke gerade an Kierkegaard). Wacht ein so im Halbschlaf lebender je für eine Minute auf so dünkt es ihn wunder was zu sein & er wäre nicht abgeneigt sich unter die Genies zu zählen."–"Es gibt einen Gedankenraum in dem man beim Einschlafen weiter oder weniger weit reisen kann & beim Erwachen gibt es eine Rückkkunft aus größerer oder geringerer Entfernung."–"Meine Gedanken sind so vergänglich, verflüchtigen sich so geschwind, wie Träume, die unmittelbar nach dem Erwachen aufgezeichnet werden müssen, wenn sie nicht gleich vergessen werden sollen."– "Heute gegen Morgen träumte mir, ich hätte eine lange philosophische Diskussion mit mehreren Anderen. Ich kam dabei zu dem Satz, den ich beim Aufwachen noch ungefähr wußte: 'Laß uns doch in unserer Muttersprache reden, & nicht glauben wir müten uns an unserem eigenen Schopf aus dem Sumpf ziehen; das war ja – Gott sein Dank – nur ein Traum. Wir wollen ja nur Miverständnisse beseitigen.' Ich glaube, das ist ein guter Satz."*

28. This refers to Wittgenstein's new quarters, into which he had moved eight days earlier, on October 8, 1930. A day after moving in, he complained "Even though I am with quite friendly people (or just because of it?) I constantly feel disturbed ... In my room I feel not alone but exiled" (*"Obwohl ich bei recht freundlichen Leuten bin (oder gerade deshalb?) fühle ich mich andauernd gestört ... Ich fühle mich in meinem Zimmer nicht allein sondern exiliert"*) (KD 47). On the day when he remarks on his ability to accommodate himself (October 16), he also notes that "he is generally feeling somewhat better," but still cannot work (*"Fühle mich im allgemeinen etwas besser"*) (KD 48).

29. *"Ich bin im Stande es mir in allen Lagen einzurichten. Wenn ich in eine neue Wohnung komme unter andere Umstände so trachte ich mir sobald als möglich eine Technik zurechtzulegen um die verschiedenen Unbequemlichkeiten zu ertragen und Reibungen zu vermeiden: Ich richte es mir in den gegebenen Umständen ein. Und so richte ich es mir nach & nach auch mit dem Denken ein nur daß*

das nicht einfach durch einen gewissen Grad Selbstüberwindung & Verstand geht. Sondern es muß sich von selbst herausbilden & zurechtlegen. Wie man endlich doch in dieser gezwungenen Lage einschläft. Und arbeiten können ähnelt in so vieler Beziehung dem einschlafen können. Wenn man an Freuds Definition des Schlafs denkt so könnte man sagen daß es sich in beiden Dingen um eine Truppenverschiebung des Interesses handelt. (Im einen Fall um ein bloßes Abziehen im andern um ein Abziehen, & Conzentrieren an einer Stelle)." One month later, Wittgenstein returns to this thought and uses the same military metaphor: "Sleep & mental work correspond to one another in many respects. Apparently in that both involve a withdrawal of attention from certain things." (*"Der Schlaf und die geistige Arbeit entsprechen einander in vieler Beziehung. Offenbar dadurch daß beide ein Abziehen der Aufmerksamkeit von gewissen Dingen enthalten"*) (KD 55f., see also 125).

30. *"Was mich im Schlafen stört stört mich auch im Arbeiten. Pfeifen & Sprechen aber nicht das Geräusch von Maschinen oder doch viel weniger."*

31. Compare KD 75 and 240, also 51.

32. *"Es gibt auch in der Kunst Menschen die glauben ihr ewiges Leben durch gute Werke erzwingen zu können & solche die sich der Gnade in die Arme werfen."*– *"Ich glaube meine Sätze sind meistens Beschreibungen visueller Bilder die mir einfallen."*–*"Ich schreibe öfters philosophische Bemerkungen die ich einst gemacht habe an der falschen Stelle ab: dort arbeiten sie nicht! Sie müssen dort stehen, wo sie ihre volle Arbeit leisten!"*

33. *"Ich könnte mich beinahe als einen amoralischen Nucleus sehen, an dem die Moralbegriffe anderer Menschen leicht kleben bleiben. So daß, was ich redete eo ipso nie mein Eigenes wäre da ja dieser Nukleus (ich sehe ihn wie einen weißen toten Ballen) nicht reden kann. Es bleiben vielmehr an ihm bedruckte Blätter hängen. Diese reden dann; freilich, nicht wie in ihrem ursprünglichen Zustand sondern durcheinander mit andern Blättern & beeinflußt durch die Lage in die sie der Nucleus bringt."* Might this be Wittgenstein's own elucidation of the remark that his movements of thought should be discernible in the history of his mind and its moral concepts and in an understanding of his situation? But compare KD 114.

34. As quoted by Norman Malcolm from one of Wittgenstein's lectures in *Ludwig Wittgenstein: A Memoir* (Oxford: Oxford University Press, new edition 1984), p. 43; see KD 65.

35. *"Ich leide unter einer Art geistiger Verstopfung. Oder ist das nur eine Einbildung ähnlich der wenn man fühlt man möchte erbrechen wenn tatsächlich nichts mehr drin ist? . . . Oft fühle ich daß etwas in mir ist wie ein Klumpen der wenn er schmelzen würde mich weinen ließe oder ich fände dann die richtigen Worte (oder vielleicht sogar eine Melodie). Aber dieses Etwas (ist es das Herz?) fühlt sich bei mir an wie Leder & kann nicht schmelzen. Oder ist es daß ich nur zu feig bin die Temperatur genügend steigen zu lassen? . . . Es gibt Menschen die zu schwach zum Brechen sind. Zu denen gehöre auch ich."*

36. *"Wie man sich in einem hohlen Zahn gut auszukennen scheint, wenn der Zahnarzt in ihm herumbohrt, so lernt man während des bohrenden Denkens jede Räumlichkeit jeden Schluff eines Gedankens kennen & wiedererkennen."* Drawing on the diaries, one could tell a second story about Wittgenstein's cultivation of the conditions of philosophical work. It would first consider his remarks about the production or creation of thoughts (KD 98f., 110, and 120), and then turn to the separate question of their proper arrangement (as discussed in KD 105, 108, and 125).

37. *"Ein Mann mit mehr Talent als ich ist der, der dann wacht, wenn ich schlafe. Und ich schlafe viel, darum ist es leicht mehr Talent zu haben als ich."*–*"Es ist in meinem Leben eine Tendenz dieses Leben zu basieren auf der Tatsache daß ich viel gescheiter bin als die Anderen Wenn aber diese Annahme zusammenzubrechen droht wenn ich sehe um wie wenig gescheiter ich bin als andere Menschen dann werde ich erst gewahr wie falsch diese Grundlage überhaupt ist auch wenn die Annahme richtig ist oder wäre."*

38. *"Man kniet & schaut nach oben & faltet die Hände & spricht, & sagt man spricht mit Gott, man sagt Gott sieht alles was ich tue, man sagt Gott spricht zu mir in meinem Herzen; man spricht von den Augen, der Hand, dem Mund Gottes, aber nicht von andern Teilen des Körpers: Lerne daraus die Grammatik des Wortes "Gott"!* [*Ich habe irgendwo gelesen, Luther hätte geschrieben, die Theologie sei die "Grammatik des Wortes Gottes", der heiligen Schrift.*]" More on the grammar of kneeling can be found in KD 183, 190f., 210, 225f.

39. See Wittgenstein's *On Certainty*, (Oxford: Basil Blackwell, 1969), remark 12 et al.

40. [Written in code:] *"Das Knien bedeutet, dass man ein Sklave ist. (Darin könnte die Religion bestehen.)"*

41. " '*Ich kann so lügen, – oder auch so, – oder vielleicht am besten, indem ich die Wahrheit ganz aufrichtig sage.' So sage ich oft zu mir selbst."*

42. This can be witnessed by his struggle with the notion of (honest) self-recognition in KD 96. First, he writes, "He did not seem to recognize that he was a poor sinner. Of course I can write now that I am one. But I do not recognize it or else I would." The remark breaks off and he crosses it out with a wavy line, writing next to it: "don't blather!" He then continues by remarking: "The word recognize is misleading, after all, for it is a deed which requires courage." "[*Er schien nicht zu erkennen daß er ein armer Sünder war. Ich kann nun natürlich schreiben ich sei einer. Aber ich erkenne es nicht sonst würde ich anders*] *schwätz nicht! Das Wort erkennen ist eben irreleitend, denn es handelt sich um eine Tat die Mut erfordert.*"

43. *"Alles oder beinahe alles was ich tue auch diese Eintragungen sind von Eitelkeit gefärbt & das beste was ich tun kann ist gleichsam die Eitelkeit abzutrennen, zu isolieren & trotz ihr das Richtige zu tun obwohl sie immer zuschaut. Verjagen kann ich sie nicht. Nur manchmal ist sie nicht anwesend."*

44. See note 42, above. The diary begins with the remark: "Without a bit of courage one cannot even write a sensible remark about oneself." (*"Ohne etwas Mut kann man nicht einmal eine vernünftige Bemerkung über sich selbst schreiben"*) (KD 1).

45. Wittgenstein consistently places the aphorisms of Georg Christoph Lichtenberg above the trenchant wit of Karl Kraus. This is due to Kraus's vanity and Lichtenberg's purity: "Lichtenberg's wit is the flame that can burn on a pure candle only."–"That is why vanity destroys the *value* of the work. *This* is how the work of Kraus, for example, has become a 'tinkling cymbal.' (Kraus was an *architect of sentences, extraordinarily* talented at that.)" (*"Der Witz Lichtenbergs ist die Flamme die nur auf einer reinen Kerze brennt."*–"[in code:] *Darum vernichtet Eitelkeit den* Wert *der Arbeit. So ist die Arbeit des Kraus, z.B. zur klingenden Schelle geworden. (Kraus war ein,* ausserordentlich *begabter,* Satzarchitekt)") (KD 114, 205; see also 104).

46. *"Ein Apostel sein ist ein Leben. Es äußert sich wohl zum Teil in dem was er sagt, aber nicht darin daß es wahr ist, sondern darin daß er es sagt. Für die Idee*

leiden macht ihn aus, aber auch hier gilt es, daß der Sinn des Satzes 'dieser ist ein Apostel' die Art seiner Verification ist. Einen Apostel beschreiben heißt ein Leben beschreiben." Cf. Wittgenstein's reflections on 'miracle' in KD 83f.

47. *"Die Leiden des Geistes los werden, das heißt die Religion los werden."*

48. *"Mir kam der Gedanke, ich solle morgen (am Charfreitag) fasten & ich dachte: das will ich tun. Aber gleich drauf schien es mir wie ein Gebot, ich habe es zu tun & dagegen sträubte ich mich. Ich sagte: 'Ich will es tun, wenn es mir von Herzen kommt & nicht weil es mir befohlen wird.' Aber dies ist doch kein Gehorsam! Es ist doch nicht* Ertötung *zu tun, was einem von Herzen kommt (auch wenn es freundlich oder in gewissem Sinne fromm ist). Dabei stirbst Du doch nicht. Dagegen stirbst Du gerade beim Gehorsam gegen einen Befehl, aus bloßem Gehorsam. Das ist eine Agonie, kann, soll, aber eine fromme Agonie sein. Wenigstens, so versteh' ich's. Aber ich selbst! – Ich gestehe, daß ich nicht absterben will, obwohl ich verstehe, daß es das Höhere ist."*

49. To be sure, not all experiments lead into dead ends or close conceptual spaces. Other experiments open them: "But if instead of 'belief in Christ' you would say 'love of Christ,' the paradox vanishes, *i.e.,* the irritation of *the intellect.* What does religion have to do with such a tickling of *the intellect.* (This too may belong for someone or another to their religion) It is not that now one could say: Yes, now everything is simple – or intelligible. Nothing at all is *intelligible,* it is just not *unintelligible."* (*"Sagst Du aber statt 'Glaube an Christus': 'Liebe zu Christus', so verschwindet das Paradox, d.i., die Reizung des* Verstandes. *Was hat die Religion mit so einem Kitzeln des Verstandes zu tun. (Auch das kann für den oder den zu seiner Religion gehören) Nicht daß man nun sagen könnte: Ja jetzt ist alles einfach-oder verständlich. Es ist gar nichts* verständlich, *es ist nur nicht* unverständlich*"* (KD 239).

50. *"Oder ist diese unbedingte Abneigung dagegen hier Worte zu gebrauchen eine Art Flucht? Eine Flucht vor einer Art Realität? Ich glaube nicht; aber ich weiß es nicht.* [from here on in code:] *Lass mich zwar vor keinem Schluss zurückscheuen, aber auch unbedingt nicht abergläubisch sein!! Ich will nicht unreinlich denken!"*

51. See p. 51 in Monk, op. cit.; Wittgenstein refers to it in his "Lecture on Ethics"; see James C. Klagge and Alfred Nordmann, eds. *Ludwig Wittgenstein: Philosophical Occasions* (Indianapolis, IN: Hackett, 1993), pp. 41f.

52. "[In code:] *Lass mich dies gestehen: Nach einem für mich schweren Tag kniete ich heute beim Abendessen & betete & sagte plötzlich kniend & in die Höhe blickend: 'Es ist niemand hier.' Dabei wurde mir wohl zu Mute als wäre ich in etwas Wichtigem aufgeklärt worden. Was es aber eigentlich bedeutet, das weiss ich noch nicht. Ich fühle mich leichter. Aber das heisst nicht etwa: ich sei früher in einem Irrtum gewesen."* Wittgenstein returns to this experience of, "There is no one here," three times: in KD 198, 220f., 222.

53. "[In code:] *Ich sage mir jetzt oft in zweifelhaften Zeiten: 'Es ist niemand hier.' und schaue um mich. Möge aber dies in mir nichts Gemeines werden."* Wittgenstein thus eludes the misleading dichotomy set up in the debate between P. M. S. Hacker on the one hand, Cora Diamond and James Conant on the other: They seem to agree that Wittgenstein's views (his doctrine?) entail an implicit judgement on whether or not there could be an unsayable "something," they disagree only on what that judgement is. See their contributions to Alice Crary and Rupert Read, eds., *The New Wittgenstein* (London: Routledge, 2000).

Letters from a Philosopher

JOACHIM SCHULTE

Why do we bother to occupy ourselves with a famous philosopher's life? As a life it is probably not especially interesting. More probably, it is rather boring – many hours of this life will have been spent working fairly hard and not always successfully. There may be family tragedies and love stories, acquisition of money and loss of money, but these are pretty general, even ubiquitous phenomena, nothing that helps us to understand this particular philosopher's writings. In the case of authors of the remote past, we may want to know more about the sociopolitical context in order to understand to what our philosopher was responding. In that case, however, what we require is information about the intellectual context in which he led his life, not about specific events of his private life.

Still, paying attention to a philosopher's more or less private relics by way of studying his correspondence may be helpful, especially in two respects. First, the correspondence may contain information about the genesis of the philosopher's work and may consequently shed light on questions of dating manuscripts and on what was (at a certain time) meant to replace what, what was regarded as superseded, and what a promising new start. This type of information may then be useful for judging the relative importance of some remarks as compared with others, and can thus help to decide questions of interpretation. A second type of information sometimes revealed by a philosopher's correspondence concerns questions of technique in writing his works. If we know more about a person's style of drafting his texts – for example, whether he spent a lot of time on revising this material or was generally rather satisfied with his first drafts – we shall be in a better position than before to assess the value to be ascribed to early manuscripts, later typescripts, revised versions, and so on.

Now, where Wittgenstein is concerned, his extant and accessible correspondence yields very little information of this second type, but that is not such a great loss, as we know so much about his way of working from the manuscripts and typescripts preserved, microfilmed and kept in various libraries. Information of the first kind, which might help with exegetical questions, is more sorely needed. Some information of this sort really is to be found in

Wittgenstein's correspondence, especially in his early exchanges with Russell, which can be quite instructive and contribute to our understanding of the *Tractatus*. Yet apart from these early letters, Wittgenstein's correspondence contains very little that might be thought to further our understanding of his philosophy in a direct way.

In an indirect fashion, however, a closer look at Wittgenstein's correspondence may help us gain a better understanding of Ludwig Wittgenstein the person, who was after all the author of a large number of philosophical works that many of us find great, challenging, or, in interesting ways, exceptional. Here I should like to stress two points variously connected with questions regarding the relevance of Wittgenstein's correspondence to his philosophical writings. The first point is that he himself believed that the life one decides to lead should always be in absolute agreement with what one considers right for oneself. Thus, as the works are works produced by the man, knowing why the man led a life of a certain kind is bound to help us understand why he produced works of this type and not another type, insofar as he strove to keep all aspects of his life – including his philosophical production – in perfect agreement. The second point is that evidently Wittgenstein thought that certain things may be expressed in contexts of one sort but not in contexts of another. You may say one thing in your philosophical writings addressed to a wide audience of fellow philosophers, and you may say another thing in a letter to a friend. Although both things should fit a certain pattern determined by, and in harmony with, one's views of what life one should lead, the things said in these different contexts should be different, but also complementary.

It is this complementarity that may allow us to profit from Wittgenstein's letters as tools by which to understand the man, and hence the writings that are our main reason for occupying ourselves with the man's life. Wittgenstein's letters are always letters written by a philosopher, even though he was a philosopher who rarely talked shop in his letters. The fact that in these letters he did not see fit to talk about certain things in a particular way may for example throw considerable light on the question of why there are so many subjects he kept silent about in his philosophy, although they were subjects he regarded as important and about which he, the man Ludwig Wittgenstein, held pronounced views.

A fair number of the letters and postcards written by Wittgenstein contain, or consist of, good wishes or congratulations addressed to relations and friends on occasions like Christmas or birthdays and so on. At first blush, many of these messages look rather conventional, but on closer inspection one will notice that conventions are often deliberately used to express kind feelings in a peculiar way, that the writer of these Christmas or birthday wishes is striving to get across that he is really thinking of, and about, the person to whom his felicitations are addressed. Even the briefest note of this kind is carefully crafted, but the care taken is not aimed at making a good impression. Wittgenstein does not say, "Look how clever I am at using these words"; what he means to show is, "I am thinking of you, and this is what I think. . . ."

A particularly nice example is a reply to a thank-you letter from Wittgenstein's brother-in-law Max Salzer:

Dear Maxl!

You old Schasian! Your dear letter has given me so much pleasure that I cannot help thanking you for it. Of course, the books were an idea of Helene's, for I myself should not have hit on anything better than flowers or victuals. – Moreover, I wish to communicate to you that shortly a book of mine will appear under the title 'Philosophical treasure for the home', dedicated to you and your wife. It will be printed in non-colouring printer's ink on fine hygienic paper, and every single sheet may be torn out separately.[1]

The first remarkable fact about this letter is that it begins with two forms of address. The first is a diminutive version of the addressee's Christian name, as it was probably used in the family. The second is the curious expression, *"alter Schasian,"* of which I am not sure whether it has ever been much in use anywhere, but whose only plausible meaning must be something like *"Scheißer."* Accordingly, the second line begins with words like "You old shitter," or "You old shit." In the jargon of Wittgenstein's family, this sort of word was evidently not regarded as completely outrageous, but rather as a sort of term of endearment. (This can be gathered from a letter by Wittgenstein's nephew John Stonborough to the former's old friend Ludwig Hänsel, in which he reports that the language in use at his school is so proper that not even the slightly daring expressions used at home are known there.)[2]

That curious word *"Schasian"* is written in a kind of code, a simple half-inversion of the alphabet, of which Wittgenstein in his letter remarks that Salzer's "dear wife," that is, Wittgenstein's sister Helene, may be able to decipher it. This code is familiar to Wittgenstein scholars used to working on the *Nachlaß* writings, whose paragraphs are more or less frequently interspersed with jottings written in this code. The general theory about these remarks written in code is that their content was by this means to be protected from the curious eyes of possible kibitzers. Of course there is something to this idea of shielding Wittgenstein's private thoughts, but the occurrence of a coded word in a family letter suggests another interpretation of its use. In view of the fact that the code was shared among members of the Wittgenstein family, employing it was a way of specifically addressing his relations. Using the code was in a sense similar to using special words and phrases common among members of the family and could thus serve the purpose of making it clear that the relevant words were meant as a family communication.

The sentence stating that Wittgenstein would not have hit on the idea of making a gift of books of course also contains a little joke, as Wittgenstein was known for his inclination to recommend and make presents of the books he regarded as suitable reading matter for the recipients of his attentions. Flowers and certain kinds of foodstuffs (humorously called "*Fressalien*" in the letter quoted) would perhaps be the more conventional type of present – and Wittgenstein was by no means beyond making, and expressing great pleasure about receiving, this conventional sort of gift – but I should think that everyone who knew him would have regarded giving books as even more in tune with his views and habits.

Then Wittgenstein goes on to the main joke of his letter, saying that he will shortly publish a book printed in non-colouring ink on toilet tissue under the title "Philosophical Treasure for the Home." Of course, Wittgenstein's real philosophical remarks were not for home use. His word "*Hausschatz*" suggests a rather antiquated kind of book consisting of well-known and profound sayings from once popular, but perhaps slightly faded, works by famous, but perhaps somewhat forgotten, sages whose names could be invoked to lend importance to one's own unimportant thoughts. At the same time, this joke alludes to an honest desire on Wittgenstein's part to express his own complicated and difficult ideas in as homely a fashion as possible. This reading is confirmed by the fact that the word "*Hausschatz*" is similar to the title of one of Wittgenstein's favourite books, Johann Peter Hebel's *Schatzkästlein des rheinischen Hausfreundes,* which in Wittgenstein's view succeeded in articulating profound thoughts in plain and unobtrusively folksy language.

The joke thus half-conceals a strong yearning Wittgenstein always felt, to produce a book that would, in spite of the rigor and depth of its insights, display the simplicity and accomplished brevity of a collection containing proverbs, folktales, and sound practical advice. This was the desire – and it always went together with the fear of not being able to fulfill it and the feeling that his writings were worthless. This is the anxiety behind the joke about having his work printed on toilet tissue. It may remind the reader of the following passage in a letter to Bertrand Russell, to whose request as to what to do about certain papers Wittgenstein had left behind in Cambridge before the outbreak of World War I Wittgenstein replied:

Please use my journals and notebooks for kindling. If you take 2 or 3 pages a day to light the fire, they will soon be used up, and I hope they burn well. Away with them, I say![3]

There are plenty of jokes in Wittgenstein's letters, and most of them are of a straightforward and harmless kind, even though often couched in rough language. Although Wittgenstein was certainly capable of hurting and offending his friends in his letters, he never used jokes to do so. Yet sometimes his jokes are of a definitely tough kind, when for example sending a short note to his Austrian friend Ludwig Hänsel containing very little more than a quotation from a French encyclopaedia, specifying the various ways in which a hanged man can die his terrible death and concluding with the words *"Herzlichste Grüße / Dein genauer / Ludwig Wittgenstein* ("Kindest regards / Yours exactly / Ludwig Wittgenstein").[4]

In certain contexts the jokes appear very difficult to separate from more serious matters. In a letter to his sister Helene (the wife of Max Salzer, the recipient of the letter addressing him as *"Schasian"*), Wittgenstein writes:

Dear Helene!

In your last letter you write that I am a great philosopher. Certainly, that's what I am, and yet I do not wish to learn this from you. Call me a striver for truth, and I shall rest contented. Certainly you are right in saying that every form of vanity is alien to me, and even the idolatrous veneration of my disciples is powerless against the relentlessness of my self-criticism. To be sure, often I myself am amazed at the extent of my greatness, and in spite of the enormous greatness of my capacity I feel incapable of grasping it. But that's enough now – words after all are empty vis-à-vis the richness of things.[5]

Quite obviously, this is an ambiguous and ambivalent letter (which probably dates from 1934). On the one hand, Wittgenstein is being ironic about the allusion to his greatness as a philosopher, while on the other his precise statement that he does not wish to hear his greatness affirmed by his sister seems to imply that he would not mind hearing this sort of thing from a different quarter. Moreover, wishing to be called a striver for truth could easily be regarded as a kind of false modesty, and it is by no means clear how much irony there is to be found in this expression of the wish. The remark about his lack of vanity, too, is at one and the same time a correct statement of fact and an admission of weakness, for Wittgenstein certainly wants to suggest that his self-criticism is by far not relentless enough. Even though the last two sentences about greatness and the emptiness of words appear, because of their play with clichés and their exaggerations, to be pure irony and fun, one still receives the impression that he who is talking here is not only a striver for truth but also a striver for greatness – an extremely ambitious man who regards most, or all, forms of ambition as bad form. At any rate, I do not think that any attentive reader of these lines can come away from them without feeling ill at ease. The end of the letter, on the other hand, where Wittgenstein thanks his sister for a recipe, stressing that his body also needs to be looked after, reflects the homely exuberance that characterizes so many of Wittgenstein's happiest letters to friends, and to relations in particular.

What comes to the fore in these exuberant remarks is an attitude, another side of which is given vent to through an activity Wittgenstein himself liked to call "*Blödeln.*" I find this word hard to translate. It means something like talking deliberate nonsense or cracking silly jokes, but I am afraid there may be certain nuances of the German word that are bound to get lost in translation.[6] Wittgenstein, at any rate, was extraordinarily partial to this activity and must have relished playing this game for hours. In a letter to his sister Helene, mailed a few weeks before his death in 1951, he writes in characteristic fashion:

Dear Helene!

Lately I have often thought of you, wishing I could once again crack silly jokes together with you. I have been born a century too early, for in a hundred years it will be possible to ring up Vienna from Cambridge to have silly fun on the telephone without spending a lot of money. For you, however, it may be a good thing that nowadays this is not possible yet.[7]

This is a moving statement, especially in view of the fact that Wittgenstein was doing everything to keep his last illness secret from his family. In many of his later letters he keeps warning those of his friends who knew about it not to let a word slip about his ill-health. The passage is also remarkable because in at least two respects it is connected with statements he made about his own way of doing philosophy and his position in the philosophical culture of his times. At one place he characterizes his philosophical remarks as "wisecracks," using a word probably picked up from the American pulp magazines he was so prone to devour as an antidote to a certain kind of seriousness he felt to be dangerous both to his work and his mood. Wisecracks, like Wittgenstein's beloved *Blödeleien* (or silly jokes cracked in the company of relations and friends), are a sort of jocular observation capable of bringing out the serious aspects of matters in a nonserious way.

The second relevant point implied by the apparently straightforward passage quoted above about having been born a century too early relates to Wittgenstein's feeling of untimeliness, of having to live and work in a cultural setting alien to him and his deepest concerns. This feeling is also expressed in Wittgenstein's Prefaces to the *Philosophical Remarks,* and in the Preface to *Philosophical Investigations.* In the latter, he speaks of the poverty and darkness of his time, in which it is unlikely that his remarks will enlighten the brains of his contemporaries. Something of the same may be seen in various observations collected in *Culture and Value,* where he wonders whether his cultural ideal is a modern one or rather one stemming from the period of Robert Schumann, thus excluding the second half of the nineteenth century and presumably much of the twentieth century, too.[8] At the same time one occasionally gets the impression that Wittgenstein is writing for the future, for generations that may find his thoughts natural and self-evident to the extent that they might complain about repetitions in his writings, which he himself finds necessary in order to penetrate what appears obscure and difficult to him.[9] It may thus turn out that he was born a century too early, not only because of the inexpensiveness of making long-distance calls, but also because of the advent of a cultural atmosphere more hospitable to Wittgenstein's ideas.

Receiving birthday or Christmas greetings from Wittgenstein was nice enough. In general, however, he was not an easy man with whom to maintain a correspondence. He would jump on his friends for not having given suffi-cient thought to their choice of words, and he was given to unburdening himself in his letters in a way that could be rather demanding for their recipients. His criticism could be more than harsh, and friends who asked for it were sometimes given advice they might have preferred not to hear. What is really interesting about this sort of criticism is that in many cases it is also criticism of himself. At the very least it is interesting because it gives us an idea of what his implicit standards were and can thus tell us what he tried to achieve in his own life and work.

A remarkable, even startling example of such criticism can be found in Wittgenstein's correspondence with his friend Ludwig Hänsel, whom he had met as a prisoner of war in Cassino in 1919. After their first meeting, Hänsel wrote to his wife:

I have made the acquaintance of a young logician (he is thirty), whose intellectual significance surpasses that of all people of roughly his age, perhaps even of any people I have met to this day. He is serious, of noble naturalness, nervous, and he has a childlike capacity to take pleasure in things. His name is Wittgenstein.[10]

Hänsel, who wrote these words of praise, was a schoolmaster with many theoretical interests. He made a partly pedagogical, partly political carreer, was a member of all kinds of associations and committees, and a dedicated catholic who even tried to persuade Wittgenstein – of all people – to read edifying books by religious authors. Hänsel, like other friends of Wittgen-stein's, was soon accepted and liked by other members of the Wittgenstein family and remained one of Ludwig Wittgenstein's closest friends for the rest of his life. One day Hänsel seems to have asked Wittgenstein to read a couple of papers he had written; moreover, he must have urged Wittgenstein to comment on them. Now in 1937, while Wittgenstein was working on the first version of what became *Philosophical Investigations,* he wrote a very long letter to Hänsel beginning with words to the effect that he did not feel able to send extensive comments; he would content himself with "mere remarks" and hoped these remarks would help rather than hurt Hänsel. Then he goes on to say:

In your first paper you write: 'Again and again allusions to contradictions are the strongest argument against everything "absolute" used by shallow and lazy minds.' At that point I inserted the words 'and in favour of the absolute too.' That, however, does not prove anything either against or for the absolute, it only means that, as long as a mind is shallow and lazy, he should not argue for or against the absolute. And, my friend, if it isn't a shallow and lazy mind which speaks from your paper, I don't know where these words are to be applied! – What a mixture of insufficiently digested and thought-through material! In addition there is lack of thoroughness, for example the fourth dimension, a paradox of science?! Who has told you that? And what do you know about 'matter which turns into energy'? Is an expression which sounds paradoxical to the uninformed a paradox?! – When I read this paper it reminds me of vomit: half-digested morsels of food and saliva. I do not want to continue this comparison. – And these big words! Any error made by a real thinker contains infinitely more truth than such tepidly served truths (supposing they are truths; or rather, supposing it's possible to express truths by means of these words). Here too what is cold stands nearer to heat than what is tepid.[11]

The principles expressed in this passage are then elaborated in the rest of the letter as well as in two further letters to Hänsel. The first point that may strike the reader is that what arouses Wittgenstein's interest is more the way one thinks or talks about a subject than the content of these thoughts or statements. According to Wittgenstein, mistakes made by real thinkers contain more truth than seemingly true sentences uttered by shallow minds. This, however, is so not for the reason that these thinkers are such important or generally valuable people, but rather because they deal with problems in a thorough fashion. They take problems seriously – in particular, they make us see that there really are problems to grapple with – and do not try to get away with superficial solutions. As Wittgenstein says in another passage of this letter, to do something well costs a very high price. This is a recurrent thought in Wittgenstein's occasional remarks: that one could put price tags on thoughts. The currency in which you pay for thoughts is courage, as he says. Cheap thoughts do not require much courage, costly thoughts demand a lot.[12] The kind of courage intended by Wittgenstein, I suppose, is chiefly the kind you need to struggle with yourself, to fight the shallowness and laziness to be found in yourself, which may recommend taking the easy road to a cheap thought that may be true in one sense but would never deserve being called true in the relevant sense.

This notion is connected with the metaphorical use of temperature – hot, cold, tepid – by Wittgenstein. He says that, in these matters, heat and coldness stand nearer to each other than either does to tepidness. Of course, here heat and coldness signify not degrees of temperature, but certain attitudes. Both are extremes whereas tepidness does not amount to having a little bit of something; it means lacking something, whether enthusiasm or seriousness or thoroughness. Heat or coldness in your attitude show that you are really participating in what is going on; they show that you are not indifferent. This comes out in remarks like the following from Wittgenstein's comments on Frazer's *Golden Bough,* where he says that "the ceremonial (hot or cold) as opposed to the haphazard (lukewarm) characterizes piety."[13] He also says that all wisdom is cold and that therefore it does not serve to put order into one's life.[14] That may mean that wisdom is not always useful, but it also means that at least it is not tepid; it does not entail an indifferent attitude, which, as we may gather, is the one most hostile to real thinking of the kind for which Wittgenstein wants us to strive.

Another important point made in the quoted passage from the letter to Hänsel is the danger of waffling, the tendency to repeat and expatiate on predigested and possibly shallow thoughts, taken for granted and never questioned. The attitude expressed here runs through all of Wittgenstein's writings. It can be found in the motto of the *Tractatus,* in remarks from all periods of his philosophical development, and in his correspondence. What is typical is that it is often connected with disgust for the seemingly philosophical pronouncements of famous scientists and the popularized science perpetrated by what Wittgenstein would have called "journalists." In a later passage of the same letter to Hänsel, Wittgenstein writes:

I have for example thoughts (and not bad ones) about the popular-scientific scribbling of modern scientists; but I do not have the capacity to let people know about my opinion in the shape of polemical writings. I do not have the relevant gift; and I have to get across my conviction, which is important to me, in a far less direct manner. – If another person is able to do this well, it does not mean that I am able to do so too; and if another person does it badly, then this is not a reason which allows me to do it equally badly! (By the way, in this case I am completely clear about my incapacity, and therefore I am not in the least tempted here to make a fool of myself.)[15]

Several points made in this passage are noteworthy. First of all, Wittgenstein evidently regards it as an essential part of the morality of good writing to abstain from saying what you feel unable to express in a suitable manner. Perhaps this sort of abstention is one of the things for which one would need the courage demanded by costly thoughts. Secondly, you should do before an audience only what you are gifted to do well. You may have fine opinions, and they may be important to you, but that does not give you a right to utter them in public unless you are able to present them in satisfactory form. I suppose that this involves a question of honesty: if you are unable to express a thought in the form demanded by this thought, then you fail to speak the entire truth. Here the quotation reveals an interesting detail. It suggests that Wittgenstein would have wished to produce polemical writings about the popularized science of his day; but he felt he should not do it because he believed himself insufficiently talented for this job. As becomes clear from this letter, he did not feel that the direct way of saying something was necessarily the best way of doing so. He thinks that he himself ought to use an indirect way to reach his goal. This is a hint commentators on Wittgenstein's work would disregard at their peril.

The tone of Wittgenstein's letters seems largely to depend on the relation that he perceives to exist between himself and the addressee in question. This impression may be generalized. He seems to have found it impossible to remain indifferent to the people with whom he had any dealings. Even people he did not have anything to do with could affect his mood – their mere presence was enough to make him feel good or, more likely, miserable. Not infrequently Wittgenstein complains in his letters that the people in whose company he finds himself are not doing him any good. On other occasions he specifically mentions the fact that the people he meets are having a positive effect on his state of mind. Thus, shortly after his arrival at Cambridge in 1929 he writes to Hänsel that people there are very nice to him and that that does him a lot of good.[16] On other occasions he writes that he feels unwell because of the people he encounters. From one of the villages in Lower Austria where he worked as a schoolmaster he writes in 1922:

Now life in this place has begun. I do not like it. – How lonely a person can be when he finds himself amongst people! In solitude one feels well and comfortable, and among these people one is isolated and left alone to an extent which I find extremely disagreeable.[17]

Similar feelings are expressed in the letters Wittgenstein writes to Russell at roughly the same time, leading to an exchange that borders on the absurd. Wittgenstein writes in October 1921:

As regards me, nothing has changed. I am still at Trattenbach, surrounded, as ever, by odiousness and baseness. I know that human beings on the average are not worth much anywhere, but here they are much more good-for-nothing and irresponsible than elsewhere.[18]

To this Russell replies in characteristic fashion:

I am very sorry you find the people of Trattenbach so trying. But I refuse to believe they are worse than the rest of the human race; my logical instinct revolts against the notion.[19]

In his next letter to Russell, Wittgenstein answers in his precise way:

You are right: The Trattenbachers are not uniquely worse than the rest of the human race. But Trattenbach is a particularly insignificant place in Austria and the Austrians have sunk so miserably low since the war that it's too dismal to talk about.[20]

Shortly afterwards, he continues in the same mode:

I have been very depressed in recent times too. Not that I find teaching in the elementary school distasteful: quite the contrary. But what's HARD is that I have to be a teacher in this country where people are so completely and utterly hopeless. In this place I have not a single soul with whom I could talk in a really sensible way. How I shall support that in the long run, God knows! I readily believe that you too found things better in China than in England, though England still is without a doubt a thousand times better than here where I am.[21]

These lamentations reach their sad culmination in a letter to Russell from Wittgenstein's next placement:

I am now in another hole, though I have to say, it is no better than the old one. Living with human beings is hard! Only they are not really human, but rather ¼ animal and ¾ human.[22]

All this does not mean that Wittgenstein was suffering from lack of contact with educated or civilized people. It was honesty and decency he needed, and it was honesty and decency he was missing in these places where he was living among "human, or rather inhuman, beings," as he writes in a letter to his friend Paul Engelmann (24.2.25). It was Engelmann who in his extremely perceptive report on Wittgenstein's Olmütz days in 1916 finds the right words to describe this side of Wittgenstein's character:

Later in life . . . [Wittgenstein] was largely indifferent to his environment and accepted the most primitive material conditions and the lowliest social milieu. He was, on the other hand, excessively sensitive to, and dependent on, the disposition of the people whom he happened to encounter.[23]

Wittgenstein himself was quite aware of his needs and difficulties with people. Thus in a letter to Norman Malcolm, written in Ireland in 1948, he says:

I haven't anyone at all to talk to here, & this is good & in a way bad. It would be good to see someone occasionally to whom one could say a really friendly word. I don't need conversations. What I'd like would be someone to smile at occasionally.[24]

Wittgenstein wanted to live in plain conditions, and he liked the company of plain people, if only they could behave in an open and friendly way.

One of the most remarkable documents of Wittgenstein's attitude to, and difficulties with, being in other people's company is a very long letter to his sister Hermine, probably written in November 1929. In this letter Wittgenstein expresses the wish to celebrate Christmas together with his family and some friends of the family. His main reason is that, without the additional presence of friends, he and his relations would not get along with each other in the right fashion. "We five brothers and sisters," he writes, "are not made in such a way that all of us together can, without the sauce of friends, be good company."[25] He then goes on to describe in detail which of the brothers and sisters can manage to talk pleasantly to each other and which other combinations make this impossible. All the brothers and sisters are rather "tough-skinned" (*scharfhäutig,* literally: "sharp-skinned"), as he says, but will mellow when together with the right sort of friends. He then continues to write:

Now I do not believe that one can say: But that's sad that we should not be able to be comfortable [*gemütlich*] by ourselves. There is nothing sad in this, but our natures are such and our most beneficial qualities are partly connected with that – We are good at talking and being sociable as long as there are only two of us – but not at playing games or things of that kind. And if you are together with others, you must do something. It is absurd to wish to be cosily [*gemütlich*] together with others if there is no connecting element – (And being companiable [*Gemütlichkeit*] as such is not an activity).[26]

In the rest of this letter Wittgenstein mentions further reasons why the presence of friends would be desirable and suggests friends who would be agreeable to most or all members of the family. He concludes by asking his sister to show this letter to his brother Paul without further comment – a request that few people except for Wittgenstein would have hit upon. This letter has many remarkable features. A particularly characteristic one is Wittgenstein's desire to spell out his reasons completely. He does not content himself with saying frankly what he thinks; he also tries hard to give all of his reasons for thinking so. What most people would find striking about this, however, is that the occasion for writing the letter seems so trifling. Most of us would probably think that a few hours together with our relations is something we can simply endure even if their company is likely to cause some strain. Wittgenstein thinks differently. In his opinion the time allotted to us is a gift, and we are responsible for making the best of it. If we do not try to do so, we are doing wrong and become open to the charge of wasting this valuable gift, that is, the time given to us. This attitude comes out in many ways in Wittgenstein's correspondence. The depth of Wittgenstein's feelings is confirmed by a story Russell tells about an afternoon spent together with Wittgenstein watching a boat race:

Wittgenstein was disgusted – said we might as well have looked on at a bull fight . . . that all was of the devil, and so on. . . . At last we got on to other topics, and I thought it was all right, but he suddenly stood still and explained that the way we had spent the afternoon was so vile that we ought not to live, or at least he ought not, that nothing is tolerable except producing great works or enjoying those of others, that he has accomplished nothing and never will, etc. – all this with a force that nearly knocks one down.[27]

In a way Russell was right. Producing great works and enjoying those of others were certainly among those activities that played a particularly important role in Wittgenstein's life and thinking. This was so not only in the sense that Wittgenstein spent a lot of time listening to music and reading books as well as trying to write a work of his own. Questions of how to produce and how to appreciate great works were in a way the model for Wittgenstein's general mode of thinking. Many moves in his strictly philosophical writings can be seen to be inspired by his way of attending to works of art.

Wittgenstein's correspondence also reflects his interest in works of art. By this I do not mean his many recommendations of certain books to friends and pupils, such as telling Russell to read Lessing, Lichtenberg, Mörike, and Goethe, or his suggesting to people that they occupy themselves with Tolstoy or study books on Mozart and Beethoven. What I do mean are remarks expressing Wittgenstein's critical appreciation of certain works and his endeavour to articulate his insights in a manner that might succeed in leading others to look at these works in a similar manner. In letters to his family one can find quite a number of remarks of this kind, wherein Wittgenstein strives to show why a certain passage in a Beethoven symphony should be played this way but not that, or passages wherein he explains why he considers it wrong to play a Bruckner symphony as it was played at yesterday's concert or was to be heard from a record he was sending as a present.

It is not only music that Wittgenstein discusses in his letters. There are many interesting and insightful remarks on works of literature, as well. An especially striking one is to be found in a well-known letter to Norman Malcolm, who, in a previous letter, had quoted from Tolstoy's *Resurrection.* To this, Wittgenstein replied:

I once tried to read 'Resurrection' but couldn't. You see, when Tolstoy just tells a story he impresses me infinitely more than when he addresses the reader. When he turns his back to the reader then he seems to me most impressive. . . . It seems to me his philosophy is most true when it's latent in the story.[28]

These lines may remind some readers of Wittgenstein's own behavior in literally turning his back on members of the Vienna Circle while reading to them poems by Rabindranath Tagore. On the other hand, it also expresses, and implies an argument for, an aesthetic judgement, which goes a little beyond aesthetics by claiming that there are occasions on which you may talk philosophy and other occasions on which you should just get on with your story, without any admixture of philosophical talk. Moreover, this passage can be read as a hint how to read Wittgenstein himself. After all, some of his philosophy is likewise latent in stories and similes and is thus bound to lose much of its force when spelled out in ordinary philosophical parlance.

It is not only music and literature that Wittgenstein mentions in his letters. He also talks about architecture and pictures, especially photographs, and about pictures he speaks in a way that strikes one as particularly instructive. In one of his last letters to his sister Helene he writes:

I received a reproduction of the drawing of [Josef] Labor, and because of that glossy paper, the badly chosen scale of reduction and the ugly tone of the black areas of the photograph it is not as beautiful as it could be. When I look at it through tissue paper it is none the less very impressive. I shall try to have the reproduction photographed on decent paper and slightly reduced in size (perhaps ¾ of the reproduction).[29]

Here as elsewhere, Wittgenstein pays attention to all manner of details, the kind of paper, the size of the picture, the shades of the colors. In similar spirit, he replies to his sister Hermine, who had sent him a drawing she had done, first by criticizing her draughtsmanship and, secondly, by pointing out that the presentation of the picture was all wrong. He then goes on to report that immediately after his reception of the gift he proceeded to improve on the picture by cutting away the margins and placing what remained after this operation on differently colored paper. Wittgenstein writes:

I straight away cut off the white parts around the drawing and then put it on brown wrapping paper, and so it has gained a certain charm for me.[30]

Now what could be a better image of Wittgenstein's own way of working on his philosophical writings? Pruning and changing the context of his re-marks, he spent an enormous amount of time cutting and reshuffling them in order to get things exactly right. Another statement of this attitude can be found in a letter to his friend Hänsel, who had sent him a photograph. Wittgenstein replies:

Thank you for the photograph! I confess that I should have liked it even better if it had been a picture on which you looked – I should almost say – less roguish. But I have trimmed it in such a way that all you can see now are the two heads and a little bit of chest and shoulders, and now I like it well enough. Of course I know that the impression of patriarchal merriness given by the picture has come about in a com-pletely unintentional way. But I always prefer a simple, sober and, if possible, serious photograph to a genre piece, however natural it may be. – I shall write a Laokoon for photographers.[31]

The mention of *Laokoon* is of course an allusion to Lessing's treatise on the limits of what can be represented by different art forms. The notion of Wittgenstein's writing a treatise of this kind seems absolutely fantastic. The idea is just as unrealistic as that of his writing a polemical piece on the declarations of scientists who try to discuss discoveries and theories in a popular manner. The allusion does show, however, that this was a subject that greatly mattered to him and upon which he would have liked to write a treatise had he possessed the gift to produce such a book. Probably it would have been a good book, as Fania Pascal suggests in her account of Wittgen-stein as a photographer and a critic of photographs. She writes that she was told by Francis Skinner that:

Wittgenstein would devote hours to shaving off tiny slivers from the small photos he took before he would be satisfied with some kind of balance achieved. Certainly when he gave me my copies they were much reduced from the original size; one was now smaller than an inch square. During the Spanish Civil War Wittgenstein, seeing in our room an enlarged photograph of John Cornford, who had just been killed in Spain, sniffed: 'They think you can just enlarge a photo. Now look. It's all trousers.' I looked, and of course, he was right.[32]

As I said, Wittgenstein's manner of treating pictures reflects that of his own philosophical remarks, but it reflects something else, too, something extremely characteristic of his general attitude. On the one hand, it is connected with his interest in our immediate reactions to certain words and situations, his emphasis on gut feelings and our instinctive reactions to expressions of pain or emotion, and his view that this kind of reaction is often more relevant to philosophy – and less misleading – than the reasoned accounts we give of our impressions. This is brought out in his reflections on aesthetics, for instance, where he focuses on rather inarticulate exclamations accompanying our directions aimed at getting a certain performance exactly right. Thus in in his Lectures on Aesthetics he said:

> 10. Perhaps the most important thing in connection with aesthetics is what may be called aesthetic reactions, e.g. discontent, disgust, discomfort. . . .

> 15. If I ask [with respect to a door I am constructing]: "If I make it lower will your discomfort cease?" you may say: "I'm sure it will." The important thing is that I say: "Too high!" It is a reaction analogous to my taking my hand away from a hot plate – which may not relieve my discomfort. The reaction peculiar to this discomfort is saying 'Too high' or whatever it is.[33]

On the other hand, Wittgenstein's way of treating pictures is connected with his extremely acute sense of what is fitting in a certain situation. This comes out in his strict views on what can, and what cannot, be said in a letter, in a conversation, or in a philosophical work. The notion of fittingness was of philosophical relevance, too. Thus in *Philosophical Investigations* he wonders, for example, in what way one may say that the meaning of a word fits the sense of a sentence.[34] In other contexts he ponders the question of why we have the feeling that certain names fit certain people or why we think that Schubert's name appears to fit his music.

Wittgenstein's remarkable sense of what is fitting colors his whole attitude toward philosophy and life in general. This becomes clear if one remembers all of the things he felt he could not talk about in his philosophy even though they were of the greatest importance to him. He could not do any kind of moral philosophy, as he knew of no fitting words to express ethical views in a philosophical context. He did not even know of words suitable to deny the possibility of ethics. Thus, in a conversation reported by Friedrich Waismann, he said – adapting a quip taken from Schopenhauer – that preaching a moral sermon is hard, but giving foundations to a system of morals is impossible.[35] This word 'impossible,' I suspect, does not merely allude to a theoretical impossibility, but also to a sense of that word in which we may say that someone is wearing an impossible hat or has chosen a tie with an impossible pattern.

As I pointed out before, Wittgenstein's remarkable sense of what is fitting puts a certain stamp on his whole attitude toward philosophy and life. His ceaseless work on pruning and arranging his philosophical remarks bears witness to this attitude. He also wanted to arrange his life in such a way that everything that did not fit was cut out and that only fitting words were said by him in suitable situations. He even wished he could arrange things in a way that his death would reach him in a fitting moment. In this mood, he wrote the following astonishing passage in a letter to his friend Paul Engelmann, with which I will conclude:

I know that brilliance – the riches of the spirit – is not the ultimate good, and yet I wish now I could die in a moment of brilliance.[36]

NOTES

1. Ludwig Wittgenstein (L W) to Max Salzer, 23.3.37, *Familienbriefe* (*FB*), ed. Brian McGuinness, Maria Concetta Ascher, Otto Pfersmann (Wien: Hölder-Pichler-Tempsky, 1996) no. 125, p. 157 (translations from *Familienbriefe* by J. Schulte). [*Lieber Maxl! Du alter Hxszhrzn!* Dein lieber Brief hat mich so gefreut, daß ich mich nicht entbrechen kann, Dir dafür zu danken. Die Bücher waren natürlich die Idee der Helene, da mir nichts Besseres eingefallen wäre, als Blumen oder Fressalien. – Noch will ich Dir mitteilen, daß in Kürze von mir ein Büchlein erscheinen wird unter dem Titel 'Philosophischer Hausschatz,' Dir und Deiner Frau zugeeignet. Es ist auf dünnem hygienischen Papier mit nicht abfärbender Druckerschwärze gedruckt und jedes Blatt kann einzeln herausgerissen werden. – . . . * Dieses Wort ist in einer Chiffre geschrieben, die vielleicht Deine liebe Frau herausbringen kann.*]

2. John Stonborough to Ludwig Hänsel (LH), 30.5.27, *Ludwig Hänsel – Ludwig Wittgenstein: Eine Freundschaft* (*Hä-Wi*), ed. Ilse Somavilla, Anton Unterkircher, Christian Paul Berger (Innsbruck, Austria: Haymon Verlag, 1994) no. 166, p. 105: *Nicht einmal unsre Haussprache mit ihren verschiedenen A, O, Sch Lauten kennt man hier.*

3. L W to Bertrand Russell (BR), [1922], *Cambridge Letters* (*CL*), ed. Brian McGuinness and Georg Henrik von Wright; trans. Brian McGuinness, (Oxford: Basil Blackwell, 1995), no. 101, p. 178. [*Meine Tagebücher und Notizen verwende, bitte, zum einheizen. Wenn Du täglich 2–3 Blätter zum Feueranzünden benützt*

*werden sie bald aufgebraucht sein und ich hoffe sie werden gut brennen. Also –
weg damit!*]

4. L W to L H [Frühjahr/Sommer 1929?], Somavilla et al., *Hä-Wi*, no. 185, p. 115
   (translations from the Hänsel correspondence by J. Schulte).

5. L W to Helene Salzer [1934], McGuinness et al., *FB*, no. 116, p. 147. [*Liebe
   Helene! Du schreibst in Deinem letzten Brief, ich sei ein großer Philosoph.
   Gewiß, ich bin's, und doch möchte ich's von Dir nicht hören. Nenn' mich einen
   Wahrheitssucher und ich will's zufrieden sein. Gewiß Du hast recht, jede Eitelkeit
   ist mir fremd und selbst die abgöttische Verehrung meiner Schüler vermag nichts
   gegen die Unerbittlichkeit meiner Selbstkritik. Freilich, ich muß es zugeben, meine
   Größe setzt mich oft selbst in Staunen und ich kann sie nicht fassen trotz der
   enormen Größe meines Fassungsvermögens. Aber nun genug der Worte, wo doch
   Worte nur leer sind gegenüber der Fülle der Dinge. Mögest Du ewig . . . Dein
   Ludwig P. S. Ich danke Dir herzlich für das Rezept, denn auch mein Leib bedarf
   der Pflege.*]

6. In an English letter to his friend Roy Fouracre he writes: "What I miss most is
   someone I can talk nonsense to by the yard" (9.11.46). Quoted in Ray Monk,
   Ludwig Wittgenstein: The Duty of Genius (London: Jonathan Cape, 1990), p. 493.

7. L W to Helene Salzer, 15.3.51, McGuinness et al., *FB*, no. 176, p. 202. [*Liebe
   Helene! Ich habe in der letzten Zeit oft an Dich gedacht, mit dem Wunsche, ich
   könnte wieder einmal mit Dir blödeln. Ich bin ein Jahrhundert zu früh auf die
   Welt gekommen, denn dann in 100 Jahren wird man ohne große Kosten Wien von
   Cambridge anrufen und ein Stündchen am Apparat blödeln können. Allerdings
   für Dich ist es vielleicht wieder gut, daß das heute noch nicht möglich ist.*]

8. Ludwig Wittgenstein, *Culture and Value,* ed. G. H. von Wright; trans. P. Winch
   (Chicago: University of Chicago Press, 1980); rev. 2d. ed. [Oxford: Basil Blackwell, 1998], p. 2/4.

9. Wittgenstein, *Culture and Value,* p. 1/3.

10. L H to Anna Hänsel, 20.2.19, Somavilla et al., *Hä-Wi*, p. 15. [*Ich habe einen
    jungen (30 jährigen) Logiker kennen glernt, der gedanklich bedeutender ist als
    alle etwa Gleichaltrigen vielleicht überhaupt als alle Menschen, die ich bis jetzt
    kennen gelernt habe – ernst, von edler Selbstverständlichkeit, nervös, von einer
    kindlichen Fähigkeit, sich zu freuen. Er heißt Wittgenstein.*]

11. L W to L H, 9.2.37, Somavilla et al., *Hä-Wi*, no. 232, p. 140. [*Du schreibst im
    ersten Aufsatz: 'Der Hinweis auf Widersprüche ist immer wieder das stärkste
    Argument in der Hand des flachen & und bequemen Geistes gegen alles "Abso-
    lute." 'Und auch für,' schrieb ich hinein. Aber das beweist natürlich nichts gegen
    oder für das Absolute, & es heißt nur, daß, solang der Geist flach & bequem ist,
    er nicht für oder gegen das Absolute argumentieren soll. Und Freund! wenn der
    flache & bequeme Geist nicht aus Deinem Aufsatz spricht, so weiß ich nicht, wo
    diese Worte anzuwenden sind! – Welch ein Gemengsel von ganz ungenügend
    Verdautem & Durchdachtem! Dazu die Ungründlichkeit: Z.B. Die vierte Dimen-
    sion, ein Paradox der Wissenschaft?! Wer hat Dir das gesagt? Und was weißt Du
    von der 'Materie, die sich in Energie verwandelt'? Ist ein, den Uninformierten
    paradox klingender Ausdruck ein Paradox?! – Wenn ich in diesem Aufsatz lese,
    so erinnert er mich an das, was einer erbricht: halbverdaute Speisebrocken &
    eigener Schleim. Ich will den Vergleich nicht fortsetzen – Und die großen Worte!
    Jeder Irrtum eines wirklichen Denkers enthält unendlich viel mehr Wahrheit als
    solche lau aufgetischte Wahrheiten (angenommen, daß es Wahrheiten sind; oder*]

*besser: angenommen, daß sich mit diesen Worten auch Wahrheiten sagen lassen.).
Auch hier ist das Kalte dem Warmen näher, als das Laue.*]

12. Wittgenstein, *Culture and Value*, p. 52/60.
13. "Remarks on Frazer's *Golden Bough*," in Ludwig Wittgenstein, *Philosophical Occasions: 1912–1951*, ed. James Klagge and Alfred Nordmann (Indianapolis, IN: Hackett, 1993), p. 127.
14. Wittgenstein, *Culture and Value*, p. 53/61.
15. L W to L H, Somavilla et al., *Hä-Wi*, no. 232, pp. 141–2. [*Ich habe z. B. Gedanken (& nicht schlechte) über die populär-wissenschaftliche Schreiberei der heutigen Wissenschaftler; aber es ist mir versagt meine Meinung in Form von polemischen Schriften Leuten mitzuteilen. Ich habe die entsprechende Gabe nicht; & muß meine Überzeugung, die mir wichtig ist, auf anderem, weit weniger direktem, Wege an den Mann bringen. – Darum, weil ein Andrer das gut kann, kann ich es noch nicht; und darum weil ein Andrer wieder es schlecht macht, darf ich es nicht auch schlecht machen! (Mir ist übrigens in diesem Falle meine Unfähigkeit ganz klar, & ich bin daher gar nicht in Versuchung hier eine Dummheit zu machen.)*]
16. L W to L H, Somavilla et al., *Hä-Wi*, no. 181, p. 113.
17. L W to L H, 21.9.22, Somavilla et al., *Hä-Wi*, no. 91, p. 68. [*Jetzt hat also das Leben hier angefangen. Es gefällt mir nicht. – Wie einsam ist doch ein Mensch, wenn er unter Menschen ist! In der Einsamkeit fühlt man sich wohl und behaglich, und unter diesen Menschen ist man so verlassen und allein, daß es mir höchst unangenehm zu mute ist.*]
18. L W to B R, 23.10.21, McGuinness and von Wright, *CL*, no. 96, p. 169.
19. B R to L W, 5.11.21, McGuinness and von Wright, *CL*, no. 97, p. 171.
20. L W to B R, 28.11.21, McGuinness and von Wright, *CL*, no. 98, p. 173. [*Du hast recht: nicht die Trattenbacher allein sind schlechter, als alle übrigen Menschen; wohl aber ist Trattenbach ein besonders minderwertiger Ort in Österreich und die Österreicher sind – seit dem Krieg – bodenlos tief gesunken, daß es zu traurig ist, davon zu reden!*]
21. L W to B R, [1922], McGuinness and von Wright, *CL*, no. 101, p. 178. [*Ich bin in der letzten Zeit auch sehr niedergeschlagen. Nicht daß mir das Lehren an der Volksschule zuwider ist. Im Gegenteil! Aber SCHWER ist es, daß ich in diesem Lande Lehrer sein muß, wo die Menschen so ganz und gar hoffnungslos sind. Ich habe in diesem Ort nicht eine Seele mit der ich ein wirklich vernünftiges Wort sprechen könnte. Wie ich das auf die Dauer aushalten werde weiß Gott! Ich glaub' Dir's gern daß auch Du es in China schöner gefunden hast als in England obwohl es in England zweifellos noch tausendmal besser ist als bei uns.*]
22. L W to B R, [November or December 1922], McGuinness and von Wright, *CL*, no. 103, p. 182. [*Ich bin jetzt in einem anderen Nest, wo es freilich auch nicht besser ist als in dem Vorigen. Es ist schwer mit den Menschen zu leben! Aber es sind ja eigentlich gar keine Menschen sondern ¼ Tiere und ¾ Menschen.*]
23. Paul Engelmann, *Letters from Ludwig Wittgenstein: With a Memoir*, ed. B. F. McGuinness; trans. L. Furtmüller (Oxford: Basil Blackwell, 1967), p. 60. [Engelmann. *Ludwig Wittgenstein: Briefe und Begegnungen*, ed. B. F. McGuinness, (Wien – München: Oldenbourg, 1970), p. 41. [. . . *später war es ihm . . . im allgemeinen gleichgültig, ob er in diesen oder jenen Umständen der äußeren Umgebung, und seien es selbst die primitivsten und gesellschaftlich niedrigsten, sich aufhalte; anderseits war er übertrieben empfindlich und abhängig von der Art der Menschen, mit denen er gerade zusammenkam.*]

24. Norman Malcolm, *Ludwig Wittgenstein: A Memoir*, 2d ed. (Oxford: Oxford University Press, 1984), no. 26, p. 107.
25. L W to Hermine Wittgenstein [November 1929], McGuinness et al., *FB*, no. 92, p. 118. [... *daß nicht einmal wir 5 Geschwister ... so geartet sind daß wir alle zusammen und ohne die Sauce der Freunde eine gute Gesellschaft geben.*]
26. McGuinness et al., *FB*, p. 119. [*Nun glaube ich durchaus nicht, daß man sagen kann: Das ist aber traurig, daß wir nicht im Stande sein sollten, unter uns allein gemütlich zu sein. Daran ist gar nichts traurig, sondern unsere Naturen sind so und unsere ersprießlichsten Eigenschaften hängen zum Teil damit zusammen. – Unter uns taugen wir zum Gespräch d. h. zur Geselligkeit zu zweit – aber nicht eigentlich zu Spielen u. dergleichen. Und wenn man beisammen ist, muß man Etwas tun. Es ist ein Unding gemütlich beisammen sein zu wollen ohne daß alle etwas verbindet. – (Und die Gemütlichkeit ist an sich keine Tätigkeit).*]
27. B R to Ottoline Morrell, 9.11.12, in Brian McGuinness, *Wittgenstein: A Life: Young Ludwig 1891–1921* (London: Duckworth, 1988), p. 112.
28. Malcolm, *Memoir*, no. 15, p. 98.
29. L W to Helene Salzer, 15.3.51, McGuinness et al., *FB*, no. 176, p. 202. [*Ich habe eine Reproduktion der Labor Zeichnung gekriegt und sie ist leider durch das glänzende Papier, eine schlecht gewählte Verkleinerung und den hässlichen Ton, den die Schwärzen auf der Photographie haben, nicht so schön, als sie sein könnte. Wenn ich sie aber durch Seidenpapier anschaue, so ist sie doch sehr eindrucksvoll. Ich will versuchen, die Reproduktion in etwas verkleinertem Maßstabe (vielleicht ¾ der Reproduktion) auf anständiges Papier photographieren zu lassen.*]
30. L W to Hermine Wittgenstein, [November 1929], McGuinness et al., *FB*, no. 90, p. 116. [*Ich habe sofort das weiße rund um die Zeichnung weggeschnitten und sie auf ein braunes Packpapier gelegt und so hat sie einen gewissen Reiz für mich ...*]
31. L W to L H, 10.9.38, Samavilla et al., *Hä-Wi*, no. 244, p. 149. [*Dank Dir für die Photographie! Ich gestehe, ein Bild, auf dem Du weniger – beinahe hätte ich gesagt – schelmisch ausschaust, wäre mir noch lieber gewesen. Aber ich habe es so beschnitten, daß nur die beiden Köpfe & etwas von Brust & Schultern zu sehen ist & jetzt gefällt es mir ganz gut. Ich weiß natürlich, daß der altväterisch lustige Eindruck des Bildes gänzlich unbeabsichtigt zustandegekommen ist; aber mir ist eine einfache, trockene &, womöglich, ernste Photographie immer lieber als eine Genrescene, so natürlich sie auch sein mag. – Ich werde einen Laokoon für Photographen schreiben.*]
32. Fania Pascal, "Wittgenstein: A Personal Memoir," in Rush Rhees, Ed., *Recollections of Wittgenstein* (Oxford: Oxford University Press, 1984), p. 28.
33. Wittgenstein, *Lectures and Conversations on Aesthetics, Psychology and Religious Belief*, ed. Cyril Barrett (Oxford: Basil Blackwell, 1970), pp. 13–14.
34. Cf. *Philosophical Investigations*, ed. G. E. M. Anscombe and R. Rhees; trans. G. E. M. Anscombe (Oxford: Basil Blackwell, 1953), § 138.
35. Friedrich Waismann, *Wittgenstein und der Wiener Kreis*, ed. B. F. McGuinness (Oxford: Basil Blackwell, 1967), p. 118.
36. Engelmann, *Letters*, no. 51, pp. 55–7. [*Ich weiß daß Geistreichtum nicht das Gute ist und doch wollte ich jetzt, ich könnte in einem geistreichen Augenblick sterben.*]

Wittgenstein and Reason

HANS-JOHANN GLOCK

Wittgenstein and reason: this is perhaps the most important topic of current Wittgenstein scholarship. Among the fundamental issues it is the most contested, and among the contested issues it is the most fundamental. There is no dearth of disagreement on, for example, the private language argument, the rule-following considerations or his philosophy of mathematics. Yet these topics are not as fundamental as Wittgenstein's attitude toward reason. For here we are dealing with the question of what kind of thinker Wittgenstein was. Was he a proponent of the claims of reason, of rational argument, justification and clarification? Or was he an enemy of such Enlightenment ideals? Was he even a philosopher in the traditional sense, or rather a sage, prophet, or guru?

Opinion on these matters divides roughly into two camps: rationalist and irrationalist interpretations.[1] Originally, Wittgenstein's work was seen simply in the context of the logical and methodological debates arising from Frege, Russell, and the logical positivists. He was treated as a member of the analytic tradition, albeit a highly exotic and troublesome one. Since that tradition prides itself on its concern with argument and justification, and even defines itself by reference to this priority, it would seem that Wittgenstein was part of *The Dialogue of Reason* (Cohen 1986; see also Føllesdal 1997). Later, through the efforts of Stenius, Pears, Hacker, and Garver, it was recognized that there is a strong Kantian element to both the early and the later work. But this did not threaten Wittgenstein's image as either an analytic philosopher or a proponent of reason. Strawson and Bennett had sanitized the *Critique of Pure Reason,* and as a result the sage of Königsberg could be treated as an honorary analytic philosopher. In any event, Kant's critical philosophy is an eminently rationalist enterprise, namely the attempt of reason to establish its own nature and limits. In so far as Wittgenstein undertakes a linguistic transformation of this critical enterprise, he is committed to the claims of reason.

Irrationalist interpretations of Wittgenstein have been equally common. This is hardly surprising, given the mystical parts of the *Tractatus* and his later exhortations that philosophy should not provide explanations or justifications. One can distinguish the following variations on the irrationalist theme:

- Existential Irrationalism: Partly fuelled by letters and by reports from personal friends like Engelmann (1967) and Drury (1984), the mystical and ethical aspects of his work are stressed and linked to existentialist thinkers like Kierkegaard, Tolstoy, and Nietzsche (Janik and Toulmin 1973).
- Nonsense Irrationalism: Because of the saying/showing distinction and the image of kicking away the ladder, the *Tractatus* is assimilated to an existentialist joke or a protracted nonsense poem with a numbering system. Its pronouncements are not attempts to gesture at ineffable truths, but plain gibberish. They are mere performances, designed, for example, to reveal the pointless nature of all philosophy (Diamond 1991; Conant 1989).
- Therapeutic Irrationalism: On account of the famous comparisons with psychoanalysis, it is held that the grammatical remarks of Wittgenstein's later work are not conceptual clarifications, but only therapeutic attempts to make us abandon philosophical problems for the sake of intellectual tranquility (Bouwsma 1986).
- Aspect Irrationalism: A related position, according to which these grammatical remarks are not part of philosophical arguments that appeal to reason, but designed to effect a conversion in outlook analogous to the change of an aspect in aspect-seeing (Baker 1991).
- Postmodern Irrationalism: A position inaugurated by Rorty (1979), according to which Wittgenstein, along with Heidegger and the pragmatists, paves the way for an "edifying philosophy" in which the traditional concern with truth and objectivity is abandoned in favor of the hermeneutic attempt to keep a conversation going. More specifically, Wittgenstein supports Dewey's and Quine's attack on the idea that philosophy is a subject distinct from the empirical sciences.

Irrationalist interpretations are not necessarily irrational. Postmodern irrationalism is indeed postmodern, that is to say, it is entertainingly ludicrous. Rorty's heroes are held together by nothing more than diverse (and often incompatible) animadversions against either Plato or Descartes or Locke or Kant; and the suggestion that Wittgenstein was keen to dissolve philosophy into science beggars belief.

By contrast to this fanciful misinterpretation, the other versions of irrationalism all have at least some foundation in the texts and in Wittgenstein's life. But the same goes for rationalist interpretations. Thus Wittgenstein insisted that philosophy should provide arguments that are "absolutely conclusive," and he described his own thought as the "rejection of wrong arguments," which is open to those feeling a need for "transparency of their own argumentation" (MS 161, 3; PO 163, 181). That both irrationalist and rationalist approaches have a *fundamentum in rebus* is no coincidence, but reflects Wittgenstein's basic ambivalence toward the claims of reason. My essay is an attempt to explore this ambivalence at an exegetical, biographical, and methodological level. I shall argue for the following three claims:

I. There is a tension in Wittgenstein's work between a rationalist strand – his radicalization of Kant's critical philosophy – on the one hand, and an irrationalist strand – his cultural hostility toward aspects of science and the Enlightenment.

II. The root of this tension lies in Wittgenstein's intellectual biography. On the one hand, it is a legacy of Schopenhauer, who combined a critical, and thereby rational, philosophical *method* à la Kant with an anti-intellectual metaphysical *doctrine,* and in particular a pessimistic anthropology. On the other, it reflects the conflict between Wittgenstein's cultural conservativism and the sometimes superficial Enlightenment ideals of Russell and the logical positivists. In fact, some of Wittgenstein's irrationalist remarks are best understood as *personal* reactions to the actual or perceived failings (both intellectual and personal) of these propagandists of reason.

III. Neither Wittgenstein's philosophical method nor his insistence on the limits of reason are inherently irrational. One must distinguish his personal ideology, which is partly inimical to science, from his philosophical methodology, which rejects not science but scientism. Even Wittgenstein's anti-intellectualism should not be equated with irrationalism: it denies that reason and the intellect have the exalted place traditionally accorded them, but it often does so by way of rational argument.

To support these claims, I shall proceed as follows: section 1 discusses the impact of Schopenhauer and Kant; section 2 Wittgenstein's interactions with Russell; and section 3 his relation to the Vienna Circle. In section 4 I turn from biographical to methodological issues, namely the relation between antiscientism, irrationalism, and anti-intellectualism.

My general aim is to defend a rationalist understanding of Wittgenstein against the currently more fashionable irrationalist interpretations. Although Wittgenstein's cultural attitudes and his spiritual and mystical tendencies are important to an understanding of his life and his work, the philosophical value of his reflections on language, mind, and philosophy itself does not depend on them. This is fortunate, since the tendencies have much less credibility than the reflections.

1. The Legacy of Schopenhauer and Kant

There are three possible standards on claims that one thinker X influenced another Y. The weakest one is to demand no more than parallels between ideas of X and ideas of Y (e.g., Dummett 1993). The most demanding insists on a demonstration that Y adopted a specific view as a direct result of noting a similar view of X (e.g., Baker/Hacker 1983). If taken seriously, this would confine attributions of intellectual influence to cases in which Y explicitly acknowledged her debt and in which we have reasons to believe that this acknowledgment was sincere.

In my view, both extremes are misguided. The weak standard simply abandons intellectual history in favor of philosophical doxography. The demanding standard is unreasonable in particular with respect to thinkers like Wittgenstein who did not conform to academic rules of citation and acknowledgment. I therefore propose the following compromise: it is probable that X influenced Y if there are clear affinities between ideas in X and ideas in Y (including affinities of opposition) *and* X was familiar with Y's ideas through reading or conversation.

By this standard, Wittgenstein was definitely influenced by Kantian ideas on the nature of philosophy, either directly or indirectly. It was only in 1918 that he read the *Critique of Pure Reason* (Monk 1990, 158). But for the early work, Schopenhauer, Mauthner, and Hertz are possible sources with which he was familiar. Of these, Schopenhauer is the most important.

It is well known that as a young man, Wittgenstein was steeped in Schopenhauer's work. According to the testimony of his pupils, Wittgenstein read Schopenhauer as a sixteen-year-old. He was familiar with *Die Welt als Wille und Vorstellung* and *Aphorismen zur Lebensweisheit,* and perhaps with *Die vierfache Wurzel des Satzes vom Grund.* Schopenhauer's version of transcendental idealism provided the basis for his first philosophical position, which he only abandoned under the influence of Frege's conceptual realism. Wittgenstein's first philosophical writings show no trace of this influence; they are exclusively concerned with problems in the philosophy of logic and mathematics inherited from Frege and Russell. To some extent, however, he returned to Schopenhauer during World War I. It is probable that Wittgenstein reread Schopenhauer sometime during the war, presumably as a result of his experiences as a front-line soldier. In any event, the *Notebooks 1914–1916,* which contain preparatory material for the *Tractatus,* increasingly combine purely logical reflections with direct allusions to Schopenhauer (von Wright 1984, 6; McGuinness 1988, 39). In the *Tractatus* the allusions are less frequent and direct, but topics such as God, ethics, aesthetics, solipsism, the will, and mysticism are discussed in a Schopenhauerian spirit.

What is less well known is that this influence did not cease after the

Tractatus. It became more transient and remote, yet also, in the area of intentionality and the will, more relevant to current debates. What has gone largely unnoticed is that affinities to Schopenhauer's work are not confined to specific topics like solipsism, ethics, or the will, but include ideas and problems concerning the nature of philosophy (see Glock 1999). Schopenhauer combined a critical, and thereby rational, philosophical method à la Kant with an anti-intellectual metaphysical doctrine: a pessimistic view of the world and a philosophical anthropology that evolves around the notions of will and action rather than those of intellect and reason.

Schopenhauer accepts not just a Kantian distinction between a phenomenal world of appearances and a world of the thing in itself, but also Kant's critique of "dogmatic metaphysics," which includes "speculative theology" and "rational psychology" (Schopenhauer 1966 Vol. I, App., especially 417–28). He is hostile to the speculations of the pre-Kantian rationalists, and scathing about the even grander speculations of the German idealists. Any attempt to derive substantive truths about the universe and our place within it from self-evident a priori premises is futile, since such derivations can amount to no more than vacuous transformations of definitions or tacitly presupposed factual claims (Schopenhauer 1966 Vol. I, 76; 1966 Vol. II, 186).

In a similar spirit, Wittgenstein, throughout his career, regarded philosophy as a critical enterprise. Like Kant, the *Tractatus* sets philosophy the task of drawing the bounds between legitimate forms of discourse – notably the "contestable sphere of science" (TLP 4.113) – and illegitimate philosophical speculation, which Kant and Schopenhauer call "dogmatic metaphysics" and Wittgenstein simply "metaphysics." Once more in line with Kant, he claims that philosophy is not so much a doctrine that extends knowledge, but a critical activity that curbs the excesses of metaphysics and clarifies nonphilosophical thoughts – their epistemic status in Kant, their logical structure in Wittgenstein (TLP 4.112, 6.53; Kant *Critique of Pure Reason* A 11–12/B 25–6, A 735/B 763, A 850–1/B 878–9). Indeed, Kant anticipated many of the subversive methodological ideas that have put Wittgenstein in the bad books of contemporary analytic philosophers, including his contention that there are no discoveries in philosophy, only the dissolution of conceptual confusions (PI § 119). For both, philosophy is a contribution not so much to human knowledge as to human understanding.

Schopenhauer and Wittgenstein develop the idea of critical philosophy in strikingly different ways. Whereas Schopenhauer seeks to circumvent Kant's antimetaphysical restrictions, Wittgenstein radicalizes them. Both, however, can be seen as reacting to a familiar tension in Kant's position. Right from the start, Kant's successors claimed that he himself had transgressed the bounds of knowledge he was trying to set. For example, Kant is committed to the idea that things in themselves *cause* sensations in us, and thereby give rise to the material aspects of the phenomenal world. But according to Kant, causal relations are structural features imposed on the world by the human mind – they can only obtain between appearances, not between things in themselves and our sensations.

Like the German idealists, Schopenhauer reacted to this predicament by concluding that it must after all be possible to achieve knowledge that transcends possible experience. Philosophy investigates the basis and limits of the empirical knowledge provided by the sciences (Schopenhauer 1966 Vol. I, § 15). But this critical enterprise is only propaedeutic. "The world is my representation" (Schopenhauer 1966 Vol. I, § 1), namely what appears to the knowing subject. It is governed by structural features (space, time, causation) that are imposed on it by that subject. But the *world as representation* is an objectification of an underlying reality. Unlike the world of experience, this noumenal reality contains no individuals, whether material objects or agents, because it lies beyond the principle of individuation, which is provided by space and time. The thing in itself is an undifferentiated unity, a cosmic "will to life" (*Wille zum Leben*) of which human individuals are mere manifestations (Schopenhauer 1966 Vol. I, §§ 18–22). Our actions are driven, if only unconsciously, by this cosmic will, a kind of blind striving directed toward the preservation and propagation of life.

According to Schopenhauer, we can know this underlying reality, since our bodies are direct manifestations of it and since, in our voluntary actions, we have access to our own *willing,* the only event we understand "from within," not merely as a phenomenon that happens to us (Schopenhauer 1966 Vol. I, § 19; Vol. II, ch. 17). More generally, we can achieve knowledge of the world of the thing in itself by extrapolating from the world of experience. The simplest and most coherent account of the empirical data is to view them as an expression of something beyond all empirical data, an underlying thing in itself that turns out to be a cosmic will. Accordingly, what Schopenhauer objects to in dogmatic metaphysics is not the fact that it purports to extend knowledge beyond experience, but rather two other features, its optimism and its rationalism. The picture of the world as the harmonious emanation of a rational principle is nothing but wishful thinking, worthy of theology but not of philosophy. Instead of putting its speculations on the sound basis of experience, dogmatic metaphysics invokes reason, distorting it into a "wholly imaginary, false and fictitious . . . faculty of the supersensuous" (Schopenhauer 1974 § 34, especially 166, 181).

Schopenhauer's attempt to derive insights into the thing in itself from empirical observations is arguably incompatible with the critical strictures to which he purports to pay tribute. Wittgenstein's reaction to the Kantian predicament avoids these difficulties. He rejects Schopenhauer's specific doctrine that we know the thing in itself through awareness of our own willing.

More importantly, he tries to reformulate critical philosophy in a way that will rescue it from a violation of its own restrictions, namely by switching from Kant's attempt to draw the limits of *human knowledge* to a more radical attempt to draw the limits of *meaningful discourse.*

Kant tried to demarcate what we can know (phenomena or possible objects of experience) from what we cannot know (things in themselves that transcend all possible experience). From Jacobi to Bradley this has provoked the complaint that one cannot draw the distinction between the knowable realm of appearances and the unknowable realm of things in themselves without tacitly presupposing some knowledge of the latter. Wittgenstein diagnosed the same problem. "In so far as people believe that they can see the 'limits of human understanding,' they naturally also believe that they can see beyond these" (CV p. 15 in 1980 ed./p. 22 in 1998 ed.).

He avoids this problem by switching from the limits of knowledge to the limits of thought, and by conceiving of the latter as limits of meaningful discourse. Philosophy can establish the limits of thought by drawing limits to the *linguistic expression of thought.* Indeed, these limits *must* be drawn in language,

for in order to be able to draw the limits of thought, we should have to find both sides of the limit thinkable (i.e. we should have to be able to think what cannot be thought). It will therefore only be in language that the limit can be drawn, and what lies on the other side of the limit will simply be nonsense (TLP, Preface).[2]

By definition, what lies beyond the limits of thought cannot be thought, and hence cannot be meaningfully talked about. As a result, the limits of thought cannot be drawn by propositions talking about both sides, but only *from the inside* (TLP 4.113–5). Instead of issuing in doctrines about where the limits of thought lie, philosophy delineates the linguistic rules that determine whether a combination of signs makes sense, that is, is capable of representing the world. Beyond these bounds lie not unknowable noumena or things in themselves, but only nonsensical combinations of signs. Metaphysical propositions are not just false or unfounded, they are literally nonsensical.

This verdict applies, however, not just to dogmatic metaphysics but equally to any attempt to state the bounds of sense. According to Wittgenstein, Russell's Theory of Types constitutes such an attempt. To forestall the set-theoretic paradoxes, Russell prohibits, for example, a statement like

(A) The class of lions is a lion.

through a rule like

(B) "The class of lions is a lion" is nonsensical.

According to Wittgenstein, such a theory is neither possible nor necessary. (B) is itself nonsensical because, unlike propositions with a sense, it does not exclude a genuine possibility. We cannot refer to something like the class of lions being a lion by means of a meaningful expression. Hence any attempt to exclude it as logically impossible is itself nonsensical (TLP 3.03, 3.32ff.).

If correct, this verdict applies not just to Russell's Theory of Types, but also to the pronouncements of the *Tractatus*. The bounds of sense cannot be *said* in philosophical propositions, but do *show* themselves in the logical form of nonphilosophical propositions, properly analyzed. Consequently, the famous or infamous saying/showing distinction is neither an expression of existential or mystical irrationalism, nor an overblown reaction to Frege's paradox concerning the concept, *horse*. Rather, it is an ingenious and heroic, if ultimately self-defeating, attempt to resolve a fundamental problem of critical philosophy in a form posed by Russell's Theory of Types.

This is not to deny that there is plenty of mysticism in the book's claim that matters of value are ineffable. In a well-known letter to von Ficker (October/November 1919, LvF 94–5), Wittgenstein even proclaimed that the *Tractatus* "consists of two parts: of the one which is here, and of everything which I have *not* written. And precisely the second part is the important one. For the Ethical is delimited from within, . . . by my book; and I'm convinced that, *strictly* speaking, it can ONLY be delimited in this way." Yet there are reasons for regarding this as a slightly hysterical piece of self-promotion vis-à-vis a potential publisher. For it is obvious from the notes dictated to Moore in 1914 that the saying/showing distinction arose not out of ethical concerns, but out of a discussion of Russell's Theory of Types (NB 108–9). In composing the *Tractatus*, Wittgenstein grafted a mystical branch (solipsism, ethics, aesthetics) onto a prior logical trunk (logical theory, picture theory, metaphysics of logical atomism, mathematics, science). The saying/showing distinction is important not just because it is Wittgenstein's solution to an antinomy of critical philosophy, but because it holds the two parts together: both propositions about the bounds of sense and pronouncements about the realm of value can be proscribed because they are not empirical pictures of reality.

In this context it should be noted that Wittgenstein later complained that the *Tractatus* along with things "good and genuine" also contained "kitsch," passages in which he filled in gaps in his own style (DB 30–1).[3] Unfortunately, he did not single out specific parts. But in the preceding paragraph he urges us to "evaporate cheap symbolism (*Symbolik*) in a higher sphere." It is plausible to conjecture, therefore, that he meant neither the theory of tautologies nor the picture theory, with its correlated metaphysics of logical atomism, but the purple passages about ethics, aesthetics, and death.

Having introduced Wittgenstein to critical philosophy is the methodological part of Schopenhauer's influence, and it is one that stands within the tradition of rational philosophical argument. The other part is Schopenhauer's emphasis on the will and on human action as its most immediate manifestation. Schopenhauer, echoing Hume, treated the intellect "as a mere tool in the service of the will" and thought as a biological function (Schopenhauer 1966 Vol. II, 205).

This emphasis on the will at the expense of the intellect was a driving force behind life-philosophy (*Lebensphilosophie*), a movement that, through Nietzsche, influenced existentialism. With respect to mathematics, this anti-intellectualist tradition was continued by Brouwer and Spengler. Spengler was (understandably) critical of Schopenhauer's contempt for history, but he commended Schopenhauer for having recognized that the will is superior to the intellect (Spengler 1928, Vol. I, chap. 5.1.2 & 5.2.10). Wittgenstein in turn acknowledged Spengler's influence on his philosophy of mathematics (see Hacker 1986, 120–1). He was presumably alluding to the discussion of the cultural diversity and relativity of mathematics in chapter 12 of *The Decline of the West*.

There is also a more general debt to Schopenhauer and Spengler. Wittgenstein's philosophy of logic and mathematics is constructivist in the general sense of treating even these abstract and inexorable disciplines as rooted in requirements of human behavior. He adopts an anthropological perspective on mathematics as part of the natural history of mankind, and views it as a family of activities for a family of purposes (RFM pp. 92–3, 176, 182, 399). At the same time, Wittgenstein replaces Schopenhauer's vitalist emphasis on the requirements of life, understood as an organic force, by an emphasis on the requirements of social human practice, which brings him closer to Marxism and American pragmatism. Logic and mathematics can play an important role in human activities only because there is a consensus about their application (see PI §§ 240–2).

2. Wittgenstein and Russell: "Good Intellectual Nursery-Training" and Bad Manners

Schopenhauer influenced Wittgenstein both directly and indirectly, insofar as he had an impact on Nietzsche and Weininger. This influence can also be felt in some of the more notorious ideas Wittgenstein shared with Weininger. Schopenhauer provided a philosophical justification for the cult of genius and for the aesthetic conception of ethics that afflicted both of them. And while Schopenhauer's misogyny and anti-Semitism were not a patch on Weininger's psychopathological ravings, they influenced the latter. In particular, the negative significance Schopenhauer attaches to Judaism is metaphysical rather than, for example, social, or racial. He accused Judaism of being crude, superficial, and lacking in "metaphysical tendency," because of its realism, optimism and the omission of immortality (Schopenhauer 1974, Vol. I, § 13n;

Vol. II, § 179). Weininger expanded this into the more general charge of an intellectual deficiency, namely that Jews lack genius and creativity. This idea much impressed young Ludwig, and, as we know from Monk (1990, 279–80), it lies behind Wittgenstein's notorious anti-Semitic remarks in *Culture and Value*.

In fact, in many ways Weininger is simply Schopenhauer without the philosophical brains. He drops the latter's critical philosophical method and the attempt at philosophical argument, while taking to extremes the metaphysical and pseudo-empirical speculations about the cosmos and human nature. In one relevant point, however, Weininger differs from Schopenhauer. He rejects the anti-intellectualism, at least officially. While he accepts the idea that the "intelligible nature" of human beings is will, he regards the latter in a Kantian light, namely as something closely linked to freedom and the intellect (Weininger 1905, 588–9, and chap. 12).

At the same time, Schopenhauer's anti-intellectualism ties in with other features of what Wittgenstein later called his "good intellectual nursery-training" (*eine gute geistige Kinderstube*; see McGuinness 1988, 32f.). This training consisted of the music of Vienna classicism on the one hand, of a particular strand of German literature, on the other. The figurehead of this movement is Goethe. It comprises Schopenhauer and (with qualifications) Nietzsche, as well as assorted Austrians like Grillparzer and Nestroy.

These figures tended to be sceptical about the ideals of the Enlightenment carried on by both neo-Kantianism and positivism. The main reaction to these ideals was provided by German idealism and romanticism. But they tended either toward nationalism (as in Fichte and romanticism), or toward an emphatic faith in progress (as in Hegel and his followers). Both came to characterize the mainstream of German culture in the nineteenth and early twentieth century, and both were shunned by Wittgenstein's intellectual heroes. Their attitude is epitomized by the quote from Nestroy that Wittgenstein chose as the motto of the *Philosophical Investigations*:

It is in the nature of every advance, that it appears much greater than it actually is. [*Überhaupt hat der Fortschritt das an sich, daß er viel größer ausschaut, als er wirklich ist.*] (*Der Schützling*, act 4, scene 10).

Wittgenstein was a cultural conservative in the same spirit. Throughout his life, he remained attached to eighteenth- and nineteenth-century German culture, especially in music. But two points need to be kept in mind here. First, Wittgenstein's intense intellectual passion and honesty prevented him from being nostalgic or parochial. Indeed, he reacted in a highly creative way to certain modern ideas, first and foremost the program of logical analysis presented by Frege and Russell. Second, cultural conservatism should not be identified with political conservatism (pace Nyíri 1982; see Schulte 1983).

In fact, Wittgenstein's cultural conservatism is nowhere more evident than in his political views, which were far from conservative. Thus he sympathized with the hard left in the 'thirties and 'forties, and even considered emigrating to the Soviet Union. Yet insofar as an underlying principle can be detected, it is precisely a conservative or even reactionary one: the Tolstoyan ideal of a simple life of manual work, coupled with a mild predilection for authoritarian ideologies – bolshevism, Catholicism – that place individual liberty and well-being below the pursuit of "higher" goals.

The contrast between Wittgenstein's cultural attitudes and the ideas that he encountered in Russell was stark. Wittgenstein, with his self-centered stress on personal integrity and genius, detested Russell's pacifism and humanist socialism (see below). Conversely, Russell deplored Wittgenstein's narrowness and lack of urbane civilization, a complaint that, as Monk (1990, 73) suggests, may have been linked to Wittgenstein's pronounced failure to apply his analytic powers to matters of public concern such as women's rights.

This cultural contrast seems to have played a major role in the growing alienation between Wittgenstein and Russell in 1913 and 1914. It became even more pronounced through developments during the war. While Wittgenstein, as a result of his experiences as a front-line soldier and under the influence of Tolstoy, underwent a religious conversion, Russell, due to his fraught dealings with D. H. Lawrence, became less tolerant of the irrational side of human life. The result was the final fallout after the meeting in Innsbruck in 1922. At that time Wittgenstein, according to Russell, was at the "height of his mystical ardour," while Russell, according to Monk, was at the "height of his atheist acerbity." Russell was contemptuous of Wittgenstein's new penchant for mysticism, and Wittgenstein was troubled by Russell's atheism, his loose sexual morals, and his lack of sincerity (see Monk, 115–6, 159, 210–11).

Their quarrels may have reached a climax in an incident that Engelmann reported to Nedo, and that must have taken place during the same ill-starred meeting.

When in the 'twenties, Russell wanted to establish, or join, a 'World Organization for Peace and Freedom' or something similar, Wittgenstein rebuked him so severely, that Russell said to him: 'Well, I suppose *you* would rather establish a World Organization for War and Slavery', to which Wittgenstein passionately assented: 'Yes, rather that, rather that!' (quoted in Monk 1990, 211).

It is not clear whether Wittgenstein was as serious as Engelmann seems to assume, but if he was, then it is clear that his conflict with Russell had gone beyond anything remotely philosophical. This kind of reaction *cannot* be explained by reference to the conflict between Wittgenstein's contemplative ethics of personal integrity on the one hand, and Russell's public ethics of responsibility on the other. Even at its worst, Wittgenstein's moral outlook could only condemn vocal support for peace and freedom on the grounds that it tries to say what can only be shown; it could not conceivably rank it below an equally vocal support for war and slavery.

I submit, therefore, that Wittgenstein's later resentment of Russell was based not just on a difference in world view or moral outlook, but also on personal animus and pique. Admittedly, there is an ideological difference between Russell's enlightened, if superficial, humanism and secularism and Wittgenstein's profound, if profoundly misguided, spirituality and mysticism. Nonetheless these ideological differences were blown out of all proportion by their personal quarrels.

Furthermore, not even the undeniable ideological differences concern questions of philosophical doctrine or philosophical method. There is no doubt, however, that other aspects of their disagreement were philosophical. Thus Wittgenstein was fond of complaining that "Russell and the parsons between them have done infinite harm" by suggesting that religions beliefs stand in need of "philosophical justification" (Drury 1984, 117).

Perhaps the greatest bone of contention between them, however, concerned the very nature of philosophy. Russell never abandoned the traditional pre-Kantian view of philosophy as a description and explanation of the most abstract features of reality; and in this attempt of delineating the furniture of the universe, he naturally regarded it as continuous with science in its task and methods. This contrasts sharply with Wittgenstein's abiding conviction that philosophy differs sharply from the sciences: it neither describes nor explains any kind of reality, but is a critical activity, namely of conceptual clarification. Monk (1996, 340–3) has conjectured plausibly that the rupture before World War I was caused by Wittgenstein's wholesale repudiation of Russell's propagation of "The Scientific Method in Philosophy" (the title of the Herbert Spencer lecture he was to give in America in 1914, reprinted entire in Russell 1918, chap. 6).

Still, even that methodological conflict is not necessarily one of irrationalism versus rationalism, mysticism versus enlightenment. To be sure, this is how Russell liked to see it, again for reasons that are partly personal. By contrast to the young Wittgenstein, Russell wrote that

the later Wittgenstein, . . . seems to have grown tired of serious thinking and to have invented a doctrine which would make such an activity unnecessary. . . . It was not by paradoxes that he wished to be known, but by a suave evasion of paradoxes (Russell 1959, 159, 161).

It is true that as early as 1912 Russell complained about Wittgenstein's failure to spell out the arguments in support of his claims. Doing so would "spoil their beauty," Wittgenstein maintained in 1912, to which Russell trenchantly replied that he should acquire a slave to take over this task (Russell to Ottoline Morrell 2.7.12, in Monk 1996, 264). Yet this contrast is more one of style than of method. On account of his aesthetic aspirations, Wittgenstein (both early and late) often condensed his insights and arguments to the point of impenetrability, but these insights and arguments can be teased out by careful interpretation and reconstruction. Furthermore, there is no indication that Wittgenstein, for his part, resented Russell on account of his penchant for philosophical argument. Throughout his life, and even at moments of greatest hostility, Wittgenstein admired Russell for being "terribly bright" and "amazingly quick" (McGuinness 1988, 87–8, 114). In fact, Wittgenstein once remarked to Drury:

Russell's works should be bound in two colours . . . those dealing with mathematical logic in red – and all students of philosophy should read them; those dealing with ethics and politics in blue – and no one should be allowed to read them (Drury 1984, 121).

Someone adverse to Russell's ideal of "dry hard reason" (see Monk 1996, 252) and to philosophical argument would surely take the opposite line. Russell's works on mathematical logic (which presumably include his writings on metaphysics and epistemology) are paradigms of analytic reasoning – they feature nine arguments for and ten against any given philosophical position. By contrast, his ethical and political reflections do not uniformly conform to these high standards. Of course, as against Wittgenstein, he was dead right to loathe Soviet Russia (Monk 1990, 247–8). Still, he limited the role of reason in ethics in a way that is not a million miles away from Wittgenstein. And in his political ruminations he often fell prey to loose thinking, for example in his claim that the Slavs are racially inferior to the Germans, or in his propagation of a preemptive nuclear strike against the Soviet Union after World War II.

3. Wittgenstein and the Vienna Circle: A Prophet Misunderstood Is a Prophet Enraged

Turning from Wittgenstein's interactions with his erstwhile teacher to those with his would-be disciples, one can detect a similar pattern. As is well known, the *Tractatus* was a major influence on the Vienna Circle. Furthermore, Wittgenstein regularly met Schlick, Waismann, Carnap, and Feigl for discussions between 1927 and 1932. The latter two were excluded in 1929, and the meetings gradually came to an end after Wittgenstein's return to Cambridge. In addition, there was an acrimonious priority dispute over physicalism with Carnap in 1932 (see Stadler 1997, 475–80), and a protracted fallout with Waismann.

Once more we find a mutual reinforcement of cultural and personal conflicts, combined with significant philosophical differences. As we shall see,
however, the methodological differences are less pronounced than in the case
of Russell. Like Ramsey, Carnap was taken aback by Wittgenstein's authoritarian style of argument, which tolerated "no critical comment" and treated
insights as a kind of divine inspiration (1963, 25–9; see Monk 1990, 241–3,
260).

I sometimes had the impression that the deliberately rational and unemotional attitude
of the scientist and likewise any idea which had the flavour of 'enlightenment' were
repugnant to Wittgenstein (Carnap 1963, 26).

It is not difficult to see why. Wittgenstein occasionally interrupted the philosophical discussion by turning his back on the others and reading aloud the
poetry of the Indian mystic Tagore, a habit that might disturb not just hard-
boiled positivists. More importantly, in discussion Wittgenstein advanced a
variety of claims that contrast with the rationalist and scientific attitude of the
logical positivists, who regarded themselves as heirs of the Enlightenment,
and in particular of the empiricist tradition in both its British (Hume) and its
Continental (Mach, Avenarius) variety. In the conversations, two conflicts
emerge.

The first concerns religion. Whereas the logical positivists treated religion
as a nonsensical, if not dangerous, form of superstition, Wittgenstein refused
to ridicule the religious attitude (WVC 117–8). He was a pious man in search
of a religion. "I am not a religious man but I cannot help seeing every
problem from a religious point of view" (Drury 79, 93; CV 2/4, 32–3/37–8,
45/51–2, 56/63; LC 63, 70; PO 119). He also rejected the "rationalist" claim
that "God wills the Good because it is good" in favor of "Good is what God
demands," on the grounds that this reveals the inexplicability of the Good,
and its independence from facts (WVC 115).

The second conflict concerns the demolition of metaphysics. The logical
positivists regarded metaphysics as theology in disguise, and hence as an
expression of superstition or of misguided artistic impulses. In truly Teutonic
fashion, they regarded themselves as "storm-troopers of anti-metaphysics"
(Frank 1935, 4). In their crusade against metaphysics, our Viennese storm-
troopers wielded three devastating weapons: Russellian logic, the *Tractatus*
claim that all necessity is tautological, and the verificationist criterion of
meaningfulness they derived from their conversations with Wittgenstein.

Yet, in spite of his designated role as a supplier of arms, Wittgenstein
disapproved of the war on metaphysics waged in his name. He criticized the
Vienna Circle on the (justified) grounds that "there was nothing new about
abolishing metaphysics" (Wittgenstein to Waismann, July 1929, in Nedo/

Ranchetti 1983, 243). And in the conversations he not only defended Schopenhauer against the attacks of Schlick, but even feigned to understand what
Heidegger means by *Sein* and *Angst* (Carnap 1963, 26–7; WVC 68). With
regard to metaphysics, it was the saying/showing distinction that separated
Wittgenstein from the logical positivists. The *Tractatus* had in fact maintained
that there are metaphysical truths about the essential structure that language
and the world must share, while at the same time maintaining that these truths
are ineffable (see Hacker 1996, 44).

In addition to these points, which surface in the conversations, three others
stand out. One is scientism. The members of the Circle characterized their
common outlook as a *Scientific World View,* as in the title of their so-called
manifesto, a programmatic pamphlet in honor of Schlick coauthored by Carnap, Hahn, and Neurath in 1929 (*Wissenschaftliche Weltauffassung: der Wiener Kreis,* see also Hacker 1996, 41; Hilmy 1987, 307–8). This scientific
world view conceives of science as the epitome of human rationality that
would in time sweep away theology and metaphysics as vestiges of the Dark
Ages. It also extols the value of science as a cooperative enterprise.

In the pamphlet, Wittgenstein, along with Russell and Einstein, is cited as
one of the three leading representatives of the scientific world view. In fact,
however, Wittgenstein strongly resented scientism and the scientific world
view (see below). He was firmly convinced of the superiority of the artistic
spirit and religious point of view. Furthermore, with regard to philosophy he
was immune to the ethos of collective work as practiced in the sciences: "The
philosopher is not a citizen of a community of ideas. That is what makes him
a philosopher" (Z § 455).

A second focus of conflict is politics. The Vienna Circle was the most
political philosophical school of the twentieth century. It certainly surpassed
the more notorious neo-Marxists of the Frankfurt School, who remained aloof
from actual political struggles. The logical positivists conceived of their
scientific world view as a vehicle not just of intellectual, but also of moral
and social change. On the left wing of the movement we find an outspoken if
unorthodox Marxist like Neurath and a humanist socialist like Carnap. By
contrast, Schlick and Waismann constituted the apolitical or right wing, not
least because of Schlick's collaboration with the Catholic fascists of Dollfuß
(Carnap 1963, 57; Geier 1992, 90–1; Hilmy 1987, 311). Yet even Schlick,
who generally resisted the attempt of harnessing logical positivism to specific
political goals, opposed Nazism as a liberal humanist, pacifist, and cosmopolitan (Schlick 1952; see Geier 1992, 57–99).

It may not be a coincidence, therefore, that these latter two were also
closest to Wittgenstein. For in the political struggle between socialism and
Catholicism that dominated the first Austrian republic, Wittgenstein occupied

an uneasy middle ground. While he had certain egalitarian tendencies, he sharply diverged from the socialists' secularism and their belief in social progress (Monk 1990, 188–9).

This takes us to the final and perhaps deepest contrast. Wittgenstein reacted positively to Spengler's attack on the Enlightenment idea of history as linear progress. By contrast, the Circle condemned Spengler's work as unscientific speculation, and insisted on the possibility and necessity of progress. On this issue, even Schlick and Neurath agreed, in spite of their numerous differences (Hilmy 1987, 260–3, 315: Stadler 1997, 552–4). Thus the manifesto opines that "the spirit of the enlightenment and *anti-metaphysical factual research* is becoming stronger today, in that it is becoming conscious of its existence and task" (Hahn 1929, 3).

The conflict between these outlooks is epitomized by two Prefaces. The first is Carnap's Preface to *Der Logische Aufbau der Welt* of 1928.

We [those with a "basic scientific attitude"] too have "emotional needs" in philosophy. But they are fulfilled by clarity of concepts, precision of methods, responsible theses, achievement through co-operation in which each individual plays his part. We do not deceive ourselves about the fact that movements in metaphysical philosophy and religion which resist such an orientation, again exert quite a strong influence today. What then, in spite of that, gives us the confidence that our call for clarity, for science without metaphysics will succeed. It is the insight, or, to put it more carefully, the belief, that those opposing powers belong to the past. We feel there is an inner kinship between the attitude on which our philosophical work is founded and the intellectual attitude which presently manifests itself in entirely different walks of life; we feel this orientation in artistic movements; especially in architecture, and in movements which strive for meaningful forms of personal and collective life, of education, and of external organization in general. We feel all around us the same basic orientation, the same style of thinking and doing. It is an orientation which demands clarity every-where, but which realizes that the fabric of life can never be quite comprehended (Carnap 1967, xvii–xviii).

Contrast an early version of the Preface that now introduces Wittgenstein's *Philosophical Remarks*:

This book is written for those who are in sympathy with the spirit in which it is written. This is not, I believe, the spirit of the main current of European and American civilization. The spirit of this civilization makes itself manifest in the industry, archi-tecture and music of our time, in its fascism and socialism, and it is alien and uncongenial to the author. This is not a value judgement. It is not, it is true, as though he accepted what nowadays passes for architecture as architecture or did not approach what is called modern music with the greatest suspicion (though without understand-ing its language), but still, the disappearance of the arts does not justify judging disparagingly of the human beings who make up this civilization. . . .

I realize then that the disappearance of a culture does not signify the disappearance of human value, but simply of certain means of expressing this value, yet the fact remains that I have no sympathy for the current of European civilization and do not understand its goals, if it has any. So I am really writing for friends who are scattered throughout the corners of the globe.

It is all one to me whether the typical western scientist understands or appreciates my work, since he will not in any case understand the spirit in which I write. Our civilization is characterized by the word "progress." Progress is its form rather than making progress being one of its features. Typically it constructs. It is occupied with building an ever more complicated structure. And even clarity is sought only as a means to this end, not as an end in itself. For me on the contrary clarity, perspicuity are valuable in themselves.

I am not interested in constructing a building, so much as having a perspicuous view of the foundations of possible buildings. So I am not aiming at the same target as the scientists and my way of thinking is different from theirs (C&V 6/8–9; cp. PR Foreword).

Wittgenstein wrote these words in 1930. Hilmy (1987, 213, 301, 307–8) has pointed out that the contrast with Carnap's Foreword and the manifesto of the Circle is hardly a coincidence. This intentional contrast with the Vienna Circle explains not just the grand topics in the Foreword of a rather technical treatise, but also the stark nature of the envisaged clash. Together with the misappropriation of his ideas on metaphysics, the fact that he had been portrayed as a representative of the scientific world view along with Russell must have incensed Wittgenstein.

Hilmy describes the political attitudes of the logical positivists as "jejune" and their expression as "spirited ejaculations" (1987, 312, 314). With regard to their politics, however, the logical positivists were always on the side of the angels, in that they rejected both Nazism and Stalinism. Unfortunately, this is more than can be said of Wittgenstein. Yeats famously remarked on the political situation in the 'thirties: "the best lack all conviction, the worst are full of passion and intensity." The members of the Vienna Circle were an honorable exception. Of course, with the benefit of hindsight we can describe their faith in the future as "tragically unwarranted" (Hacker 1996, 40). As Carnap's Foreword shows, however, this faith was not a naïve prediction, but a defiant hope. If that hope was disappointed, it was not the fault of the Vienna Circle.

To be sure, contemporary readers may be taken aback by the view, vocally expressed by Neurath, that the obstacle to political progress lies in theological or metaphysical thought systems. It should, however, be kept in mind that some of the metaphysical thinkers they combated – Weininger, Spengler, Heidegger – provided ideological and/or political support for the Nazis. It is one thing to imbibe ideas about the relation of logic and ethics from these authors, or about morphological method, but quite another to follow their views on race and politics.

This takes me from areas of conflict to equally important points of contact. The position of most logical positivists was not just inspired by the *Tractatus,* but indeed is actually reasonably close to the logical and methodological letter, if not the mystical spirit. If one leaves aside the explosive mixture of personal resentment and the clash of ideologies, Carnap and Wittgenstein agree on a variety of points. This chimes with the former's remark that ideological differences apart, with respect to "philosophical problems, about knowledge, language and the world, I was usually in agreement with his views and certainly his remarks were always illuminating and stimulating" (Carnap 1963, 27).

In my view, this assessment is closer to the mark than many would grant. Although there are important differences, both Wittgenstein and the Vienna Circle came to develop a (loosely speaking) conventionalist account of logical necessity in the early 'thirties: logical truths are neither inductive generalizations (Mill), nor descriptions of how humans tend to think (psychologism), nor truths about a Platonist hinterland (Frege) or the most abstract features of reality (Russell). Rather, their special a priori status is to be explained by reference to linguistic rules.[4]

Closely linked to this point of contact is a crucial metaphilosophical parallel, which has for the most part gone unnoticed. All of the forementioned members of the circle follow Wittgenstein's linguistic turn and the (surprisingly Kantian) conception of philosophy to which it leads. Unlike science or common sense, philosophy does not itself describe or explain reality; it is a second-order discipline that *reflects* on the conceptual scheme employed by science and common sense (see Glock 1997). There is a qualitative difference between science, which is concerned with factual issues and hence a posteriori, and philosophy or logic, which is concerned with conceptual issues, and hence a priori.

This kind of picture was explicitly preached by Schlick ("The Future of Philosophy") and Waismann (*Principles of Linguistic Philosophy*); but in a more technical and science-oriented manner, it is also evident in Carnap. Philosophy is not a doctrine consisting of propositions but a method, namely of logical analysis. Negatively, it reveals metaphysical nonsense. Positively, it turns into the "logic of science," namely the linguistic analysis or explication of scientific propositions, concepts, and methods (Carnap 1937, 279). This demarcation of philosophy and science underlies Carnap's distinction between analytic and synthetic propositions in *The Logical Syntax of Language* and his distinction between internal and external questions in "Empiricism, Semantics and Ontology" (in Carnap 1956). Both are unjustly ridiculed by contemporary orthodoxy, and both are in important respects close to ideas in Wittgenstein, early and late.

Regarding the fundamental question of how philosophy stands to science, the front lines within the Vienna Circle run not between the conservatives (Schlick, Waismann) and the progressives (Neurath, Carnap), or between the phenomenalists (Schlick, early Carnap) and the physicalists (Neurath, later Carnap), but between the Wittgensteinians (Schlick, Waismann, and Carnap) on the one hand, and Neurath on the other, who, as is well-known, anticipated Quine's assimilation of philosophy to science.

4. Scientism, Irrationalism and Anti-Intellectualism

Even though the *Tractatus* presupposes an ineffable metaphysics, it confines meaningful discourse to science no less than the logical positivists (TLP 4.1, 4.5). Wittgenstein later abandoned this restriction and acknowledged the existence of meaningful uses of language outside science. According to MS 134 (143–6; Hilmy 1987, 186), "The use of the word 'science' for 'everything that can be meaningfully said' constitutes an 'overrating of science.' "

At the same time, Wittgenstein held on to the idea of philosophy as a critical activity in pursuit of conceptual clarity. That idea was equally shared by Carnap, and this explains Wittgenstein's subtle allusion to clarity in the above quotation. For better or worse, Carnap pursued clarity for the sake of scientific theory-building, in this respect echoing Locke's conception of the philosopher as an under-laborer of science. By contrast, Wittgenstein regarded conceptual clarity as an end in itself. It is all the more ironic, therefore, that he should pursue this end in a fashion that is at times extremely obscure.

Contacts with members of the Vienna Circle may, to use Hilmy's words, have stimulated Wittgenstein "more through provocation than through inspiration" (1987, 214). In fact, they may have provoked Wittgenstein to gloss his position in a way that is more hostile to science and more sympathetic to irrationalist tendencies than his philosophy warrants. As in the case of Russell, genuine philosophical contrasts were magnified by differences extrinsic to philosophy as Wittgenstein understood it, namely as the attempt to resolve metaphysical problems by way of conceptual clarification (e.g., Z § 458).

It is crucial to distinguish between Wittgenstein's *personal ideology,* on the one hand, and his *philosophical methodology,* on the other. This holds in particular with respect to his attitude toward science. It is also important to remember that Wittgenstein had a background in engineering and an *abiding* interest in certain kinds of scientific investigation. At the same time, he was hostile to the scientific spirit of the twentieth century. He rejected the belief in progress, and abhorred the "idol worship" of science, which he regarded as both a symptom and a cause of cultural decline (CV 6–7/9, 49/56, 56/64, 63/72; Drury 1984, 112).

Partly this reaction indicates his cultural conservativism, and partly it reflects his personal experiences, including his rows with Russell and the logical positivists. It also expresses, however, a humanistic worry that the predominance of science and the advance of technology marginalize ethics and the arts, and thereby endanger the human spirit. Yet even while regretting the pernicious influence of the scientific spirit, Wittgenstein distinguished between good and bad scientific works (LC 27–8; CV 42/48; Drury 1984, 117). The former follow ideals of clarity and intellectual honesty, and involve detailed empirical investigations like Faraday's *The Chemical History of a Candle.* The latter, like Jean's *The Mysterious Universe,* pander to a craving for mystery, and engage in speculation.

In any event, Wittgenstein's philosophical methodology rejects not science but *scientism,* the imperialist tendencies of scientific thinking that result from the idea that science is the measure of all things. Wittgenstein insists that *philosophy* cannot adopt the tasks and methods of science. Scientific theories and hypotheses try to provide causal explanations of empirical phenomena. Philosophical problems, by contrast, cannot be solved by experience or causal explanation since they are conceptual, not factual. They require not new information or discoveries, but greater clarity about what Wittgenstein, somewhat misleadingly, calls "grammar," that is, about the constitutive rules of our language. This means that there should be a *division of labor* between science and philosophy's second-order reflection on our conceptual apparatus (CV 16/23). Alas, the twentieth-century obsession with science makes it difficult to uphold this division, and thereby obstructs philosophy (PR 7; BB 17–8).

Although philosophy is a critical activity rather than a scientific doctrine, it can be entirely rational. To be sure, there are no causal explanations or factual *discoveries.* Indeed, "If one tried to advance *theses* in philosophy, it would never be possible to debate them, because everyone would agree to them" (PI § 128, see § 599). Yet this remark does not evince a mystical quietism or a refusal to engage in rational philosophical argument. On the contrary, it alludes to the idea of criticizing philosophical positions in a way that is immanent, that is, does not rely on dogmatic assumptions of one's own. Wittgenstein spelled out this "undogmatic procedure" in his conversations with the Vienna Circle (WVC 183–6; see PR 54–5; PI §§ 89–90, 127; PO 179, 185–189).

With regard to your theses [Waismann's attempt to summarize TLP in WVC App. B] I once wrote: were there theses in philosophy they should occasion no debate. That is, they would have to be so stated that everyone would say: yes, yes, that is obvious. [WVC 183]

I once wrote, "The only correct method of doing philosophy consists in not saying anything and leaving it to the other person to make a claim." That is the method I now adhere to. What the other person is not able to do is to arrange the rules step by step and in the right order so that all questions are solved automatically. . . . The only thing we can do is to tabulate rules. If by questioning I have found out concerning a word that the other person at one time recognizes these rules and, at another time, those rules, I will tell him. In that case you will have to distinguish exactly how you use it; and there is nothing else I wanted to say. [WVC 183–4]

Thus I simply draw the other person's attention to what he is really doing and refrain from any assertion. Everything is then to go on within grammar. [WVC 186; see PR 54–5]

Conceptual clarification proceeds by way of 'grammatical reminders,' namely of how the relevant words are used outside the context of philosophical puzzles and theories. Philosophical theses would have to be indisputable because they remind us of linguistic rules with which we are already familiar outside philosophical reflection. Nevertheless, such theses are part of a rational philosophical debate because they are invoked to show that metaphysical philosophers use words according to conflicting rules (see Glock 1991). Whether this procedure does justice to metaphysical positions is debatable, but it stands in the wholly rational tradition of the Socratic *elenchos* and of Kant's Transcendental Dialectic. In both we find the idea that philosophical views can be criticized because their tacit assumptions lead to inconsistency.

I am not denying that there are irrationalist elements in Wittgenstein's remarks on philosophy, notably in the early saying/showing distinction and in the later stress on the need for therapy and conversion. Unlike his ideological outbursts, which are confined to conversations and lectures, these ideas can be found in his major works, notably the *Tractatus* and the *Philosophical Investigations,* and they do form part of his methodological views. In my view, however, many of these passages can be glossed in a way that brings them closer to a more rational conception of philosophy, and some of them, like *Philosophical Investigations* § 128, *must* be glossed on this way.

It should have transpired that Wittgenstein's philosophical position combines a Kantian project of avoiding confusion and nonsense with an un-Kantian anti-intellectualism influenced by Schopenhauer and Spengler. But even this anti-intellectualism should not simply be equated with irrationalism. The "tradition of continental anti-rationalist thought" for which, as Monk (1990, 250) rightly notes, Wittgenstein "had a great deal of sympathy," actually comprises two distinct positions:

- irrationalism – a neglect of empirical science, logic and rational argument in favor or religious, political, or artistic styles of thinking;
- anti-intellectualism or voluntarism – the denial that reason and intellect have the exalted position accorded to them by philosophical tradition.

These two positions do not coincide, either intensionally or even extensionally. Some of the most vocal proponents of reason present their case in a completely irrational manner. This holds true, for example, of Hegel, whose writings Einstein rightly compared to the "drivel of a drunk," but also of Weininger's defense of the intellect. Conversely, it is possible to attack the intellectualist picture of human beings by way of rational argument. This holds true of Hume and the American pragmatists, and, to a lesser extent, of Schopenhauer.

Wittgenstein is more of a voluntarist than an irrationalist. In fact, he can be seen as a pragmatist, though not in the vein of Peirce, James, and Dewey. There are numerous places in which he emphasizes action and the will in place of theory and intellect, yet for him the initial lesson is not that intellect and reason are useless or even dangerous (as it would be for Nietzsche), but that they are features of, and grounded in, human activity: *Im Anfang war die Tat* ("In the beginning was the deed"), as he approvingly quotes from Goethe (PO 395; CV 31/36; OC 402; & cf. RPP I § 151). The foundations of the human intellect lie in the exigencies and possibilities of human practice.

There is, however, a more specific moral: partly because of its foundation in practice, the scope of reason is necessarily limited. This moral underlies some of the most interesting claims of Wittgenstein's later work. In the rule-following considerations we find the famous claim that justifications come to an end. "Once I have exhausted the justifications, I have reached bedrock, and my spade is turned. Then I am inclined to say: 'this is simply what I do' " (PI § 217). A similar idea underlies his claim that teaching through explanation presupposes certain fundamental linguistic and cognitive skills that are engendered by training (PI §§ 6, 27; PG 62). Finally, there is the claim, directed against the *Tractatus,* that insofar as language has foundations, they are not metaphysical but lie in shared communal practices or "forms of life" (PI II p. 226).

None of these claims are an expression of irrationalism. Although they may not be tenable, they are the result of painstaking and intricate reflections that combine dialectical acuity with imaginative analogical thought. Ever since Plato, many philosophers have identified human reason with a "quest for the unconditioned," as Kant put it. They have maintained that our beliefs are rational only if they can be grounded in foundations that are in some way self-evident or self-authenticating. This strategy is, however, self-defeating in an important respect. In the name of dubious notions like self-evidence, the demand for rational justification is suspended precisely at the alleged foundations. This suggests that the quest for the unconditioned is doomed to fail. Human reason is of necessity limited, and, if Wittgenstein is right, its foundations are not self-grounding but practical. Far from being irrational, it is perhaps the pinnacle of human rationality to recognize such limitations, as Kant and Wittgenstein have done in their different ways.

Unlike Wittgenstein's reflections on the nature of philosophy and of reason, his ruminations on wider artistic, cultural, and political issues are a mixed blessing. They combine valuable insights into the dangers of progress with noxious views such as anti-Semitism, misogyny, and the wholly misguided hope that bolshevism would create a morally superior breed of human beings. To be fair, many of these objectionable remarks were made in conversation, and none of them were intended for publication. As a philosophical dialectician, Wittgenstein was a genius, but as a cultural critic and moral mentor, he was a loose cannon.[5]

LIST OF ABBREVIATIONS OF FREQUENTLY CITED REFERENCES

I use the following abbreviations for Wittgenstein's work:

NB: *Notebooks 1914–16,* rev. ed. Oxford: Basil Blackwell, 1979.

TLP: *Tractatus Logico-Philosophicus.* London: Routledge and Kegan Paul, 1961.

LvF: "Letters to L. von Ficker," in *Wittgenstein: Sources and Perspectives,* ed. C. G. Luckhardt. Hassocks: Harvester Press, 1979.

PR: *Philosophical Remarks.* Oxford: Basil Blackwell, 1975.

DB: *Denkbewegungen: Tagebücher 1930–1932, 1936–37* Frankfurt: Fischer Verlag, 1999.

PG: *Philosophical Grammar.* Oxford: Basil Blackwell, 1974.

LC: *Lectures and Conversations on Aesthetics, Psychology and Religious Belief.* Oxford: Basil Blackwell, 1996.

BB: *Blue and Brown Books.* Oxford: Basil Blackwell, 1958.

RFM: *Remarks on the Foundations of Mathematics,* rev. ed. Oxford: Basil Blackwell, 1978.

PI: *Philosophical Investigations.* Oxford: Basil Blackwell, 1958; first edition 1953.

RPP I: *Remarks on the Philosophy of Psychology,* Vol. I Oxford: Basil Blackwell, 1980.

Z: *Zettel.* Oxford: Basil Blackwell, 1967.

CV: *Culture and Value.* Oxford: Basil Blackwell, 1980; rev. ed. 1998.

PO: *Philosophical Occasions.* Indianapolis, IN: Hackett, 1993.

References to the *Nachlass* follow von Wright's catalogue. (Where necessary, I have provided my own translations from the German.)

REFERENCES

Baker, G. P. (1991) "Wittgenstein: neglected aspects," in R. L. Arrington and H. J. Glock, eds., *Wittgenstein's Philosophical Investigations: Text and Context*. London: Routledge.

Baker, G. P. and Hacker, P. M. S. (1983) *Frege: Logical Excavations*. Oxford: Basil Blackwell.

Boghossian, P. A. (1997) "Analyticity," in B. Hale and C. Wright, eds., *A Companion to the Philosophy of Language*. Oxford: Basil Blackwell.

Bouwsma, O. K. (1986) *Wittgenstein: Conversations*. Indianapolis, IN: Hackett.

Carnap, R. (1937) *The Logical Syntax of Language*. London: Routledge.

   (1956) *Meaning and Necessity*. Chicago: University of Chicago Press.

   (1963) "Intellectual Autobiography," in P. A. Schilpp, ed., *The Philosophy of Rudolf Carnap*. La Salle, IL: Open Court.

   (1967) *The Logical Structure of the World*. Berkeley: University of California Press; German original 1928.

Cohen, J. L. (1986) *The Dialogue of Reason*. Oxford: Clarendon.

Conant, J. (1989) "Must we show what we cannot say?," in R. Fleming and M. Payne, eds.. *The Senses of Stanley Cavell*. Lewisburg, PA: Bucknell University Press.

Diamond, C. (1991) *The Realistic Spirit*. Cambridge, MA: MIT Press.

Drury, M. (1984) "Some Notes on Conversations with Wittgenstein," in R. Rhees, ed. *Recollections of Wittgenstein*. Oxford: Oxford University Press.

Dummett, M. A. E. (1993) *Origins of Analytic Philosophy*. London: Duckworth.

Engelmann, P. (1967) *Letters from Wittgenstein, With a Memoir*. Oxford: Basil Blackwell.

Føllesdal, D. (1997) "Analytic Philosophy: What Is It, and Why Should One Engage In It?," in H. J. Glock, ed. *The Rise of Analytic Philosophy*. Oxford: Blackwell.

Frank, P. (1935) *"Wissenschaftliche Weltauffassung und Metaphysik," Erkenntnis* 5, 1–12.

Geier, M. (1992) *Der Wiener Kreis in Selbstzeugnissen und Bilddokumenten*. Hamburg: RoRoRo.

Glock, H. J. (1991), "Investigations § 128: Theses in Philosophy and Undogmatic Procedure," in R. Arrington and H. Glock, eds.. *Wittgenstein's Philosophical Investigations*. London: Routledge.

   (1996) "Necessity and Normativity," in H. Sluga and D. Stern, eds. *The Cambridge Companion to Wittgenstein*. New York: Cambridge University Press.

   (1997) "Kant and Wittgenstein: Philosophy, Necessity and Representation," *International Journal of Philosophical Studies*, 5 285–305.

   (1999) "Schopenhauer and Wittgenstein: Language as Representation and Will," in C. Janaway, ed. *The Cambridge Companion to Schopenhauer*. New York: Cambridge University Press.

Hacker, P. M. S. (1986) *Insight and Illusion*. Oxford: Clarendon Press; first edition 1972.

Hahn, H., O. Neurath and R. Carnap (1929) *Wissenschaftliche Weltauffassung: Der Weiner Kreis* (Vienna: Artur Wolf Verlag).

   (1996) *Wittgenstein's Place in Twentieth Century Analytic Philosophy*. Oxford: Basil Blackwell.

Hilmy, S. (1987) *The Later Wittgenstein.* Oxford: Basil Blackwell.

Janick, A., and Toulmin, S. (1983) *Wittgenstein's Vienna.* New York: Simon and Schuster.

McGuinness, B. (1988) *Wittgenstein, A Life: Young Ludwig.* London: Penguin.

Monk, R. (1990) *Wittgenstein: the Duty of Genius.* London: Jonathan Cape.

(1996) *Bertrand Russell: The Spirit of Solitude.* New York: The Free Press.

Nedo, M., and Ranchetti, M. (1983) *Ludwig Wittgenstein: sein Leben in Bildern und Texten.* Frankfurt: Suhrkamp.

Nyíri, C. (1982), "Wittgenstein's later Work in its Relation to Conservatism," in B. F. McGuinness, ed. *Wittgenstein and his Times.* Oxford: Basil Blackwell.

Rorty, R. (1979) *Philosophy and the Mirror of Nature.* Princeton: Princeton University Press.

Russell, B. (1959) *My Philosophical Development.* London: Unwin.

Schlick, M. (1952) *Natur und Kultur.* Wien: Humboldt.

Schopenhauer, A. (1966) *The World as Will and Representation.* New York: Dover.

(1974) *On the Fourfold Root of the Principle of Sufficient Reason.* Le Salle, IL: Open Court.

Schulte, J. (1983) "Wittgenstein and Conservatism", *Ratio,* 25 69–80:

Sidelle, A. (1989) *Necessity, Essence and Individuation.* Ithaca: Cornell University Press.

Spengler, O. (1928) *The Decline of the West.* London: Unwin; first edition 1923.

Stadler, F. (1997) *Studien zum Wiener Kreis.* Frankfurt: Suhrkamp.

Weininger, O. (1905) *Geschlecht und Charakter.* Wien and Leipzig: Braunmüller; first edition 1903.

von Wright, G. H. (1984) "Biographical Sketch", in N. Malcolm, *Ludwig Wittgenstein. A Memoir.* Oxford: Oxford University Press; first edition, 1958.

NOTES

1. Two terminological remarks: I shall use the term "rationalist" to include not just the continental rationalists, with their emphasis on innate ideas and a priori knowledge, but also any position that stresses that our beliefs should be subject to critical scrutiny and supported by argument, no matter whether these arguments invoke reason or experience. Similarly, I use the term "reason" for the general ability to justify one's actions and beliefs by way of argument, and not in the narrow (and, in my view, misguided) sense employed by modern theories of rationality, in which it refers to a disposition to act exclusively in one's own interest.

2. This passage nicely illustrates the problems in detecting Kantian influences on Wittgenstein's early work. It clearly alludes to an antinomy of critical philosophy, but there is no way of telling where precisely Wittgenstein encountered this paradox. On the one hand, there are remote parallels in authors he definitely read, namely Schopenhauer and Mauthner, and on the other there are immediate parallels in Bradley, an author he may have read.

3. Note, incidentally, that this remark is utterly incompatible with nonsense irrationalism, which treats the whole of the *Tractatus* as deliberate nonsense. To a lesser extent, the same goes for many other remarks Wittgenstein later made about his

first book. If Diamond and Conant know what the *Tractatus* is all about, then Wittgenstein himself didn't.

4. This account has recently been both rediscovered and rehabilitated against the prevailing Quinean and Kripkean orthodoxies. See, for example, Hacker 1996, chap. 8; Glock 1996; Boghassian 1997; Sidelle 1989.

5. This paper was written during the tenure of a research fellowship of the Alexander von Humboldt Foundation at the University of Bielefeld. I should like to express my gratitude to both. For comments and advice thanks are also due to Peter Hacker, Ray Monk, Eike von Savigny, Joachim Schulte, and David Stern, as well as to the participants at the conference, "Wittgenstein: Biography and Philosophy," held at Virginia Tech, March 25–28, 1999.

Wittgenstein and the Idea of Jewishness*

BRIAN McGUINNESS

Wittgenstein, in a confessional phase, reproached himself bitterly for having minimized his Jewish ancestry. Yet he was right to minimize it, if a correct impression of his family and its influence on him was the aim. No one at the turn of the century would have thought of characterizing that large cousin-hood as a Jewish family, as it is occasionally described today. Karl Menger, who knew them and was a particular friend of Wittgenstein's Aunt Clara, comments, that insofar as there was any difference between Jewish and non-Jewish households, they seemed to belong rather to the latter.[1]

They (Ludwig's parents and his uncles and aunts and their children after them) were Protestant or Catholic and married to Protestants or Catholics. Theirs was not a life with any Jewish dimension, or consciousness of their remote Jewish ancestry, a diminishing proportion in any case as the generations passed. Nor did they live among, consort with, or feel a special affinity for other families with a Jewish element in their background. Such a possibility did not really exist in the Christian circles to which they did belong, since Jewishness as a family characteristic vanished on conversion and intermarriage: often only a name remained, on the male side.[2]

Ludwig himself came at the intersection of two such families, since Karl alone of that generation married one whose father had Jewish ancestors. The result still is that, of Ludwig's three grandparents, only one was herself demonstrably a member of the Jewish community, in, as it happens, Vienna, and her marriage – her marriage out, so to speak – was registered there as well as in Dresden, where it actually took place.[3]

She was a Figdor, from a family of bankers who had been financiers to court circles and later to the city of Vienna. Such families were in fact often the last to convert, if they did so at all: to belong to a supernational community was an advantage for them. Yet Fanny did convert, and when she went to Dresden to be married, she was also, the day before, baptized.

* This is an English version of "Wittgenstein und das Judentum," in *Paul Engelmann (1891–1965): Architektur, Judentum, Wiener Moderne,* ed. Ursula A. Schneider (Vienna: Folio Verlag, 1999).

The story of the Wittgenstein family into which she married is an interest-ing, because so typical, one for the historian of what is sometimes called assimilation, though (borrowing a metaphor from Lewis Namier) the evapo-ration of Jewishness might in this case be a more appropriate term.[4] Their ancestors, not yet called Wittgenstein, had been court Jews in Hesse since at least the mid-18th century. We can infer two lines, one signalized by the alternation Meyer Moses, Moses Meyer, the other Hirsch Meyer, Meyer Hirsch, going back to a Meyer born in the 17th century. Living in Laasphe, near the castle of one line of the Sayn-Wittgensteins, they were agents and factors to that family: one of them, Ahron Meyer Moses, our Hermann Christian's grandfather, leader of the community, must have been among the Laasphe Jews sent to England to collect the payment for mercenaries used in the Seven Years War. Probably it was the mediatization of the Sayn-Wittgensteins that brought the family to Korbach, though the second line mentioned also spent some time in Gütersloh. About this time, too, they all took the name Wittgenstein. Associated now with the Waldeck-Pyrmonts (for they were still known as Court Jews), they soon embarked on trade of their own.

The years 1815–48 into which Hermann Christian's youth fell were years of emancipation for the Jews throughout Germany, but in many regions, particularly in Hesse, this met with much resistance and nowhere more than in the little center of Korbach. No doubt the town's decline as a trade center was partly responsible for this. It was impossible for most Jews to assert their rights and difficult even for the Wittgensteins and Simons (the family of Hermann Christian's mother, who were also Court Jews). Most members of the Wittgenstein connection went off, taking their business with them – some to Bielefeld, even more to Leipzig. All became Christians. We know of only one, Jakob, son of a much older brother, who remained in the Jewish religion: he stayed on in Korbach and fought through to civic equality, being elected to the Waldeck assembly in 1848.[5]

In centers such as Korbach, conversion tended to mean exclusion from both of the local communities. Hermann Christian himself may have had difficulties with his line of the family, perhaps on this very account and went to join his cousins and uncles (in a wide sense) in Leipzig, the city of Felix Mendelssohn.[6] When exactly he left the Jewish community and professed himself a Christian is not clear, but he certainly had no regrets: "We are glad to be out of the East!" he is reported to have said.[7] By the time of his courtship and marriage he was already a prosperous wool merchant, mature, severe and of impressive culture.[8]

His own sub-branch of the Wittgenstein family, moving yet again, to Austria-Hungary, retained much of a family tradition of benefactions and support for worthy causes, no longer of course with the function of providing for needy and vagrant Jews arrived from the East (as had been the case in Korbach). That sort of community was left behind and they now found another one among the quietly prosperous Lutheran or Zwinglian burghers of their new country. Intermarriage was to bring in Catholic elements as well: perhaps it is significant that there was some fluidity as to confessional adherence, which varied according to marriage and the convictions of the other party, apparently without generating friction. Their friends and protegés and social lions might be of any stripe – Mendelssohn and Joachim, yes, but also Clara Schumann and Brahms, Hebbel and Bonitz – very often Germans, who, like themselves, found Austria congenial.[9]

The existence of a number of Jewish ancestors was of little significance for most of the family. When Carl heard that his son Paul was studying their ancestry, he laughed, saying, "As long as he doesn't find that one of them was hanged!" Only for very particular purposes did the non-"German" element in their ancestry create any hindrance, as in the case of a boyhood wish of Ludwig's to join a distinctively German gymnastic club.

The period of Ludwig's boyhood and youth is one regarding which it has become customary to stress the contribution of "the Jews" to Viennese culture. There are severe limitations to such an approach. If Vienna itself, and the concentration of science and culture there, attracted many from outside, and if, for sociological reasons, many of these had at diverse periods been set loose from a Jewish background, this by no means implies any uniformity in their contribution, and certainly not any Jewish coloring of the science and culture itself. How could it, indeed, saving the exceptional case – a Chagall, an Else Lasker-Schüler? As Max Liebermann said when Jewish origins were mentioned: "But good heavens, what has that got to do with drawing?" Just as for every Liebermann there was a Corinth, so, closer to our hero, for every Mach there was a Boltzmann, for every Kraus a Loos. Above all, the things said or produced, the cultural content, was generally above such classification. A Jewish element – there might be one: for Freud, it has been claimed that there was one – would have to be proved in each case.

These are very general considerations and to a considerable degree obscured by the affections and passions of our own half of the century, but it is essential to have some objective basis for this sort of discussion. Ludwig, at all events, thought himself in 1914 completely German. He was aware, it is true, of the Jewish predominance in his ancestry. If he denied it (how flatly we cannot from his confessions absolutely know), this will at that time have been from a sense of its irrelevance. He was pained perhaps by a detail of descent that objectively meant nothing, but might give others a wrong impression of him. He was, we might almost say, ashamed of being ashamed of it – an irrational reaction he perhaps shared with Hofmannsthal.[10] Wittgenstein's much later self-examination on the question of being Jewish is a

different phenomenon to which we shall return. In youth he felt he was not a
Jew, rightly, as I have tried to say. At his school the Jewish boys (defined, of
course, confessionally) were a small minority and he notes some tension, not
further specified, in his relation with them – "with the Jews," not "with the
other Jews."

It was at the outbreak of the First World War that Wittgenstein made his
remark about feeling completely German. Whether this will have changed
during the first two years of the war, as the differences between Germans and
Austrians became clearer, is a matter for speculation: it may have gone either
way. At all events, at the end of August 1916 he came, after perhaps his
hardest-fought battles, to Olmütz and found himself for the first time in a
Jewish circle – found himself *tout court,* we may say, since their thinking
chimed so well with his own. The town was small and the intellectuals were
mostly of Jewish origin, now perfect examples of assimilation, yet not min-
gling much with the few other German-speaking bourgeoisie. In Prossnitz,
where many of their families originated, there was even a Jewish municipality,
a remnant of the ghetto (Max Zweig came from there, and Stefan Zweig's
family also, and the mother of Paul Engelmann). In Brünn, the city of Loos
and of Gödel, there was still a German cultured class, alongside the emerging
Czechs, for whom Janacek may serve as a symbol. Olmütz was a special
case, betwixt and between one might say. Engelmann himself speaks of the
cultural past still recognizable from its buildings, and indeed it had once been
the capital of Moravia, with its own university (closed in 1858), and it was
still home to a well-endowed metropolitan see, where the canons of the
cathedral had the unique privilege of electing the archbishop rather than
accepting the nomination of the emperor. (This circumstance may have put
an edge on Franz Josef's tongue when they elected a worthy Msgr. Cohen:
Ist er wenigstens getauft?, "I hope he's baptized," he is reputed to have said.)
Yet Engelmann's account of the town (and Max Zweig's, too, of the gymnasium there) suggests that there was no lively intellectual life outside this
group of sons and daughters of professional or merchant families that were at
the height of their development and, as it happened, of Jewish descent,
whereas the older German burgher families were, like the town itself, in
decline.

To Olmütz then came Wittgenstein and after a summer of isolation and
hostile relations with his comrades he found a circle that dedicated itself to
things of the mind. Like his own family in happier days they spent their time
making music, staging plays, and discussing books and poems. I have described elsewhere this circle and the effect Wittgenstein had on it, as others
have also. Engelmann's memoir is a testimony to the profundity of that effect.
Arrived in Vienna after completing his training in Olmütz, Wittgenstein was

to hear from Max Zweig that he had won from the latter the deepest respect of the heart.[11]

The message he brought them is obviously too complex to express in a single formula, but its main effect was to confer an intellectual legitimacy upon their aspirations. The question of the part played by their Jewish ancestry in these is a rather artificial one, since the enthusiasms of youth appear in every part of our culture and are very similar in all of them. But perhaps that ancestry played some part indirectly: the main need they felt, the keystone missing for their devotion to culture and to good causes, was a religion, so to speak, a natural one. Many felt this need but perhaps membership of an assimilated, but not converted, Jewry particularly predisposed these Olmützers to feel it. They certainly wanted something more than *Schöngeistigkeit* and *Schwärmerei.* They were readers of Karl Kraus (Engelmann had been his assistant), they were or were preparing to be competent and serious practitioners in their own professions – architecture, music, drawing. They would look for standards in their intellectual life, too.

Wittgenstein's earlier attitude toward religion I have attempted to describe elsewhere.[12] His loss of faith was not due to a general lack of faith in his family, which had many devout members, but perhaps to the mocking attitude of his father and the enlightenment of his advanced sister, Margaret Stonborough. Russell reports him as a fierce critic of organized religion, or, at any rate, of clerics. One such was told that he would do better to "read some good book on some exact science and see what honest thought is." Still Wittgenstein's interest in William James's *Varieties of Religious Experience* antedates the war as does (almost certainly) the performance of Anzengruber's *Kreuzelschreiber,* where the slogan "*Es kann dir nix g'schehen*" ("Nothing can happen to you") in its context of nature mysticism awoke echoes in him.

I will not repeat here how he came, in the first year of the war, to an intense living of the Tolstoyan gospels and a belief in the Spirit, but will only say that all this is described in the coded or personal part of his diaries.[13] When Wittgenstein came to Olmütz, however, he was at a crucial point in his reflections. Resuming his philosophical notes after the summer's battles – 1 or 4 July 1916, misdated 11.6.16 in all editions[14] – he asks more directly than before, "What do I know about God and the purpose of life? [*Was weiß ich über Gott und den Zweck des Lebens?*]" and then continues with reflections on God, prayer, good and evil, all themes that he had excluded from the chaste first version of the *Prototractatus* (a much more stratified text than we at first thought), which really leaves unsaid all that is unsayable.[15] That he was aware of this shift appears in the coded part of his diary, where he says, on 6 and 7 July 1916:

Have thought a lot about everything possible. But, strangely enough, cannot establish the connexion with my mathematical lines of thought. But the connexion will be established. What cannot be said, *cannot* be said.[16]

(Here we have, probably, the first version of the concluding proposition of the *Tractatus*). Wittgenstein's position here may seem a self-contradictory one. If the religious realm is inexpressible, will it not be all the harder, indeed impossible, to connect it with "mathematical lines of thought"?

This brings us, however, straight to the conversations that then took place in Olmütz. A main theme, indeed the main theme, of Engelmann's reminiscences is that Wittgenstein brought the others to see, by strict attention to the nature of science and mathematics, that the realm of religion was indeed inexpressible. And that not because it happens to be inexpressible, but because that is its very essence, just as an irrational number can have no rational expression nor can the velocity and position of a particle both be determined. The converse is even true: the inexpressible *is* the mystical: it is in seeing what cannot be expressed that we come near to the nature of the mystical. This body of thought has been characterized as negative theology, as man's urge to run up against the limits of language, and in various other ways. For Engelmann and Wittgenstein it entailed, in particular, a certain way of expressing what can be expressed, which takes account of what cannot, and it was in such a light, we can see from their letters, that the two talked of poetry, as of other matters.

This jejune characterization is not intended to recommend their way of thinking. Quite the contrary: its main point is to indicate that the conclusions reached have sense only in the light of the route followed in reaching them.[17]

This was the lesson of Olmütz, this the corrective to the occasionally "lukewarm atmosphere" of the Engelmann home.[18] It is equally important to note that it was a lesson for Wittgenstein, too. It was in these months that he added to his treatise two series of remarks: on the nature of science, and on the inexpressibility of ethics. These are to be found on pp. 71–8 of the *Prototractatus* manuscript, but he continued to make considerable additions in the early months of 1917, shortly after his departure from Olmütz. These additions reflect the nature of his interaction with his friends there, Engelmann in particular. While his logical insights gave them an underpinning for their philosophy of life, he learned from them how he could say something about his deepest convictions without running counter to those same insights. Hence, in part, his remark, reported by Engelmann, "If I can't manage to bring forth a proposition, along comes Engelmann with his forceps and pulls it out of me!"[19]

But in all of this, what role was played by the "Jewishness" of the Olmütz circle and by the Jewish ancestry of Wittgenstein? The common factor seems to have been the need for a self-made religion, the ethical equivalent of

Christianity.[20] Here Tolstoy, too, played his part, and no doubt readings of the *Brenner* before the war, where there were translations of Kierkegaard and other writings of similar inspiration.[21] Finally, for all of them, the war was the great catalyst, making it imperative to come to terms with these questions. At all events, the Olmützers, objectively speaking, were looking for an alternative to a Jewishness that no longer meant anything to them, while Wittgenstein was making good the failure of his Christian upbringing to take root. Such in essence was the nature of Wittgenstein's first and only adventure into an environment that can in an intelligible sense be called Jewish.

Time was to bring its changes: most obviously when the plague of Nazi anti-Semitism struck. Fritz Zweig emigrated. Max Zweig and Peter Eng had to abandon cosmopolitan Berlin, where perhaps they had never thought they were Jews. Eng committed suicide. Zweig began to write plays relating to the persecution and the resistance of the Jews. The success of one of these took him to Palestine, fortunately at exactly the time when the Germans occupied the Czech lands, where he had taken refuge from them. He spent the rest of his long life there, much of it in the company of Engelmann.[22]

Engelmann's own return to Judaism, or perhaps rather his turn to Zionism, came earlier. His correspondence with Wittgenstein and his notebooks from the years 1928 to 1932 have yet to be studied in depth, but it is, at any rate, clear that he was not content with the measure of success as an architect that was or might have been open to him, and certainly not with the relative comfort of the life he could live in Olmütz.[23] He felt a strong call to live also, ideally it would have been entirely, for others, both by intervening in difficult or desperate cases and also by seeking to have an influence at the social level. At the same time (and to some extent for the same reason) he wanted to write, to carry further the work of his mentors: Kraus, Loos, and Wittgenstein. It was natural to think of the new society that it was hoped to build in Palestine and to share the hopes of many of the early Zionists; and there, in 1933, he went. Who can say with what success? First of all, of course, it in fact ensured his survival in a decade of persecution. His life was both modest and full of idealism. He found some work in Tel Aviv as an architect, but could afford to live only in the poorest circumstances. He composed, but did not publish, a great deal of material: it was, in some sense, a seamless web, moving from logic, to psychology, to social organization inspired by ideals of the higher life, and (to complete the circle) to town-planning and architecture. His practical activity issued from this thinking, since he was active in promoting cultural groups and discussions, which (as he explains in his writings) are the first step to creating the mentality required for his ideal state. Needless to say his was no religious Zionism. He happened to be a Jew so it was among Jews in Palestine that he sought to promote universal ideals. At one point, he says that he feels for the welfare of Jewish workers in

Palestine exactly as a Spaniard or a Swede would. He also envisages a
government of Palestine by separate Arab and Jewish chambers. He himself
says about his work that it was not so completely without effect as might be
thought, and this must be respected, but there were elements reminiscent of
his address to the Czech conscripts in the Mauritzkirche.[24] Here, too he spoke
only the language of a minority, and a distrusted minority at that.

In 1925, when Engelmann first broached the idea (not yet very concrete)
of going to Palestine, Wittgenstein was half-inclined to go with him.[25] The
idea of a new start, a tabula rasa, no doubt appealed to him: we see this in
his frequent impulses of flight, to Norway (more than once), to Russia, to
Ireland (more than once): there was even talk of Brünn. By the time Engelmann actually went, Wittgenstein was principally in Cambridge and the two
men seem hardly to have been in contact (though in 1937 Wittgenstein found
a way to send one of his confessions to Engelmann).[26]

We leave here the sphere of Wittgenstein's actual contact with Jewish
culture, though how "Jewish" it was is, as we have seen, debatable, and turn
to two different spheres: his thoughts about his own Jewishness at the beginning of the 1930s and the effect on him of racial discrimination in the late
1930s. That these themes need to be treated together, and in the same context
as those touched on above, is evidence of the artificiality of the concept of
Jewishness. We have here at least five different sets of phenomena, or supposed phenomena: the religion; descent from persons professing it; the culture
of assimilated Jews who still formed something of a community; the common
genetic heritage of Jews (thought to exist); and (distinct from this) the supposition of such a heritage, typically the assumption by the anti-Semitic that
it did exist and was an excrescence on European culture, with which we may
class the mirror-image of this assumption, which finds in Jewish consciousness the origins of the modern world view. Of these five, only the first and
the last are reasonably clearly definable and certainly existed, though they are
by no means identical or very closely related. Jewishness, *"das Judentum"*, is
surely one of those words of which Heinrich Hertz spoke in a favorite passage
of Wittgenstein's:

We have accumulated around the terms "force" and "electricity" more relations than
can be completely reconciled amongst themselves. . . . It is not by finding out more
and fresh relations that it [the question as to the nature of force and electricity] can be
answered; but by removing the contradictions existing between those already known
and thus [this?] perhaps by reducing their number.[27]

So far we have considered Wittgenstein's actual ancestry and the extent to
which Jewish religion and culture entered – (very indirectly, as it turned out)
– into his life. In the early 1930s Wittgenstein, who had played down his
ancestry to others, and who had made no reference to it previously in his

private diaries, began, only for this period as far as I know, to think that his own work was marked by Jewishness. One passage will serve as an illustration:

Amongst Jews "genius" is found only in the holy man. Even the greatest of Jewish thinkers is no more than talented. (Myself for instance.) I think there is some truth in my idea that I really only think reproductively. I don't believe I have ever *invented* a line of thinking, I have always taken one over from someone else. I have simply straightaway seized on it with enthusiasm for my work of clarification. That is how Boltzmann, Hertz, Schopenhauer, Frege, Russell, Kraus, Loos, Weininger, Spengler, Sraffa have influenced me. Can one take the case of Breuer and Freud as an example of Jewish reproductiveness? . . . [28]

Even read with the caution we should bring to every self-assessment, the passage is fascinating, for the characterization of Wittgenstein's work and for his list of influences, but our main concern here is with the importance attached to Jewishness.[29] Wolfgang Kienzler has pointed out that the sense of such passages would not be materially altered if for "Jews" we read "philosophers".[30] There is much in the idea that philosophy is of necessity a second-order activity, and perhaps Wittgenstein made this even clearer than before. Whether this excludes originality is more questionable – or perhaps the very idea of originality is questionable.[31] Moreover, the idea that lack of originality should be associated with race, when differences within a race, whatever a race may be, are greater than differences between races is hard indeed to accept. At all events it suffices to read, for example, Mach's *Principles of the Theory of Heat,* not of course written with such as its theme, to see how the most original of scientists depended on their predecessors and how little room for chauvinism there is in basic science. *All* contributions were necessary to get us as far as we have come. Of course a place and a period may for reasons hard to divine witness a surprising efflorescence: in England the Elizabethan poets are a striking example.

Yet Wittgenstein, for a while at least, subscribed both to the myth of genius, the absolutely original thinker, and to the idea that a national character was transmitted in the blood – the genes, we would perhaps now say, with vague thoughts of selection, but on such matters Wittgenstein was happier with utterances that flew in the face of science (let alone of scientism). They better corresponded to an emotional truth. One might almost say, alas, that he was thinking with the blood. Thus later in 1931 he writes:

It has sometimes been said that the Jews' secretive and cunning nature is a result of their long persecution. That is certainly untrue: on the other hand it is certain that they continue to exist despite this persecution only because they have an inclination towards such secretiveness.[32]

These characteristics do indeed belong to the *picture* of the Jew, as in Shylock's, "For sufferance is the badge of all our tribe." No one today, with the example of the State of Israel before him, would choose this picture, or perhaps any single picture, but Wittgenstein accepted it and indeed spoke as if it corresponded to characteristics that had been in the Jewish race from the start and would remain so for ever.

At least he spoke in such a way for a time in 1931: later he discusses the same moral problems without the reference to Jewishness. Even so, why? Note that with this question we are engaged in a different enterprise from that so far undertaken. We are no longer talking about what Jews are really like (if there is such a thing), but solely about how Wittgenstein imagined them. We should surely also go on to ask, What conclusions for his life or thought did he draw from this picture? It will be seen, I think, that the answers to these two questions are closely connected.

We are speaking of a time when Hitler's ideas were in the air, but not yet put into practice (which, of course, more clearly revealed their repulsive and self-stultifying nature, but also their dangerous fascination), we are speaking of a time when Wittgenstein was reading, or at any rate discussing with Moore, Weininger's *Sex and Character*.[33] It was also a time (but then, when was not?) in which he was questioning his own relation to the world. He spoke of himself as living in a more rarified atmosphere than others, of his cowardliness, of his need to hide himself behind his words.[34] As always with Wittgenstein, the direction of thought is from his own soul outwards. He accepts the picture of the Jew not because Jews are such, but because he thinks that he himself is. So he does not accept it on historical grounds, nor because he takes pleasure in preferring a folk belief to the lucubrations of the historian or the social scientist – though no doubt that did give him pleasure – but because it serves his purpose of self-examination. Something similar can be seen in his "Remarks on Frazer's *Golden Bough*"[35]: we understand a primitive rite when it makes us shudder, and in his remarks about religion, where believing in God is quite different from being convinced by a philosophical or historical argument.[36]

The upshot of such thought, then, the effect that it had on him, was precisely to provide themes for his self-criticism, though, as we have said, he contrived to continue this throughout his life without reverting often to this particular device. But in 1931, at any rate, Jewishness was a moral category, whose concrete manifestations are of secondary importance.[37] Much more important is the seriousness of the whole issue. Wittgenstein writes (shortly after the main passages we have been discussing):

Jewishness is deeply problematic but not cozy or warm-hearted. Woe betide the author who stresses the warm-hearted side. I was thinking of Freud when he talks about the Jewish joke.[38]

We, too, can enter into this discourse of Wittgenstein's. One is tempted to say, for example, that there is something in this last criticism of Freud. But such discourse will be anything but historical. We are saying rather that the emphasis on jokes, or to take a related example, the sentimentality, the *Schmaltz,* in this or that sketch or film does not represent Jewishness as we should wish it to be. For everyone can feel a fascination (the converse of that mentioned above) in this picture of an alternative smaller world in which all questions are resoluble, cut off, a secret garden. Whether this fascination is healthy is another question.

We return to history to round out our account. Objectively, but perhaps only objectively, Wittgenstein entered into a different relationship to Jewishness with the annexation of Austria, when his family (in some cases to their surprise) found themselves to differing degrees subject to the racial laws. Their story can be followed in letters exchanged at the time.[39] As others paid the emigration tax (*Reichsfluchtsteuer*) or used some similar device, so they were prepared to repatriate a part of their monies held abroad to purchase a racial status that permitted them to remain in Austria but in safety. Wittgenstein involved himself energetically in making these arrangements: like his sisters he fell out with the other brother, who chose the path of exile.[40] They made themselves, what they had always thought they were, non-Jewish, and in their talk and discussions made the distinctions they had always made:[41] for them a "Jew" meant an *Ostjude,* a Jew from Eastern Europe, with the corresponding, or rather supposed, appearance and manners.[42] Some such they indeed helped, and they continued to consort as before with friends who were Jews, or half-Jewish in the Nazi sense. Their help to all categories must have been risky. But there is no trace – why should there be?, one might ask – of solidarity with Jews as such. It had always been the family practice to help those in need (and to help in a direct and personal way). The race did not count.

So, too, Wittgenstein in England was active in helping individual refugees, many of whom were, of course, Jewish. His diaries contain a number of their addresses and he wrote letters to bring them to England, or, to help them while there, he contributed to their upkeep, insisting that the source of the money not be revealed – all the things that one would hope or expect. But as one human being to another. It was as a human being that he reacted to the revelations as the concentration camps were opened; Buchenwald was perhaps the first. "Do you believe that?," he said to Peter Stern with horror and a sort of unbelief, although the truth was by now established, and, of course, because they did these things to human beings.[43]

In the end, then, Wittgenstein did not think of himself as Jewish, nor need we do so. The concept is an attractive, although, or because, a confused one. It is possible to think that it would have been well if all "Jews" had felt solidarity, or to think that they now ought to do so – it is also possible to think the contradictory or even the opposite of these things. But in any case these are aspirations, not realities.[44]

REFERENCES

Berlin, Isaiah. 1992. *Fra filosofia e storia delle idee,* ed. Steven Lukes, Florence: Ponte alle Grazie.

Bettelheim, Samuel, ed., 1935. "Aus der Geschichte der Juden in Waldeck," *Judaica,* 5–6.

Bezzel, Chris et al. 1989. *Wittgenstein/Wiener Secession,* Vol. 1 "Biographie, Philosophie, Praxis" (an exhibition catalogue, no apparent editor), Vienna.

Bolz, Robert. 1992. "Notice of German translation of *Wittgenstein, A Life, Vol. 1,* by Brian McGuinness," *Philosophische Rundschau,* Tübingen 334f.

Engelmann, Paul. 1967. *Letters from Ludwig Wittgenstein with a Memoir,* Oxford: Basil Blackwell.

Gombrich, Ernst. 1996. "The Visual Arts in Vienna circa 1900 & Reflections on the Jewish Catastrophe," *Occasions,* 1, Austrian Cultural Institute, London.

Hertz, Heinrich. 1899. *Principles of Mechanics.* London: Macmillan.

Kienzler, Wolfgang. 1997. *Wittgensteins Wendung zu seiner Spätphilosophie.* Frankfurt: Suhrkamp Verlag.

Laqueur, Walter. 1996. *"Ich will Zeugnis ablegen bis zum letzten Tag"* in *Holocaust and Genocide Studies,* (Winter).

McGuinness, Brian. 1988. *Wittgenstein, A Life.* Vol. 1. *Young Ludwig 1889–1921.* London: Duckworth.

Mann, Golo. 1962. *Geschichte und Geschichten.* Frankfurt.

Medding, W. 1951. *Korbach: die Geschichte einer deutschen Stadt.* Korbach.

Menger, Karl. 1994. *Reminiscences of the Vienna Circle.* Dordrecht: Kluwer.

Rhees, Rush, ed. 1984. *Recollections of Wittgenstein,* rev. ed. Oxford: Oxford University Press.

Rieckmann, J. 1993. "Zwischen Bewußtsein und Verdrängung / Hofmannsthals jüdisches Erbe," *Deutsche Vierteljahresschrift* 67, (1993).

Toury, Jakob. 1965. "Die Juden im Vormärz," *Bulletin of the Leo Baeck Institute,* 8.

Toury, Jakob. 1972. *Der Eintritt der Juden in das Bürgertum.* Tel Aviv.

Weininger, Otto. 1906. *Sex and Character,* New York: Heinemann.

——— 1907. *Über die letzten Dinge.* Vienna: W. Braumüller Verlag.

Wittgenstein, Hermine. 1944. *Familienerinnerungen* (typescript circulated privately), Vienna.

Wittgenstein, Ludwig. 1979a. *Notebooks 1914–16* (actually 1914–17), 2d ed., ed. G. H. von Wright and G. E. M. Anscombe. Oxford: Basil Blackwell.

——— 1979b. *Remarks on Frazer's* Golden Bough, ed. R. Rhees, Retford: Brynmill.

——— 1980/1998. *Culture and Value,* ed. G. H. von Wright, trans. P. Winch. Oxford: Basil Blackwell; rev. ed. 1998.

——— 1989. *Logisch-philosophische Abhandlung/Tractatus Logico-Philosophicus,* Kritische Edition, ed. B. McGuinness and J. Schulte, Frankfurt: Suhrkamp.

——— 1995. *Cambridge Letters.* ed. B. McGuinness and G. H. von Wright. Oxford: Basil Blackwell.

Wittgenstein, Ludwig. 1996a. *Familienbriefe,* ed. B. McGuinness, M. C. Ascher, and O. Pfersmann. Vienna: Verlag Hölder-Pichler-Tempsky.

——— 1996b. *Prototractatus,* 2nd ed., ed. B. F. McGuinness, T. Nyberg & G. H. von Wright. London: Routledge.

1997. *Denkbewegungen: Tagebücher 1930–32/1936–37*, ed. by Ilse Somavilla. Innsbruck, Austria: Haymon Verlag.

Zweig, Max: 1992. *Lebenserinnerungen*. Gerlinger: Bleicher Verlag.

NOTES

1. Menger 1994, 74.
2. It is relevant to this discussion that in Austria-Hungary registration for civic purposes was on a confessional basis. (Thus, for instance, it was a baptismal, not strictly a birth-, certificate that Wittgenstein presented to the Home Office when seeking naturalization in Great Britain.) In Austria, therefore, the term "Jew" had a precise legal significance.
3. Whether as a result of a change in his first name or of his leaving the community, or for some other reason, Wittgenstein's paternal grandfather could not be identified in any Jewish register in Korbach when a search was made in 1938 in connection with the racial laws: this of course was anything but a disadvantage at the time.
4. Quoted from Lewis Namier in Berlin 1992, 34. Cf. also what Golo Mann says of his maternal grandfather in "*Über Antisemitismus*" (1960), in Mann 1962, 169–70: "*In seinem Fall wie in hunderttausend anderen, hat es kaum Sinn von Assimilierung zu sprechen, weil sie langst vollzogen war.*" ("In his case, as in a hundred thousand others, it scarcely makes sense to talk of assimilation, since that had been accomplished long ago.")
5. Jakob's real prosperity, however, came after removal to Berlin. The account in the last two paragraphs is largely based on Bettelheim 1935 (which revolves round Jakob) and Medding 1951, 348–50 and 402–3. I have also seen useful correspondence between the late W. W. Bartley and the late Thomas Stonborough.
6. In his will, he speaks of difficult circumstances and being thrown back on his own resources at the beginning of his career: see Wittgenstein, Hermine 1944, 17 (*"Ich habe unter anderen sorgenvollen Umständen meine Carrière begonnen; auf eigene Kraft angewiesen etc."*) This may have to do with his father's death in 1822 and some disagreement with Jakob's father, Simson, for no further contact with this, his own line of the family, is recorded.
7. The family tradition is no more precise than that he was "*stehend getauft*" ("baptised standing") i.e., not in infancy.
8. See Laqueur 1996, 257, on assimilation as a perfectly natural process. "Traditional Judaism had become irrelevant, certainly for the educated Jews. There was no Jewish culture outside religion, which put greater emphasis on ritual than on anything else." The Old Orthodox of the day (the *Vormärz* or *Biedermeierzeit*) put the same thought in a different way: "*Vor allem emanzipiert die Emanzipation die Juden vom Judentum*" ("The immediate effect of the emancipation of the Jews is to emancipate them from Jewishness"); see Toury 1965, 65f.
9. This account adds some details to that in McGuinness 1988, 1–23; for references to the Wittgensteins of Korbach, see "*Ein Bürgerrechtsstreit in Korbach*" in Toury, 1972, 105–12, Bettelheim 1935; and Medding 1951.
10. Dr. Ritchie Robinson of Oxford kindly drew my attention to Rieckmann 1993.
11. Letter of 27.12.16, copy in the Brenner Archiv. Thus the warm but more measured account in Zweig 1992, written more than 75 years after the events, probably does less than justice to the original effect that Wittgenstein had on the circle.

12. McGuinness 1988, 84, 111.
13. It will be recalled that in these early notebooks the code passages are entered separately on the versos and rapidly fall behind, so far as date is concerned, the philosophical notes on the rectos. After 1929, Wittgenstein generally interspersed the two types of entry. (Wittgenstein 1997 is an exception: it has indeed remarks both in code and in clear, but none are philosophical. Conceivably but by no means necessarily, other such notebooks have been lost or were destroyed by Wittgenstein.)
14. This can even be seen in the photograph of the relevant passage now added to Wittgenstein 1979a.
15. I have dated the composition of this to the period from October 1915 (Wittgenstein tells Russell he is working on a treatise) to March 1916 (he goes off to the Front). Its content will have been the first 70 pages, in Wittgenstein's numbering, of MS 104, Trinity College Library. Wittgenstein probably brought a typescript based on this to Olmütz and may there have added in manuscript the passages from pp. 71–8 referred to below in the text. See also my Preface to Wittgenstein 1996b and an earlier article of mine in *Grazer Philosophische Studien,* 1989, largely incorporated into the preface to Wittgenstein 1989.
16. *"Habe viel über alles Mögliche nachgedacht. Kann aber merkwürdigerweise nicht die Verbindung mit meinen mathematischen Gedankengängen herstellen. Aber die Verbindung wird hergestellt werden. Was sich nicht sagen läßt, läßt sich nicht sagen."* From MS 103, Trinity College Library. Publication of code passages is planned by the Brenner Archiv.
17. Thus Wittgenstein's cousin, Lydia Oser, who said to Karl Menger (Menger 1992, 83f), "Is there really any merit in saying, 'Whereof one cannot speak thereof one must be silent'?" was in a sense right. The conclusion in isolation is banal. Ramsey's reported criticism "What can't be said, can't be said, and it can't be whistled either," if genuine, is unwontedly superficial, not only because it, too, treats the upshot of the *Tractatus* as if it stood on its own, a procedure questionable even with the last line of a mathematical proof, but because it involves a *petitio principii*: indirect ways of making manifest may be possible, the *Tractatus* is itself meant as a way of making this itself manifest.
18. *"Lauwarme Atmosphäre"* – the phrase is Heinrich Groag's in a postcard of 1917 to Wittgenstein, original in the Brenner Archiv.
19. Engelmann 1967, 94.
20. Engelmann in particular was clearly influenced by Christianity: witness his quotations from the Fourth Gospel, his appeals to the Holy Spirit, and his certainty that the sayings of Christ in the Gospels cannot be of purely human origin. (References to Christianity, and to the relative incompleteness of the Jewish religion, are quite frequent in later, as in earlier, notes by Wittgenstein, but are sufficiently known not to need citation here.)
21. The *Brenner* was avowedly a Christian periodical. Adolf Loos, who introduced Wittgenstein to Engelmann, was himself introduced to Wittgenstein by Ludwig von Ficker, the editor of the *Brenner.* To complete the circle, Wittgenstein came to Ficker through a favorable mention of him by Karl Kraus, also a Christian at this period.
22. See Zweig 1992.
23. Available in the Jewish National and University Library.
24. At a *Feldmesse* – a Mass before they went off to the Front – he exhorted them, in the name of the Holy Ghost, to lay down their arms. Information from the late H. Groag.

25. Engelmann 1967, 54–5.
26. We have a copy of Engelmann's reply among Wittgenstein's papers (and of Wittgenstein's reply to that in Engelmann 1967, 58–9), but Engelmann seems to have tactfully suppressed the confession itself.
27. Hertz 1899 8. As a motto for the *Philosophical Investigations,* Wittgenstein originally thought of the passage from which this is taken, which he also used in both of the general talks he gave to the Cambridge University Moral Science Club, in 1939 (on taking up the Professorship) and in 1946 (his counterblast to Popper); minutes of the Moral Science Club in Cambridge University Library. For a lucid discussion of the concept of Jewishness, see Gombrich 1997. (I am grateful to Dr. Emil Brix for a copy of this pamphlet.)
28. Wittgenstein 1980/1998, 19/16: *Das jüdische "Genie" ist nur ein Heiliger. Der größte jüdische Denker ist nur ein Talent. (Ich z.B.) Es ist, glaube ich, eine Wahrheit darin, wenn ich denke, daß ich eigentlich in meinem Denken nur reproduktiv bin. Ich glaube ich habe nie eine Gedankenbewegung erfunden, sondern sie wurde mir immer von jemand anderem gegeben & ich habe sie nur sogleich zu meinem Klärungswerk aufgegriffen. So haben mich Boltzmann, Hertz, Schopenhauer, Frege, Russell, Kraus, Loos, Weininger, Spengler, Sraffa beeinflußt. Kann man als ein Beispiel jüdischer Reproduktivität Breuer & Freud heranziehen? . . . Es ist dem jüdischen Geist typisch das Werk eines Andern besser zu verstehen als der es selbst versteht.*
    Note the order (clearly chronological) in which influences are listed: we can infer that Weininger became important to Wittgenstein *later* than his first meeting with Loos in July 1914, and thus not as a result of a reading in boyhood or youth. See also note 30, below.
29. In a previous discussion (McGuinness 1988, 84) I dismissed this element out of hand, which earned me an accusation of "positivism" in the *Philosophische Rundschau* (Bolz 1992). This may serve as an excuse for here arguing for what I think to be obvious.
30. Kienzler 1997, xxx.
31. A remark dating from 1939–40, Wittgenstein 1980/1998, 36/42, repeating the example of Freud and Breuer (but was not Breuer also "Jewish"?), distinguishes between an originality "of the soil" (Wittgenstein's own and Freud's) and an originality "of the seed." There, however, no reference is made to Jewishness.
32. Wittgenstein 1980/1998, 22/19: *Man hat manchmal gesagt, daß die Heimlichkeit & Verstecktheit der Juden durch die lange Verfolgung hervorgebracht worden sei. Das ist gewiß unwahr; dagegen ist es gewiß, daß sie, trotz dieser Verfolgung, nur darum noch existieren, weil sie die Neigung zu dieser Heimlichkeit haben.*
33. See Wittgenstein 1995, 250. I have given some account of how Wittgenstein viewed this book in McGuinness 1988, 40–3. I suspect, however, that when listing influences (text above) Wittgenstein was thinking of Weininger's other book, *Über die letzten Dinge* (Weininger 1907). See note 25 above; also the parallels adduced in McGuinness 1988, 40–1; Wittgenstein 1996a, 30 and 83, which suggest that the later book is what Hermine Wittgenstein refers to as "Dein Weininger" in 1916.
34. In Wittgenstein 1997, 72, 87, 97: cf. Wittgenstein 1980/1998, 12/14, which expresses the idea that abstractness is a particularly Jewish characteristic. (Of course one might just as well say the opposite.)
35. Wittgenstein 1979b, *passim.*
36. Wittgenstein 1980/1998, 32/37.
37. This is of a piece with Wittgenstein's remark to Moore (Wittgenstein 1995, 250)

about Weininger 1906: "It isn't necessary or rather not possible to agree with him but his greatness lies in that with which we disagree." Similarly, Jewishness, for Wittgenstein, is an interesting *idea*. See also Rush Rhees's discussion of Weininger, Rhees 1984, 177–82.

38. Wittgenstein 1997, 141: *Das Judentum ist hochproblematisch, aber nicht gemütlich. Und wehe, wenn ein Schreiber die gemütvolle Seite betont. Ich dachte an Freud, wenn er vom jüdischen Witz redet.*

39. Wittgenstein 1996a, 162f., see also Wittgenstein, Hermine, 1944, 154–80. It will be seen that there was something in the apparently naive remark about his sisters that Wittgenstein made to Drury, "They are too much respected, no one would dare to touch them," see Rhees 1984, 139.

40. He was against giving so much to the Nazis, but to his brother and sisters this seemed a self-serving pretext. I have summarized in the text a process fraught with passion.

41. In February 1940, the *Reichsstelle für Sippenforschung* told the *Gauamt für Sippenforschung* in Vienna that the declaration of Hermann Christian's German blood, or *Deutschblütigkeit,* went back to a decision of the Führer and Reichskanzler. Thus they enjoyed a high degree of protection.

42. See, for example Wittgenstein 1996a, 166.

43. *"Die Erinnerung an jene Frage hat mich nie verlassen"* ("The memory of that question has never left me") says Stern, in Bezzel 1989, 17. Anyone who remembers England at that date will confirm that the specificity of Jewish suffering under Hitler was not present to most minds, even in 1945. Similarly, the refugees seemed, as they indeed were, *Germans* driven away by their own government.

44. Having arrived so far, I have the impression that the polemical part of what I have said has, in essence, been said before. I should mention in particular "Wittgenstein's Judaism," a paper shown me by J. J. Ross of Tel Aviv University and (quoted by him) Yuval Lurie, "The Jew as Parable," *Iyyun* 37, 1988. It seems always necessary to repeat it, and yet by airing the topic one risks nourishing it. This is part of the fascination I speak of. Gombrich 1997 is more incisive about such considerations.

Was Wittgenstein a Jew?*

DAVID STERN

In my mind's eye, I can already hear posterity talking about me, instead of listening to me, those, who if they knew me, would certainly be a much more ungrateful public.

And I must do this: not hear the other in my imagination, but rather myself. I.e., not watch the other, as he watches me – for that is what I do – rather, watch myself. What a trick, and how unending the constant temptation to look to the other, and away from myself.

– (Wittgenstein, *Denkbewegungen: Tagebücher 1930–1932/1936–1937,*
15 November or 15 December, 1931

1. Was Wittgenstein Jewish?

Did Ludwig Wittgenstein consider himself a Jew? Should we? Wittgenstein repeatedly wrote about Jews and Judaism in the 1930s (Wittgenstein 1980/ 1998, 1997) and the biographical studies of Wittgenstein by Brian Mc-Guinness (1988), Ray Monk (1990), and Béla Szabados (1992, 1995, 1997, 1999) make it clear that this writing about Jewishness was a way in which he thought about the kind of person he was and the nature of his philosophical work. On the other hand, many philosophers regard Wittgenstein's thoughts about the Jews as relatively unimportant. Many studies of Wittgenstein's philosophy as a whole do not even mention the matter, and those that do usually give it little attention. For instance, Joachim Schulte recognizes that "Jewishness was an important theme for Wittgenstein" (1992, 16–17) but says very little more, except that the available evidence makes precise statements difficult. Rudolf Haller's approach in his paper, "What do Wittgenstein and Weininger have in Common?," is probably more representative of the received wisdom among Wittgenstein experts. In the very first paragraph, he

* This paper is based on a talk given at the conference, "Wittgenstein: Biography and Philosophy," at Virginia Polytechnic Institute & State University, Blacksburg, VA, March 25–28, 1999. An abridged version of § 1 and § 4–7, on the connections between Wittgenstein's thoughts about his Jewishness and his philosophy, "The Significance of Jewishness for Wittgenstein's Philosophy," was published in *Inquiry,* December 2000. That material is reprinted with the kind permission of the editor and publishers of *Inquiry.*

makes it clear that the sole concern of his paper is the question of "deeper philosophical common ground" between Wittgenstein and Weininger, and not "attitudes on feminity or Jewishness" (Haller 1988, 90). Those who have written about Wittgenstein on the Jews have drawn very different conclusions. He has been lauded as a "rabbinical" thinker (Nieli 1987) and a far-sighted critic of anti-Semitism (Szabados 1999), and criticized as a self-hating anti-Semite (Lurie 1989), as well as condemned for uncritically accepting the worst racist prejudices (Wasserman 1990). Monk (1990) provides a rather more nuanced reading of the evidence. He presents Wittgenstein as briefly attracted to using anti-Semitic expressions in the early 1930s, but only as a way of thinking about his own failings. Most discussions of the topic take it for granted that Wittgenstein was a Jew, but recently McGuinness (1999/ 2001) has contended that even this is a mistake.

In this essay, I argue that much of this debate is confused, because the notion of being a Jew, of Jewishness, is itself ambiguous and problematic. Instead, we would do better to start by asking in what senses Wittgenstein was, or was not, a Jew. Another way of putting this is to say that we should first consider different ways of seeing Wittgenstein as a Jew. Before rushing to judgment, we need to consider what it could mean to say that Wittgenstein was, or was not, a Jew, or an anti-Semite. This is not just a matter of tabulating various possible definitions of these expressions, but of considering the different contexts – cultural, social, personal – in which those terms can be used, and their significance in those contexts. In doing so, we need to give critical attention not only to the various criteria for being a Jew that Wittgenstein would have been acquainted with, and the presuppositions he might have taken for granted about Jews and Judaism, but also the ones that we use in our discussion of Wittgenstein as a Jew, and our motives for doing so. One of the great dangers in writing philosophical biography is the risk of turning the study of a philosopher's life and work into vicarious autobiography, wishful thinking, or worse.

I begin my discussion of the question of Wittgenstein's Jewishness by looking at two passages by Brian McGuinness that offer very different answers. The first, from the first volume of his biography of Wittgenstein, subtitled "*Young Ludwig (1889–1921),*" takes it for granted that Wittgenstein did think of himself as a Jew, at least during the first half of his life, and gives some indication of how important that fact was to him. The passage begins with a reference to Otto Weininger, who Wittgenstein identified, in a passage written in 1931 (1980/1998, 18–19/16–17), as an important influence. In the same piece of writing, Wittgenstein also discussed the connection between his Jewishness, his character, and his way of doing philosophy. Wittgenstein repeatedly recommended Weininger's pseudoscientific and anti-Semitic *Sex and Character* (1903) to friends, including G. E. Moore in the early 1930s and G. E. M. Anscombe in the late 1940s. As we shall see, Monk's biography also emphasizes Wittgenstein's indebtedness to Weininger's ideas about talent and genius, and their close connection to his views about Jewishness and femininity.

> Weininger had yet two important features in common with the young Ludwig. First he was Jewish. He suffered from the consciousness of that fact. He identified the Jewish with all that was (on his theory) feminine and negative. . . . The theme of the stamp put on a man's life and thought by his Jewishness often recurs in Ludwig's later notes, though, to be sure, he saw it more as an intellectual than as a moral limitation. Already in childhood he was preoccupied on a more practical level with dissociating himself for social and even moral reasons from all the different strata of Judaism in Austria. We shall see what remorse that cost him and can measure in that way how compelling the need for dissociation was. (McGuinness 1988, 42)

In the passage quoted above, McGuinness puts his finger on two leading themes that must be addressed by anyone interested in the question of whether Wittgenstein was a Jew, or his views about the Jews: the nature of the Weininger connection, and the nature of Wittgenstein's "dissociation" from Judaism. First, Wittgenstein did, on occasion, speak of himself as a Jew, and the understanding of what it means to be a Jew we find in his writings – his conception of Jewishness, so to speak – makes use of ideas of Weininger's. Most of his surviving writing on this topic dates from the early 1930s, and much of it has been published in *Culture and Value*: these are the "later notes" McGuinness (1988, 42) refers to above in passing, and discusses in some detail in (1999/2001). (I examine this material in §§ 4 f. below.)

The second important point McGuinness touches on in the passage above is that Wittgenstein did, on occasion, deny his Jewishness, and this was a charged matter for him. In his last sentence, McGuinness alludes to Wittgenstein's confessions to friends and family in 1936 and 1937 that he had misrepresented his Jewish ancestry. In 1935, the German government enacted the Nuremberg Laws, which specified that only those people with three or more Jewish grandparents were to be classified as Jews; those with one or two Jewish grandparents were classified as different grades of mixed race. In 1936 and 1937, while at work on what would become the first 180 sections of the *Philosophical Investigations,* Wittgenstein confessed to friends and family that he had misrepresented the extent of his Jewish descent, claiming that one grandparent had been a Jew, when actually three of them were. In 1938, as a result of the *Anschluss* with Austria, the Nuremberg Laws became applicable to the Wittgenstein family. Wittgenstein, who was living in Britain at the time, took British citizenship. His brother Paul fled to Switzerland in July 1938. Meanwhile his sisters stayed in Austria, eventually making a deal with the Berlin authorities, under which they repatriated very substantial foreign assets in exchange for classifying them as non-Jewish, an arrangement

Wittgenstein actively supported. (McGuinness 1999, 74–75; 2001, 231; Monk 1990, 396–400.)

The discussion of Wittgenstein's views about the Jews and his own Jewishness in McGuinness' *Young Ludwig* (1988) does not address the ways in which these terms have been used. In "Wittgenstein and the Idea of Jewishness," McGuinness (1999/2001) touches on this issue. He distinguishes various religious, scientific, and racial criteria for Jewishness and reviews the biographical evidence that he considers most relevant, including passages from *Culture and Value*. The second passage from McGuinness that I want to take as a point of departure, the final paragraph of that paper, takes a sharply different position to the first. There he concludes that:

In the end, then, Wittgenstein did not think of himself as Jewish, nor need we do so. The concept is an attractive, although, or because, a confused one. It is possible to think that it would have been well if all "Jews" had felt solidarity, or to think that they now ought to do so – it is also possible to think the contradictory or even the opposite of these things. In any case these are aspirations, not realities (McGuinness 1999, 76; 2001, 231).

At first sight, the two passages seem to offer diametrically opposed answers to the question of whether Wittgenstein thought of himself as a Jew: the first says that he did, the second, that he didn't. Taking a cue from the words "in the end," which can be used to sum up a person's overall outlook, or their view at the end of their life, the apparent contradiction could be resolved if the passages referred to different phases of Wittgenstein's life. The first is taken from a chapter on Wittgenstein's childhood and schooldays, while the second sums up a piece about his life as a whole. The first passage mentions "later writings," written when Wittgenstein was in his early forties, and alludes to confessions made in his late forties, and these are topics in the more recent piece, too. The second passage certainly suggests that when McGuinness had earlier talked of Wittgenstein's Jewishness, he, too, had fallen prey to a certain kind of muddled thinking, taking Wittgenstein to have thought of himself as a Jew because it cast him in a sympathetic light, and had mistaken an attractive interpretation for the truth.

McGuinness does not say who he has in mind when he speaks of the "attractions" of thinking of Wittgenstein as a Jew, but in a note to the paper he speaks disparagingly of others who have made this error, not his own earlier work. In that note, at the end of the paragraph quoted above, he writes:

Having arrived so far, I have the impression that the polemical part of what I have said has in essence, been said before. . . . It seems always necessary to repeat it, and yet by airing the topic one risks nourishing it. This is part of the fascination I speak of. (McGuinness 1999, 76, n. 40; 2001, n. 44).

He gives, however, very little indication of the principal targets of his polemic; the only writings he explicitly mentions are an unpublished paper by J. J. Ross and a piece published in Hebrew by Yuval Lurie. Nor does he include references to those he is criticizing in his bibliography. This is, on the face of it, odd, for the scholarly literature on Wittgenstein's Jewishness is, for the most part, not well known. Perhaps this is because of McGuinness's concern that "by airing the topic one risks nourishing it," an obscure object of fascination that he apparently considers best left unnamed. Cornish's (1998) speculative and imaginative account of Wittgenstein's Jewishness as the driving force behind Hitler's anti-Semitism is a good example of the dangers of applying the conspiracy theory approach to Wittgenstein, but it seems unlikely that it was the focus of McGuinness's attention. Perhaps his principal target here is Ray Monk's biography of Wittgenstein, *Ludwig Wittgenstein: The Duty of Genius,* which takes the Weiningerian conception of the "duty of genius" as its leading theme in interpreting Wittgenstein's life and work, even though Monk's excellent biography, which rightly gives Wittgenstein's Jewishness and his relationship to Weininger a central place, is never cited or mentioned in McGuinness's paper.

Wittgenstein's favorite passage, which he quoted frequently, came from the introduction to Hertz's *Principles of Mechanics.* There, Hertz summed up his answer to debates over the meaning of terms such as 'force' or 'electricity': because the term has accumulated contradictory meanings, the only solution is to give some of them up. "When these painful contradictions are removed, the question as to the nature of force will not have been answered; but our minds, no longer vexed, will cease to ask illegitimate questions" (1899, 8). Wittgenstein thought of his philosophy as analogous: a matter of uncovering inconsistencies in our use of everyday terms that lead us to talk nonsense yet think we make sense. In "Wittgenstein and the Idea of Jewishness," McGuinness rightly observes that 'Jewishness' is just such a term. Yet instead of developing a Hertzian critique of 'Jewishness,' he tries to show that Jews and Jewishness in any sense were of very little significance for Wittgenstein. As part of his discussion of this issue, he gives a list of meanings of 'Jewishness' that reads as follows:

We have here at least five different sets of phenomena, or supposed phenomena: [1] the religion; [2] descent from persons professing it; [3] the culture of assimilated Jews who still formed something of a community; [4] the common genetic heritage of Jews (thought to exist); [5] and (distinct from this) the supposition of such a heritage, typically the assumption by the anti-Semitic that it did exist and was an excrescence on European culture, with which we may class the mirror-image of this assumption, which finds in Jewish consciousness the origins of the modern world view. Of these five, only the first and the last are reasonably clearly definable and certainly existed, though they are by no means identical or very closely related. Jewishness, *"das Judentum"*, is surely one of those words of which Heinrich Hertz spoke in a favorite passage of Wittgenstein's. (McGuinness 1999, 70; 2001, 228. I have added the bracketed numbering).

This list not only omits some important senses of the term; the answers it offers raise more problems than they solve. McGuinness gives no reason for thinking that either "the religion" or the suppositions of the anti-Semitic can be clearly defined. The Jewish religion has a history spanning several millenia, and has comprised many competing sects and splinter groups, each of which have argued both among themselves and with their rivals about what it means to be a Jew. Anti-semitism is also an extremely variable phenomenon, and has taken very different forms. Oddly, the definitions of being Jewish that most Jews would offer, if asked – either being born of a Jewish mother, or having converted to Judaism – are not on McGuinness's list. Nor does he mention the idea that anyone with a Jewish ancestor is a Jew – akin to the "one-drop" rule favored by white American racists – or the 1935 Nuremburg Laws' definition of a Jew: having at least three Jewish grandparents. Finally, in talking about anti-Semitism, he only mentions a hereditary conception of Jewishness, passing over the Weiningerian idea of Jewishness as a personality syndrome, akin to effeminacy, a connection of traits that could equally well be manifested by those with little or no Jewish ancestry – for instance, both Wittgenstein and Weininger were prepared to extend the concept of Jewishness to other groups, such as the English (cf. Monk 1990, 313). The drawing of distinctions between races, and the principles on which racial boundaries are demarcated, are among the most charged questions one can ask about race, not only for those who apply them, and to whom they are applied, but also for those who study race. No list of definitions could do justice to the historical and genealogical dimension of this issue.

Unfortunately, much of the rest of McGuinness's recent discussion of Wittgenstein's Jewishness (1999/2001), leading up to his conclusion that Wittgenstein was not a Jew, loses sight of the rich possibilities suggested by Wittgenstein's favorite passage from Hertz, and is highly selective and tendentious: he seems determined to cut through this Gordian knot by doing the best he can to show that Jews and Jewishness in any sense were of very little significance for Wittgenstein. In particular, McGuinness seems to lay considerable stress on the claim that the Wittgenstein family would not have identified themselves as Jews, and neither would their immediate circle have done so. For instance, in the first paragraph of that paper, McGuinness emphasizes that no one at the turn of the century would have thought of describing Wittgenstein's relatives as a Jewish family (1999, 57; 2001, 221). Yet his insistence on the Hertzian – and Wittgensteinian – insight that the concept of a "Jew" is ambiguous and inconsistent suggests that "Was Wittgenstein a

Jew?" is a question that stands in need of philosophical treatment, rather than a direct answer.

Indeed, the rapid and insistent move from the descriptive – "Wittgenstein was not a Jew" – to the prescriptive – "we don't need to do so" – suggests that we need to look more closely at his motivation for this overly insistent conclusion. Comparing McGuinness's two accounts, one gets the impression that he has followed the path of dissociation from Jewishness that he originally saw in Wittgenstein; he begins by insisting on Wittgenstein's need to deny that he was a Jew, and ends up denying that Wittgenstein was a Jew. Contradictions between different conceptions of Jewishness are not so much the subject of McGuinness's discussion as enacted in its development. Indeed, we might well ask what could have motivated someone as well-informed as McGuinness to make such an injudicious claim. Why is McGuinness so eager to silence those he disagrees with that he does not even name them? To answer these questions, we must look more closely at the connections between what Wittgenstein had to say about the Jews, his life, and his philosophical work. The principal biographical reasons for rejecting the claim that Wittgenstein was not a Jew can be summarized quickly, however. Wittgenstein was certainly not, in any sense, a practicing Jew; he, his parents, and three of his grandparents, were baptized by the Catholic Church. On the other hand, he, and his brothers and sisters, knew that three of their four grandparents were of Jewish descent, and this fact was known to others. For instance, both Monk (1990, 14) and McGuinness (1988, 49) tell the story of how the young Wittgenstein wanted to lie about his Jewish background in order to join a Viennese gymnastic club, and had to be dissuaded by his brother Paul. Both biographers make it clear that while the Wittgenstein family presented themselves in public as Christians, it was widely known that they were of Jewish descent. In a diary entry written after the German-Austrian *Anschluss,* he described the prospect of holding a German *Judenpass,* Jewish identity papers, as an "extraordinarily difficult situation" and compared it to "hot iron" that would burn in his pocket (MS 120, 14.3.1938; cf. Monk 1990, 389 f.) To simply say that Wittgenstein was not a Jew, and didn't think of himself as a Jew, hardly does justice to this complex state of affairs. It is Wittgenstein's response to this predicament that is the principal concern of this essay.

After looking at the relationship between biography and philosophy (§ 2) and Wittgenstein's own thoughts on the topic (§ 3), the remainder of the essay considers two periods from the 1930s in which Wittgenstein's Jewishness occupied center-stage. First, in the early 1930s, his Jewishness was a recurrent theme in his writing and in his dreams. In 1931, he discussed the Jews and Jewishness at some length, connecting his character as a "Jewish thinker" with the nature of his philosophical work (§ 4; cf. Wittgenstein 1980/1998, 12, 13, 16, 18–21, 22/14, 15, 16–19, 23). In 1929 and 1932, he wrote down dreams about his Jewish descent and racial identity (§ 5; cf. MS 107, 219, 1.12.29; MS 183, 137, 28.1.32.) Second, in the latter half of the 1930s, Wittgenstein's Jewishness once again became a problem for him. In 1936 and 1937 he made a point of confessing to family and friends that he had misled others about the extent of his Jewish descent (Monk 1990, 367 f.) and in 1938 and 1939, he had to confront the implications of the German invasion of his homeland, both for himself and his immediate family (§ 6).

2.   Life and Work, Biography and Philosophy

As these passages already make clear, asking whether Wittgenstein saw himself as a Jew, and whether we should, are questions of considerable interest in their own right. They also raise more general problems both for the writing of biography in general, and philosophical biography in particular. Any biography turns the chaotic and conflicting events of a person's life into a coherent story. Biographers usually aim at a balanced and comprehensive account of the life of their subject, but that has proved to be an extremely elusive goal. Lives are rarely consistent, and are colored by changing motives and conflicting concerns. Those who write about them are tempted to give them greater coherence than they had when they were lived, a coherence that may be as much a product of the biographer as the life in question. There is a further problem in the case of philosophical biography. Biographers are constitutionally inclined to explain the principal features of a person's philosophical writing in terms of the person's life – his or her character, or formative experience, or social circumstances. Most philosophers, on the other hand, regard any such explanation as a particularly egregious form of the naturalistic fallacy, holding that the values, or reasons, expressed in a philosopher's work cannot be understood in causal terms.

The question of the relationship between a philosopher's life and philosophy rarely receives the careful attention it deserves. Usually, the answers that are offered favor one extreme or the other – either the work is to be explained by the life, or the life and work are independent – and these diametrically opposed answers are usually taken for granted by their supporters. Many nonphilosophers, and some biographically minded philosophers, find it attractive to explain the philosopher's work in terms of the philosopher's life. A very wide range of positions fit under this broad heading, but they all maintain that some aspect of the person's life determines, explains, or is important for an understanding of the content of the work. Psychoanalytic accounts of the origins of philosophical views in the unconscious, or the claim that a philosopher's unreasoned convictions, class, or social interests underpin his or her arguments, are leading examples of this kind of approach.

If asked, most philosophers would sharply separate the arguments a philosopher gave from a discussion of his or her biography. In particular, they would insist that a philosopher's arguments stand or fall quite independently of what we know about his or her life. Life and work must be kept apart, at least when it comes to assessing the content and significance of the philosopher's work. While a philosopher's life undoubtedly plays a part in the causal processes that lead to the production of his or her writings, such matters are not relevant to the reasoned evaluation of the resultant philosophical position. Mixing one's account of a philosopher's life experience, convictions, and influences, on the one hand, and his or her philosophy, on the other, is a category mistake.

Insofar as this view, on which there is a sharp distinction between a philosopher's life and arguments, is usually taken for granted by most analytic philosophers and historians of philosophy, it is rarely defended or even discussed explicitly in the current philosophical literature. For the most part, those who accept this position do so by refraining from drawing connections between life and work, without explicitly arguing against them. Thus, most books and journal articles on Wittgenstein's philosophy either do not discuss his life, or keep it entirely separate from discussion of his philosophy. Most of those who do discuss the relationship between life and work do so because they reject the separation of biography and philosophy, and hold that a philosopher's biography can be fruitfully connected with his or her philosophy (propenents would include Engelmann, McGuinness, Monk, Szabados, Nevo, Nyiri, Lurie, Cornish, Nieli, Sass, Scharfstein).

Popper is perhaps the best-known defender of the view that the philosopher's life is irrelevant to the appraisal of his or her arguments, but his views are seldom mentioned in the literature on the relationship between Wittgenstein's life and work, perhaps because Popper and Wittgenstein were enemies, and represent approaches to philosophy that have often been contrasted with each other (cf. Munz 1985). There are wildly conflicting stories over how their confrontation at the Cambridge Moral Science Club, where Popper was a visiting speaker in 1946, ended, but what is most interesting for our purposes is that Popper was there to defend the view that there are substantive philosophical problems, and this was the point over which they fell out. The only Wittgenstein interpreter who appeals to Popper's views on the independence of biography and philosophy is Bartley (1973/1985), who maintains that Wittgenstein's character helps to explain his personal influence, but is irrelevant to his philosophy.

One of the rare exceptions to this rule is Hans-Johann Glock (2001), who maintains that any attempt to understand philosophical writing in general, and Wittgenstein's writing in particular, in biographical terms fails to do justice to its reasoned and argumentative character. (Another exception is Conant [1991], discussed in § 3.) Glock's argument proceeds from the premise that Wittgenstein's writing, early and late, includes many passages that must be read as philosophical arguments, arguments that must be taken seriously. Due to the central role of argument in Wittgenstein's writing, Glock classifies him as a "rationalist." Rationalists, in his sense of the term, provide an argumentative and reasoned defense of their position. "Irrationalists" appeal to something unreasoned, such as religious or existential commitment, or the idea that different philosophies are different ways of seeing things.

Glock is certainly right that Wittgenstein wrote arguments, and took them very seriously, but this is only a problem for an extreme irrationalist reading of Wittgenstein, one that denies that arguments have any real significance in Wittgenstein's philosophy. This does nothing to undermine a quietist irrationalism, in which the point of the arguments in Wittgenstein's writing is to make problematic, and so subvert, the power of philosophical argument. It is possible that Wittgenstein's use of argument should be interpreted as defending a positive philosophical position, and that it is unconnected with the way he lived his life. If it is to be a plausible claim about Wittgenstein's own views, it must be backed up not just with philosophical argument, but with evidence that Wittgenstein accepted that argument, and this is not provided in Glock's argument.

My own reading of Wittgenstein, and the position I defend in this paper, is a quietist irrationalism, a position that draws on both the rationalist and irrationalist approaches to philosophy as characterized by Glock. Like the rationalist, I read Wittgenstein's writing argumentatively, as giving a reasoned defense of certain philosophical positions. Like the irrationalist, I read Wittgenstein's writing as trying to show that the unreasoned, the outer limits of philosophical argument, play a much greater part in philosophy than the rationalist thinks. Philosophical argument rarely gets the last word in Wittgenstein's writing. Philosophy for Wittgenstein, when it is not criticizing the argumentative hubris of the rationalist, is a matter of description, not explanation. A philosopher who wishes to show the limitations of argument can hardly help making use of arguments – the works of the ancient skeptics, or Plato's early dialogues, perhaps the principal source of Glock's "irrationalist" tradition, are full of arguments. For someone who thinks that differences in philosophy come down to different ways of looking at things, or world views, or matters of temperament and character, may still depend on argument to defend the view that argument is not, ultimately, what matters in philosophy.

In a conversation with Oets Bouwsma about the difficulties involved in writing a completely honest autobiography, Wittgenstein argued that the author's motives will inevitably get in the way of the autobiographical project of giving an account of oneself and maintaining "a consistent attitude towards that account" (Bouwsma 1986, 70). The autobiographer aims to give a balanced survey of what happened to him or her, how he or she acted, and the motives for those actions. But no one can maintain an impartial attitude towards him or herself, for no one can be indifferent to one's own weaknesses or failings, and so any account one gives of oneself will inevitably be unstable:

No one can write objectively about himself and this is because there will always be some motive for doing so. And the motives will change as you write. And this becomes complicated, for the more intent one is on being "objective" the more one will notice the varying motives that enter in (Bouwsma 1986, 71).

Wittgenstein was not just suggesting that self-serving motives will lead the autobiographer who tries to tell the truth to put the best possible light on whatever he or she is impelled to relate. He was also casting doubt on the very idea that telling the truth about onself can ever be a matter of simply providing accurate information about one's past, for the reason that whatever story one tells will always be colored by one's current preoccupations and concerns, which will, in turn, be affected by the telling of that story. Objectivity, which at first sight might seem to be a matter of impartially separating onself from one's involvement in what one did, turns out, on closer inspection, to be a particularly charged stance, precisely because of its claim to stand above the fray. The very effort to give a balanced and consistent account of the difficult questions about oneself will inevitably be marked by a certain instability and inconsistency in what one says, because no one can be indifferent about such charged matters.

In "Autobiography after Wittgenstein," a perceptive discussion of these concerns, Béla Szabados contends that

what Wittgenstein brings to our attention is that the very attempt to maintain such a consistent and coherent attitude, as if time had stopped and the writer is dead, involves the autobiographer in some form of myopia or self-deception. Such an aim fuels omissions, rationalizations, inventions: suppressions of salient, raw, stubborn memories which confound this imperial attitude of pretended wholeness or single-mindedness. It also masks the present concerns of the writer. So the traditional autobiographical project appears to contain inherently its seeds of self-destruction. Its aim, disengaged self-knowledge, objective stock-taking and cataloguing of truths about oneself is turned on its head; its goal ends up in self-deceit; its primary intention is frustrated (Szabados 1992, 7).

Szabados' essay explores the strategies of confession, self-acceptance, and self-transformation with which Wittgenstein attempted to overcome these difficulties, and closes by bringing out some of the similarities between Wittgenstein's way of doing philosophy and his ideas about autobiography. Traditionally, both autobiography and philosophy aim at objectivity, detachment, and self-understanding, and for this reason, both are fraught with the risk of self-deception. Like philosophy, autobiography is "a working on oneself, on one's own way of seeing things, on one's own interpretation and what one expects of it" (Szabados 1992, 10, paraphrasing Wittgenstein 1980/ 1998, 16/24).

At the very end of his discussion, Szabados uneasily brings up the topic of his own role in the essay he has just written about Wittgenstein's reflections on autobiography: he points out that he has, in effect, been impersonating Wittgenstein, claiming Wittgenstein's voice as his own, with the aim of evoking the reader's interest in his own concerns about autobiography as a kind of writing (Szabados 1992, 11). These final remarks touch on a point that is a central concern in this paper, for they make it clear that Szabados' problem is only a special case of a problem that arises for anyone writing about Wittgenstein's life or thought, regardless of whether that writing is autobiographical, biographical, or philosophical in character. For any attempt to write about Wittgenstein's life and thought – and for that matter, anyone else's life and thought – must face the very issues that make autobiography particularly problematic. While it is true that the biographer writes about someone else's life, rather than his or her own, this is no guarantee that he or she will be any more capable of Olympian impartiality than the autobiographer. Indeed, if Wittgenstein's train of thought about the impossibility of giving a consistent account of one's own motivations is correct, then anyone who aims at a coherent account of the life of another will have to confront that hermeneutic pitfall twice over. The biographer will not only have to come to terms with the inconsistencies and tensions in the subject's life, but will also have his or her own vested interests in the project – interests that may well be just as complex as the conflicting motivations that pull at the autobiographer.

In "Philosophical Biography: The Very Idea," Ray Monk (2001) draws a contrast between two ideal types of philosophical biography, which one might call "explanatory" and "descriptive." An explanatory biography takes the life of its subject as grist for the author's mill, setting the events of the subject's life within the context of the author's pet theories about the nature of life. Monk gives the example of Sartre's biography of Baudelaire, and Sartre's use of Baudelaire's abandonment by his mother as an opportunity to advance his existentialist thesis that we all choose our fate – a thesis that is argued at length, but not supported by quotations from Baudelaire, or other evidence that he believed the views Sartre attributes to him. Such a biography is not really a biography at all, Monk argues, but rather a covert and self-aggrandizing argument for the author's own views. A descriptive biography, on the other hand, presents the events of the subject's life in rich detail, carefully choosing the most telling stories and drawing connections between them, but self-effacingly avoids moralizing or drawing conclusions from the material it presents. The author of such a biographer aims to be "part of the frame," rather than "part of the picture." Such a biography does not have its form imposed on it by the biographer, as the "frame" simile initially suggests, but is rather due to the interconnected character of the life that is being described.

Monk cites Boswell's life of Johnson as his paradigmatic instance of a good descriptive biography, and said this was the method he had followed in his life of Wittgenstein. He notes, however, that he had found it much harder to follow this method successfully in the case of his Russell biography. In part, this was because Wittgenstein's was an unusually unified life. He never married, had few close friends, almost no possessions, and preferred to live alone. Monk's life of Wittgenstein, *Ludwig Wittgenstein: The Duty of Genius,* takes as its leading theme the notion of the "duty of genius," an ethical imperative inspired by Wittgenstein's reading of Otto Weininger, an Austrian fin de siècle popular psychologist and philosopher.

Perhaps Wittgenstein's unusual sensitivity to the paradoxes and inconsistencies involved in trying to tell a coherent and consistent life story was partly due to the intensity with which he strove to lead such a life. Monk's self-effacing approach to Wittgenstein's biography is particularly appropriate to the life that Wittgenstein led, or wished to lead. Yet to attempt to tell the story of someone's life in such a unified way runs the danger that it will pass over, or smooth over, the cracks and fissures that signal the inconsistencies and incoherences in even the most single-minded of lives. Indeed, it may well be the case that the impossibility of arriving at an entirely settled perspective on a life emerges most clearly precisely when one attempts to fit the whole life into a single frame.

3. Wittgenstein on Philosophy and Biography

There were times when Wittgenstein gave forceful expression to the irrationalist views that a person's philosophy is a matter of temperament, or a person's ethics a product of circumstance:

If it is said on occasion that (*someone's*) philosophy is a matter of temperament, there is some truth in this. A preference for certain comparisons [*Gleichnisse*] is something we call a matter of temperament & far more disagreements rest on this than appears at first sight // could be called a matter of temperament & a much larger proportion of disagreements rest on this than may appear// (Wittgenstein, 1980/1998, 20/17–18, 1931).

It is not unheard of that someone's character may be influenced by the external world (Weininger). For that only means that, as we know from experience, people change with circumstances. If someone asks: How *could* the environment coerce someone, the ethical in someone? – the answer is that he may indeed say "No human being has to give way to coercion," but all the same under such circumstances someone *will* do such & such.

"You don't HAVE to, I can show you a (different) way out, – but you won't take it" (Wittgenstein 1980/1998, 84/95, 30.3.50).

The first of these two quotations is from 1931, a time when he was particularly preoccupied with Weiningerian questions about the relationship between originality and influence. Thus this paragraph immediately precedes a passage on how the Jews are "experienced as a sort of disease" within European history. This passage is quoted and discussed toward the end of section 4. Comparisons [*Gleichnisse*] play an important role in Wittgenstein's philosophical writing, and in his understanding of the particular character of his approach to philosophy, another topic discussed further in section 4. The second quotation, which includes an explicit parenthetical reference to Weininger, is an example of how the topic of influence still attracted Wittgenstein's attention many years later. The reference to Weininger is by way of contrast, not agreement: Weininger did regard character as necessarily inner, and so did think it outrageous to say that character is a product of circumstance.

Yet, on other occasions, Wittgenstein gave voice to the rationalist conviction that philosophy and life are separate, and philosophy primary. Perhaps this is because it is much easier to think of philosophy, or character, as a product of temperament, or external circumstances, when one is thinking about others' convictions – and naturally adopts an external perspective – than in one's own case. In a manuscript written in 1948, he expressed his conviction that he should not publish a philosophical autobiography in which the specific difficulties he had felt were "chewed over." The real importance of his work, he thought, lay in the "remedies" he had developed, not the particular causes that had occasioned them:

These difficulties are interesting for me, who am caught up in them, but not necessarily for other people. They are difficulties of *my* thinking, brought about by *my* development. They belong, so to speak, in a diary, not in a book. And even if this diary might be interesting for someone some day, I cannot publish it. My stomach-aches are not what is interesting but the remedies – if any – that I've found for them (Wittgenstein, MS 136, 144, 24.1.48).

Notice that Wittgenstein's autobiographical difficulties are figured in vivid bodily terms, both as something that should not be "chewed over," and as the cause of his "stomach-aches." Perhaps Wittgenstein thought that overly close attention to his personal predicament would detract from the dignity and seriousness of the work he had written. As a result, he claims that his specific difficulties are really only of interest to himself, but not to others, and so should not be published.

Despite his inability to publish them – or any of the other writing that he did after 1929 – he did leave the corpus of his writing for his literary trustees to publish "as they see fit." (The words quoted are from Wittgenstein's will.)

As a result, it was his literary heirs who had to distinguish between his "philosophical" work on the one hand and the "nonphilosophical" work on the other, as though these dismembered limbs could be surgically separated from the corpus of typescripts and manuscripts that Wittgenstein left to posterity. As a matter of fact, the majority of that material does take the form of a diary, a dated sequence of notes, first drafts, and revisions that provides an intimate record of his struggle with the difficulties that occasioned his more polished philosophical writing. If one turns to this (still mostly unpublished) source material, one can see that Wittgenstein's writing arises out of a struggle between opposing intuitions and his attempts to resolve that struggle. One of the strongest currents of thought in his later philosophy is the idea that one cannot dissociate the first impulses toward a philosophical train of thought from its most finished expression, an idea that motivates the fragmentary arguments one finds in the opening sections of the *Philosophical Investigations.* The debate that animates so much of his writing is a conversation with interlocutory voices that express intuitions and instinctive convictions, not polished philosophical theories.

In the *Philosophical Investigations,* Wittgenstein says that what he does is to bring words back from their metaphysical to their everyday use (1953, § 116): but what is the everyday use of a word that we are led back to, the "language which is its original home"? (Ibid., my translation) Most biographically based accounts of Wittgenstein's thought find an esoteric doctrine at this point, a concealed view that supposedly animates his philosophical writing, a view that is extracted from one aspect or another of his life. Leading candidates have included his religious convictions, which have been variously construed as mysticism, rabbinicism, Catholic, Tolstoyan or Kierkegaardian Christianity, or his ascetic and self-denying ethical outlook. (There is a substantial literature along these lines. Representative examples include Chatterjee 1996, Cornish 1998, Edwards 1982, Engelmann 1967, McGuinness 1988, Janik and Toulmin 1973, and Nieli 1987.) Such biographically motivated readings depend on the premise that the real philosophy lies outside of the texts that Wittgenstein wrote, and that Wittgenstein's writing is to be decoded by attributing to him views that can be found in the books he read and admired.

James Conant's "Throwing Away the Top of the Ladder" (1991), a critical review of McGuinness (1988) and Duffy (1987), argues that approaching Wittgenstein's philosophy in terms of his biography does not do justice to his views about the nature of his writing. In other words, he maintains that the answers McGuinness and Duffy look for in their reading of Wittgenstein's life are to be found in the books he wrote, and the quite unusual way in which they are written. Conant charges them with using "the philosopher's life to decipher the ethical teaching that they know on independent grounds must be buried somewhere in his work" (1991, 351). Their claim, he replies, that Wittgenstein's values were those of the authors he read or admired mistakenly presupposes that influence must take the form of accepting, or adapting, another's views. They overlook the possibility that Wittgenstein criticized the ideas he took from his reading. By prioritizing biography over philosophy in this way they deny that Wittgenstein's own writing could itself provide an answer to our questions about the point of his work. With regard to the *Tractatus,* Conant argues that the ethical point of the book is not be found in any particular doctrine, either within the text or in one of the philosophers who influenced its author, but rather in the overall project of the book, which is a matter of helping its reader "to achieve genuine clarity":

The achievement of such clarity inevitably requires learning how to overcome one's own innermost tendencies to evade such clarity, and this presupposes the attainment of an understanding of the sources and natures of these tendencies themselves. It is a kind of self-knowledge that exacts a high standard of honesty. In this sense of *ethical,* if any of the *Tractatus* is engaged in an ethical activity, then all of it is. The reason the ethical teaching of the work has eluded its commentators is that they have looked for it somewhere in the text rather than everywhere. They evade the pervasiveness of the ethical demand by attempting to locate it in some particular region of the text. When their externally imposed requirement for a discrete ethical doctrine is frustrated by the text itself, they are forced to flee outside the text into biographical detail (Conant 1991, 353–4).

Yet if Conant is right that an ethical imperative permeates Wittgenstein's work, one should also expect to find it expressed in his life, too; not as an esoteric doctrine, but rather as an activity, a way of being in the world, that Wittgenstein regarded as being of a piece with the point of his philosophical work. Norman Malcolm's memoir of Wittgenstein provides testimony that he did see his teaching and ordinary life as continuous in just this way. He tells the story of how he and Wittgenstein had a serious break in their friendship as the result of a disagreement over the German accusation, shortly after the start of World War II, that the British government had been behind a recent attempt to assassinate Hitler. Wittgenstein said that it would not surprise him at all if it were true, while Malcolm believed the British were "too civilized and decent to attempt anything so underhand" and that "such an act was incompatible with the British 'national character'." Malcolm's remark "made Wittgenstein extremely angry. He considered it to be a great stupidity and also an indication that I was not learning anything from the philosophical training he was trying to give me" (1984, 30).

Until this event, Wittgenstein had regularly gone for a short walk with Malcolm before giving his lectures; afterward he gave up the practice and the friendship cooled. In a letter written from Trinity College, Cambridge, in November 1944, Wittgenstein wrote that he:

couldn't help thinking of a particular incident which seemed to me very important. You & I were walking along the river towards the railway bridge & we had a heated discussion in which you made a remark about "national character" that shocked me by it's primitiveness. I then thought: what is the use of studying philosophy if all that it does for you is to enable you to talk with some plausibility about some abstruse questions of logic, etc., & if it does not improve your thinking about the important questions of everyday life, if it does not make you more conscientious than any journalist in the use of the DANGEROUS phrases such people use for their own ends. You see, I know that it's difficult to think *well* about "certainty," "probability," "perception," etc. But it is, if possible, still more difficult to think, or *try* to think, really honestly about your life & other peoples lives. And the trouble is that thinking about these things is *not thrilling,* but often downright nasty. And when it's nasty then it's *most* important (Malcolm 1984, 93–4).

Much of Wittgenstein's work in the early 1930s takes the form of a struggle with traditional philosophical conceptions of the essence of language. When he wrote the *Tractatus,* he was convinced that everyday language must have an underlying logical structure, and that philosophy had the task of clarifying that structure. The *Tractatus,* however, does very little to actually analyze our ordinary language. After he returned to philosophical work in 1929, Wittgenstein came to see that the notion of an underlying essential structure was a demand imposed by a certain way of seeing things, rather than something given to us by the nature of things. In the early 1930s, he applied this critique not only to his own earlier work, but also to the work of figures such as Spengler and Freud, arguing that they betrayed their own insights into particular cultural formations by transforming them into ahistorical claims about human nature (cf. Wittgenstein 1980/1998; Monk 1990; Bouveresse 1995; Szabados 1999).

One aspect of the later Wittgenstein's legacy that is of particular value here arises out of his critique of the traditional philosophical search for clear-cut, ahistorical essences: he offers a positive characterization of our language as a loosely interrelated network of activities, that are not unified by any one essence, and that have to be located within a particular practical context. This critique of essentialism is, in turn, the product of an attraction to essentialism, and it would be a mistake to assume that Wittgenstein easily overcame the traditional ways of thinking that preoccupied him. These developments in Wittgenstein's work emerge at a time when he was rereading, and recommending to his friends, Otto Weininger's *Sex and Character.* In this connection, Monk aptly observes that

What is perhaps most ironic is that, just as Wittgenstein was beginning to develop an entirely new method for tackling philosophical problems – a method that has no precedent in the entire tradition of Western philosophy (unless one finds a place for Goethe and Spengler in that tradition) – he should be inclined to asssess his own philosophical contribution within the framework of the absurd charge that the Jew was incapable of original thought (Monk 1990, 316).

4.   Wittgenstein and Weininger

In 1931, Wittgenstein included Weininger on a short list of writers who had influenced him, in the context of a discussion of the relationship between originality and influence, a discussion which clearly echoes Weininger's own views about the relationship between merely reproductive talent and genuinely creative genius. The Wittgenstein-Weininger connection thus not only provides an opportunity for examining the influence of one philosopher on another, but also has the topic of originality and influence as one of its foci. Unfortunately, Wittgenstein never specified the nature of his debt to Weininger. The topic has become a matter of considerable speculation in recent years, especially following the publication of Ray Monk's biography, with its emphasis on the Weiningerian theme of the "duty of genius" as a key to understanding Wittgenstein's life and work.

Weininger's *Sex and Character* (1903/1906), an extraordinarily popular and much-discussed book, contains an extremely misogynistic, anti-Semitic, and homophobic theory of human nature. Weininger held that everyone is bisexual, by which he meant that we all are partially feminine and partially masculine. Masculinity and femininity are, in turn, to be understood as ideal types that are only partially instantiated in any given person. This provided the basis for an "explanation" of homosexuality and heterosexuality as products of the mathematical combination of these components. Each person seeks out a partner within the complementary amount of masculinity and feminity; homosexuals, having less than the usual amount of masculinity, if male, or feminity, if female, find the complementary balance in another person of the same sex.

In the opening chapters of *Sex and Character,* Weininger elaborates his fundamental law of sexual attraction, in the form of a pseudoscientific equation, complete with Greek letters and mathematical formalism. Weininger contrasted masculine originality with feminine reproductiveness, and held that the latter traits are particularly exemplified by Jews; race, sexuality, and gender are all closely aligned in the Weiningerian economy. Women, according to Weininger, are governed by the imperative to reproduce, and are constitutionally incapable of thinking clearly. Only the rare genius can overcome his feminine component and avoid the snares of physical sexuality; the only honorable alternative is suicide. Weininger, like Spengler and Kraus, was preoccupied with the decay of modern times, and took an aristocratic view of the rise of science and business and the decline of art and music, a time without originality. The worst aspects of modernity are identified in terms of their Jewishness and femininity.

Little of this was new, but it did set out a synthesis of contemporary prejudices that captured the attention of a huge readership. Shortly after the publication of his book, at the age of 23, Weininger killed himself in the room in Beethoven's house where Beethoven died, thus assuring himself of the fame that eluded him during his lifetime. Later, Hitler was to refer to him as the only good Jew, because he killed himself when he realized that the Jew lives upon the decay of peoples (Hitler 1980, 148, cited by Janik 1985, 101). Wittgenstein was well-acquainted with both *Sex and Character* and *On The Last Things,* and discussed them with friends and family.

Most of the Weininger literature is polarized, and constrained, by the dispute between those who find it necessary to condemn, and those who find it necessary to excuse, Weininger's use of such stereotypes (see Hyams and Harrowitz 1995). Those who read Weininger sympathetically – let us call them Weininger's apologists – emphasize his observation that no human being is a pure instantiation of masculinity or femininity, heterosexuality or homosexuality, Jew or non-Jew. Rather, these are to be understood as ideal types that we all exemplify to varying degrees; it would, on this construal, be a grave misunderstanding to take Weininger to be setting out crudely racist, sexist, or homophobic views. Thus, according to Allan Janik: "Weininger goes out of his way to insist that he does not identify the Jew as a member of a race. Judaism is a possibility for all men in his eyes" (1985, 101. Cf. 1985 87 f., 98 f., and 1995).

Those who read Weininger unsympathetically – let us call them Weininger's critics – argue that his writings implicitly invite and encourage such bigoted uses, even as they explicitly reject them. On this approach, defending his stereotypes as heuristic devices is comparable to the familiar defense that "some of my best friends are Jews," when it is used to set out prejudiced views while ostensibly denying that the speaker is prejudiced.

There is a striking congruence between Wittgenstein's remarks about the Jews, and the significance of his Jewishness, and Weininger's views on the topic. In a note written in 1931, Wittgenstein discusses his own reproductiveness and lack of originality, describing it as a characteristically Jewish trait. After distinguishing creative genius from mere talent, which is only reproductive, he wrote:

The saint is the only Jewish "genius." Even the greatest Jewish thinker is no more than talented. (Myself for instance.)

I think there is some truth in my idea that I am really only reproductive in my thinking. I think I have never *invented* a line of thinking but that it was always provided for me by someone else & I have done no more than passionately take it up for my work of clarification. That is how Boltzmann Hertz Schopenhauer Frege, Russell, Kraus, Loos Weininger Spengler, Sraffa have influenced me. Can one take Breuer & Freud as an example of Jewish reproductive thinking? – What I invent are new *comparisons*.

. . . It might be said (rightly or wrongly) that the Jewish mind is not in a position to produce even so much as a tiny blade of grass or flower but that its way is to make a drawing of the blade of grass or the flower that has grown in the mind of another & then use it to sketch a comprehensive picture. This is not to *allege* a vice & everything is all right as long as what is being done is quite clear. Danger only arises when someone confuses the nature of a Jewish work with that of a non-Jewish work & especially when the author of the former does so himself, as he so easily may. (Doesn't he look as proud as though he were being milked himself?)

It is typical of the Jewish mind to understand someone else's work better than he understands it himself (Wittgenstein 1980/1998, 19/16–17, 1931).

In an apologetic reading, Wittgenstein's talk of 'Jewishness' here, and in similar passages, should not be taken literally as a claim about all and only those people who are Jews – however one ultimately understands that term – but rather as a metaphor that Wittgenstein uses to think about issues of creativity and originality, and different kinds of intellectual activity, a topic to which he repeatedly returned. In this reading, he is really talking about his particular way of approaching philosophical problems, which he connects with his temperament. Certainly, the four paragraphs that immediately follow the passage just quoted explore further his conviction that he is constitution- ally incapable of producing anything fundamentally new, that his talent rather consists in rearranging and making good use of materials provided by others. We shall see that at the end of the 1930s he expressed much the same ideas without making explicit use of the image of the Jew (§ 6).

McGuinness (1999, 71; 2001, 229) tries to minimize the role of Jewishness in the earlier passages by drawing on Kienzler's observation that in such places "one can replace 'Jew' by 'philosopher' without essentially changing the sense [*Sinn*]" (Kienzler 1997, 43). Given a narrowly Fregean notion of sense, this may be strictly true, but it all depends on what one takes to be essential. Wittgenstein's talk of *"Jewish* reproductiveness" here contributes a metaphorical dimension to this passage that would be missing if he had instead chosen to speak of "philosophical reproductiveness." Even Mc- Guinness does acknowledge that there are prejudicial pictures of the Jews in a few places in Wittgenstein's writing – for instance, where he speaks of "the Jews' secretive & cunning nature" as innate, rather than a result of persecution (Wittgenstein 1980/1998, 22/19).

On a critical reading, what is most troubling about the lengthy passage quoted above, and a number of others written in 1931, is that they take Weininger's prototypically anti-Semitic ideas about the Jewish mind so much for granted. As Monk puts it, "what is most shocking about Wittgenstein's remarks on Jewishness is his use of the language – indeed, the slogans – of racial anti-Semitism. The echo that really disturbs is not that of *Sex and Character,* but that of *Mein Kampf*" (1990, 313).

Around the same time, Wittgenstein recommended Weininger's book to several friends, including G. E. Moore. According to Ray Monk, "Their response was understandably cool. The work that had excited the imagination of pre-war Vienna looked, in the cold light of post-war Cambridge, simply bizarre. Wittgenstein was forced to explain" (1990, 312). In response to Moore's lack of sympathy for the book, Wittgenstein wrote:

I can quite imagine that you don't admire Weininger very much what with that beastly translation and the fact that W. must feel very foreign to you. It is true that he is fantastic but he is *great* and fantastic. It isn't necessary or rather not possible to agree with him but the greatness lies in that with which we disagree. It is his enormous mistake which is great. I.e. roughly speaking if you just add a "~" to the whole book it says an important truth (Wittgenstein 1995, 250; letter dated 23.8.31).

Unfortunately, Wittgenstein's letter does not further explain what he means by negating the whole book, or identify what he takes to be the "important truth" that emerges. Monk pointedly sets out the questions raised by this silence:

But why did Wittgenstein admire the book so much? What did he learn from it? Indeed, given that its claims to scientific biology are transparently spurious, its epistemology obviously nonsense, its psychology primitive, and its ethical prescriptions odious, what could he *possibly* have learnt from it? (Monk 1990, 23)

Monk's own answer to this question is contained in the subtitle of his biography of Wittgenstein, namely "the duty of genius"; he argues that Wittgenstein identified with Weininger's valorization of the figure of the male genius. Monk is right to stress that the later Wittgenstein rejected Weininger's view of Woman; on one occasion, he said of Weininger's views on this topic: "How wrong he was, my God he was wrong" (Drury, in Rhees 1984, 91). Consequently, Monk emphasizes the affinities between Wittgenstein's and Weininger's positive views about love and self-knowledge: man can choose between the masculine and the feminine, love and sexuality; to find oneself is to find one's higher self, and escape the empirical self. The only love that is of value in the end is love of the divine in oneself, of the idea of God.

Another suggestion as to how to understand Wittgenstein's response to Weininger can be found in a recent article by Béla Szabados. He finds it implausible that what Wittgenstein meant by negating Weininger was simply a matter of replacing his prejudicial attack on Woman with an equally one-sided denigration of Man, for that would amount to retaining Weininger's Platonism, with the proviso that he charged the wrong suspect:

That the mature Wittgenstein would give the nod to stipulative, evaluatively loaded definitions of Man and Woman strains credulity. The suggestion is completely out of alignment with the resolute anti-essentialism of the late philosophy. So "Man and masculinity are the sources of all evil" is not the important truth that we are supposed to get out of negating Weininger's book. For this is as much of an absurdity as his central theme, and between two absurdities there is nothing to choose. It rests on a kind of essentialism that the later Wittgenstein rejects simply in virtue of its prejudicial nature. The author of the *Investigations* is devoted to a method of *looking and seeing* how things are rather than saying and prejudging how things are. Both absurdities reveal a deep prejudice and distort the particularity and individuality of people. (Szabados 1997, 492–3; the closely parallel passage in "Was Wittgenstein an Anti-Semite?" (1999, 16–17) indicates how important this claim is for his reading.)

I want to agree with this reading of the text of the *Philosophical Investigations,* but there is no guarantee that the views of the person who wrote the book are as congenial. This is an attractive reading, but it is "attractive" in just the sense that McGuinness (1999/2001, 76/236; cited above, 240) warns against: it would have been good if Wittgenstein had freed himself of the deeply prejudicial, evaluatively loaded definitions of Man and Woman, Jew and non-Jew, that one finds in Weininger, but we should be wary of arguing from what we think our philosophical heroes should have believed to what they actually believed.

Furthermore, Monk's sanitized attempt to recuperate a positive vision from the Weiningerian cesspool, and Szabados's suggestion that it is just a matter of two "absurdities," both involve a failure to see how much Wittgenstein identified with the complementary image of the abjectly feminine – both as Jew and homosexual (cf. Cavell 1990). Part of Weininger's achievement in Wittgenstein's eyes, I believe, was to clearly and honestly set out the prejudices of his age. In the late 1940s, Wittgenstein explained his admiration for Weininger to G. E. M. Anscombe by contrasting him with Kafka: Kafka, he said, "gave himself a great deal of trouble *not* writing about his trouble," while Weininger, whatever his faults, was a man who really did write about his. Anscombe had lent Wittgenstein some of Kafka's novels; Wittgenstein, on returning them, compared Kafka unfavorably to Weininger, and recommended "Weininger's *Sex and Character* and *The Four Last Things*" (Monk 1990, 498). The latter is presumably a mistranslation, or misplaced memory of Weininger's *Über Die Letzte Dinge* [*On the Last Things*], a posthumous miscellany of his other writings. Weininger's pronouncements about Jews, gender, national character and sexuality are the kind of stereotypes about how people and culture "must be" that Wittgenstein criticized in his attacks on "dogmatism" and the use of "prototypes" in the early 1930s (cf. Wittgenstein's "Notes on Frazer's *Golden Bough*" and his discussions of Schopenhauer, Freud, and Spengler in *Culture and Value*; Lurie; Szabados). Another aspect of Wittgenstein's debt to Weininger was the central role Weininger accorded to what Freud called "projection" in the construction of stereotypes: Weininger contends that the conception of women as either virgins or whores he sets out is a product of male needs, not of women's nature.

Monk and Szabados read Wittgenstein's image of negating Weininger's book as a matter of denying its odious components. It is hard, however, to avoid the conclusion that the negation we are discussing here is not the notion of Fregean logic, but rather the Freudian notion of denying that with which one cannot help identifying. One can see this in the ambiguous reference to "W." in the first sentence of Wittgenstein's letter – "I can quite imagine that you don't admire Weininger very much, what with that beastly translation and the fact that W. must feel very foreign to you" – a "W." that both names and does not name its author. Wittgenstein saw in Weininger, and Weininger's anti-Semitism, a mirror of his own self-hatred, a way of figuring a relationship of identification and denial that he both had to and could not confront. During the question period after the presentation of this paper at the Virginia Tech conference on Wittgenstein, Monk challenged this reading, pointing out that Wittgenstein explicitly used a "~", the Fregean negation sign, not the word "not." Certainly, there is no evidence that his conscious intention was to make use of the Freudian notion of denial; equally, there is good reason to think that Wittgenstein's fascination with Weininger at this time arose out of an uneasy identification with that famously Jewish, homosexual philosopher who was himself deeply troubled by his own identity.

One can see the same tension between identification and denial in a problematic discussion of anti-Semitism from the same period, where he explores the idea of comparing the Jews to a disease in the body of Europe.

"Look on this wart //swelling// [*Warze // Beule//*] as a regular limb of your body!" Can one do that, to order?

Do I have the power to decide *at will* to have, or not to have, a certain ideal conception of my body?

Within the history of the peoples of Europe the history of the Jews is not treated so circumstantially as their intervention in European affairs would actually merit, because within this history they are experienced as a sort of disease, anomaly, & nobody wants to put a disease on the same level as normal life //& nobody wants to speak of a disease as though it had the same rights as healthy bodily processes (even painful ones.)//

We may say: this bump [*Beule*] can be regarded as a limb of one's body only if our whole feeling for the body changes (if the whole national feeling for the body changes.) Otherwise the best we can do is *put up with* it.

You may expect an individual to display this sort of tolerance or even to disregard such things; but you cannot expect this of a nation since it is only a nation by virtue of not disregarding such things. I.e. there is a contradiction in expecting someone to retain the original aesthetic feeling for his body & also to make the swelling [*Beule*] welcome (Wittgenstein 1980/1998, 20/18, 1931).

Peter Winch's 1980 translation for the German *Beule* was "tumor." Presumably the change was made because "tumor" is not supported by current German dictionaries or usage: in contemporary German, a *Beule* is a bump or swelling, with no implication of malignancy. There is a clear etymological connection with the English "boil" – a "hard inflamed suppurating tumor" (Little et al. 1973, vol. I, 212). Jacob and Wilhelm Grimm's historic dictionary makes it clear that the principal senses of the term in the nineteenth century were far from benign: their two leading definitions of the term both characterize it as a tumor (Grimm and Grimm 1854, 1745–6). That sense was still alive in the 1960s, although by then it was no longer the leading meaning. The entry for "*Beule*" in a German-English dictionary first published in the 1960s begins as follows: "bump, lump, swelling; (*Geschwür*) boil, tumo(u)r; . . ." (Messinger and Rüdenberg 1964, 114.) This strongly suggests that Wittgenstein must have been aware of the negative connotations of the term, and that "tumor" is the correct translation. The context in which Wittgenstein used the word does provide additional support for the original translation: he first wrote "wart," an unhealthy growth, and compares the *Beule* with a disease. This passage has attracted attention in the secondary literature, and several English readers have been quick to condemn it for its noxious racist similes. Thus Monk reads this, and related material, as "anti-Semitic paranoia in its most undiluted form" (1990 314, 315). Isaac Nevo's reading of this passage stresses that the anti-Semitism is primarily self-directed, but also part of an intolerant nationalism:

The genocidal fantasy with respect to the Jewish tumour, which in the period this was written was being acted out on the European scene, is articulated by Wittgenstein from within. The analogies and judgments here are his own. The Jewish anomaly could, after all, be portrayed as a curable, rather than incurable, disease. . . . But the nationalism Wittgenstein displays in this passage is defined by intolerance (Nevo 1987–8, 238).

Szabados, on the other hand, working from Winch's first translation, takes the passage to be laying bare, in a philosophically critical spirit, racist ideas that Wittgenstein most certainly does not accept. He lays great stress on Wittgenstein's use of certain distancing devices in setting out these dangerous ideas. The opening sentence is an instruction to see things in a certain way, placed within quotation marks; the second asks us whether it is possible to carry out the instruction. This is followed by a further question, an outline of a way of looking at European history that is about to be rejected, then a "we may say" and a "you may expect." On Szabados' reading, Wittgenstein is bringing up racist ideas to help us see how they hang together with some of the most dangerous problems that liberal democracies currently face, and proposing philosophical therapy for the idea of the nation-state.

What we have here is an attempt at a precise description and diagnosis of the conceptual and political roots of the problem the liberal democracies found themselves in, in the wake of the Holocaust: how to restructure and reinscribe the nation-state and what it is to belong to it, so that the conditions leading to intolerance of difference and subsequent genocide do not recur (Szabados 1999, 7–8).

Szabados is right that Wittgenstein does not straightforwardly endorse the anti-Semitic ideas he explores in this passage, and Wittgenstein's critics have been far too ready to assume that he accepted the prejudicial views he discusses. Also, one must remember that these were private notes, not intended for publication; however, while it is possible to imagine that Wittgenstein might have expanded the proposals and questions just quoted with the sensitive exploration of nationalism and racism Szabados sketches, he did not, as far as we know, ever do so. Instead he follows it up in his manuscript with Weiningerian reflections on how Jews supposedly are only interested in money as a form of power, not in possessions for their own sake.

Power & possession are not the *same* thing. Even though possession also gives us power. If Jews are said not to have any sense for possession that is presumably compatible with their liking to be rich; for money is for them a particular sort of power not possession. (I should for instance not like my people to be poor, since I wish them to have a certain power. Naturally I wish them to use this power properly too.) (Wittgenstein 1980/1998, 21/18, 1931)

The use of "people" in this translation is potentially misleading, for at first sight it suggests that Wittgenstein is talking about the Jewish people as a whole, but the German word in question is *Leute,* and so the people in question are rather Wittgenstein's own family. In this connection, it is important to note that this remark is not only a reflection of his conception of Jewishness, power, and possession, but also a matter of thinking over his feelings about his extraordinarily wealthy family. As we have already seen, seven years later his sense of the proper use of power would lead him to side with his sisters in their dispute with his brother over how best to respond to the German annexation of Austria, in favor of his sisters' paying for non-Jewish identity papers.

Another passage about the Jews, also from 1931, makes it clear how little Wittgenstein was able to transcend the stereotypes about Jews and nation that were current at the time.

"Fatherlandless rabble" (applied to the Jews) is on the same level as "crooked-nosed rabble," for giving yourself a fatherland is just as little in your power, as it is to give yourself a particular nose (Wittgenstein 1997, 59, 2.11.31).

This passage takes certain prevalent negative stereotypes about the Jews –
that they are a rabble, lack a fatherland, are crooked-nosed – as a point of
departure, and does nothing to challenge them. These are hardly the words
one would expect of the critic of "intolerance of difference" Szabados describes. A critique of intolerance of difference may well draw on Wittgenstein's writings, but that critique is not articulated there.

5. Wittgenstein's Peculiar Dreams

There is reason to think that Wittgenstein's uneasy relationship to his own
racial identity, a relationship framed in terms of the prevalent anti-Semitic
discourse of his times, also figures in his relationship to his sexuality. First,
Weininger's racial and sexual theories are themselves mutually congruent,
and both depend on drawing a binary contrast between a valorized and a
denigrated term, a contrast that is drawn in strikingly similar ways in each
case. Recent work on the anti-Semitism of this period by Nancy Stepan
(1986) and Sander Gilman (1986, 1993) has made clear the ways in which
racial and gender theories draw on each other, so that the racial other, the
feminine, and the homosexual are all constructed in terms of the same set of
distinctions. Second, Wittgenstein's virulent racial self-hatred, recorded in
1931, occurs at the same time that he was considering marrying Marguerite
Respinger, a friend of his family. Her visit to him in Norway in 1931 was
conducted on strikingly Weiningerian lines. He found her a room of her own
at a neighbor's house, and proposed that they prepare for a new spiritual life
by reading the Bible together. Even Monk, who minimizes the links between
Wittgenstein's attraction to the darker side of Weininger's thought and his
own self-hatred, notes the connection between Wittgenstein's anti-Semitic
writing in 1931 and his proposed marriage:

Wittgenstein's remarks on Jewishness, like his projected autobiography, were essentially confessional, and both seem in some way linked to the "sacred" union he
planned for himself and Marguerite. They coincide with the year in which his intention to marry Marguerite was pursued with its greatest earnestness (Monk 1990, 317–
8).

Monk, presumably relying on Marguerite's testimony, presents the "union"
as an idea of Wittgenstein's that she never took very seriously.

The themes of race, gender, guilt, and identity all converge in a "strange
dream" of Wittgenstein's, which he wrote down, in code, in one of his
manuscript volumes, on 1 December 1929. The dream concerns a character
named "Vertsagt" or "Vertsag"; the name is the only word *not* written in
code.

A peculiar dream. Today toward morning I dreamt: I see in an illustrated newspaper a photograph of Vertsagt, who is a much discussed hero of the day. The picture shows him in his car. There is talk of his disgraceful deeds; Hänsel is standing next to me and also someone else, similar to my brother Kurt. The latter says that Vertsag is a Jew but has enjoyed the upbringing of a rich Scottish lord; now he is a workers' leader. He has not changed his name because it is not the custom there. It is new to me that Vertsagt, which I pronounce with the stress on the first syllable, is a Jew, and I see that his name simply means "verzagt" [German for "faint-hearted."] It doesn't strike me that it is written with "ts" which I see printed a little bolder than the other letters. I think: must there be a Jew behind every indecency? Now Hänsel and I are on the terrace of a house, perhaps the big log-cabin on the Hochreit, and along the street comes Vertsag in his motor-car; he has an angry face, slightly reddish fair hair and a similar moustache (he does not look Jewish.) He opens fire with a machine-gun at a cyclist behind him who writhes with pain and is mercilessly gunned to death with many shots. Versag has driven past, and now comes a young poor-looking girl on a cycle and she too receives Vertsag's fire as he drives on. And these shots, when they hit her breast make a bubbling sound like an almost-empty kettle over a flame. I felt sympathy for the girl and thought: only in Austria could it happen that this girl would find no helpful sympathy and people watch as she suffers and is killed. I myself am afraid to help her because I fear Vertsag's shots. I go towards her, but look for cover behind a plant. Then I wake up. I must add that in the conversation with Hänsel, first in the presence of the other person and then after he had left us, I am embarassed and do not want to say that I myself am descended from Jews or that Vertsag's case is my own case too. . . . I wrote the dream down immediately after waking up (MS 107, 219, 1.12.29. The passage is also translated in Monk 1990, 279–80, and the German text is provided on pp. 612–3. See also the transcription of the text in Wittgenstein 1993–, vol. 2, 127).

Hänsel was a close friend, the first person he wrote to in 1936 to confess he had concealed his Jewishness, asking Hänsel to pass on his confession to his family (see the correspondence between Wittgenstein and Hänsel, recently published in Somavilla 1994). In his notes on the dream, Wittgenstein tries, three times, to interpret the significance of Vertsagt's name. In the dream, he thought he saw "that his name simply means 'verzagt'," which is German for "faint-hearted." After waking, he came to think that it was really written "Pferzagt," which means nothing at all. His closing attempt suggests that "the name as I pronounced it in the dream, 'Vèrt-sagt' is Hungarian. The name had for me something evil, spiteful and very masculine about it."

Clearly, the dream is connected with Wittgenstein's pervasive sense of guilt, and its connection with his discomfort with his sexuality and racial origins. Monk takes the dream to be about Wittgenstein's sense that he was "hiding something . . . allowing people to think of him as an aristocrat when in fact he was a Jew" (1990, 279). Consequently, he treats the trail of associations as a distraction from the manifest content of the dream, and the initial thought that the case of Vertsagt is his own case, the case of a man who hides his origins, and is too faint-hearted to admit it (1990, 280). It is surely right to take Wittgenstein's attempts to make sense of the name as themselves faint-hearted, and a distraction from thinking about the fact that the predicament of the protagonist is his predicament. Yet the search for the meaning of the name is not just a screen: looked at one way, the names are nonsensical; looked at in another way, they all have similar and connected sounds and meanings. Christoph Nyíri has pointed out that, despite Wittgenstein's repeated attempts to decode the name, he fails to consider a striking alternative: that the word is "*versagt*", from *versagen,* the German word not only for "failed," "denied," – an obvious construal under the circumstances – but also "betrothed." The usage in the sense of "betrothed" is no longer common – it is not in the current *Duden* – but it is in the 1967 *Langenscheidt,* and it would have been familiar to Wittgenstein (Nyíri 1992, 22).

Nyíri's piece, written before he had seen Monk's biography, takes it for granted that Wittgenstein was not betrothed. Monk's account, presumably based on his conversations with Marguerite Respinger – specific sources for such matters are not given in his biography – gives the impression that while Wittgenstein might have desired a celibate marriage with her, this was never a realistic possibility. Wittgenstein's diary from this period presents a rather different picture, which is that Marguerite needed him at a time of personal crisis, but that this could not be a permanent relationship. Another complicated dream, a few weeks earlier, is interpreted by Wittgenstein as being about how he imagines he is bound to Marguerite by a thousand ties, but as a matter of fact, it is easy for him to walk away from her (Wittgenstein 1997, 63–4). In any case, it seems fair to say that the Vertsagt dream epitomizes Wittgenstein's sense of failure at the time, and particularly the failure of their proposed "union."

The theme of struggling to make sense of nonsense, and in particular of a name containing consonants with similar sounds, recurs in another dream that Wittgenstein wrote down early in 1932:

Today I dreamt the following strange dream. Someone (was it Lettice? [Ramsey]) said to me that someone was called Hobbson "with mixed b"; which meant, that one pronounced it "Hobpson." I woke and remembered that Gilbert [Pattison] once told me about the pronunciation of a word that it was "pronounced with mixed b," which I had understood as "mixed beef" [in English] and didn't know what he meant, but it sounded as if he meant that one would have to have a dish called "mixed beef" in one's mouth when saying the word, and I had understood Gilbert to have said it as a joke. I remembered all that immediately on waking. Then it sounded less and less plausible to me, and by the time I'd got dressed it seemed obvious nonsense. (By the way, if one went into this dream, it leads to thoughts about racial mixing, and what that means to me.) (Wittgenstein 1997, 67; MS 183, 137–8; 28.1.32)

Lettice Ramsey was a close friend and confidante of Wittgenstein's, with whom he could discuss his feelings for Marguerite (Monk 1990, 258); Pattison, a friend with whom he joked and played with nonsensical language (Monk 1990, 265 f.). Wittgenstein does not explain the connection he sees between this dream and his thoughts about mixed race, but both dreams give great significance to almost imperceptible differences in pronouncing a name that is difficult to say correctly, a name whose meaning seems clear during the dream, then elusive, and ultimately nonsensical. In each dream, racial difference, and differences in meaning between nonsense words, play a central part. A name takes on a racially charged significance, but the significance resists his analytic efforts. One further connection here is that both nonsense and racial mixing arise out of combinations that are not permitted; both are offenses against the normal ways of going on. Both seem to make sense within Wittgenstein's "strange" (1.12.29) and "peculiar" (28.1.32) dreams, but turn into nonsense when he tries to reconstruct their meaning. Wittgenstein's unsuccessful struggle to make sense of the nonsense names in the Vertsagt and Hobbson dreams is an uncanny parody of the traditional philosophical quest to explain a name's meaning in terms of what it stands for.

6. Jewishness, Anti-Semitism and Philosophy

Is there a connection between Wittgenstein's writing on Jews and his philosophy? What did he mean when he spoke of himself as a "Jewish thinker" in 1931? Monk takes Wittgenstein to be engaging in a form of self-directed anti-Semitism, humbling himself by describing his own work as nothing more than clarifying the ideas he had taken from others, or reminding himself of "his limitations, of his 'Jewishness' " (1990, 317).

It is as though, for a brief time (after 1931 there are, thankfully, no more remarks about Jewishness in his notebooks), he was attracted to using the then current language of anti-Semitism as a kind of metaphor for himself (just as, in the dream of Vertsagt, the image of the Jew that was propagated by the Nazis – an image of a cunning and deceptive scoundrel who hides behind a cloak of respectability while committing the most dreadful crimes – found a ready response in his fears about his own 'real' nature.) . . . So long as he lived, Wittgenstein never ceased to struggle against his own pride, and to express doubts about his philosophical achievement and his own moral decency. After 1931, however, he dropped the language of anti-Semitism as a means of expressing those doubts. (Monk 1990, 316–17)

Yuval Lurie sees a direct connection between developments in Wittgenstein's views about meaning and his giving up talk of Jewishness in this way.

For it was around this time that Wittgenstein began to talk about family resemblances, the similarities that things of certain kinds have in common with each other without sharing a comon essence.

Is this simultaneity coincidental? I think not. It seems to me that he found he could no longer hide behind the claim that he was merely conducting a metaphysical discussion about the ideal Jew when he spoke of Jews as he did (Lurie 1989, 340).

Lurie, like Szabados (1999), supports this reading by connecting Wittgenstein's particular use of the concept of Jewishness with the Weiningerian notion of a prototype, a conception of an idealized instance of the concept in question that can be used to organize empirical evidence, a notion that Wittgenstein rejected shortly after these discussions of the Jews in 1931. Lurie also goes on to show that many of Wittgenstein's subsequent and closely related discussions of talent and genius, creativity and originality, make use of other metaphors, such as talk of how seeds grown in different soils will produce different plants.

Strictly speaking, Monk is correct in saying that there are no more remarks about Jewishness, per se, after 1931 in Wittgenstein's surviving notebooks, and that he no longer used the language of anti-Semitism as a means of doubting his own decency; and Lurie is right that Wittgenstein did develop other ways of thinking about reproductiveness and originality. Yet there are remarks about Jews and the bible, dating from a series of notebooks from 1939 or 1940, that show that the anti-Semitic metaphors and connections that he had made in the early 1930s were still alive for him. In these passages, Wittgenstein returned to the themes of the difference between genius and talent, and how courage and character distinguish genius from talent. Thus we find him asking himself the question, "What does Mendelssohn's music lack? A 'courageous' melody?" (Wittgenstein 1980/1998, 35/40, 1939–1940). In 1929, Mendelssohn is introduced as an exemplar of Wittgenstein's idea of Jewishness, and used as a way of thinking about Wittgenstein's own ideals, which he thinks of as akin to Mendelssohn's. Wittgenstein compares the Jew to a tree that avoids tragedy by bending, rather than breaking: "Tragedy is something unjewish. Mendelssohn is perhaps the most untragic of composers" (1980/1998, 1/3). Wittgenstein takes it for granted that the Jew lacks the courage, or resistance, that is required for tragedy. Indeed, he identifies his own ideal in these terms, for the passage, which up till now has been in ordinary German, continues in code: "Tragically holding on, defiantly holding on to a tragic situation in love always seems quite alien to my ideal. Does that mean my ideal is feeble? I cannot & *should not judge*" (Wittgenstein 1980/1998, 3–4; the passage is not included in the pre-1994 editions).

In another notebook from the same period, he writes:

The Old Testament seen as the body without its head; the New T[estament]: the head; the Epistles of the Apostles: the crown on the head.

If I think of the Jewish Bible, the Old Testament on its own, I should like to say: the head is (*still*) missing from this body The solution to these problems is missing. The fulfilment of these hopes is missing. But I do not necessarily think of a head as having a *crown.*

The measure of genius is character, – even if character on its own does *not* amount to genius

Genius is not 'talent *and* character', but character manifesting itself in the form of a special talent. Where one man will show courage by jumping into the water, another will show courage by writing a symphony. (This is a weak example.)

There is no more light in a genius than in any other honest human being – but the genius concentrates this light into a burning point by means of a particular lens (Wittgenstein 1980/1998, 35/40–1. 1939–1940).

My originality (if that is the right word) is, I believe, an originality that belongs to the soil, not the seed. (Perhaps I have no seed of my own.) Sow a seed in my soil, & it will grow differently than it would in any other soil.

Freud's originality too was like this, I think. I have always believed – without knowing why – that the original seed of psychoanalysis was due to Breuer, not Freud. Of course, Breuer's seed-grain can only have been quite tiny.

(*Courage* is always original.) (Wittgenstein 1980/1998, 36/42, 1939–40)

Although he does not explicitly make any of the claims about "the Jews" that one finds in the earlier remarks, he continues to talk in terms that take those earlier ideas for granted. The biblical analogy makes it clear that Wittgenstein cannot entirely let go of using the Jews as a way of thinking about his identity: his Bible, the Jew's, and the Catholic's are compared to a body, a headless body, and a crowned body. Apparently, it is integral to Wittgenstein's conception of his Christianity that it be seen as contrasted with the supposed shortcomings of Judaism. Isaac Nevo reads this passage as a figure of the Jewish faith as "a living death":

The essential point is that variation, or even schism within Christianity does not constitute an anomaly, or a disturbance. . . . The "Jewish Bible," on the other hand, constitutes a real disturbance: a (living?) body without a head (1987–8, 236).

While the passage as a whole is not as strikingly anti-Semitic as the earlier writing on the Jews, the fact remains that he is still writing about the difference between genius and talent in terms of a stock example of a Jewish composer who lacks the un-Jewish virtue of courage, interspersing it with a biblical analogy that cannot help but suggest the image of the Jews who lost their heads, and worse, as the result of the Shoah.

7. Conclusion

Wittgenstein's later philosophy, with its far-reaching criticism of essentialism and Platonism about meaning, certainly lends itself to a critique of anti-Semitic stereotypes, and his falling-out with Malcolm makes it clear that he saw a close connection between his more technically philosophical work and a critical attitude toward nationalistic stereotypes. On the other hand, his continued uncritical use of Jewish stereotypes in material from the same time as his dispute with Malcolm show that he was far from being fully successful in applying his own methods to his use of anti-Semitic discourse. Indeed, his final recorded reflection on anti-Semitism, written three years after the Second World War, begins by comparing anti-Semitism to a tangle, a knot he was unable to untie:

If you cannot unravel a tangle, the most sensible thing you can do is to recognize this; & the most decent thing, to admit it. [Antisemitism.]

What you should do to cure the evil is *not* clear. What is *not* permissible is clear from one case to another (Wittgenstein 1980/1998, 74/95, 4.11.48).

It is hard to know what to make of this passage. Nevo reads it as Wittgenstein's confession that he could not unravel the tangle of anti-Semitism, that he was still entangled in it, and suggests that he was contemplating suicide, the "honourable" Weiningerian way out (1987–8, 242). Yet, given the available evidence, such a reading is extremely speculative. Wittgenstein neither says what unravelling the tangle would be, nor specifies what one "must *not* do." The reference to unravelling a tangle evokes an image that Wittgenstein repeatedly used in talking about the nature of philosophy. In section 2 of the *Philosophical Remarks,* written in 1930, he writes:

Why is philosophy so complicated? It ought, after all, to be *completely* simple. – Philosophy unties the knots in our thinking, which we have tangled up in an absurd way; but to do that, it must make movements which are just as complicated as the knots. Although the *result* of philosophy is simple, its methods for arriving there cannot be so.

The complexity of philosophy is not in its matter, but in our tangled understanding.

This passage is the basis for Big Typescript, § 90 (pp. 183–9 in Wittgenstein 1993), and can also be found in the company of much post-1945 writing in *Zettel,* § 452. This suggests that the talk of a tangle one cannot unravel was a way of acknowledging that anti-Semitism was a philosophical problem that Wittgenstein was not able to resolve, or cure. Wittgenstein's confidence that it was clear what *not* to do in particular cases is hardly reassuring, in view of what we have seen of his own actions. Anti-Semitism is strikingly akin to a Wittgensteinian philosophical problem: it arises from taken-for-granted prejudices and the misuse of langage, and can only be resolved by a change in the way people lead their lives. The philosophical significance of Jewishness for Wittgenstein is not primarily that he thought of his philosophy as Jewish, but that Jewishness was not a problem that he was able to write about philosophically.

Finally, we can briefly return to the question: was Wittgenstein a Jew? My Hertzian answer is that we would be better off distinguishing different senses of the term, and reflecting on their role in his life and in our own. Wittgenstein's problematic Jewishness is as much a product of our problematic concerns as his. There is no doubt that Wittgenstein was of Jewish descent; it is equally clear that he was not a practicing Jew. Insofar as he thought of himself as Jewish, he did so in terms of the anti-Semitic prejudices of his time. It would have been good if he could have untangled those prejudices, but he did not do so.[1]

REFERENCES

Bartley, W. W. III (1973/1985) *Wittgenstein.* First ed., by J. B. Lippincott; rev. 2d ed. 1985. LaSalle, IL: Open Court Press.

Bouveresse, Jacques (1995) *Wittgenstein Reads Freud: The Myth of the Unconscious.* Trans. Carol Cosman. Princeton, NJ: Princeton University Press.

Bouwsma, Oets (1986) *Wittgenstein: Conversations, 1949–1951.* Indianapolis, IN: Hackett.

Cavell, Stanley (1990) "Postscript (1989): To Whom It May Concern." *Critical Inquiry* 16: 248–290.

Chatterjee, Ranjit (1996) *Philosophy as Atonement: Judaic Themes in Wittgenstein's Linguistic Thought.* Unpublished typescript, 300 pp.

Conant, James (1991) "Throwing Away the Top of the Ladder." *The Yale Review* 79: 328–64.

Cornish, Kimberly (1998) *The Jew of Linz: Wittgenstein, Hitler and Their Secret Battle for the Mind.* London: Century Books.

Duffy, Bruce (1987) *The World As I Found It.* New York: Ticknor and Fields.

Edwards, James C. (1982) *Ethics Without Philosophy: Wittgenstein and the Moral Life.* Tampa: University of South Florida Press.

Engelmann, Paul (1967) *Letters from Ludwig Wittgenstein, with a Memoir,* ed. B. F. McGuinness; trans. L. Furtmueller. Oxford: Basil Blackwell.

Gilman, Sander (1986) *Jewish Self-Hatred: Anti-Semitism and the Hidden Language of the Jews.* Baltimore, MD: Johns Hopkins University Press.

Gilman, Sander (1993) *Freud, Race and Gender.* Princeton, NJ: Princeton University Press.

Glock, Hans-Johann (2001) "Wittgenstein and Reason" in this volume.

Grimm, Jacob and Wilhelm (1854) *Deutches Wörterbuch.* Leipzig: Hirzel.

Haller, Rudolf (1988) "What Do Wittgenstein and Weininger Have in Common?" in Haller, *Questions on Wittgenstein,* 90–99. Lincoln: University of Nebraska Press.

Harrowitz, Nancy A. and Hyams, Barbara (eds.) (1995) *Jews and Gender: Responses to Otto Weininger.* Philadelphia: Temple University Press.

Hertz, Heinrich (1899) *The Principles of Mechanics,* trans. D. Jones and J. Walley. London: Macmillan.

Hitler, Adolf (1980) *Monologe in Fuehrerhauptquartier, 1941–1944.* ed. Werner Jochmann. Hamburg: Orbis.

Hyams, Barbara and Harrowitz, Nancy A. (1995) "A Critical Introduction to the History of Weininger Reception," in Harrowitz and Hyams, *Jews and Gender: Responses to Otto Weininger.* Philadelphia: Temple University Press. 3–20.

Janik, Allen and Stephen Toulmin (1973) *Wittgenstein's Vienna.* New York: Simon and Schuster.

Janik, Allen (1985) *Essays on Wittgenstein and Weininger.* Amsterdam: Rodolpi.

Janik, Allen (1995) "How did Weininger influence Wittgenstein?" in Harrowitz and Hyams, *Jews and Gender: Responses to Otto Weininger.* Philadelphia: Temple University Press. 61–72.

Kienzler, Wolfgang (1997) *Wittgenstein's Wende zu seiner Spaetphilosophie 1930–1932: Eine historische und systematische Darstellung.* Frankfurt am Main: Suhrkamp.

Little, William et. al. (1973) *Shorter Oxford English Dictionary.* Oxford: Oxford University Press.

Lurie, Yuval (1989) "Jews as a Metaphysical Species," *Philosophy* 64: 323–47.

Lurie, Yuval (1989a) "Wittgenstein on Culture and Civilization," *Inquiry* 32: 375–97.

Malcolm, Norman (1984) *Ludwig Wittgenstein: A Memoir,* 2d ed. Oxford: Oxford University Press.

McGuinness, Brian (ed.) (1982) *Wittgenstein and his times.* Oxford: Basil Blackwell.

McGuinness, Brian (1999/2001) "Wittgenstein und Judentum," in *Paul Engelmann (1891–1965) Architektur Judentum Wiener Moderne,* ed. Ursula A. Schneider, Vienna: Folio Verlag, 57–78. English version: "Wittgenstein and the Idea of Jewishness," in this volume.

Messinger, Heinz and Werner Rüdenberg (1964) *Langenscheidt Concise German Dictionary English-German.* Langenscheidt, 1964; New York: McGraw Hill, 1969.

Monk, Ray (1990) *Ludwig Wittgenstein: The Duty of Genius.* New York: The Free Press.

Monk, Ray (2001) "Philosophical Biography: The Very Idea" in this volume.

Munz, Peter (1985) *Our knowledge of the growth of knowledge. Popper or Wittgenstein?* London: Routledge and Kegan Paul.

Nevo, I (1987–8) "Religious belief and Jewish identity in Wittgenstein's philosophy." *Philosophy Research Archives* 13: 225–43.

Nieli, Russell (1987) *Wittgenstein: From Mysticism to Ordinary Language.* Albany, NY: SUNY Press.

Nyíri, J. C. (1982) "Wittgenstein's later work in relation to conservatism," in McGuinness (1982), *Wittenstein and his times.* Oxford: Basil Blackwell, 44–68.

Nyíri, J. C. (1984) "Ludwig Wittgenstein as a conservative philosopher." *Continuity: a journal of history* 8: 1–23. Reprinted in S. G. Shanker, *Ludwig Wittgenstein:*

Critical Assessments, vol. 4. Wolfeboro, NH: Croom Helm, 1986 as "Wittgenstein 1929–31: The Turning Back," 29–59.

Nyíri, J. C. (1992) "Wittgenstein 1929–31: Conservatism and Jewishness," in *Tradition and Individuality.* Dordrecht: Kluwer, 9–24.

Rhees, Rush (1974) Review of W. W. Bartley's *Wittgenstein, The Human World,* 14 (February).

Rhees, Rush, ed. (1984) *Recollections of Wittgenstein.* Oxford: Oxford University Press.

Sass, Louis (1994) *The Paradoxes of Delusion: Wittgenstein, Schreber and the Schizophrenic Mind.* Ithaca: Cornell University Press.

Scharfstein, Ben-Ami (1980) *The Philosophers: Their Lives and the Nature of Their Thought.* Oxford: Oxford University Press.

Schulte, Joachim (1992) *Wittgenstein: an introduction,* trans. William Brenner and John Foley. Albany, NY: SUNY Press.

Sedgwick, Eve Kosofsky (1990) *Epistemology of the Closet.* Berkeley: University of California Press.

Shanker, S. G. (1986) *Ludwig Wittgenstein: Critical Assessments,* volumes 1–4. Wolfeboro, NH: Croom Helm.

Somavilla, Ilse, ed. (1994) *Ludwig Hänsel – Ludwig Wittgenstein. Ein Freundschaft* Innsbruck, Austria: Brenner Studien, vol. 14.

Stepan, Nancy (1986) "Race and Gender: The Role of Analogy in Science." *Isis* 77. Reprinted in *The "Racial" Economy of Science*, ed. Sandra Harding, Bloomington, IN: Indiana University Press, 1993, 359–76.

Szabados, Béla (1992) "Autobiography after Wittgenstein," *The Journal of Aesthetics and Art Criticism* 50: 1–12.

Szabados, Béla (1995) "Autobiography and Philosophy: Variations on a Theme of Wittgenstein" *Metaphilosophy* 26: 63–80.

Szabados, Béla (1997) "Wittgenstein's Women: The Philosophical Significance of Wittgenstein's Misogyny" *Journal of Philosophical Research* 22 (1997): 483–508.

Szabados, Béla (1999) "Was Wittgenstein an Anti-Semite? The Significance of Anti-Semitism for Wittgenstein's Philosophy," *Canadian Journal of Philosophy* 29: 1–28.

Wasserman, Gerhard (1990) "Wittgenstein on Jews: Some Counter-examples," *Philosophy* 65: 355–65.

Weininger, Otto (1903/1906) *Geschlecht und Charakter.* Translated (without footnotes) as *Sex and Character.* New York: Heineman, 1906.

Weininger, Otto (1904) *Über Die Letzte Dinge [On the Last Things].* Vienna & Leipzig: W. Braumüller.

Wittgenstein, Ludwig (1922) *Tractatus Logico-Philosophicus,* trans. C. K. Ogden. London: Routledge and Kegan Paul. Second edition, 1933.

Wittgenstein, Ludwig (1953) *Philosophical Investigations,* ed. G. E. M. Anscombe and R. Rhees; trans. G. E. M. Anscombe. Oxford: Basil Blackwell. Second edition, 1958; third edition, 1973.

Wittgenstein, Ludwig (1968) *The Wittgenstein Papers,* microfilm and/or bound photocopies. Ithaca, NY: Cornell University Libraries. Revised 1982.

Wittgenstein, Ludwig (1980/1998) *Culture and Value.* First published as *Vermischte Bemerkungen,* German text only, ed. G. H. von Wright and Heikki Nyman. Frankfurt: Suhrkamp, 1977: Amended 2d ed., trans. P. Winch. Oxford: Basil Blackwell, 1980; rev. 2d ed., German text only, edited by G. H. von Wright and Heikki Nyman, with revisions by Alois Pichler. Frankfurt: Suhrkamp, 1994, rev. 2d ed., new trans. P. Winch. Oxford: Basil Blackwell, 1998. (References will give the pagination for the 1980 and 1998 editions of the book; translations are taken from the 1998 edition.)

Wittgenstein, Ludwig (1993) *Philosophical Occasions, 1912–1951,* ed. James Klagge and Alfred Nordmann. Indianapolis, IN: Hackett.

Wittgenstein, Ludwig (1993-) *Wiener Ausgabe [Vienna Edition],* ed. Michael Nedo. Vienna: Springer Verlag.

Wittgenstein, Ludwig (1995) *Ludwig Wittgenstein, Cambridge Letters: Correspondence with Russell, Keynes, Moore, Ramsey and Sraffa,* ed. Brian McGuinness and G. H. von Wright. Oxford: Basil Blackwell.

Wittgenstein, Ludwig (1997) *Denkbewegungen: Tagebücher 1930–1932 1936–1937* (*MS 183*) ed. Ilse Somavilla. Innsbruck, Austria: Haymon Verlag.

Wittgenstein, Ludwig (1998) *Bergen Electronic Edition* Oxford: Oxford University Press, 1998–2000.

NOTES

1. Earlier versions of this paper were presented to the 6th North American Lesbian, Gay and Bisexual Studies Conference; a conference on "Body Matters" at the University of Hull, North Humberside, England; the Society for Lesbian and Gay Philosophy; the History of Science and Technology program, UC Berkeley; the Iowa Philosophical Society; a conference on Russell and Wittgenstein at American University; and the Canadian Philosophical Association meeting in Edmonton, Alberta.

   I particularly want to thank Geeta Patel, who encouraged me to write a four page paper on Wittgenstein and Weininger, the many people whose constructive comments led me to keep on rewriting that paper until it turned into this one, and the University of Iowa, the Alexander von Humboldt Foundation, and the Department of Philosophy at the University of Bielefeld for fellowship support during which this paper was completed.